ATLAS OF
CHINA

CHINA CARTOGRAPHIC PUBLISHING HOUSE
BEIJING·CHINA

CONTENTS

LEGEND

SETTLEMENT

◎ **BEIJING** Capital

◎ **Shanghai** Province-level administrative centre

Yanji Administrative centre of autonomous prefectures, prefectures and leagues

◎ Qingdao Administrative centre of prefecture - level cities (Important city outside China)

◎ Xinji (city) Fengyang County - level administrative centre

○ Nankou Township or village (City outside China)

TOPOGRAPHICAL MAP

◎ **BEIJING** Capital

◎ Shanghai Province-level administrative centre

○ Suzhou Other city

COMMUNICATIONS

Railway

Motorway, Highway

Track

× Pass

Canal

200nm (370km) Shipping route and mileage nm (km)

Shipping terminal

⚓ Port

BOUNDARIES

International boundary, undefined

Boundary of provinces autonomous regions and municipalities

Boundary of special administrative region

Boundary of autonomous prefectures, prefectures, leagues and prefecture level cities

Regional boundary

Military demarcation line

HYDROGRAPHY & TOPOGRAPHY

Coastline

Sandbank, shoal

Coral reefs

Freshwater lake

Salt lake and surface elevation (m) 4718

Seasonal lake, seasonal river

Perennial river

Underground river

Waterfall

Irrigation canal

Reservoir, lock and dam

Flood storage area

Well, karez

Spring, hot spring

Contour, snowfield and glacier

Isobath

Loess gully

Karst cave, needle karst

☆ Volcano

▲ 8848 Peak and elevation (m)

· 583   3803 Elevation point and elevation (m) Sea depth (m)

Dry bed, dry lake

Desert (crescent dunes, longitudinal dunes, honeycomb dunes, sand mound, flat sand)

Gravel desert

Wind-eroded unaka (monadrock) yardang

Swamp

Salt marsh

OTHERS

The Great Wall

∴ Place of interest

INSET CITY MAP

Street and block

Park, greenbelt

Railway and station

City wall

Bridge

Monument

⊥ Pagoda

⊂⊃ Stadium

The national boundaries of China in this atlas are drawn after the 1:4M "Relief Map of the People's Republic of China" Published by China Cartographic Publishing House in 1989

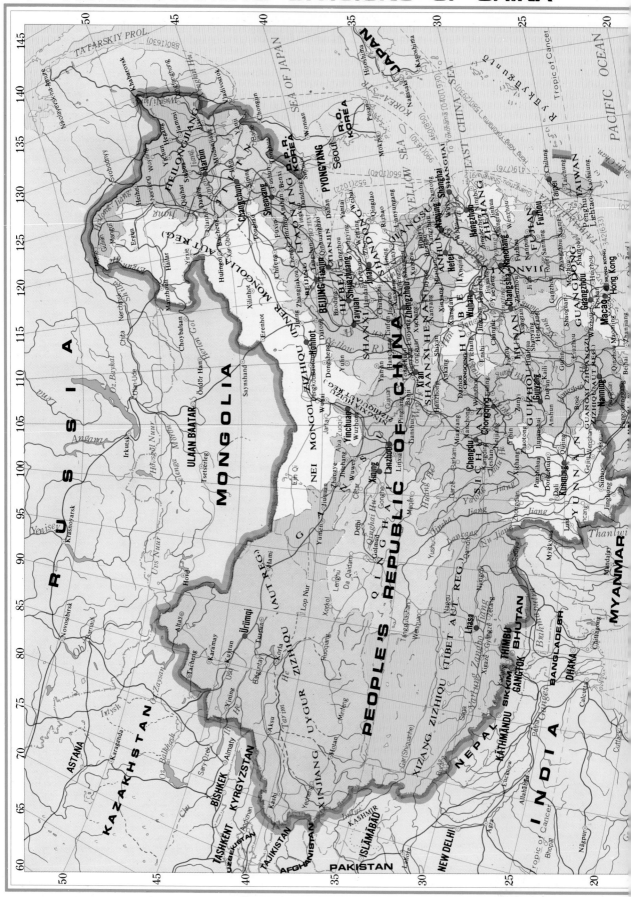

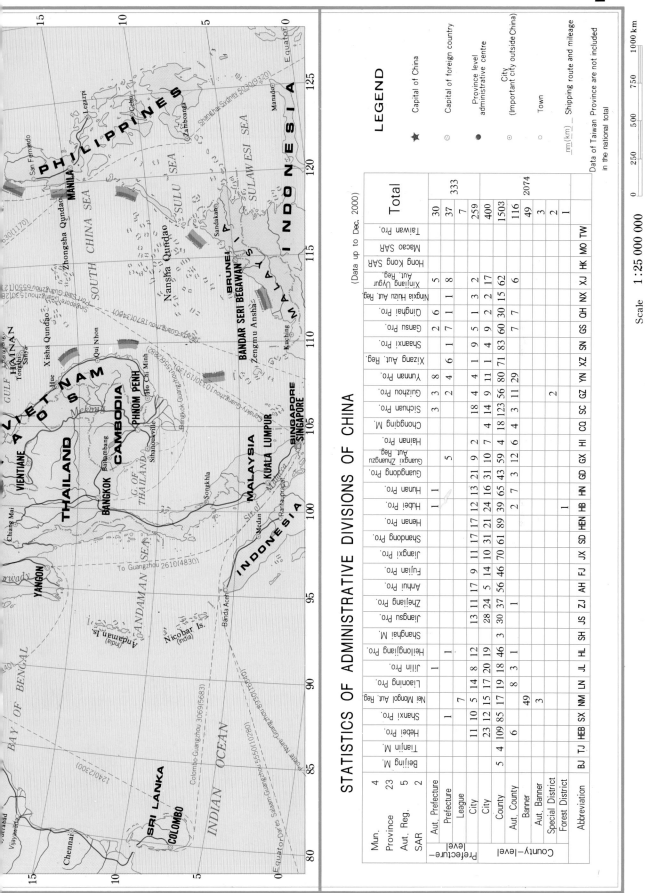

STATISTICS OF ADMINISTRATIVE DIVISIONS OF CHINA

(Data up to Dec. 2000)

Province level

	Count
Mun.	4
Province	23
Aut. Reg.	5
SAR	2

Province	Aut. Prefecture	Prefecture	League	City (prefecture-level)	City (county-level)	County	Aut. County	Banner	Aut. Banner	Special District	Forest District	Abbreviation
Beijing M.												BJ
Tianjin M.												TJ
Hebei Pro.				11	23	109	6					HEB
Shanxi Pro.				10	12	85						SX
Nei Mongol Aut. Reg.			7	5	15	17		49	3			NM
Liaoning Pro.				14	17	19	8					LN
Jilin Pro.	1			8	20	18	3					JL
Heilongjiang Pro.		1		12	19	46	1					HL
Shanghai M.												SH
Jiangsu Pro.				13	28	30						JS
Zhejiang Pro.				11	24	37	1					ZJ
Anhui Pro.				17	5	56						AH
Fujian Pro.				9	14	46						FJ
Jiangxi Pro.				11	10	70						JX
Shandong Pro.				17	31	61						SD
Henan Pro.				17	21	89						HEN
Hubei Pro.	1			12	24	39	2				1	HB
Hunan Pro.	1			13	16	65	7					HN
Guangdong Pro.				21	31	43	3					GD
Guangxi Zhuangzu Aut. Reg.				9	10	59	12					GX
Hainan Pro.				2	7	4	6					HI
Chongqing M.						18	4					CQ
Sichuan Pro.	3			18	14	123	3					SC
Guizhou Pro.	3	2		4	9	56	11			2		GZ
Yunnan Pro.	8	4		4	11	80	29					YN
Xizang Aut. Reg.		6		1		71						XZ
Shaanxi Pro.				9	4	83						SN
Gansu Pro.	2	5		5	9	60	7					GS
Qinghai Pro.	6	1		1	2	30	7					QH
Ningxia Huizu Aut. Reg.				3	2	15						NX
Xinjiang Uygur Aut. Reg.	5	8		2	17	62	6					XJ
Hong Kong SAR												HK
Macao SAR												MO
Taiwan Pro.												TW
Total	30	37	7	259	400	1503	116	49	3	2	1	

Prefecture-level total: 333   County-level total: 2074

LEGEND

- ★ Capital of China
- ◎ Capital of foreign country
- ● Province level administrative centre
- ◉ City (Important city outside China)
- ○ Town
- ___nm(km)___ Shipping route and mileage

Data of Taiwan Province are not included in the national total

Scale 1 : 25 000 000

0   250   500   750   1000 km

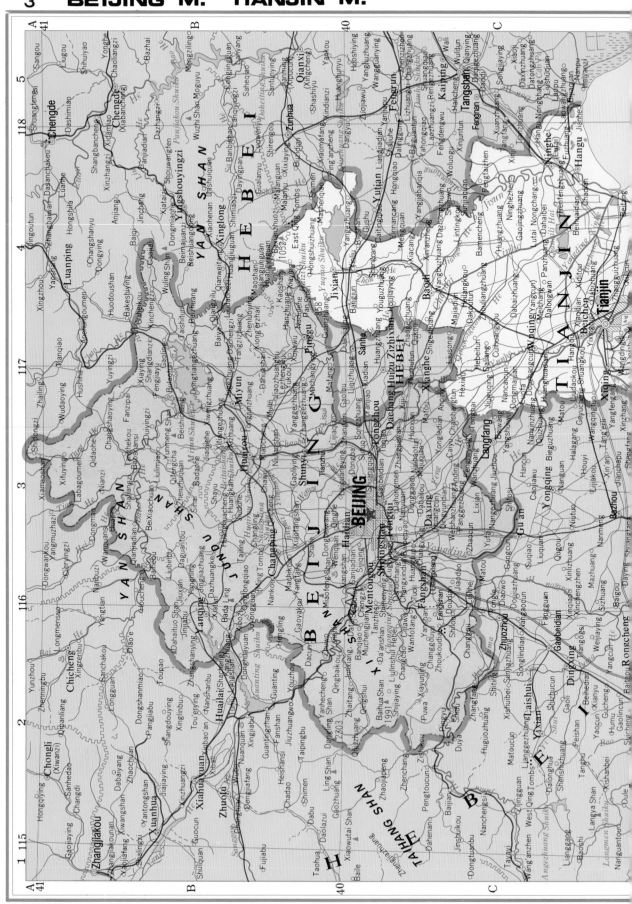

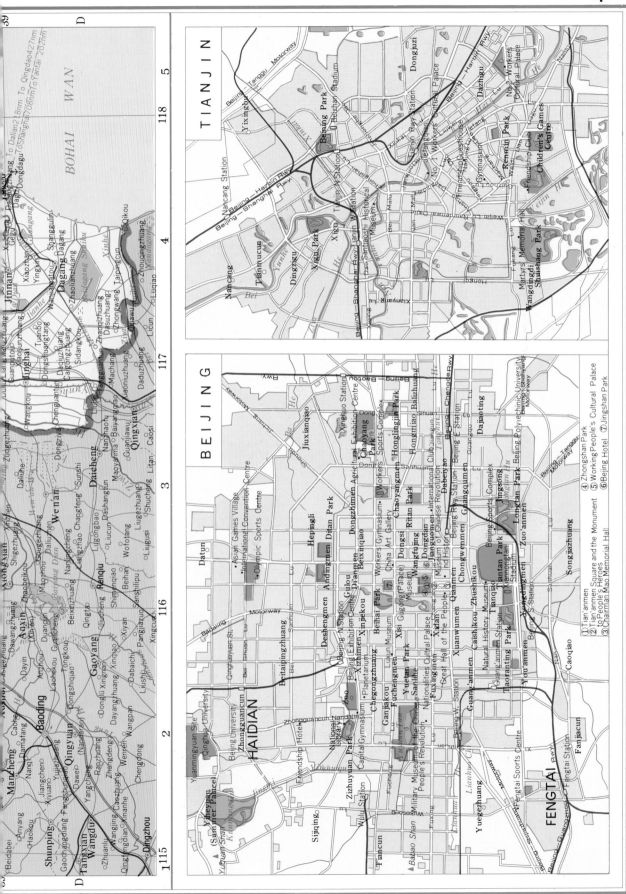

4

Scale 1:1 333 000

0   10   20   30   40   5.0 km

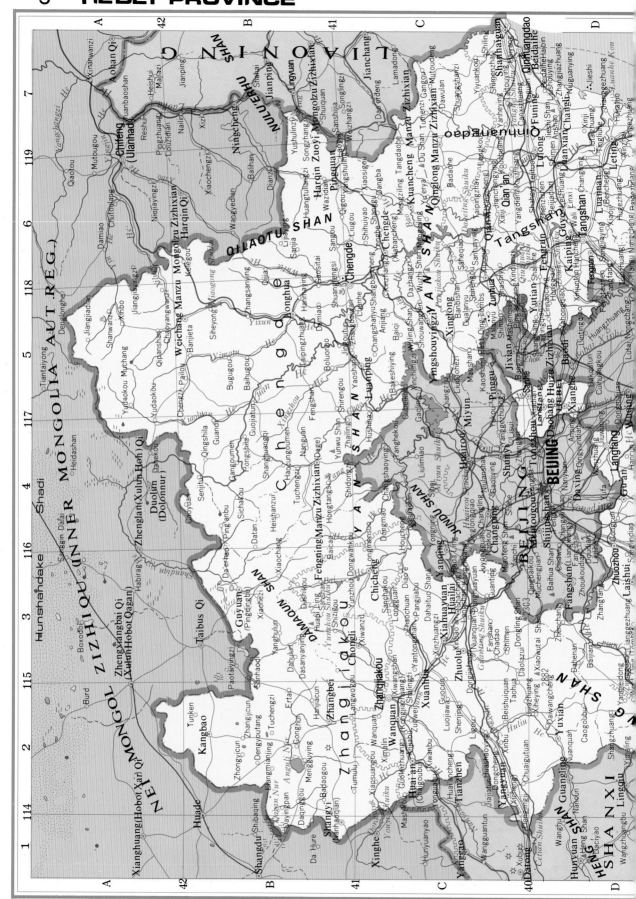

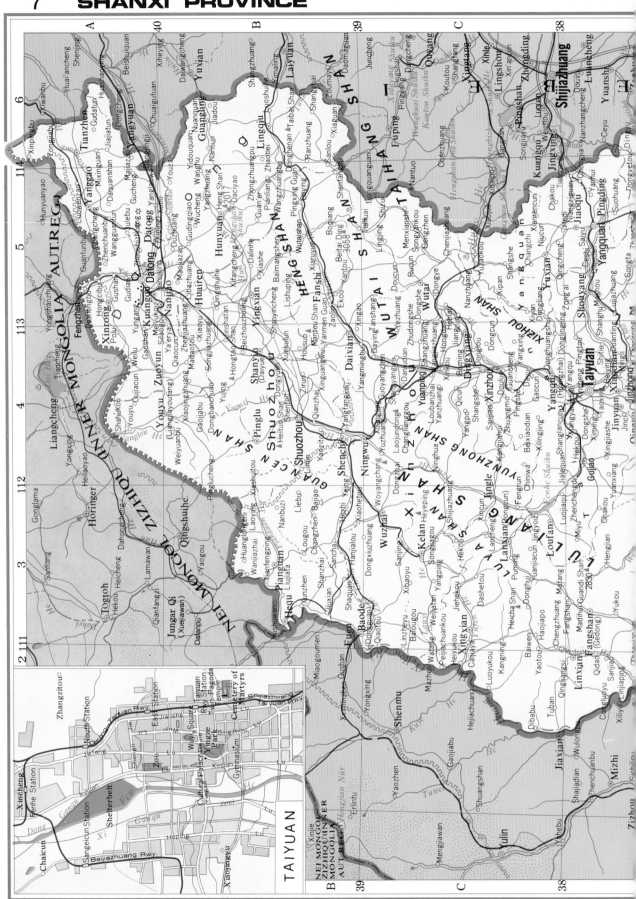

TAIYUAN

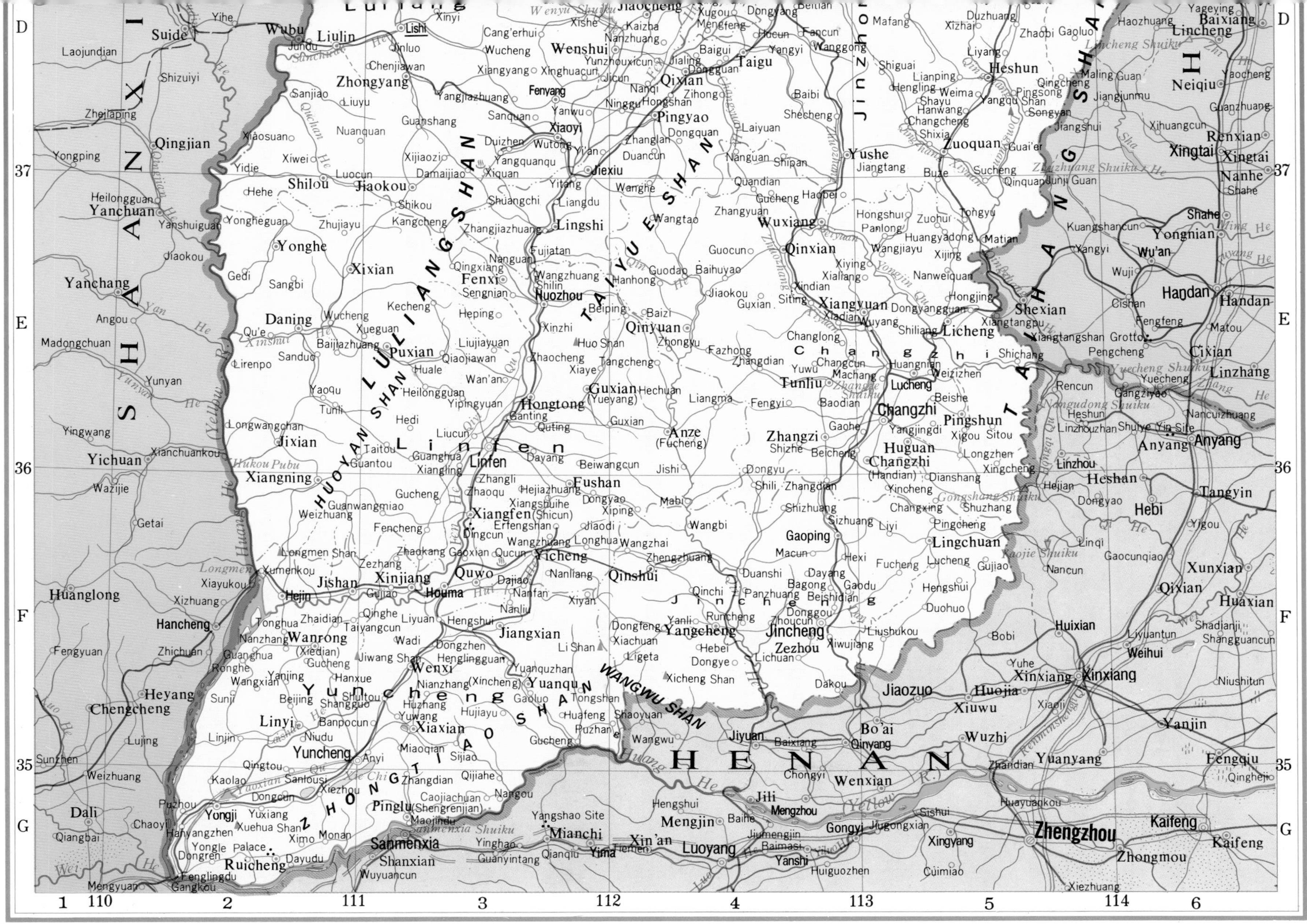

Scale 1:2 000 000

0 25 50 75 km

SHANXI HEBEI HENAN SHAANXI

TAIHANG SHAN LÜLIANG SHAN HUOYAN SHAN WANGWU SHAN ZHONGTIAO SHAN

Zhengzhou Kaifeng Xinxiang Anyang Handan Xingtai Heshun Changzhi Linfen Yuncheng Luoyang Jincheng Sanmenxia

Baixiang Lincheng Neiqiu Renxian Nanhe Wuan Cixian Linzhang Tangyin Tangyin Huaxian Xunxian Qixian Weihui Huojia Huixian Bo'ai Qinyang Wenxian Mengzhou Jiyuan Jiaozuo

Yushe Qinxian Wuxiang Xiangyuan Licheng Lucheng Pingshun Huguan Gaoping Zezhou Yangcheng Qinshui Jiangxian Yicheng Quwo Houma Xinjiang Wanrong Jishan Linyi Ruicheng Yongji Heyang Hancheng Chengcheng Huanglong Yichuan Daning Yonghe Xixian Puxian Jixian Xiangning

Taigu Qixian Pingyao Jiexiu Lingshi Huozhou Hongtong Fenxi Qinxian Anze Gucheng Fushan Xiangfen Hongdong Yangquan Pingyang

Pingyao Fenyang Wenshui Xiaoyi Zhongyang Liulin Wubu Suide Qingjian Yanchuan Yanchang

Zhengzhou

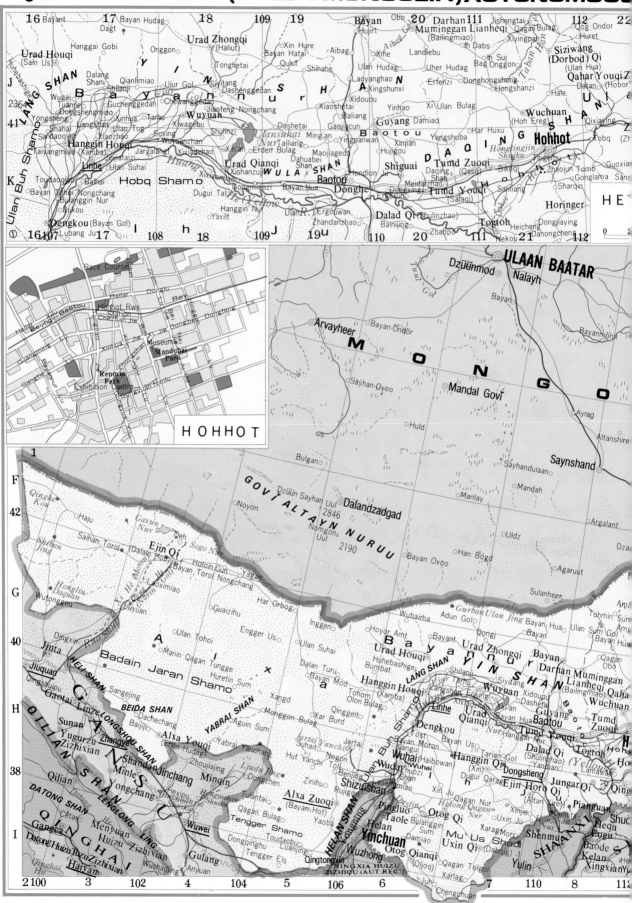

① Alxa League

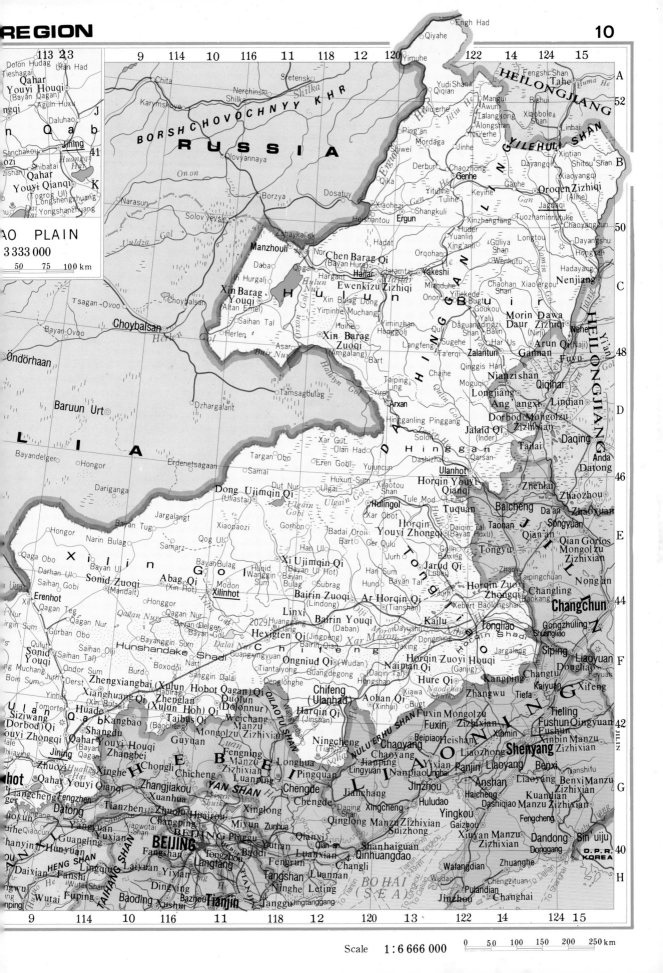

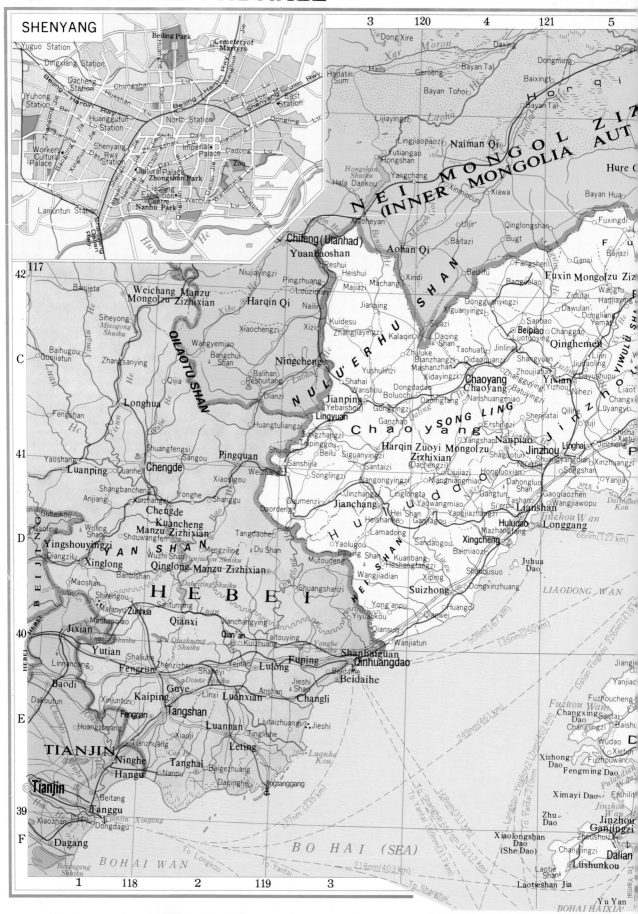

SHENYANG

Yuguo Station
Dingxiang Station
Dacheng Station
Huashan
Yuhong Station
Huanggutun Station
Workers' Cultural Palace
Shenyang Rwy Station
Nanhu Park
Lanjuntun Station

Beijing Park
Cemetery of Martyrs
North Station
Shenyang East Station
Dongling
Imperial Palace
Zoo
Dadong
Zhongshan Park
Cultural Palace
Liaoning Exhibition Centre
Wenhua
Hun He

42 117
Banjieta
Weichang Manzu Mongolzu Zizhixian
Siheyong
Baihugou
Guojiatun
Zhangsanying
Qijia
Longhua
Fengshan
Yaoshang
Luanping
Luanhe
Shangbancheng
Anjiang
Gubeikou
Gaoling
Yingshouyingzi
Qiangzilu
Xinglong
Maoshan
Shinengou
Zunhua
Mashenpao
Jixian
Linnancang
Yutian
Fengrun
Baodi
Dakoutun
Kaiping
Fengnan
Huangzhuang
TIANJIN
Ninghe
Hangu
Tianjin
Beitang
Tanggu
Xiaozhan
Dagu
Dongdagu
Dagang
Beidagang Shuiku

Dong Xire
Hadatin Sum
Lijiayingzi
Lingjiaopaozi
Hala Daokou
Xibo
Xiaochengzi
Wangyemiao
Bangchui Shan
Balihan
Reshuitang
Dianzi
Huangtuliangzi
Songzhangzi
Taipinggou
Sanshijia
Songlingzi
Nangongyingzi
Jinzhangzi
Linglongta
Jianchang
Hei Shan
Heishanke
Lamadong
Yaolugou
Daqing Shan
Mutoudeng
Wangjiadian
Shuangshanzi
Yong'anpu
Yiyuankou
Qiansuo
Wanjiatun

BO HAI (SEA)

BOHAI WAN

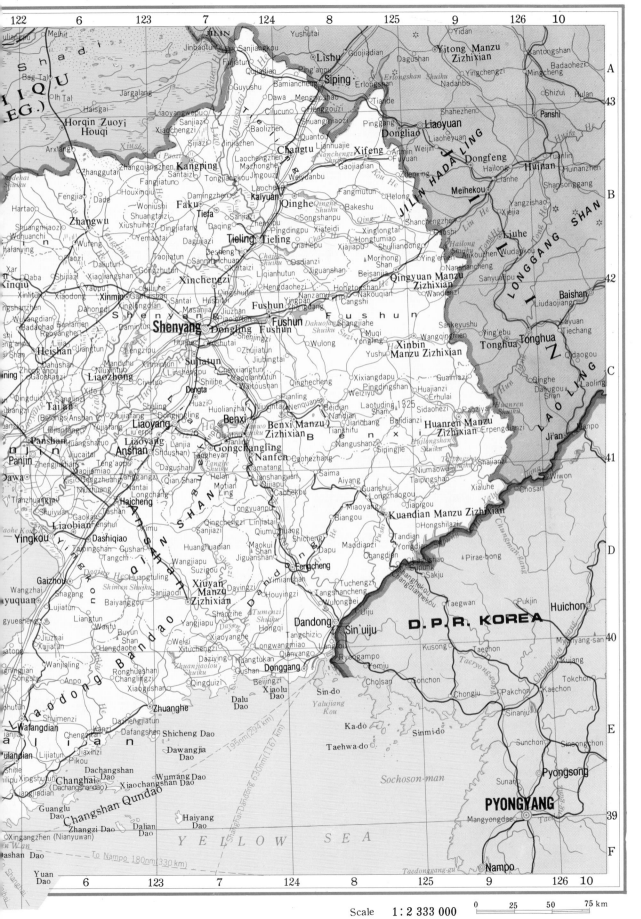

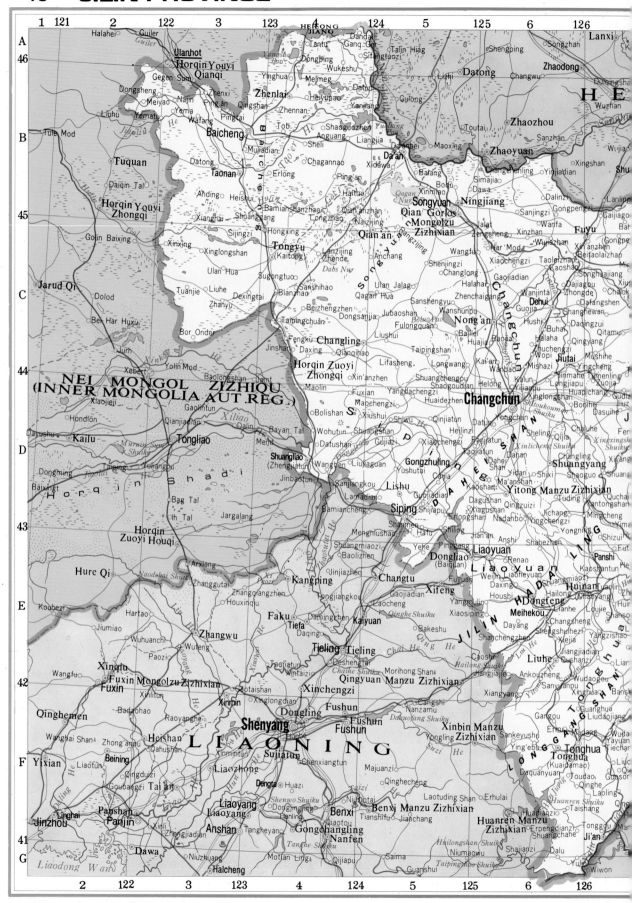

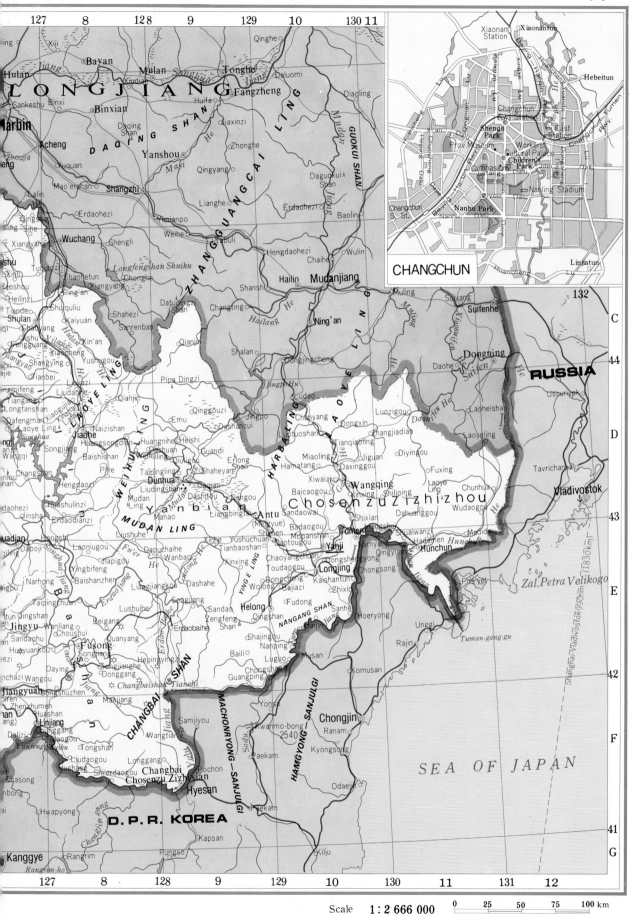

CHANGCHUN

127 8 128 9 129 10 130 11

L O N G J I A N G

Xiji · Qinghe
Bayan
Hulan · Mulan · Tonghe · Daluomi
Xindian · Songhua Jiang · Huifa · Fangzheng · Diaoling
Binxi · Daqiao · Daqing Shan · Jiaxinzi · Guokui Shan
Sankeshu · Binxian · Zhonghe · Daguokui Shan
Harbin · Acheng · Yanshou · Erdaohezi · Baolin
Zhoujia · Xuquan · Qingyang · Lianghe
Mao'erhan · Shangzhi · Yimianpo · Weihe · Hengdaohezi · Chaihe · Wulin
Lalin · Erdaohezi · Shengli · Hailin · Mudanjiang · Muling · Suyang · Suifenhe
Xiangyang · Wuchang · Longfengshan Shuiku · Shanshi · Ning'an · Muling He · Dongning · RUSSIA
Shulan · Shanhetun · Qianjin · Dongjingcheng · Daohe · Suifen He · Laoheishan · Ussuriysk
Kaiyuan · Datuchangzi Shan · Changting · Hailang · Shalan · Jingpo Hu · Chunyang · Luozigou · Laoyeling
Yushugou · Pipa Dingzi · Jingpo · Dongxin · Zhangjiadian · Tavrichanka
Emu · Qinggouzi · Dashanzui · Tianqiaoling · Diyingou · Fuxing · Vladivostok
Naizishan · Huangnihe · Heishi · Guandi · Miaoling · Jiguan · Daxinggou · Laoye Ling · Chunhua · Wudaogou
Jiaohe · Weihuling · Qiujia · Erlong Shan · Hamatang · Xiwaizi · Baicaogou · Wangqing · Shiliping · Dahuanggou
Dunhua · Taipingling · Daqiao · Shaheyanzi · Mopanshan · Shixian · Shuaiwanzi · Madida
Mudan · Dashitou · Nangou · Liangbingtai · Antu (Mingyue) · Sandaowai · Tumen · Namyang · Qingyuan · Hunchun
Liudingshan · Mahao · Yushuchuan · Shihen · Badaogou · Maotougou · Yanji · Hadamen · Hunchun
Xinhe · Tianbaoshan · Chaoyangchuan · Dongshengyong · Posyet
Xinxing · Toudaogou · Longjing · Chongsong
Rongcheng · Kaishantun · Zhixin
Wolong · Bajiazi
Helong · Fudong · Sanhe · Hoeryong
Zengfeng · Qingshan · Unggi
Erdaobaihe · Shajingou · Nanping · Tuman-gang-gu
Baili · Luguo · Musan · Komusan
Changshan · Rajin
Guangping · Chongshan
Changbaishan Tianchi · Yonsa · Chongjin
Songshuzhen · Ranam
Manjiang · Samjiyou · Kwanmo-bong 2540 · Kyongsong
Wangtian · Paekam · Odaejin
Changbai · Pochon
Hyesan · Sepam
Hwapyong · D. P. R. KOREA · Kilju
Kanggye · Rangrim · Pungso
Rangrim-ho

SEA OF JAPAN

Zal. Petra Velikogo (1830 km)

Scale 1 : 2 666 000

0 25 50 75 100 km

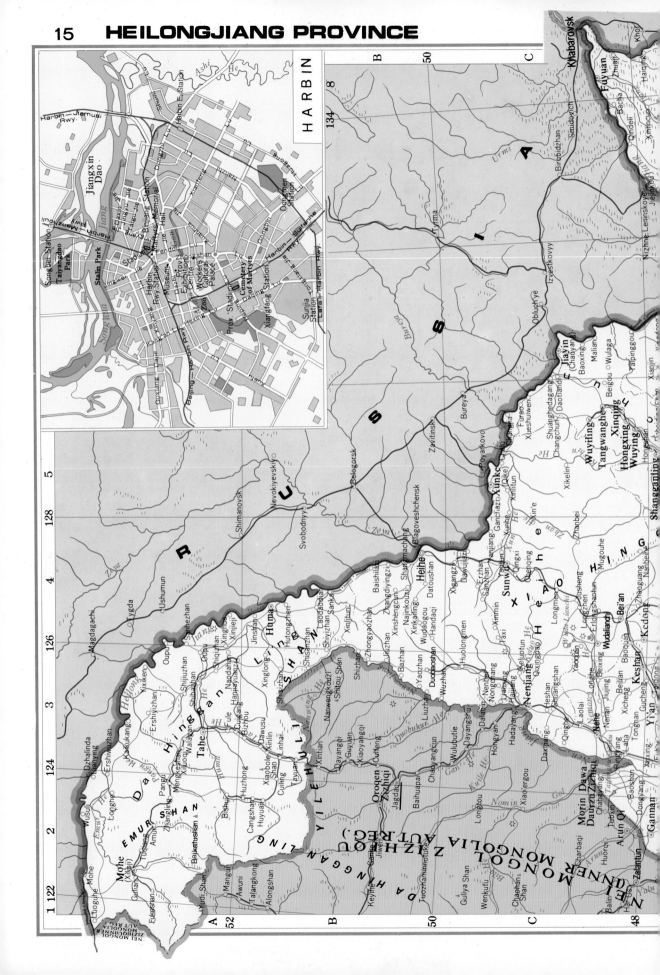

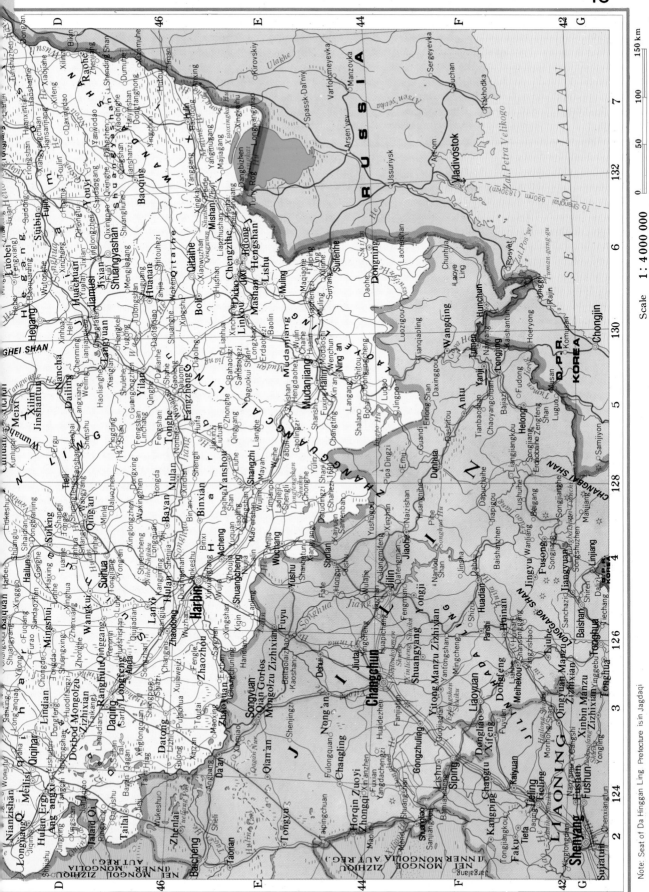

Note: Seat of Da Hinggan Ling Prefecture is in Jagdaqi

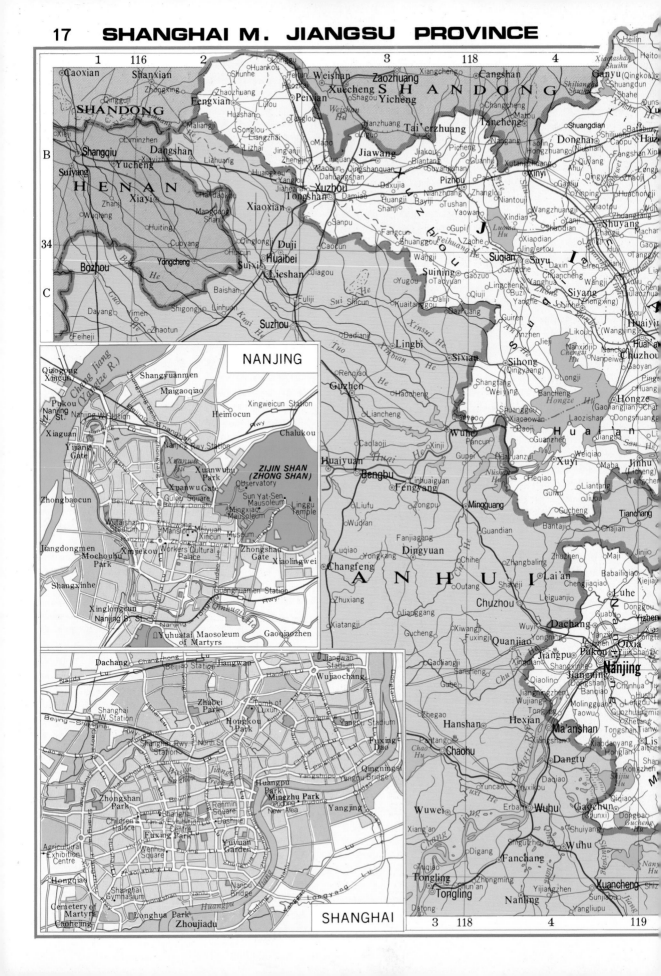

Caoxian • Shanxian •   Huankou   Weishan • Zaozhuang • Xiangcheng • Cangshan •   Ganyu (Qingkou)
Shunhe   Peilun   Xuecheng • S H A N D O N G   Shuangquan • Shahe • Haito
Qingguji   Zhongxing   Zhaozhuang • Haozhuang • Peixian • Yicheng •   Changcheng •   Yu • Xia
SHANDONG   Fengxian • Huashan • Lufou • Shagou • Tai'erzhuang • Tancheng •   Matou • Shuangdian •
Shangqiu • Dangshan • Malianggi • Songlou • Tanglou • Jiawang • Biantang • Nangang • Taoin • Donghai • Haiz
Suiyang • Yucheng • Liangzhai • Jingji • Zhenji • Daoun • Qingshanquan • Xutangzhuang • Hongzhuang • Quyang • Fangshan Xin •
H E N A N   Xiayi • Handaoku • Xuzhou • Tongshan • Damiao • Huangji • Bayji • Tushan • Yaowan • Wangzhuangji • Miaotou • Shuyang •
Zhanji • Manggang Shan • Xiaoxian • Sanji • Gupi • Niantouji • Zanji •
Wuqiang • Huiting • Qinglongji • Duji • Caocun • Fangcun • Shuangqou • Zaohe • Xindian • Xiaodian • Jing'ertou • Suqian • Suyu • Daxin •
Cupyang • Yongcheng • Suixi • Huaibei • Jiagou • Yugou • Qiuji • Buzi • Zhong • Ling • Siyang •
Bozhou • Baishan • Lieshan • Fuliji • Shicun • Dazhuang • Guiren • Likou • Huaiyi •
Dayang • Yimen • Shigongji • Linhuan • He • Dalji • Xinsui He • Anzhen • Jieji • Chengzi Hu • Chuzhou •
Feiheji • Zhaotun • Suzhou • Dadianji • Lingbi • Sixian • Sihong •

SHANGHAI

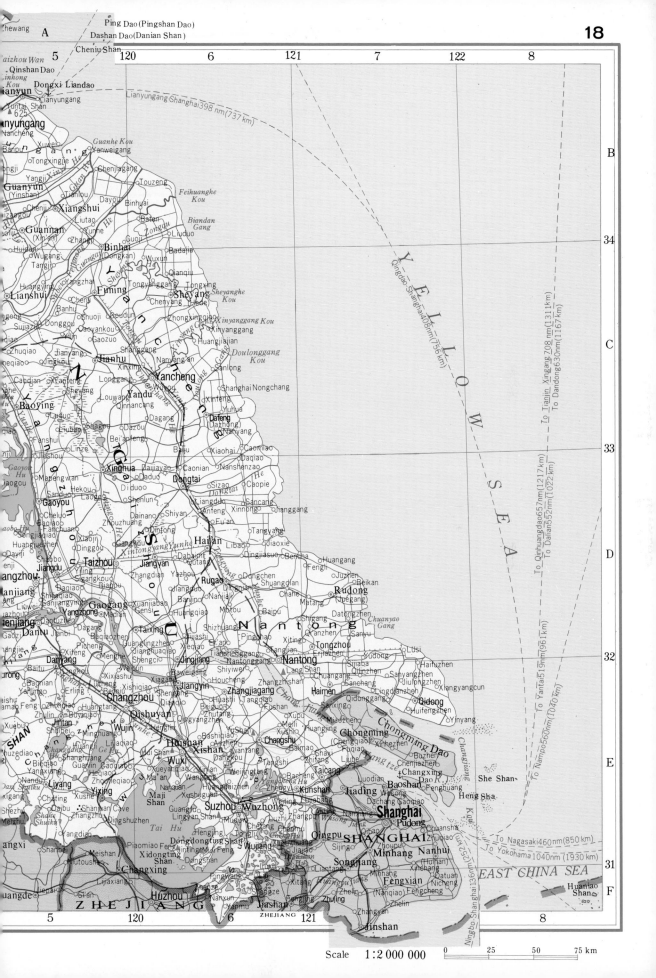

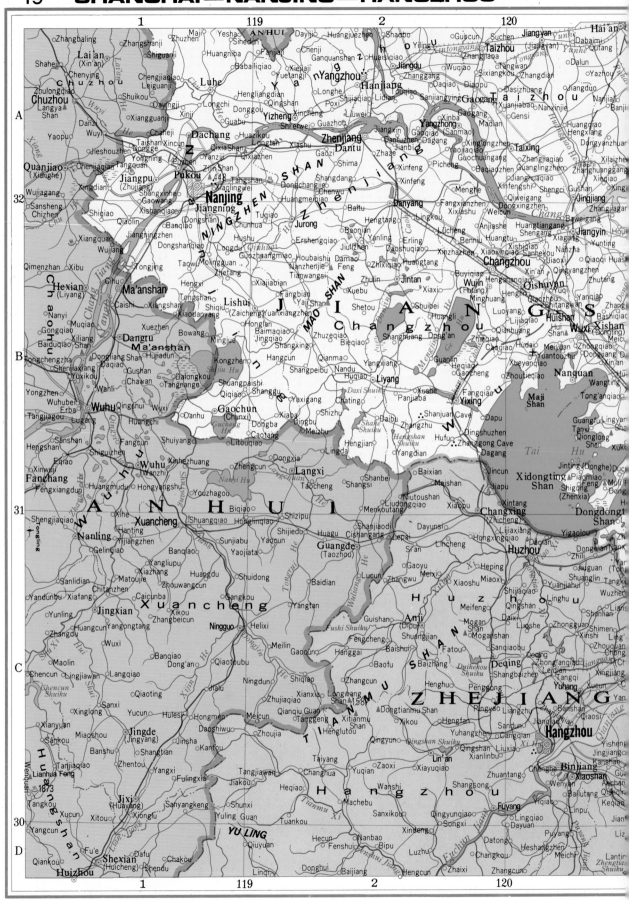

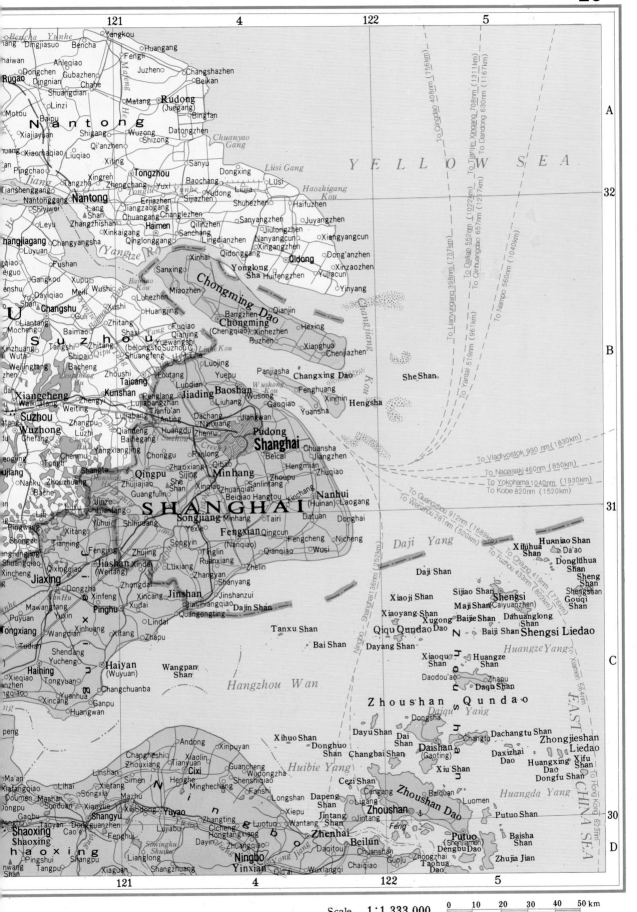

Scale   1:1 333 000   0   10   20   30   40   50 km

HANGZHOU

Gudang
Tianmushan Lu
Zhejiang
Exhibition Centre
Huanglong Cave
Baochu Pagoda
Ziyun Cave
Jade Spring
Yue Fei Temple
Botanical Garden
Beigao Feng
Lingyin Temple
Feilai Feng
Xiatianzhu
Zhongtianzhu
Gu Shan
Autumn Moon on Calm Lake
Mid-Lake Pavilion
Xiaoyingzhou Isle
Three Pools Mirroring the Moon
Huagang Park
Nangao Feng
Shangtianzhu
Dragon Well
Yanxia Cave
Shuile Cave
Fenghuang Shan
ShiwuCave
Tiger Spring
Zoo
Yuhuang Shan
Zilai Cave
Nine Creeks and Eighteen Gullies
Nine Creeks
Exhibition Hall of the Deedsof Martyr Cai Yongxiang
Liuhe Pagoda
Wuyun Shan
Zhejiang
Jiangxi
Fuxing
Qiantangjiang Bridge
Qiantang Jiang
Xixing Jiangbian
Nanxingqiao Station
Genshanmen Station
Gymnasium
Children's Palace
Huangcheng
Hangzhou Rwy. Station
Wu Shan
Xi Hu (West L.)

ANHUI

Shiguizhen
Wuhu (Wanzhi)
Langxi
Fanchang
Shanbei
Niutoushan
Chang
Meishan
Xuancheng
Guangde
Nanling
Yijiangzhen
Sunjiabu
Shuangqiao
Yanglinpu
Jingxian
Yangtan
Helixi
Fusui Shuiku
Fengcheng (Dipu)
Ningguo
Maolin
Sanlidian
Langqiao
Yucun
Daoshiwu
Zhoujia
Hengloutou Shan
Qingyun
Lin'an
Jingde
Jinsha
Shexian
Datu
Huizhou
Huangshan (Tunxi)
Wucheng

TIANMU SHAN
YU LING

QIANLI GANG
BAIJI SHAN
HUANG SHAN

Kaihua
Quzhou
Qu Jiang
Jinhua
Changshan
Jiangshan

XIANXIA LING

JIANGXI

Jingdezhen
Boyang
Poyang Hu
Leping
Dexing
Wannian
Yugan
Yiyang
Shangrao
Guangfeng
Dongxiang
Yujiang
Yingtan
Guixi
Yanshan
Jinxi
Nancheng
Zixi
Guangze
Nanfeng
Lichuan

WUYI SHAN
SHAN LING

FUJIAN

Pucheng
Wuyishan
Zhenghe
Shouning
Songxi
Qingyuan
Longquan
Yunhe
Songyang
Suichang
Lishu

Shaowu
Jianyang

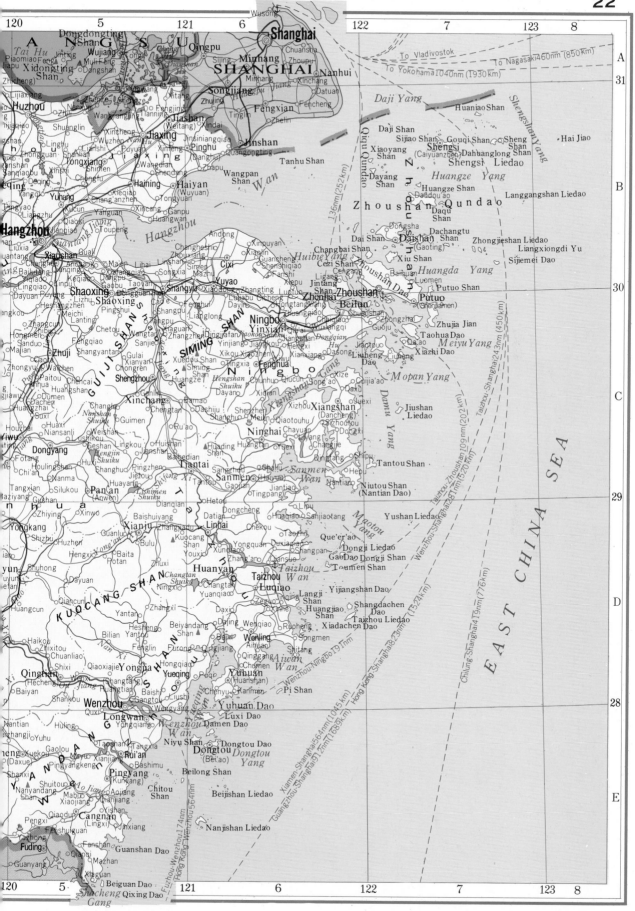

Scale 1:2 000 000

0   25   50   75 km

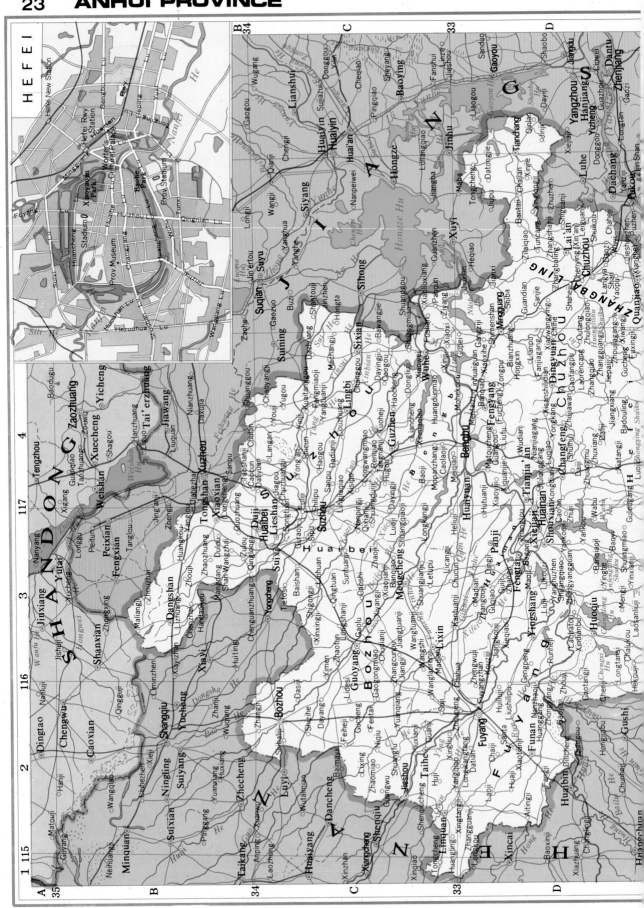

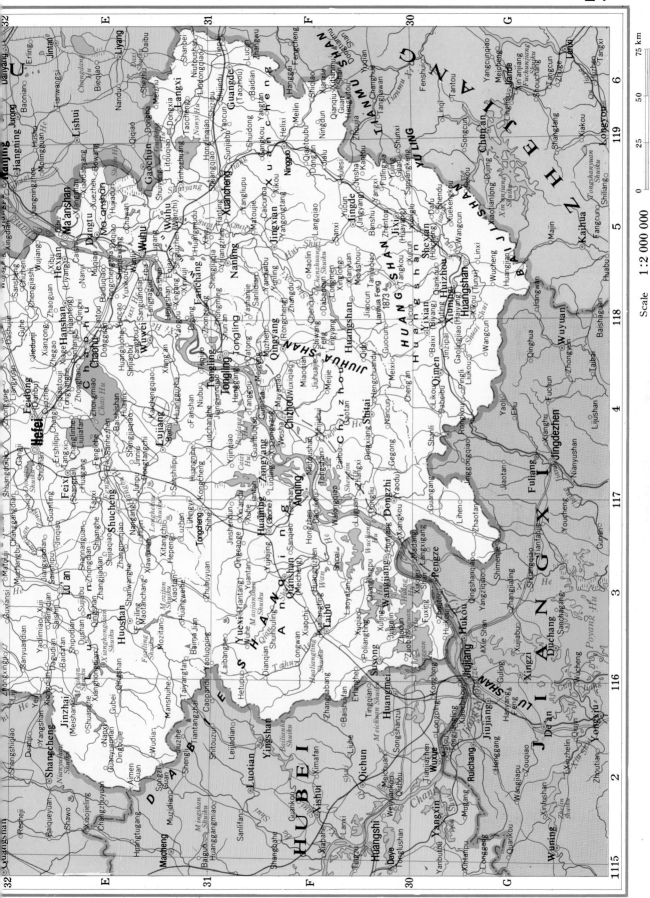

Scale 1:2 000 000

0   25   50   75 km

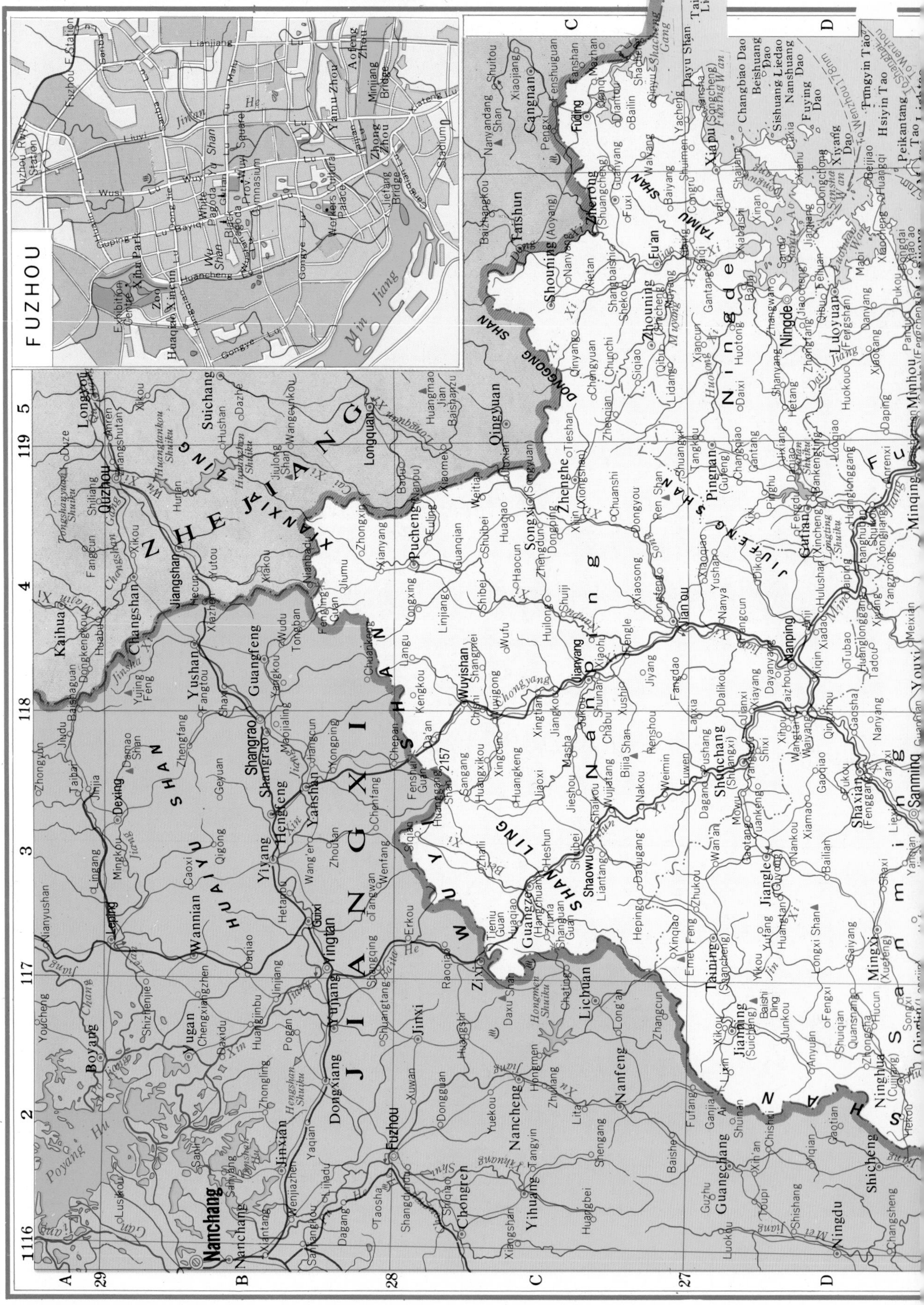

FUZHOU

ZHEJIANG

JIANGXI

Ningde

Nanping

Sanming

Nanchang

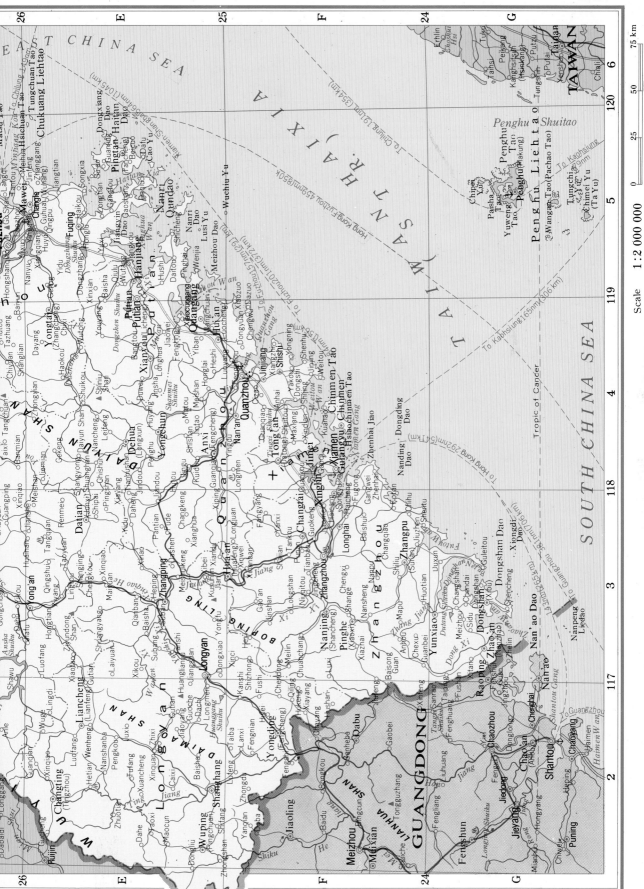

EAST CHINA SEA

SOUTH CHINA SEA

TAIWAN

TAIWAN STRAIT (TAIWAN HAIXIA)

GUANGDONG

Penghu Liehtao

Penghu Shuitao

Scale   1:2 000 000

Tropic of Cancer

0   25   50   75 km

QUANZHOU

ZHANGZHOU

LONGYAN

DAIYUN SHAN

DAIMAO SHAN

BOPING LING

LIANHUA SHAN

Xiamen

Quanzhou

Putian

Fuqing

Zhangzhou

Longyan

Meizhou

Shantou

Chaozhou

Chaoyang

Jieyang

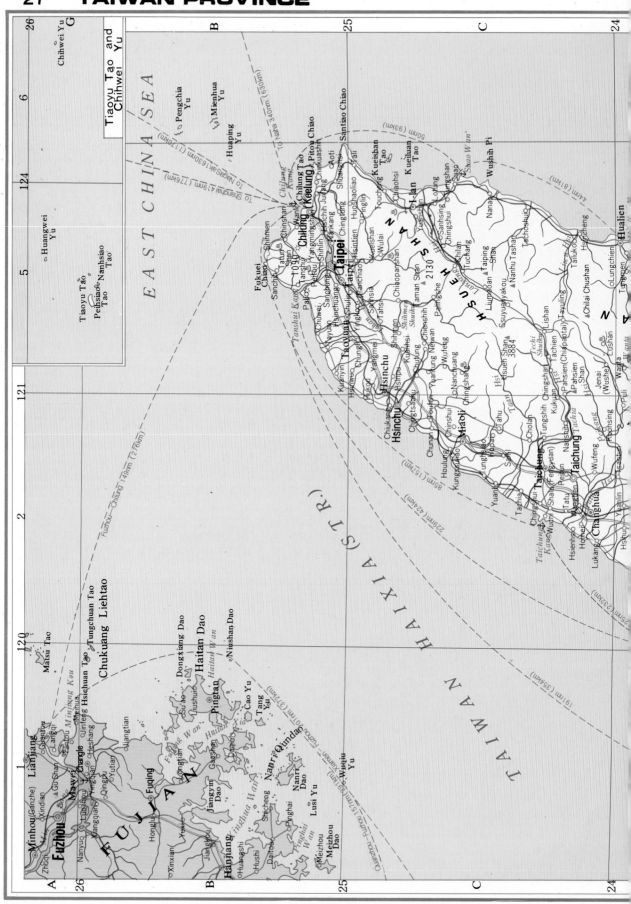

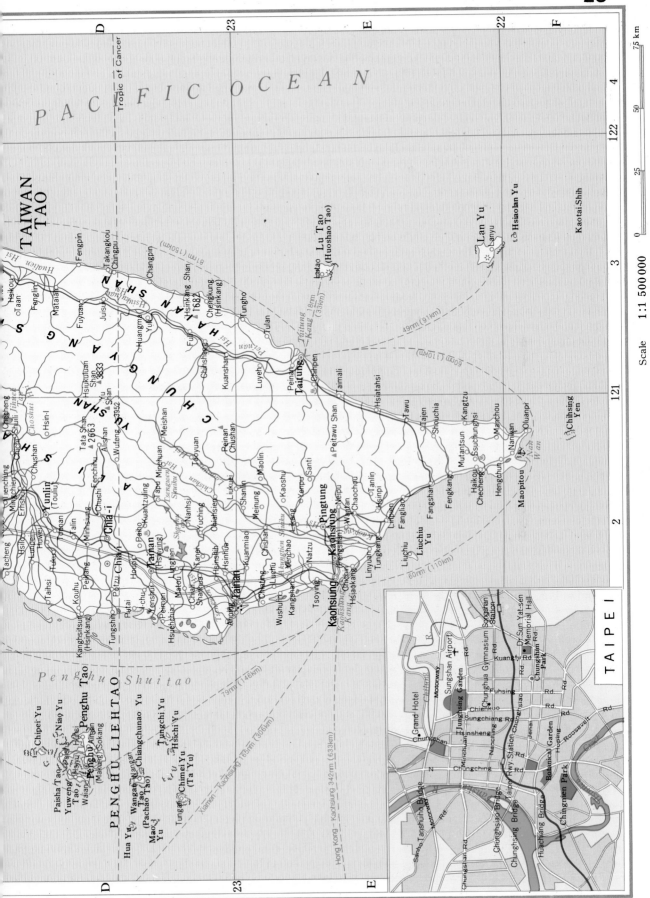

PACIFIC OCEAN

TAIWAN TAO

Scale   1:1 500 000

75 km

TAIPEI

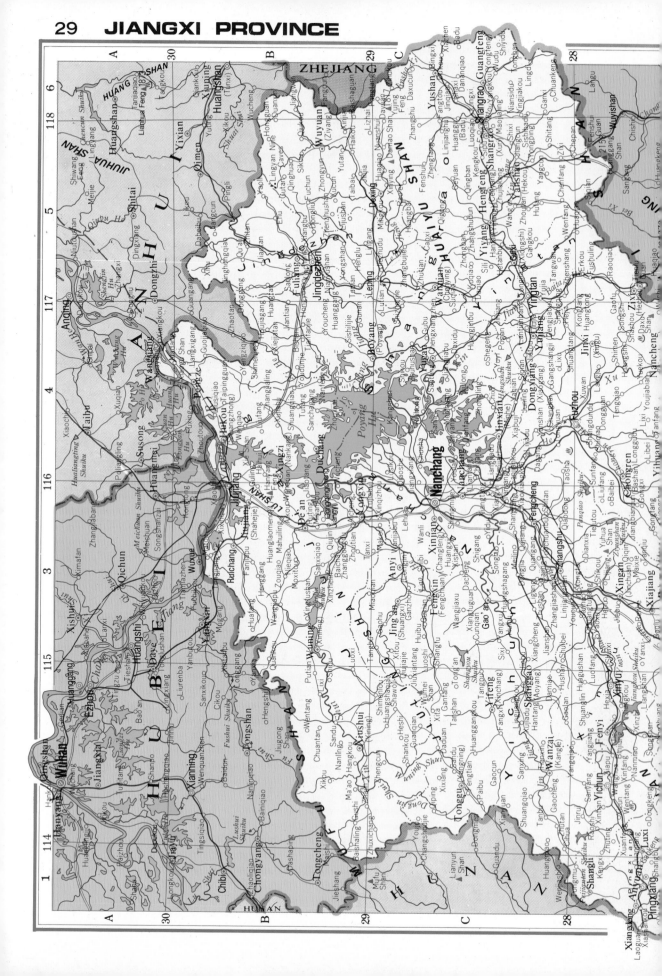

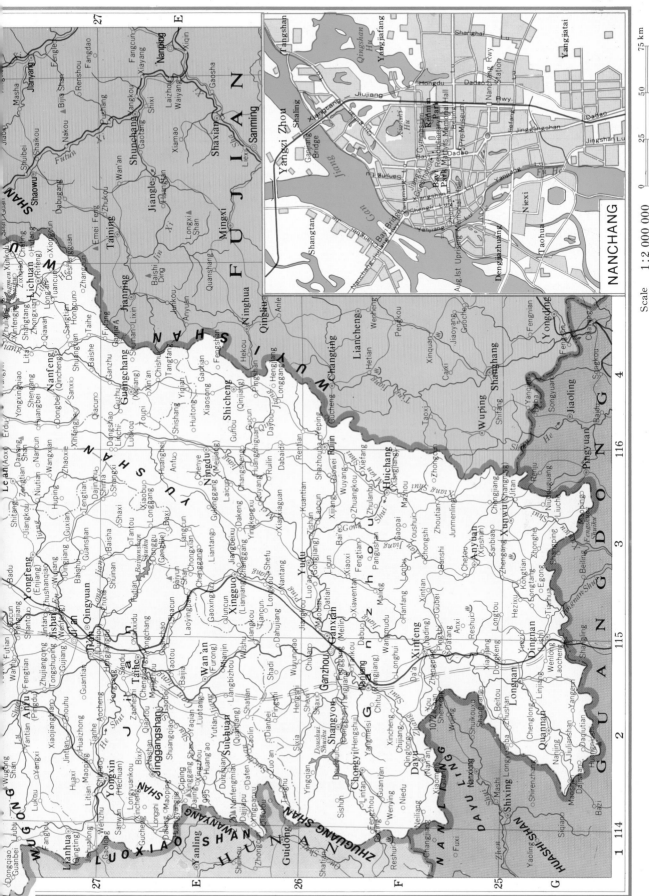

NANCHANG   Scale   1:2 000 000

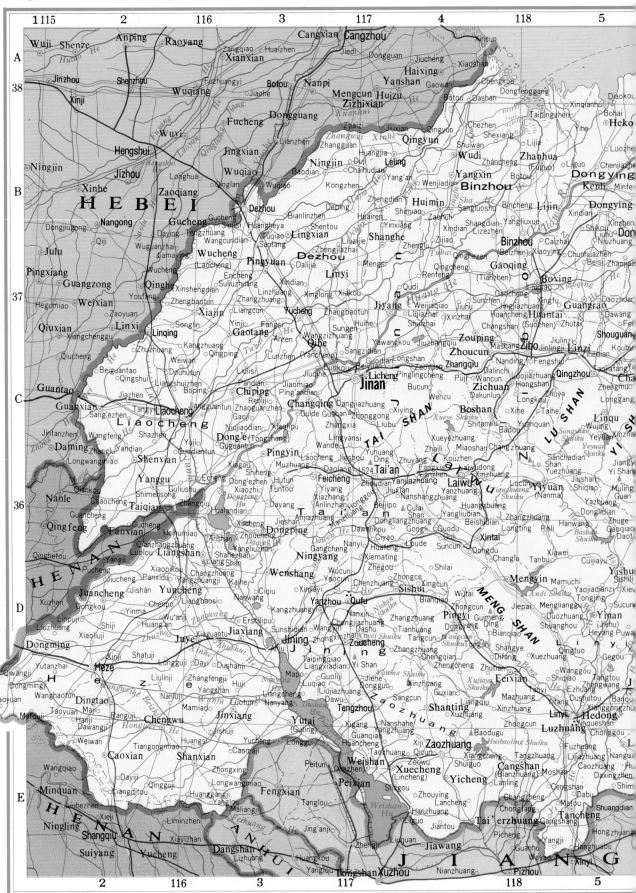

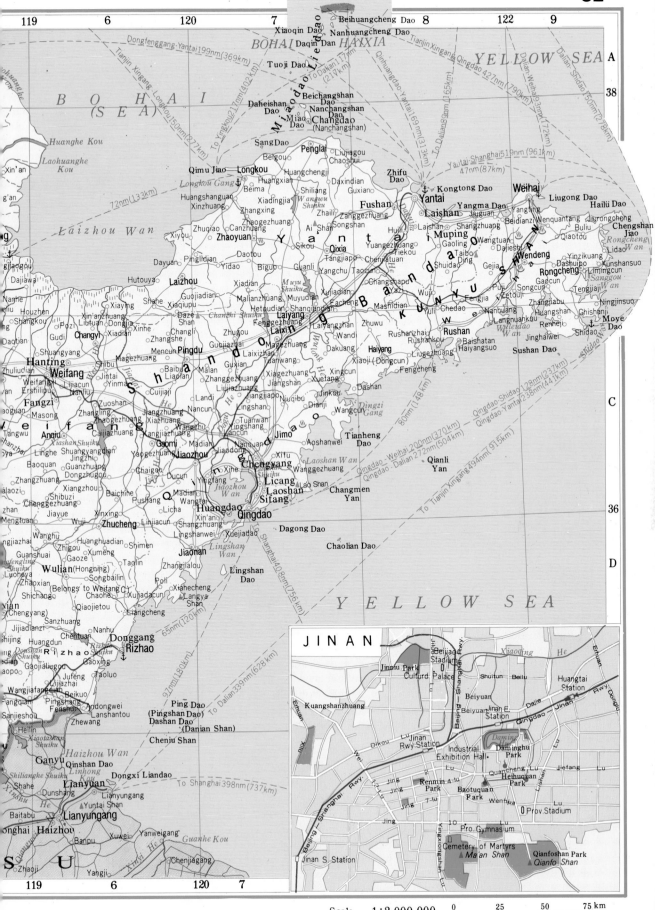

BOHAI HAIXIA

Xiaoqin Dao　Beihuangcheng Dao　8　122　9

Daqin Dan　Nanhuangcheng Dao

Dongfenggang-Yantai199nm(369km)

Tianjin Xingang Qingdao 427nm(790km)

Dalian-Shidao150nm(278km) A

Tuoji Dao

YELLOW SEA

38

B O H A I
(SEA)

Huanghe Kou

Laohuanghe Kou

Xin'an

g'an

gilaogou

Daheishan Dao
Nanchangshan Dao
Miao Dao
Changdao (Nanchangshan)

SangDao

Belgou

Penglai

Liujiagou
Chaoshui

Zhifu Dao

Kongtong Dao

Yantai

Weihai

Liugong Dao
Hailü Dao

Laizhou Wan

72nm(133km)

Qimu Jiao　Longkou
Longkou Gang
Huangxian
Beima
Xiadingjia

Huangchengji
Daxindian
Guxian

Fushan

Laishan

Yangma Dao
Jiguan
Yangting
Beidianzi Wenquantang

Jirongcheng

Chengshan Jiao

Rongcheng
Lidao

Rongcheng Wan

Huangshanguan
Xinzhuang
Zhangxing

Zhaili

Zanggezhuang
Songshan

Huili
Shangzhuang

Muping
Gaoling

Wangtuan

Daliesh

Yinzikuang
Dashuipo

Xunshansuo

Ningjinsuo

Ai Shan

Zhaili

Taibo Ding

Gejia

Puji

Wendeng

Limingcun

Zhuqiao
Canzhuang

Zhaoyuan

Xiyou
Daotou

Pingliddian
Yidao

Qixia

Yuangezhuang
Chenjiatuan
Tiekou

Shuidao

Zetouji
Songcun

Dashuipo
Gaocun

Sanggou Wan

Tengjiaji

Dayuan

Hutouya

Laizhou

Xiadian
Xiaqiupu

Guojiadian

Biguo
Guanli

Changshapu

Yazi

Wuji
Chedao

Fengjia

Nanhuang
Zhangjiabu

Chishanji

Huangshan

Xiaying
Shahe

Daze Shan

Mallanzhuang
Muyudian
Xujiadian

Yangchu

Langnuankou

Renheji

Moye
Dao

Shangkou

Houzhen

Gudi

Shuangyang

Changyi

Xiadian
Xinhe

Hetoudian
Fenggezhuang
Shanqiandish

Laiyang
Laiyangzhan

Mashidian
Yuli

Shidao

Dongtai

Daojan

Pingdu

Mencun

Magezhuang
Changli
Zhangshe

Zhugou

Laixi

Magezhuang
Dakuang

Zhuwu

Wandi

Rusharizhai
Rushankou

Rushan

Baishatan
Haiyangsuo

Sushan Dao

Hanting

Weifang

Shibu
Libuan
Dongjia

Baibua
Liaofan

Guojiazhai
Guxian

Malan

Xiagezhuang
Jiangshan

Haiyang

Liugezhuang

Fengcheng

Zhuliudian

Weifang
Ershilibu

Jintai
Yinma

Cuijiaji

Zhanggezhuang
Liujiazhuang
Landi

Xuefang

Xingcun

Dashan

Fangzi

Masong

Zuoshan
Zhangjia

Nancun

Lingshan

Niuqibu

Jjinkou

Dianji

Wangcun

Dingzi Gang

80nm(148km)

Qingdao-Shidao128nm(237km)

Qingdao-Yantai238nm(441km)

C

Anqiu

Caijiazhuang
Yaogezhuang
Xianjiazhuang

Gaomi
Madian

Jiaozhou
Jiaodong

Xihe
Nanquan

Tuanwan
Wanggezhuang

Tianheng Dao

Aoshanwei

Qingdao-Weihai200nm(370km)

Qingdao-Dalian272nm(504km)

Qianli
Yan

Jingzhi

Chaigezhuang
BaichHe

Guanzhuang
Dongzhugou

Ducun

Yingfang

Chengyang

Laoshan Wan

Licang

Laoshan

Changmen
Yan

Xiangzhou

Pushang

Madian
Wangtai
Licha

Sifang

Qingdao

Qingdao-Dalian494nm(915km)

Chenggezhuang

Jiayue
Xinxing

Huangdao

Dagong Dao

36

Zhucheng
Linjiacun

Lingshanwei
Xuejiadao

Chaolian Dao

Wanghu

Huanghuadian
Zhigou

Shimen

Lingshan Wan

D

Guanshuai

Xumeng
Gaoze

Taglin

Jiaonan

To Shanghai408nm(756km)

Wulian(Hongning)

Songbailin

Zhaoxian
Shichang

Chaohe
Qiaojietou

Poli

Xiahecheng
Langya Shan

Lingshan
Dao

65nm(120km)

Sanzhuang

Chentuan

Nanhu

Liangcheng

YELLOW SEA

JINAN

Jijiadianzi
Shijing
Huangdun

Donggang

Rizhao

97nm(180km)

To Dalian339nm(628km)

Gaojialiugou

Jufeng
Lijiazhai

Baoxing
Taoluo

Wangjiafangqian

Andongwei
Lanshantou

Ping Dao
(Pingshan Dao)

Pingshang
Fenshu

Zhewang

Dashan Dao
(Danian Shan)

Fanqian

Sanjieshou

Heilin

Chenju Shan

Ganyu

Haizhou Wan

Qinshan Dao

Lianyuan

Shilianghe Shuiku

Dongxi Liandao

Lianyungang

Dunshang

Lianyungang

Baitabu

Yuntai Shan

Lianyungang

S U

Shanghai

Haizhou

Banpu

Xuwei
Yanweigang

Guanhe Kou

Zhaoji

Yangji

Chenjiagang

Scale　1:2 000 000　　0　25　50　75 km

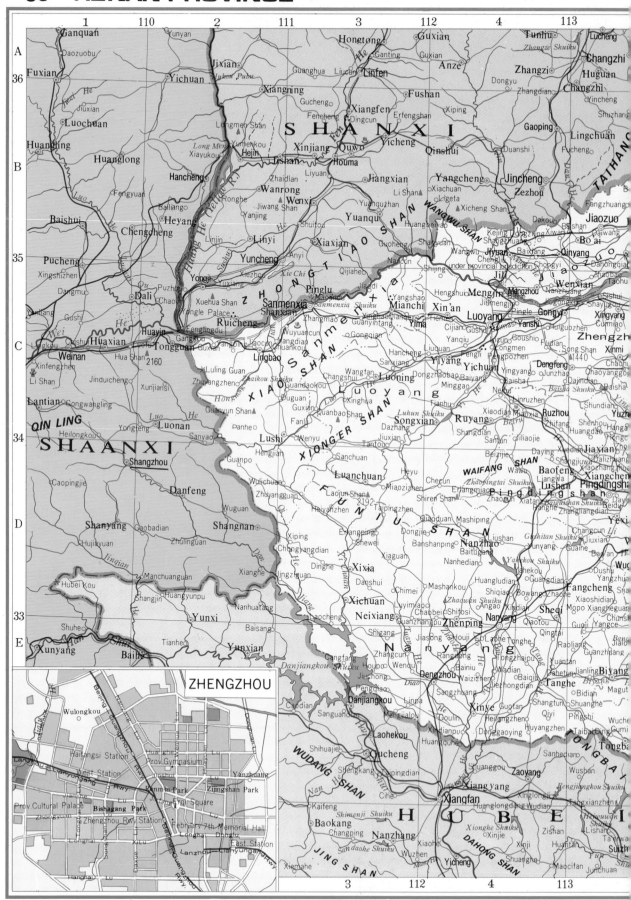

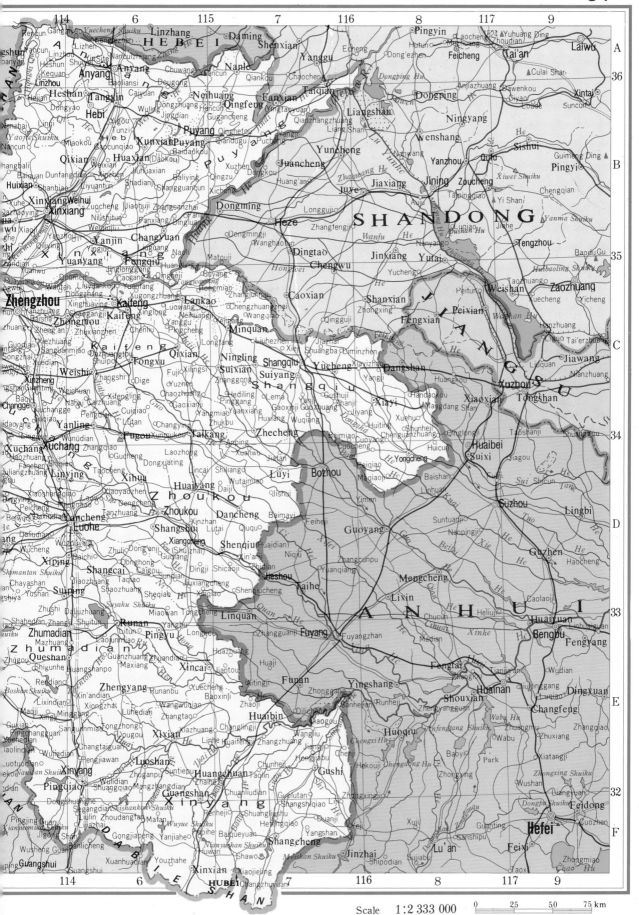

Scale   1:2 333 000   0 25 50 75 km

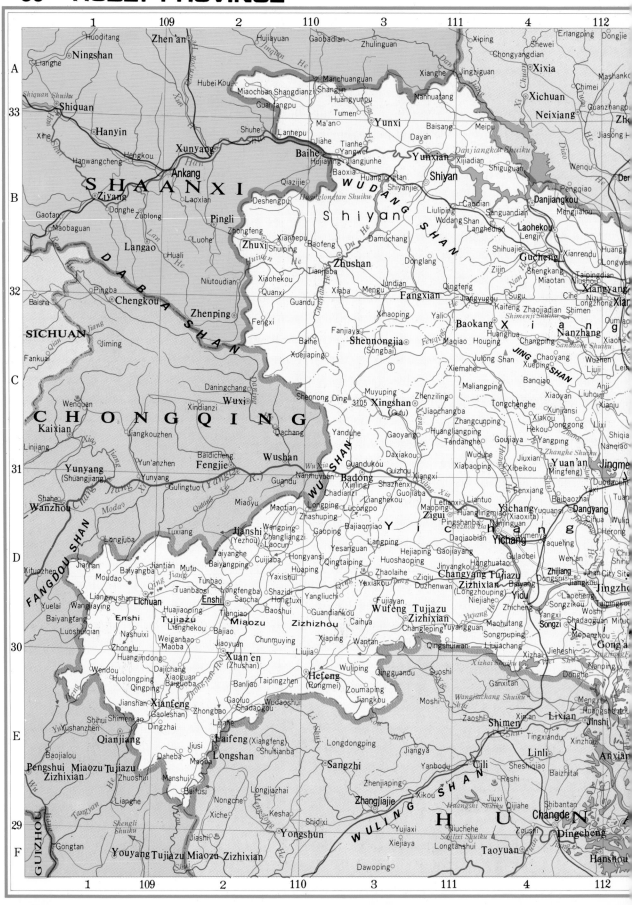

Scale 1:2 333 000

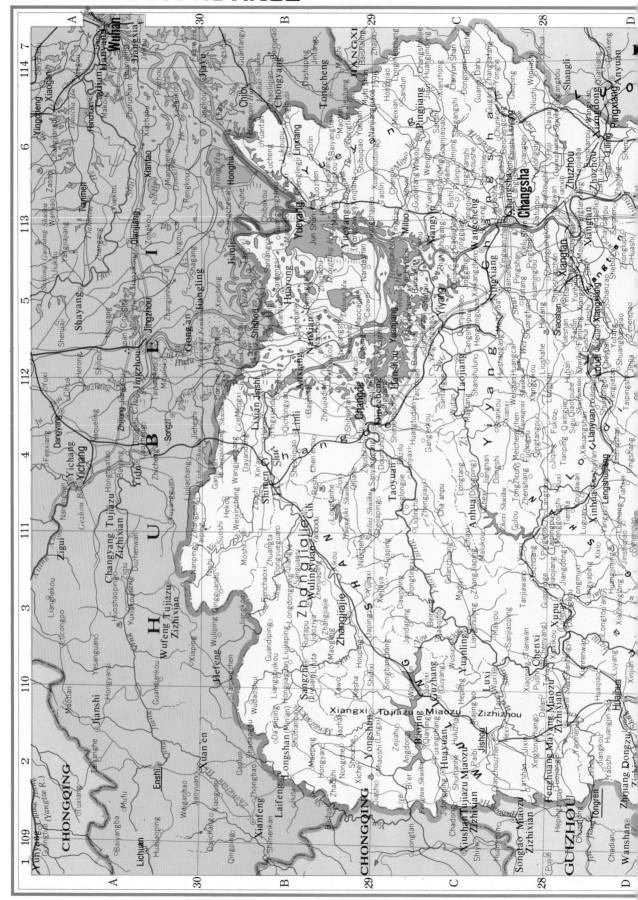

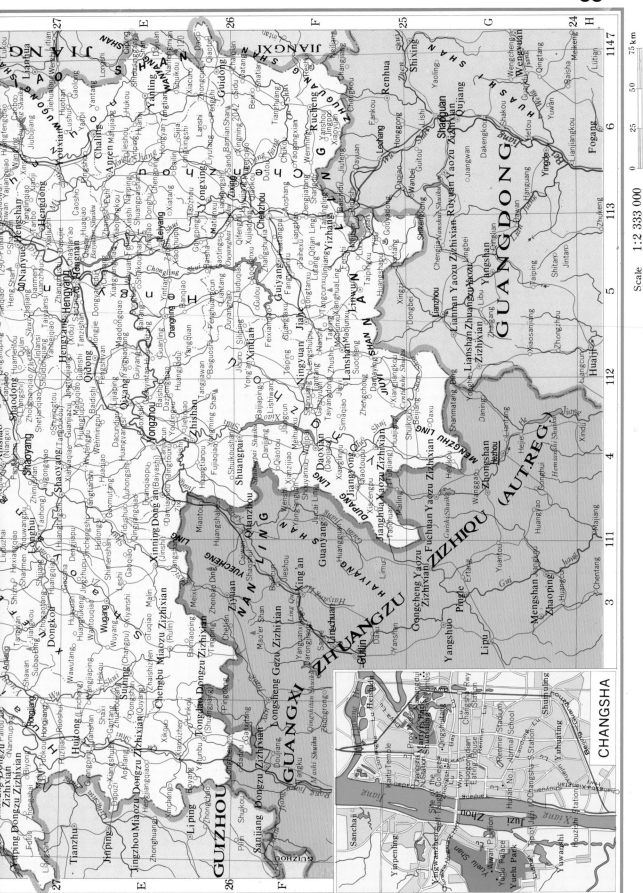

Scale 1:2 333 000

CHANGSHA

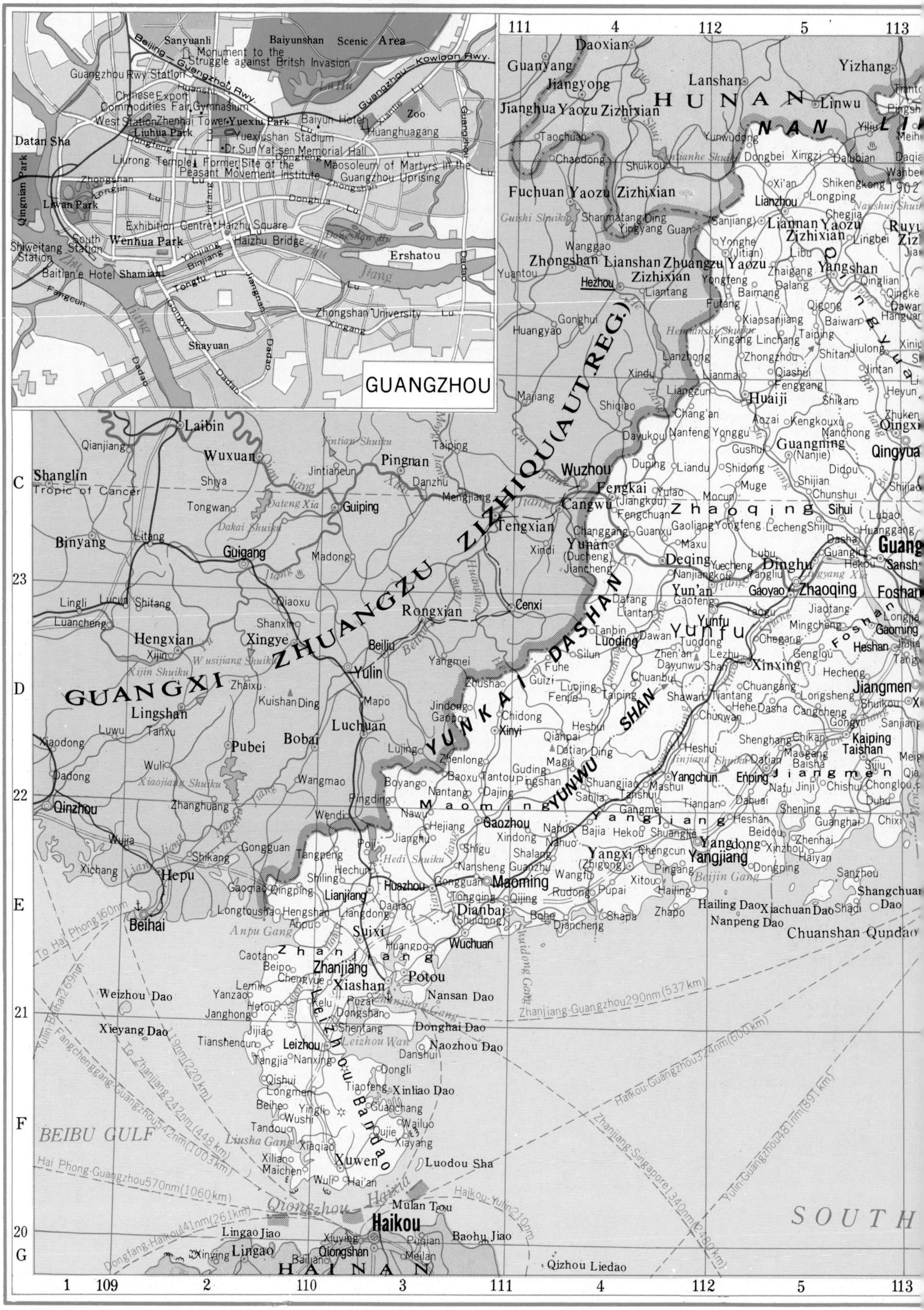
GUANGZHOU
Baiyunshan Scenic Area
Sanyuanli
Monument to the Struggle against Britsh Invasion
Beijing-Guangzhou Rwy.
Guangzhou-Kowloon Rwy.
Guangzhou Rwy. Station
Chinese Export Commodities Fair
Gymnasium
West Station
Zhenhai Tower
Yuexiu Park
Liuhua Park
Baiyun Hotel
Zoo
Huanghuagang
Yuexiushan Stadium
Dr. Sun Yat-sen Memorial Hall
Liurong Temple
Former Site of the Peasant Movement Institute
Maosoleum of Martyrs in the Guangzhou Uprising
Datan Sha
Qingnian Park
Liwan Park
Exhibition Centre
Haizhu Square
Haizhu Bridge
Wenhua Park
South Station
Shiweitang Station
Baitian'e Hotel
Shamian
Ershatou
Zhongshan University
Shayuan
Zhu Jiang
111
4
112
5
113
Daoxian
Guanyang
Jiangyong
Jianghua Yaozu Zizhixian
HUNAN
Lanshan
Linwu
Yizhang
Taochuan
Chaodong
Shuikou
Fuchuan Yaozu Zizhixian
Zhongshan
Lianshan Zhuangzu Yaozu Zizhixian
Hezhou
Lianzhou
Liannan Yaozu Zizhixian
Yangshan
Huaiji
Guangning
Qingyuan
Wuzhou
Cangwu
Fengkai
Zhaoqing
Sihui
Deqing
Dinghu
Zhaoqing
Yunfu
Yun'an
Foshan
Xinxing
Jiangmen
Heshan
Kaiping
Taishan
Enping
Yangchun
Yangjiang
Yangdong
Yangxi
Maoming
Gaozhou
Huazhou
Dianbai
Wuchuan
Lianjiang
Suixi
Zhanjiang
Potou
Xiashan
Leizhou
Xuwen
Leizhou Bandao
Nansan Dao
Donghai Dao
Naozhou Dao
Hailing Dao
Chuanshan Qundao
YUNKAI DASHAN
YUNWU SHAN
GUANGXI ZHUANGZU ZIZHIQU (AUT. REG.)
Laibin
Wuxuan
Pingnan
Guiping
Guigang
Tengxian
Cenxi
Rongxian
Yulin
Beiliu
Luchuan
Bobai
Pubei
Lingshan
Hengxian
Binyang
Shanglin
Tropic of Cancer
Qinzhou
Hepu
Beihai
Weizhou Dao
Xieyang Dao
BEIBU GULF
Qiongzhou Haixia
Haikou
Lingao
Qiongshan
HAINAN
SOUTH
Qizhou Liedao
Zhanjiang-Guangzhou 290nm (537 km)
Haikou-Guangzhou 324nm (600 km)
Hai Phong-Guangzhou 570nm (1060 km)
Zhanjiang-Singapore 1340nm (2480 km)
Yulin-Guangzhou 481nm (891 km)
C
D
E
F
G
23
22
21
20
1
109
2
110
3
111
4
112
5
113

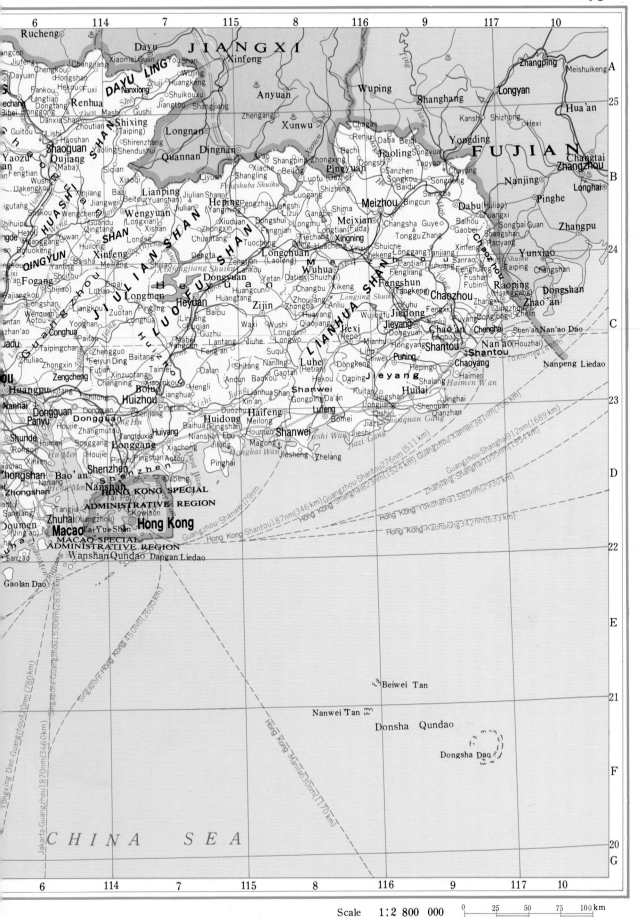

Scale 1:2 800 000

0   25   50   75   100 km

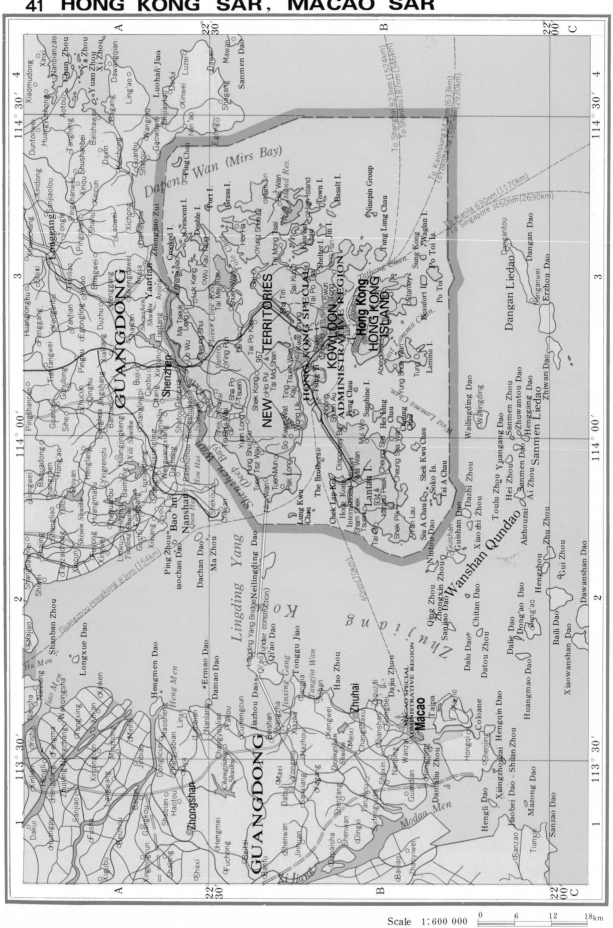

Scale 1:600 000

0   6   12   18km

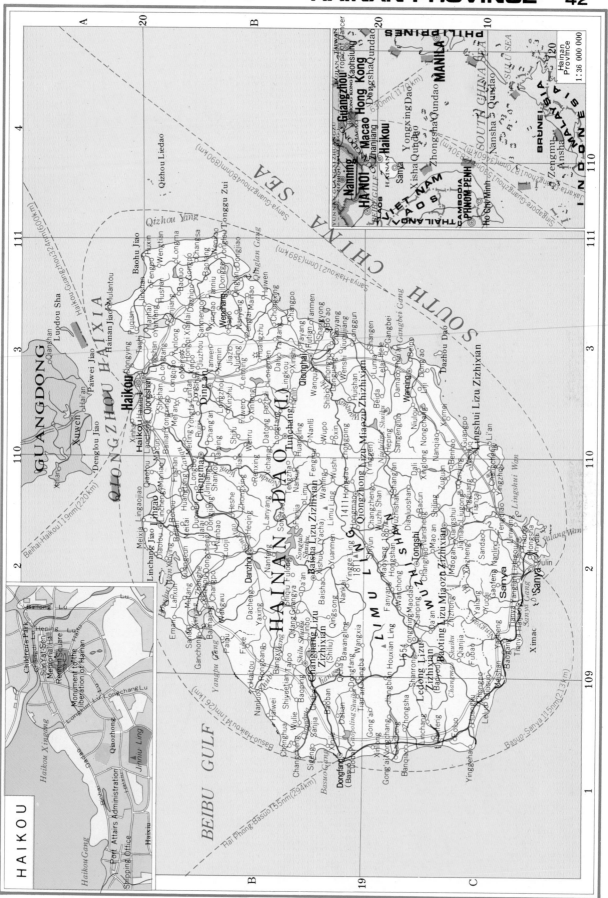

NANNING

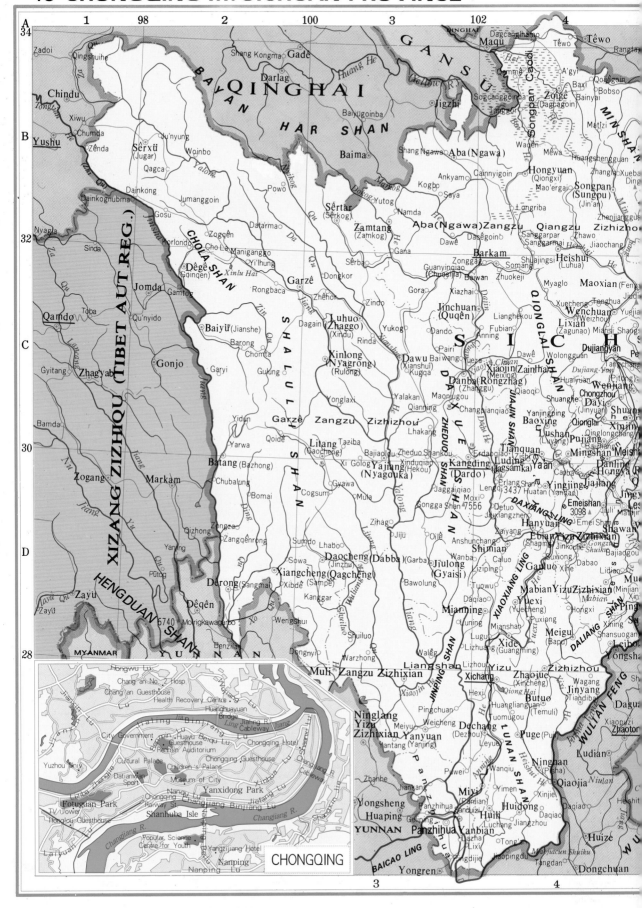

CHONGQING

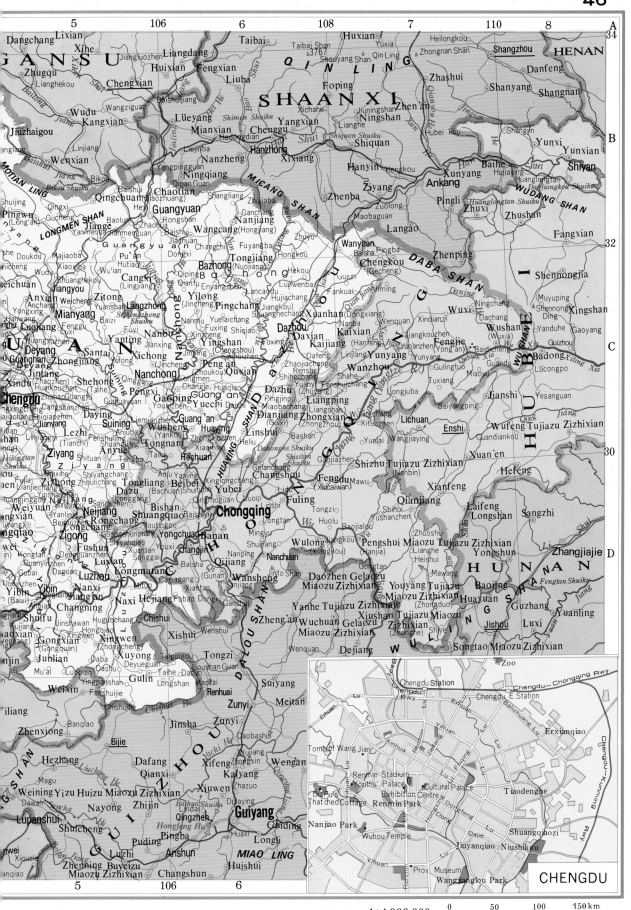

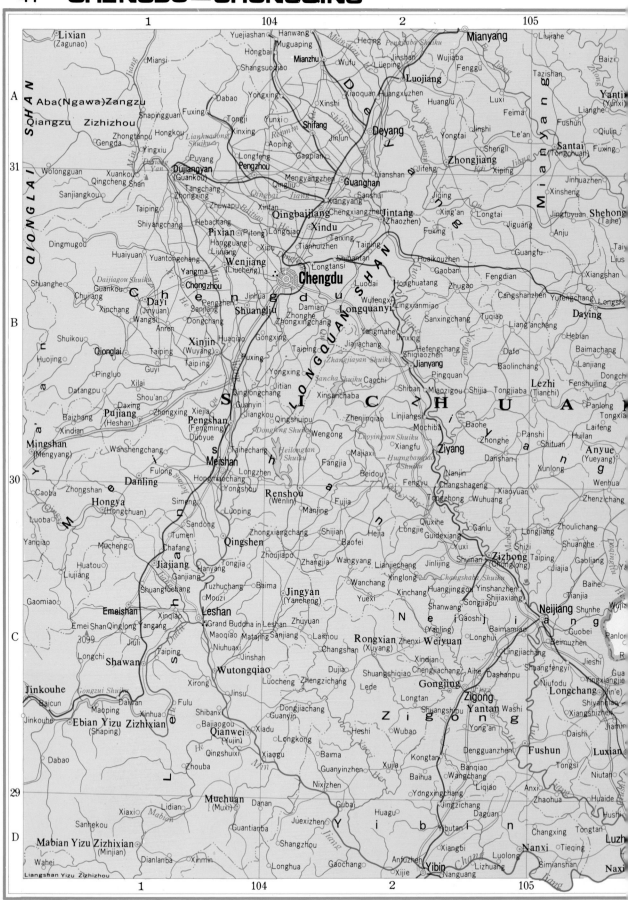

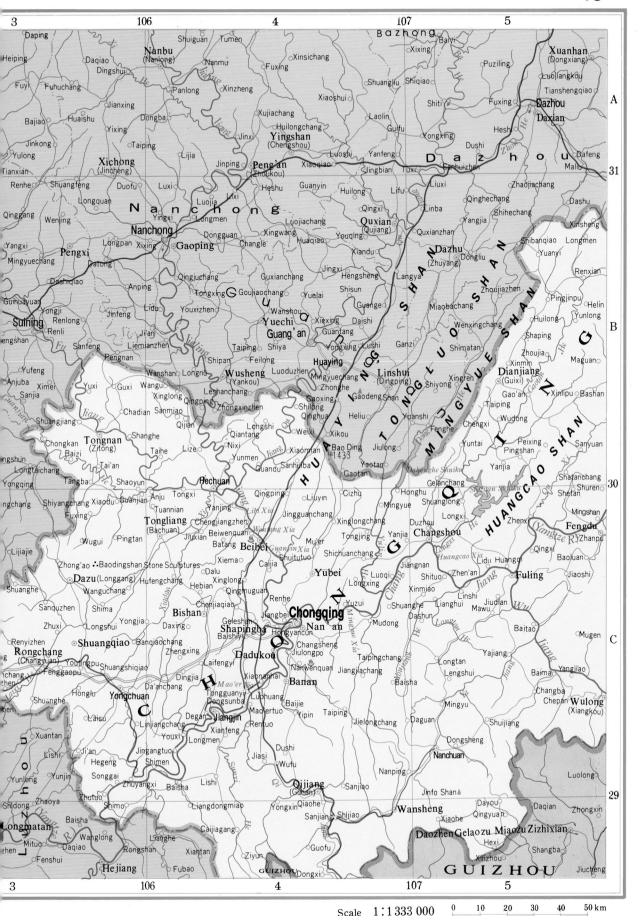

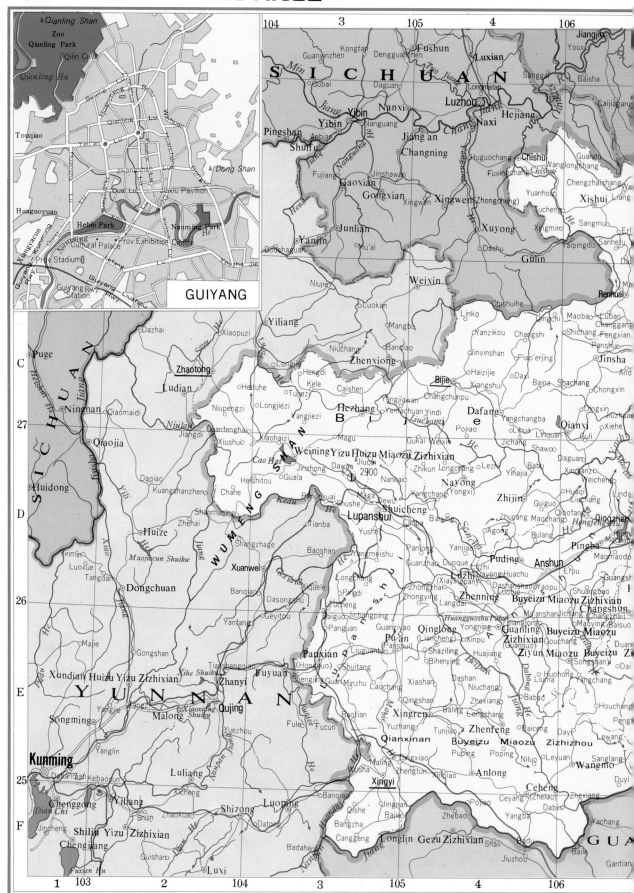

① belongs to Lupanshui C

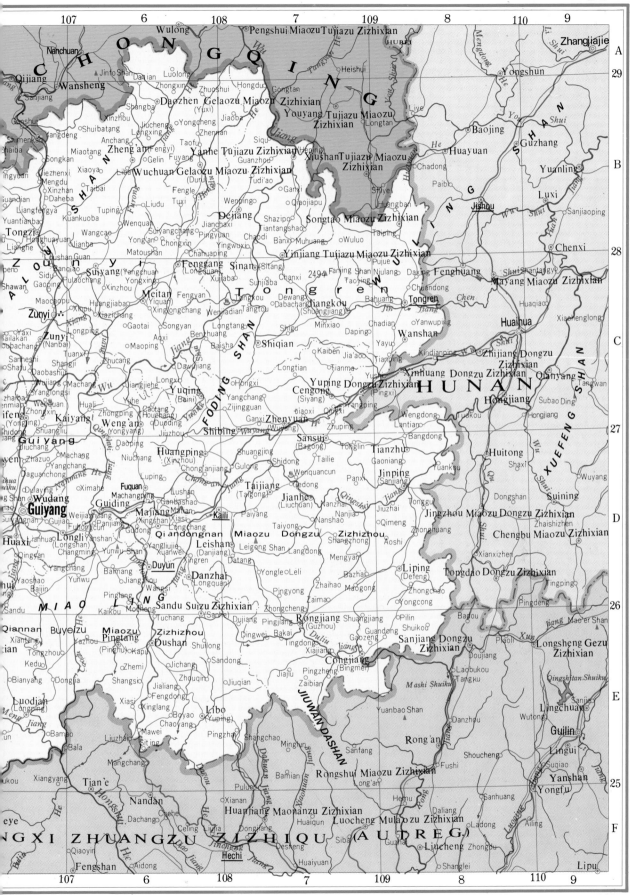

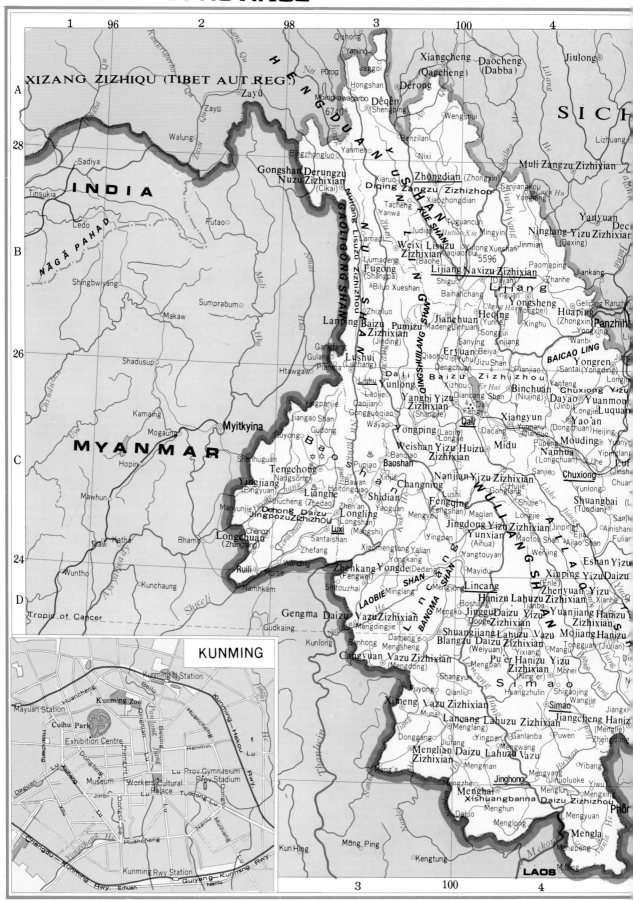

Shimian　Ankouhe　Ebian Yizu　Qianwei　Fushun　Nanchuan　CHONGQING　Jinfo Shan　CHONGQING
Zizhixian　Baisha　Sanjiang　Qijiang　Wansheng Daozhen Gelaozu Miaozu
Ganluo　Muchuan　Luzhou　Ganshui　Zizhixian　Youyang Tujiazu Miaozu
Mabian Yizu Zizhixian　Yibin　Nanxi　Naxi　Hejiang　Zheng'an　Wuchuan Gelaozu　Zizhixian
Yuexi　Meigu　Suijiang　Pingshan　Jiang'an　Chishui　Wenshui　Yinjiang Tujiazu Miaozu Zizhixian
Mianning　Xinshizhen(Zhongcheng)　Anbian　Changning　Xishui　Miaozu Zizhixian　Yanhe
Xichang　Xide　Leibo　Gaoxian　Gongxian　Xingwen(Zhongcheng)　Xuyong　Tongzi　Dejiang
Zhaojue　Yongshan(Jingxin)　Guixi　Tianchi　Ru'erdu　Taipingdu　Loushan Guan　Suiyang Fenggang
Butuo　Jinyang　Daxing　Juhlian　Yanjin(Yanjing)　Weixin(Zhaxi)　Gulin　Maotai　Meitan
Puge　Zhaotong　Shoushan　Niujie　Chishuihe　Renhuai　Zunyi　Jiangkou
Ningnan　Huidong　Ludian(Wenping)　Mangbu　Dawan　Banqiao　Zhenxiong　Dafang　Qianxi　Xifeng　Huangping
Weining Yizu Huizu Miaozu　Nayong　Zhijin　Guiyang　Guiding　Kaili
GUIZHOU　Guiyang　Jianhe
Lupanshui Shuicheng　Anshun　Huishui　Duyun Danzhai
Dongchuan(Xincun)　Zhenning　Guanling Buyeizu Miaozu　Sandu Suizu Zizhixian
Kunming　Qujing　Panxian　Xingren　Zhenfeng　Wangmou　Libo
Chenggong　Shizong　Xingyi　Longlin Gezu Zizhixian　Leye　Hechi
Kaiyuan　Wenshan　Funing　Napo　Nanning
Gejiu　Mengzi　Malipo
VIET NAM　HA NOI

Scale　**1:4 000 000**　0　50　100　150 km

1 78 2 80 3 82 4 84 5 86 6 88

XINJIANG UYGUR ZIZHIQU （AUT.REG.）

Moyu(Karakax)
Hotan
Lop
Qira
Yutian(Keriya)
Minfeng (Niya)
Yawatonggurzlangar
Aqqikkol Hu

Xaidulla

Dahongliutan
6638 Muz Tag
Pulu
Nur
Yeyik
6973 Muz Tag
Karamiran Shankou

K U N L U N   S H A N (M T S.)

HOH

Quanshuigou
Chaoyang Hu
Rola Co
Rolagang
Dogaiçor

Aksayqin Hu
Tielongtan
Gozha Co
Keriya Shankou
Bangdag Co
Bairab Co
Margai Caka
Mano

Changmar
Sumxi
Lazhuglung
Wenquan Hu
Laxong Co
Maqmupo
Dogai Corin

Orba Co
Mêmar Co
Duomula
Tuoheping Co
6148
Chagdo Kangri

Bangong Co
Gyipug
Lumajangdong Co
Aru Co
Gyaco
Gomo
Gomo Co
Shuanghu

Rutög
Zapug
Qangdoi
Lugu
Nishan
Kangro

Jaggang
Rabang
Xaxa
Dinggo
Yibug Caka
Zoidê Lha

Demqog
Nganglong Kangri
6596
Qagcaka
Oma
Gêrzê (Luring)
Kangtog
Zhaxigang
Gar (Shiquanhe)
Zoco
Yanhu (Caka)
Dong Co
Zhaxi Co
Dongco
Gase
Dagzê Co
N

Sogmai
Napug
Gê'gyai
Xangdong
Marmê
Yumco
Gowaqungo
Nyima
Zabduq

Qangzê
Garyarsa
Goicangmai
Ngangla Ringco
Ringtor
Xardong
Dawaxung
Ombu
Ngangzê Co
Richoi
Doijang
Xungba

Zanda (Toling)
Sêngdui
Yagra
Sêlêpug
Chahyêr Caka
Taro Co
Coqên (Maindong)
Cêri Tangra Yumco
Juri Namco
Qumigxung
Tomra
Têring
Gyaring Co

Daba
Kangrinboqê Feng
6638
Lunggar
Gyangdrag
Coqên
Namoding
Xain

Mapam Yumco
Barga
Kunggyü Co
Gyangrang
Qulho
Xuru Co

Burang
Hordag
Mayum La
Samsang
Norcang
Dêlêg
Lungsang

Kotdwara
Biling La
Bünsum
Namsê La
Paryang
Loinbo Kangri 7095
Raka
Dogxung Zangbo
Mükangsar
Xaitongmoin (Kaika Xam

Partol
Zhongba
Zhabdün
Sagaa (Gya'gya)
Püncogling
Xigaze

Morādābād
Pêdo La
Mustang
Xarru
Ngamring
Zêsum
Bai

Bareilly
Gyirong (Zongga)
Dya La
Paiku Co
Gaqung
Lhaze (Quxar)
Sa'gya
War

Pokhara
Gyirong Xixabangma Feng
Tingri
Tingri (Xêgar)
Jênlung
Dobzha

Shāhjahānpur
8027
Rongpu Si (Gyangkar)
Dinggyê
Gamba

Lucknow
Naugarh
Nyalam
Qomolangma Feng (Gyangkar)
8848
Dêgyi
Rabca

Kānpur
KĀTHMĀNDU
Lalitpur
Bhaktapur
8586
Kangchenjunga

Amlekhganj
SIKKIM
GANGTOK

Garakhpur
Kalimpong
Darjeeling
Dhankuta
Siliguri

Muzaffarpur
I N D I A
Kishanganj
BANGLA

Allahābād
Patna
Hājipur
Parbatis

2 80 3 82 4 84 5 86 6 88

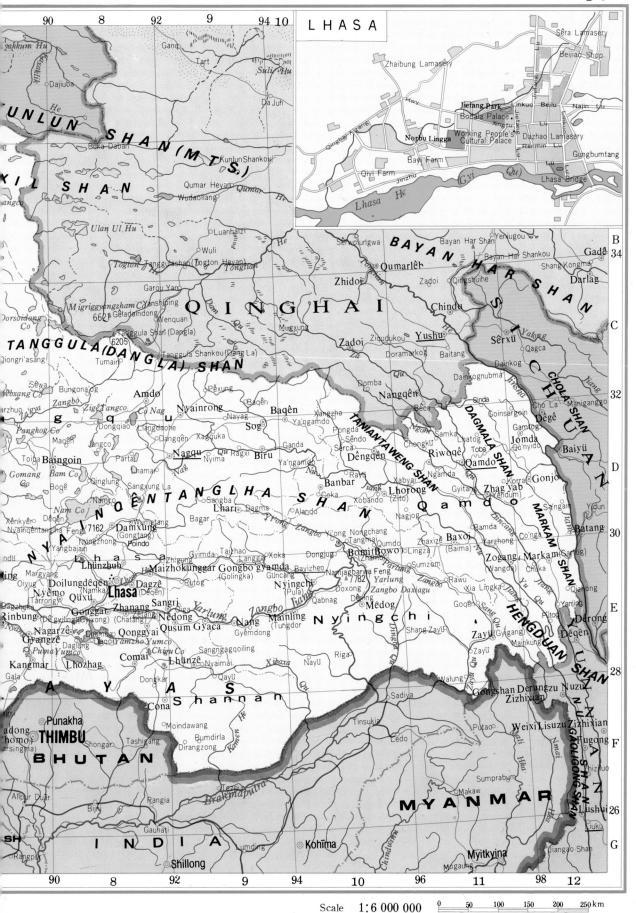

LHASA inset:

Sêra Lamasery
Beijiao Shop
Zhaibung Lamasery
Jiefang Park
Bodala Palace
Linkuo Beilu
Najin Lu
Working People's Cultural Palace
Dazhao Lamasery
Norbu Lingga
Renmin Lu
Gungbumtang
Qiyi Farm
Bayi Farm
Jinzhu
Lhasa Bridge
Lhasa He
Gyi Qu

Main map:

KUNLUN SHAN (MTS.)
yakkum Hu
Kezaitik
Dajiuba
Buka Daban
Kunlun Shankou
XI SHAN
Gand
Tart
Suli Hu
Da Juh

Ulan Ul Hu
Luanhaizi
Wuli
Togton (Togton Heyan)
Tanggulashan
Tongtian

Dorsoidong Co
Migriggyangzham
6621
Geladaindong
Cyanshiping
Wenquan
Mugxung

QINGHAI

Serwolungwa
Bayan Har Shan
Yeniugou
Bayan Har Shankou
Shang Kongma
Gadê
Darlag

Zhidoi
Qumarlêb
Zadoi
Qingshuihe
Chindu

TANGGULA (DANGLA) SHAN
Tanggula Shan (Dangla)
Tanggula Shankou (Dang La)
Tumain

Qiongri'asang
Sêwa Co
Bungona'o
Ziga Tangco
Co Nag
Amdo
Pêxung
Bagên
Zadoi
Ziqudukou
Yushu
Doramarkog
Baitang
Sêrxü
Qagca
Dainkog

Zangbo
Nyainrong
Nagya
Sog
Ya'ngamdo
Xiangzha
Pongda
Sêndo
Serca
Chengku
Domba
Nangqên
Bêca
Sinda
Dainkognubma
Ngom
Samka
Jinsha
Cho La
Goinsargoin
Dêgê
Gamtog
Manigango

Dongqiao
Liangdaohe
Danggên
Xagquka
Qu
Ragxi
Nyima
Biru
Ya'ngamdo
Ganda
Dêngqên
Riwoqê
Qamdo
Jomda
Qu'nyido
Baiyü

Partal
Lhamar
Nam
Qinglung
Sangxung La
Qu
Banbar
Ravti
Coka
Ngamda
Gyitang
Zhag'yab
Korra
Yendum
Gonjo
Sa'ngain
Yidun

Gomang Co
Boğê
Namco
Lunpola
Nam Co
Sangba
Dagma
Alando
Lhari
Xobando
(Zito)
Lhorong
Nagjog
Ramda
Banda
Co'nga
Batang

Xênkyêr
Dêqên
Nyainqêntangla Feng 7162 (Gongtang)
Damxung
Nyingzhong
Yangbajain
Poindo
NYAINQÊNTANGLHA SHAN
Bagar
Yi'ong Nongchang
Tangmai
Qumdo
Zhaxizê
Baxoi
(Baima)
Yarzhong
Zogang
Markam (Sarnog)
Wangda
Chuka
Qiahong

Margyang
Oiyug
Nyêmo
Tarrong
Qusu
Doilungdêqen
(Namka)
Lho
Dagzê
(Dêqen)
Zhigung
Gyimda
Taizhao
Langgar
Xoka
Dongjug
Bomi (Bowo)
(Zhamo)
Lingza
Sumzom
Rawu
Xia Lingka
Yanjing
Dêrong

Lhünzhub
Maizhokunggar
Gongbo gyamda
(Golingka)
Butog
Bayizhen
Namjagbarwa Feng
7782
Doxong
Yarlung
Zangbo
Yu Qu
Pitog
Dêqên

Rinbung
Gonggar
Zhanang
Sangri
Nêdong
Nang
Mainling
Tungdor
Nyingchi
(Pula)
Qabnag
Dêxing
Zayü
(Gyigang)
Mainkung

Nagarzê
Gyangzê
Daglung
Qonggyai
Qusum
Gyaca
Gyêmdong
NYINGCHI
Shang Zayü
Goqên
Zayü Qu
Riga

Kangmar
Lhozhag
Comai
Lhünzê
Nyaimai
Xibaxa
Nayü
Walung
Gongshan
Derungzu Nuzu
Zizhixian

Puma Yumco
Dongkar
Qayü
Sadiya
Weixi Lisuzu Zizhixian

HAYA
Cona
SHANNAN
Tinsukia
Putao
Hugong
Shizhuo

Punakha
THIMBU
Shongar
Tashigang
Bumdirla
Dirangzong
Moindawang
Ledo
GAOLIGONG SHAN
Lushui
Liuku

BHUTAN
Rangia
Tezpur
Sumprabum
Makaw
Jiangao Shan

Alipur Duar
Biji
Brahmaputra
MYANMAR
Lushui

SH
INDIA
Gauhati
Lumding
Kohima
Shillong
Kohima
Myitkyina
Mogaung

Scale 1 : 6 000 000   0   50   100   150   200   250 km

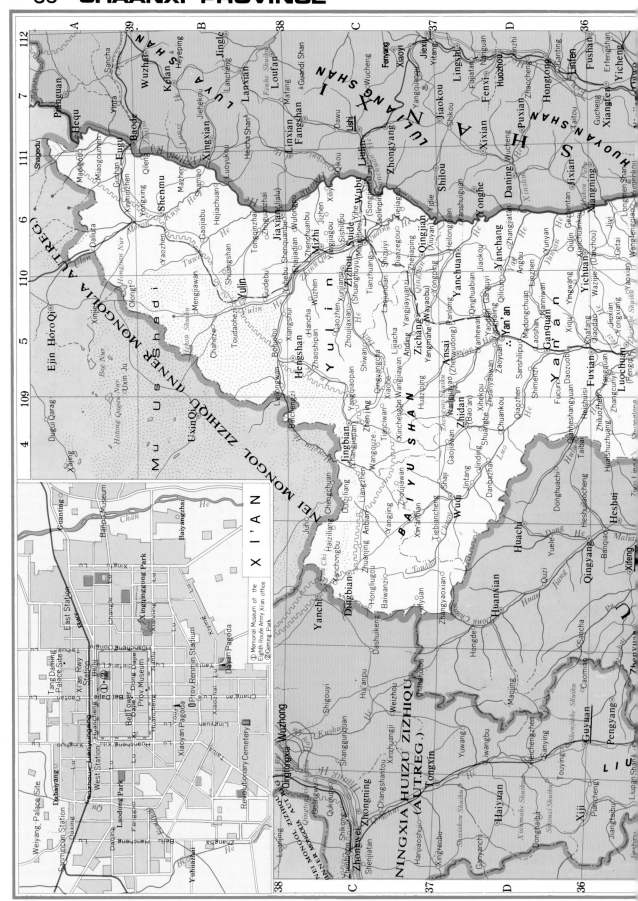

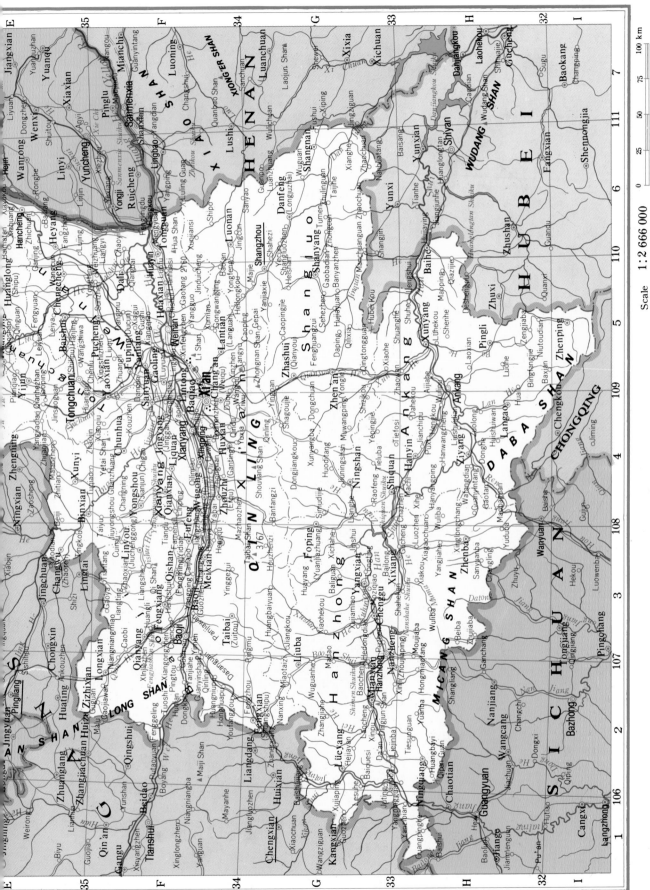

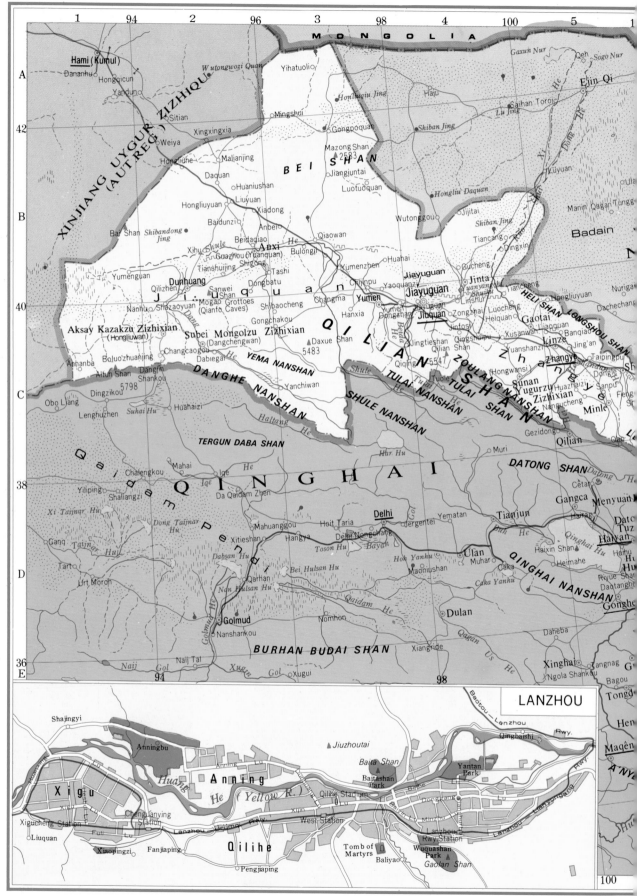

① b longs to Lanzhou C.

Scale 1 : 4 666 000

0   50   100   150 km

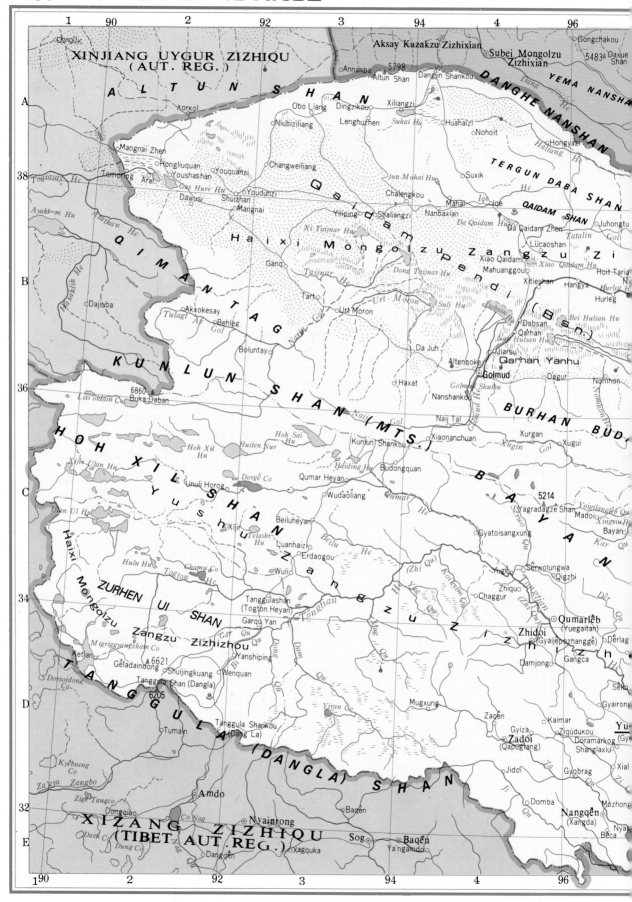

XINING

Scale 1 : 4 000 000   0   50   100   150 km

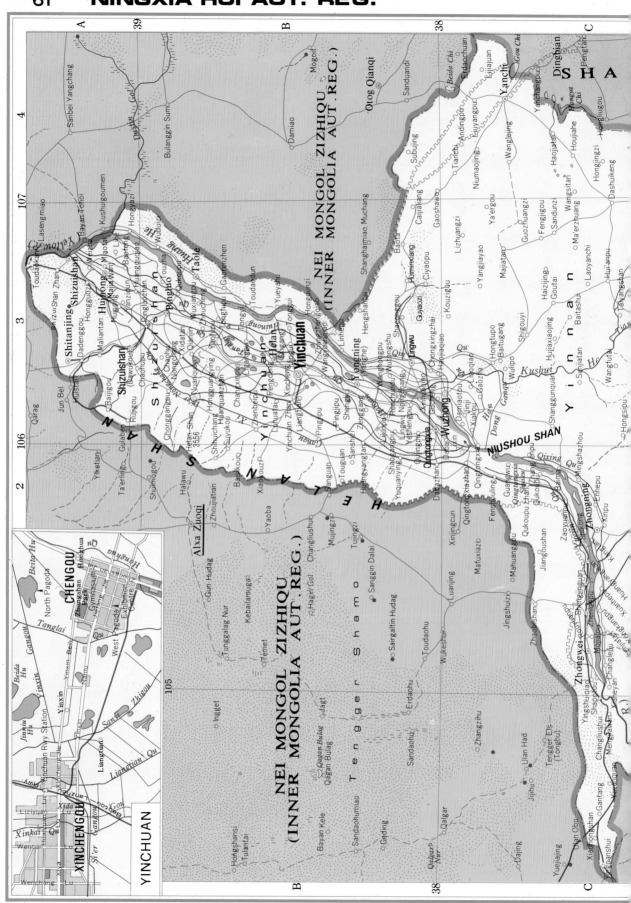

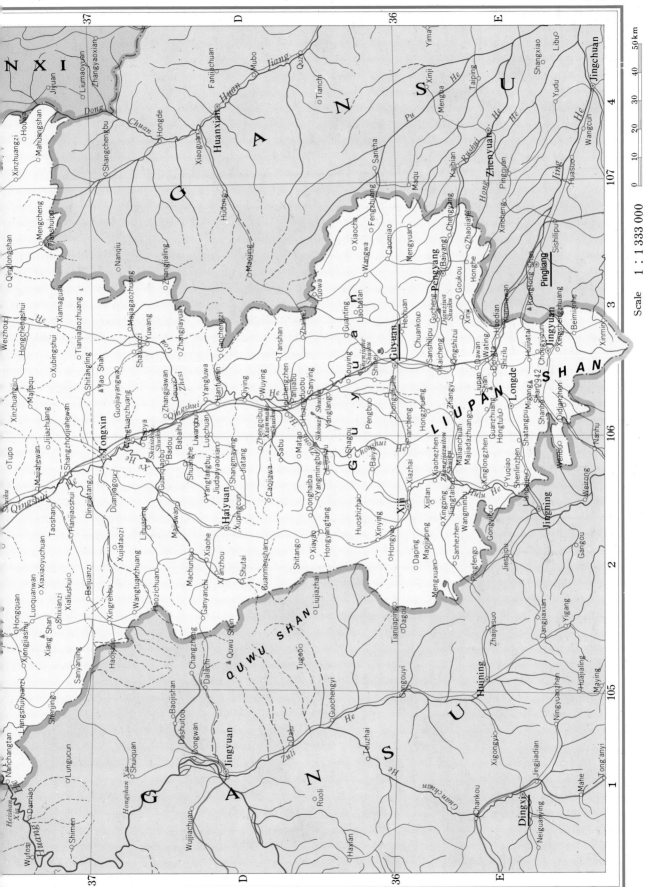

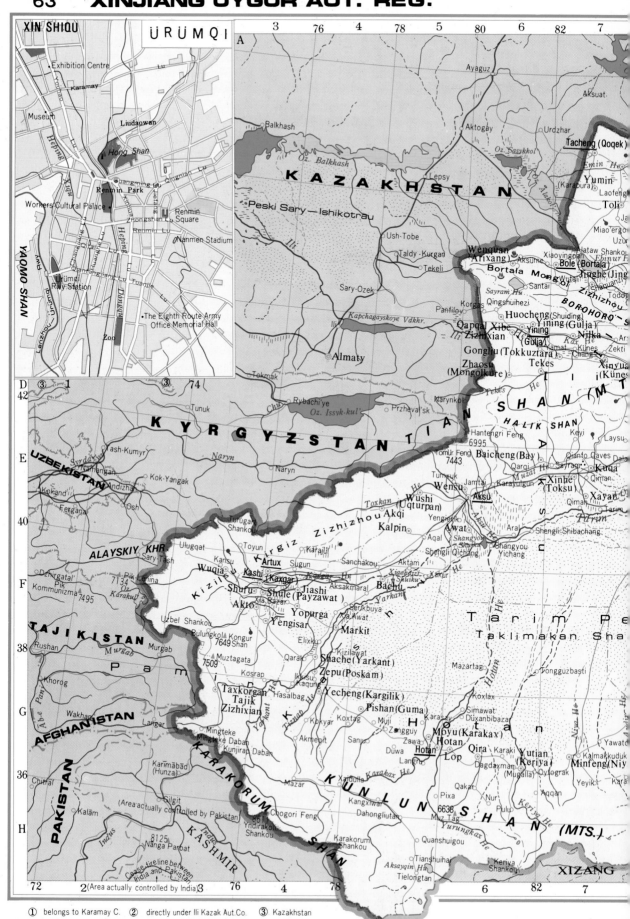

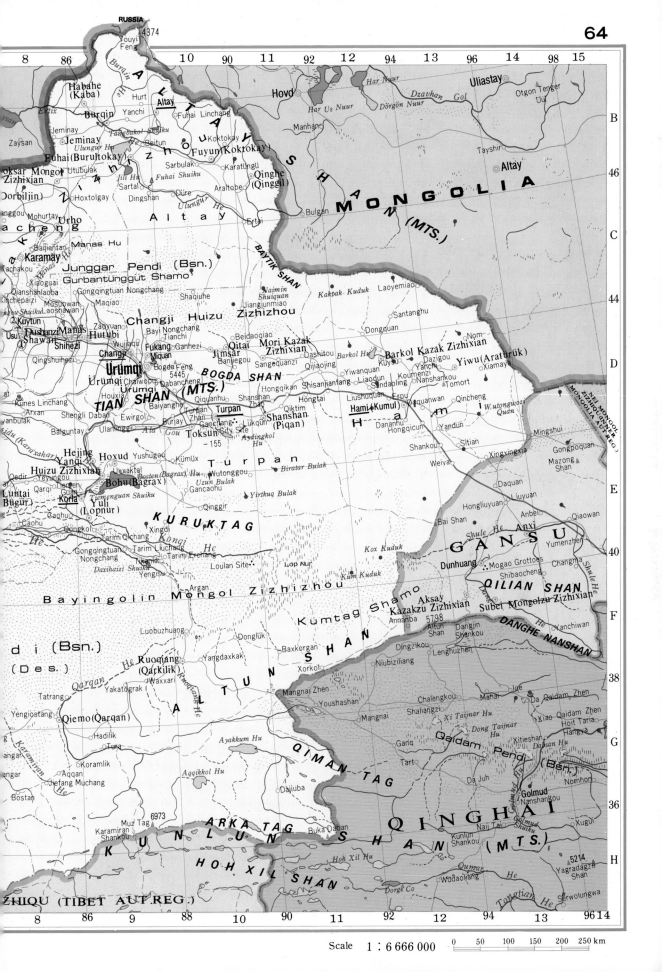

RUSSIA

Youyi
Feng 4374

8 86   10 90   11 92   12 94   13 96   14 98   15

Habahe
(Kaba)   Hovd   Uliastay   B

Burqin   Yanchi   Fuhai Linchang   Har Us Nuur   Dzavhan   Gol   Otgon Tenger
Jeminay   Koktokay   Manhan   Uul
Jeminay   Ulungur He Beitun   46
Fuhai(Burultokay)   Fuyun(Koktokay)   Altay
Oksar Mongol   Utubulak   Sarbulak   Karatüngü   Qinghe   MONGOLIA
Zizhixian   Jil Ha   Fuhai Shuiku Araltobe (Qinggil)
Dorbiljin   Hoxtolgay   Dingshan   Düre   Bulgan   (MTS.)   C
Mohurtay Urho   Altay   Ulungur He   Ertai
acheng   Baytik Shan
Baijiantan   Manas Hu   Laoyemiao
Karamay   Kakpak Kuduk   44
Tachakou   Xiaoguai   Junggar Pendi (Bsn.)   Naimin   Santanghu
Qianshanlaoba   Gurbantünggüt Shamo   Shuiquan
Mosuowan Gongqingtuan Nongchang Maqiao   Shaqiuhe   Dongquan
Laoshawan   Jiangjunmiao   Nom
Kuytun Dushanzi Manas Changji Huizu Zizhizhou   Beidaoqiao   Barkol Hu
Usu Shawan Hutubi Tianchi Bayi Nongchang   Dashitou   Kuysu Barkol Kazak Zizhixian
Qingshuihezi Shihezi Wujiaqu Ganhezi Qitai Mori Kazak   Sangequanzi Dazigou Yiwu(Aratürük)   D
Changji Miquan Jimsar Zizhixian Yiwanquan   Koumenzi Xiamaya
Ürümqi Fukang   Banjiegou Yiwanquan Liaodun Nanshankou Tomort
Bogda Feng   Shisanjianfang Sandaoling
Ürümqi 5445 BOGDA SHAN Qiquanhu   Hongqikan   Erpu
TIAN SHAN Dabancheng   Shanshan Hongtai   Liushuquan Daquanwan Qincheng
Baiyanghe (MTS.) Turpan Zhan Qiktim   Hami(Kumul) Wutongwozi
Kunes Linchang Shengli Daban Burjay lükun Shanshan H a m i Quan
Arxan Ewirgol Turpan Zhan (Piqan) Dananhu   Yandun
anbulak Balguntay Ulanlinggi Ata Gou Gaochang Hongqicun   Shankou   Sitian Mingshui
Kara'axahar Toksun City Site   Aydingkol   Weiya   Gongpoquan
Hejing Hoxud Yushugou   -155 Hu   Mazong Shan
Yanqi Kümüx   Turpan   Biratar Bulak   Xingxingxia
Huizu Zizhixian Uxxaktal Bosten(Bagrax) Hu Wutonggou   Daquan
Qedir Yeyungou Qarqi Uzun Bulak Gancaohu   Hongliuyuan Liuyuan
Luntai Bohu(Bagrax) Uli Temenguan Shuiku   Yirtkuq Bulak   Bai Shan Anbei
Bügür) Korla (Lopnur) Qinggir   Kox Kuduk   Qiaowan E
Caohu Dongkol   KURUKTAG   GANSU
He Tarim Qkhang Kongi He   Yumenzhen
Gongqingtuan Tarim Liuchang   Neirmk He   Loulan Site   Dunhuang Mogao Grottoes Changma 40
Nongchang Daxihaizi Shuiku Yengisu   Argan Lop Nur Kum Kuduk Bai Shan Shibaochena
Bayingolin Mongol Zizhizhou   Qilian Shan
di (Bsn.) Luobuzhuang Donglük Kumtag Shamo Aksay Subei Mongolzu Zizhixian F
(Des.) Ruoqiang Baxkorgan Xorkol Annanba 5798   Danghe Nanshan
He (Qarkilik) Yangdaxkak   Dingzikou Altun Dangjin Yanchiwan
Qarqan Waxxari   Niubiziliang Shan Shankou Lenghuzhen   38
Yengiostang Yakatograk   Mangnai Zhen   Youshashan
Tatrang Qiemo(Qarqan) ALTUN SHAN Mangnai Shaliangzi Xi Taijnar Hu Da Qaidam Zhen
Hadilik Tura Ayakkum Hu QIMAN-TAG Dong Taijnar Xiao Qaidam Zhen Hoit Taria G
angar Koramlik   Gariq Hu Qaidam Pendi Dabsan Hu Hangya
Aqqan Jiefang Muchang Aqqikkol Hu Dajiuba Tart   Xitieshan   (Bsn.)
Bostan   Muz Tag 6973 ARKA TAG Da Juh   Golmud Nomhon
Karamiran   Karamiran KUNLUN SHAN Buka Daban Kunlun   Nanshankou   36
Shankou HOH XIL SHAN (MTS.) Shankou QINGHAI Xugui
ZHIQU (TIBET AUT.REG.) Hoh Xil Hu   Qumar He Wudaokang Yagradagzê 5214
Dorge Co Tongtian He   Serwolungwa Shan H

8 86   9 88   10 90   11 92   12 94   13 96 14

Scale   1 : 6 666 000   0   50   100 150 200 250 km

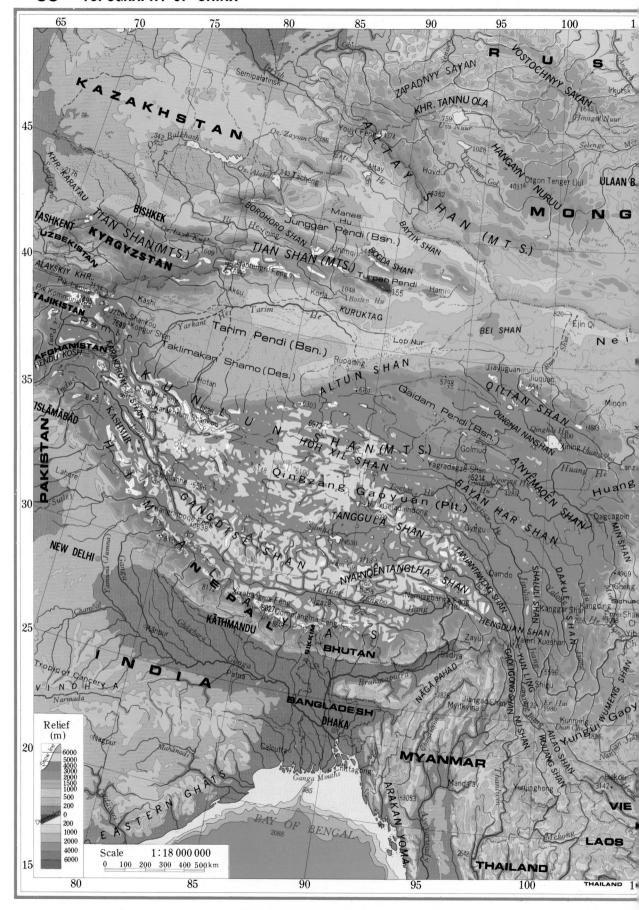

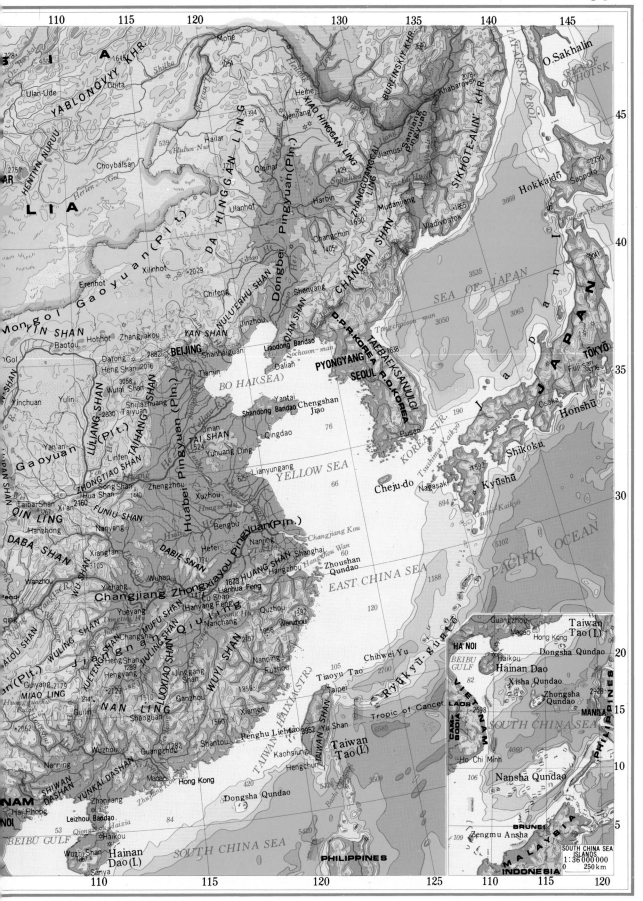

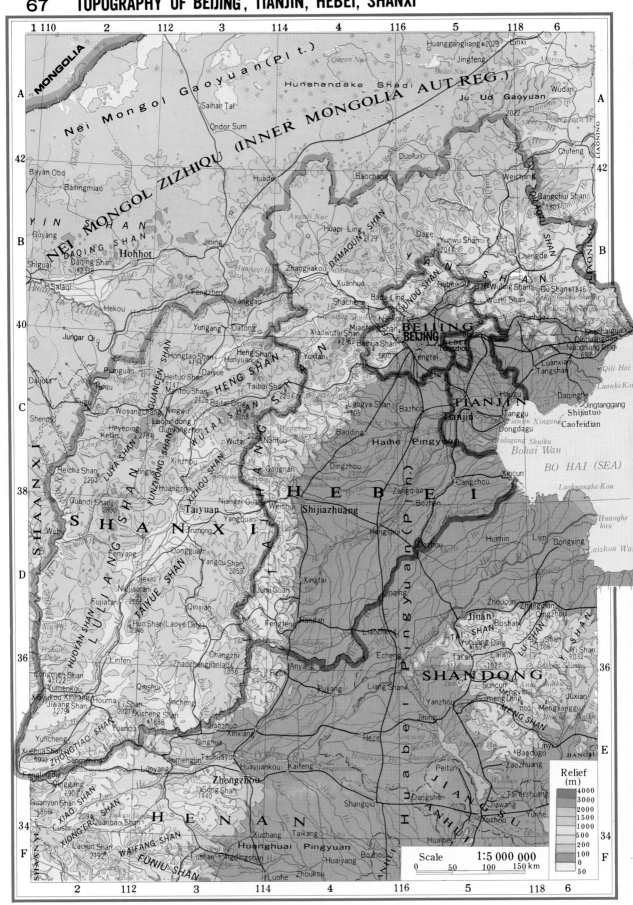

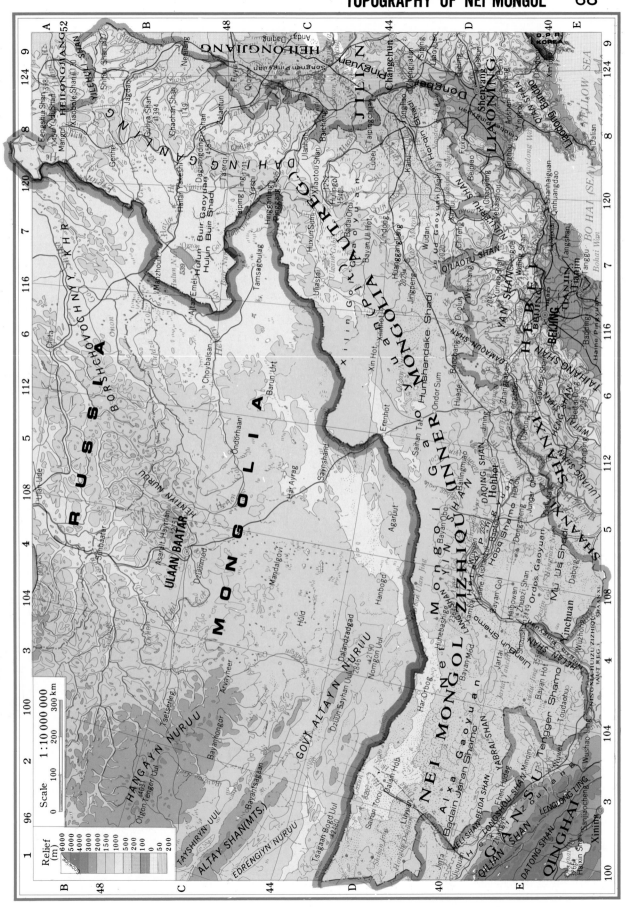

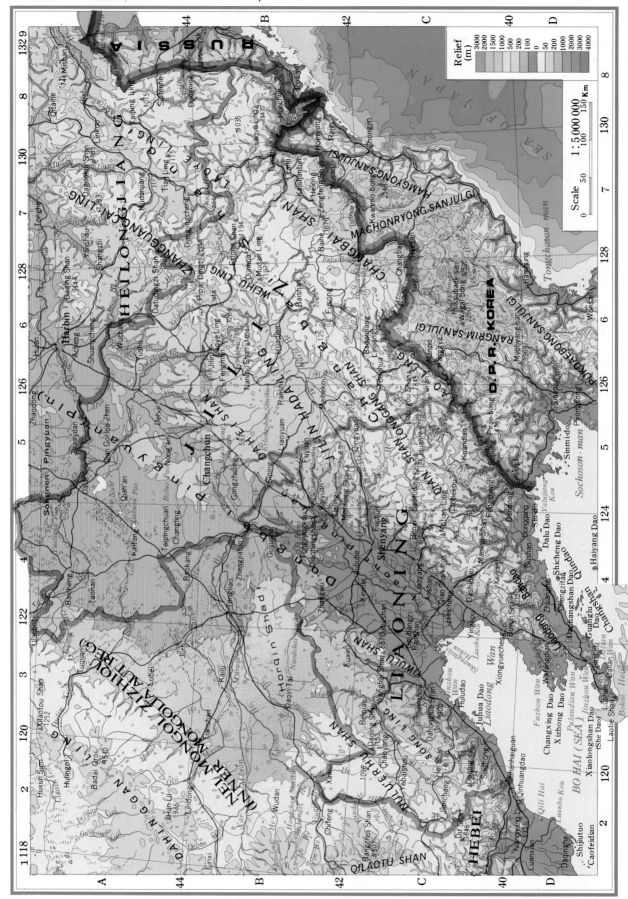

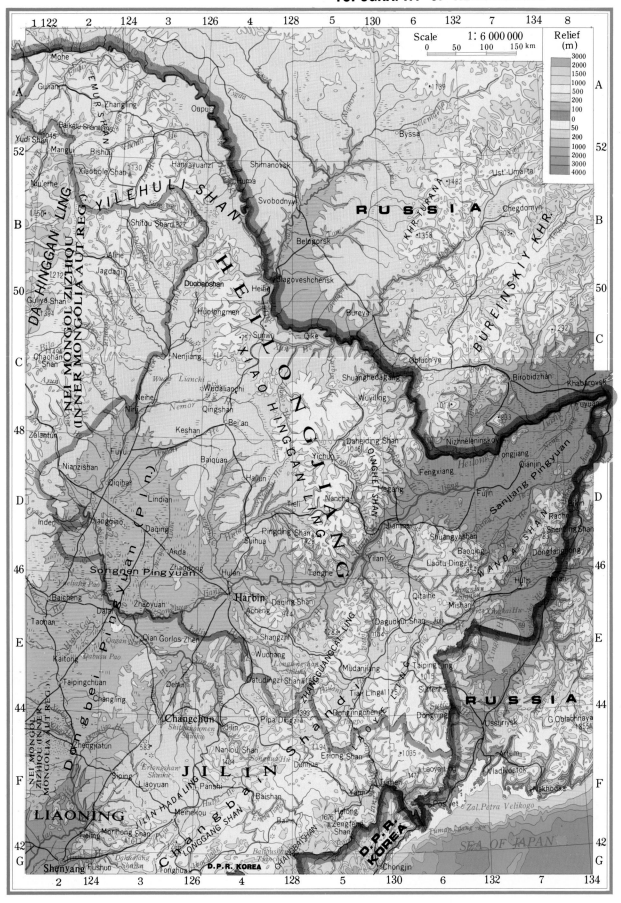

Scale 1 : 6 000 000

0　50　100　150 km

Relief (m)

3000
2000
1500
1000
500
200
100
0
50
200
1000
2000
3000
4000

RUSSIA

BUREINSKIY KHR.

KHR. TURANA

DA HINGGAN LING

NEI MONGOL ZIZHIQU (INNER MONGOLIA AUT. REG.)

YILEHULI SHAN

HEILONGJIANG

XIAO HINGGAN LING

QINGHE SHAN

WANDA SHAN

Sanjiang Pingyuan

Songnen Pingyuan

Songnen Pingyuan (Pln.)

Dongbei Pingyuan (Pln.)

ZHANGGUANGCAI LING

Changbai Shan

JILIN HADA LING

LONGGANG SHAN

JILIN

LIAONING

D.P.R. KOREA

RUSSIA

SEA OF JAPAN

Mohe
Gulian
Zhangling
Oupu
Baikalu Shan 1396
Yudi Shan
1045
Mangui
Bishui
Mu'erhe
Xiaobole Shan 1130
Hanjiayuanzi
Huma
Shimanovsk
Svobodnyy
1139
Byssa
Ust'-Umal'ta
1482
Chegdomyn
1150
Alihe
Shitou Shan 1827
Belogorsk
1358
1303
Jagdaqi
Duobaoshan
Blagoveshchensk
757 Sunwu
Heihe
Bureya
Qike
1292
Huolongmen
Guliya Shan
394
Chaohan Shan 1494
Nenjiang
Obluch'ye
Shuanghedagang
Birobidzhan
Khabarovsk
Neihe
Wudalianchi
Wuyiling
1014
Fuyuan
Niru
Qingshan
Daheiding Shan 1046
Fengxiang
Nizhneleninskoye
833
Tongjiang
Qianjin
Zalantun
Keshan
Bei'an
Yichun
Nancha
Hegang
Fujin
Nianzishan
Baiquan
Hallun
Tieli
Jiamusi
Qiqihar
Lindian
Shuangyashan
Baoqing
Inder
Liangqiao
Daqing
Pingding Shan 1429
Shenling Shan 831
Suihua
Yilan
Laotu Dingzi 855
Raohe
Dongfanghong
Anda
Zhaodong
Hulan
Tonghe
Huljn
Baicheng
Zhaoyuan
Qitaihe
Mishan
Dalai
Daqing Shan 924
Daguokui Shan 1184
Jixi
Taonan
Harbin
Acheng
Shangzhi
1283
Sumian
Qian Gorlos Zhen
Wuchang
Mudanjiang
Taiping Ling 1015
Suifenhe
Kaitong
Dongjingcheng
Tian Ling 1155
Dongning
Ussuriysk
Taipingchuan
Dehui
Datudingzi Shan 1669
1393
G. Oblachnaya 1855
Changling
Pipa Dingzi
Erlong Shan
1035
Laoye Ling
Artem
Changchun
Jilin
1194
Dunhua
1477
Vladivostok
Zhengjiatun
583
Nanlou Shan
Siping
Erlongshan Shuiku
1404
Songhua Hu
Yanji
Tumen
Laoyeling
Nakhodka
Liaoyuan
Panshi
Baishan
Helong
Pos'yet
Meihekou
1676
Zengfeng Shan
Tieling
Morihong Shan 1613
Baihe
Chongjin
Shenyang
Fushun
Tonghua
Changbai Shan 2744
D.P.R. KOREA

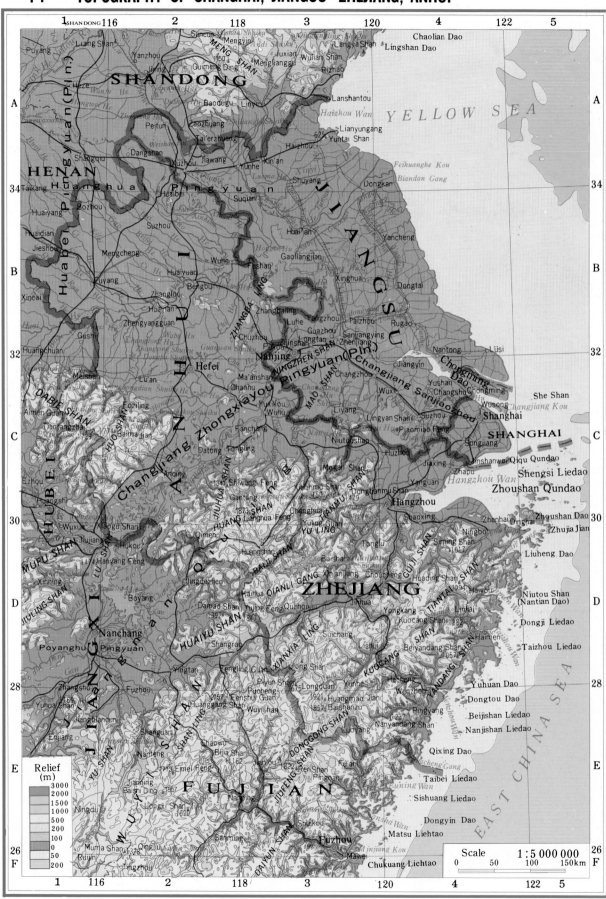

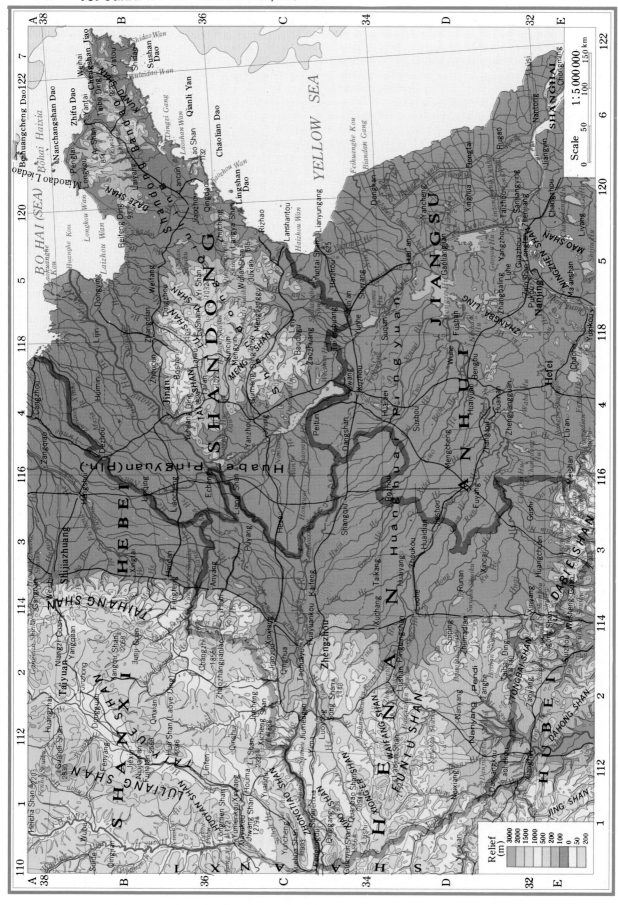

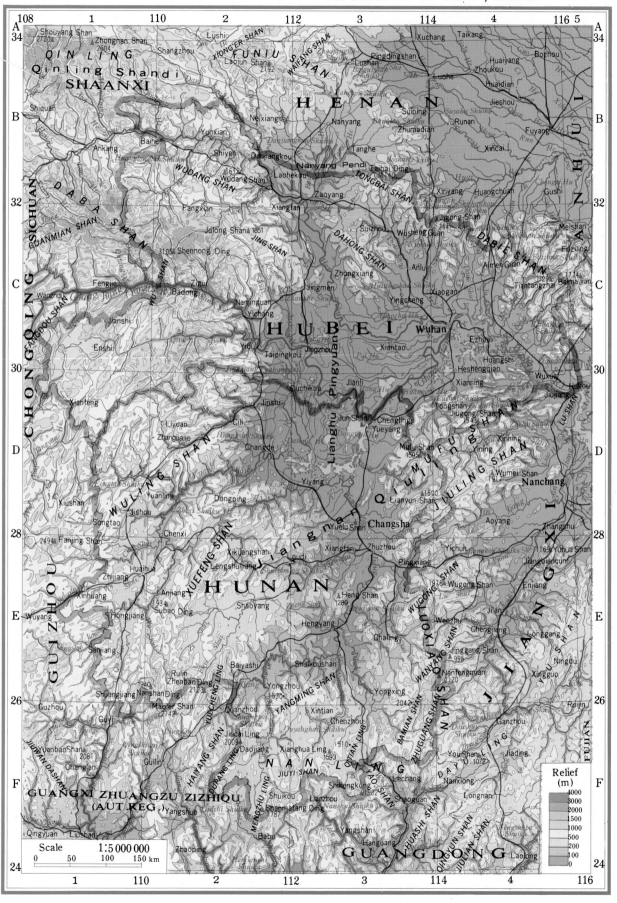

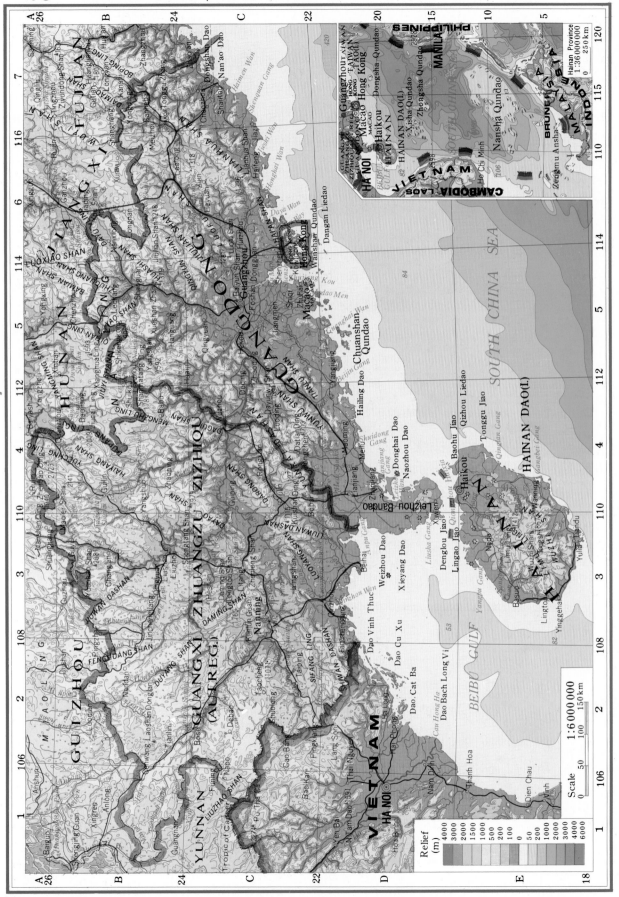

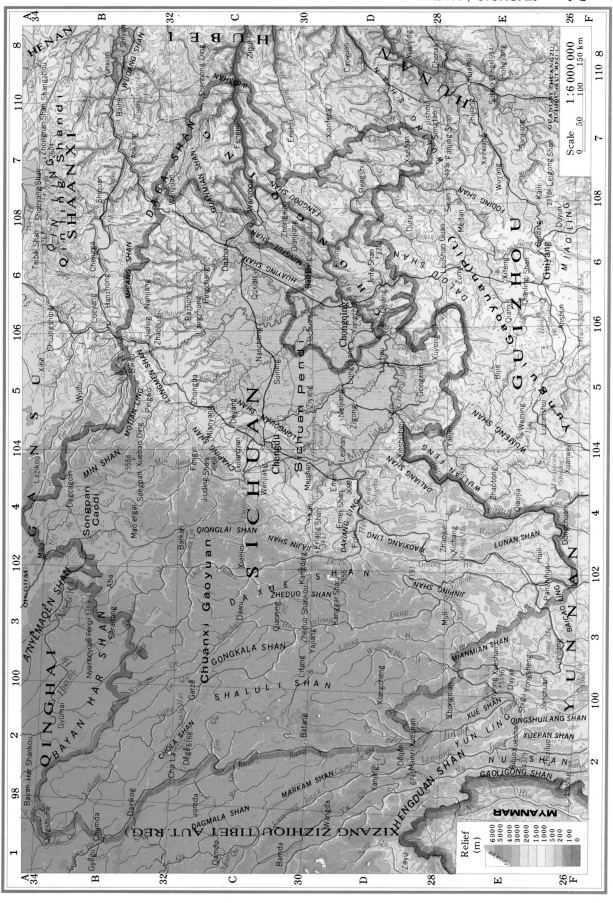

Scale 1:6 000 000

Relief (m)
6000
5000
4000
3000
2000
1500
1000
500
200
100
0

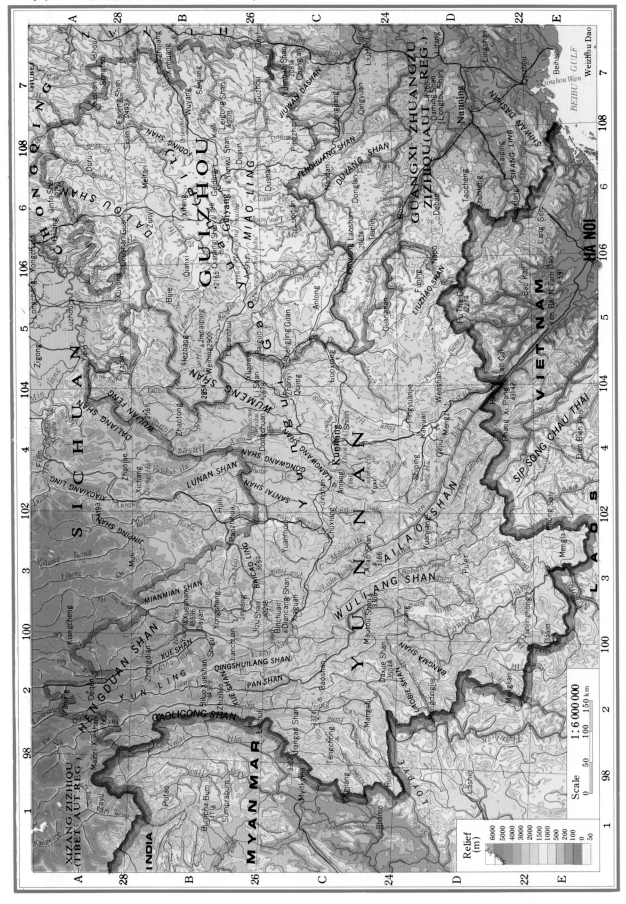

Scale 1:6 000 000

Relief (m)
6000 5000 4000 3000 2000 1500 1000 500 200 100 0 50

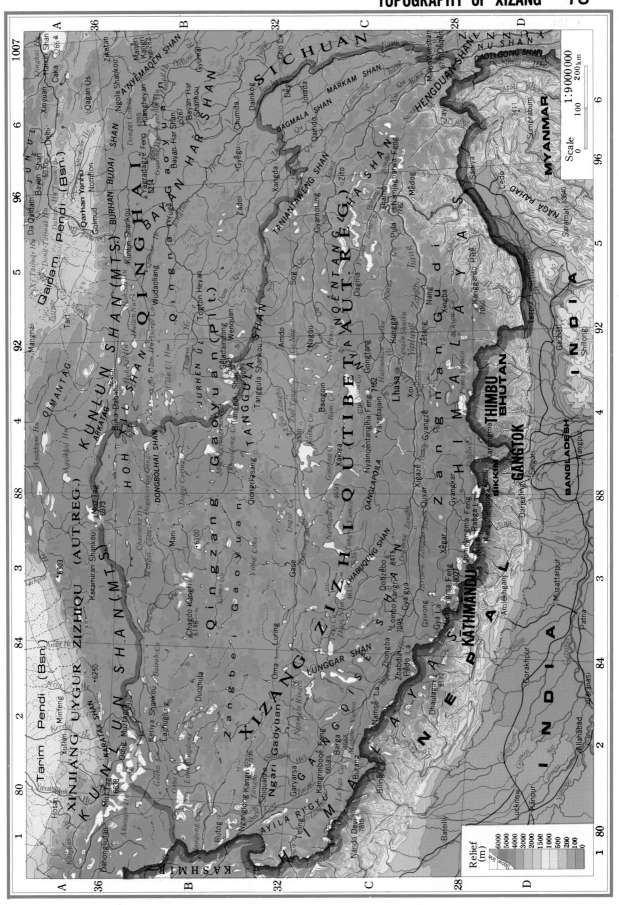

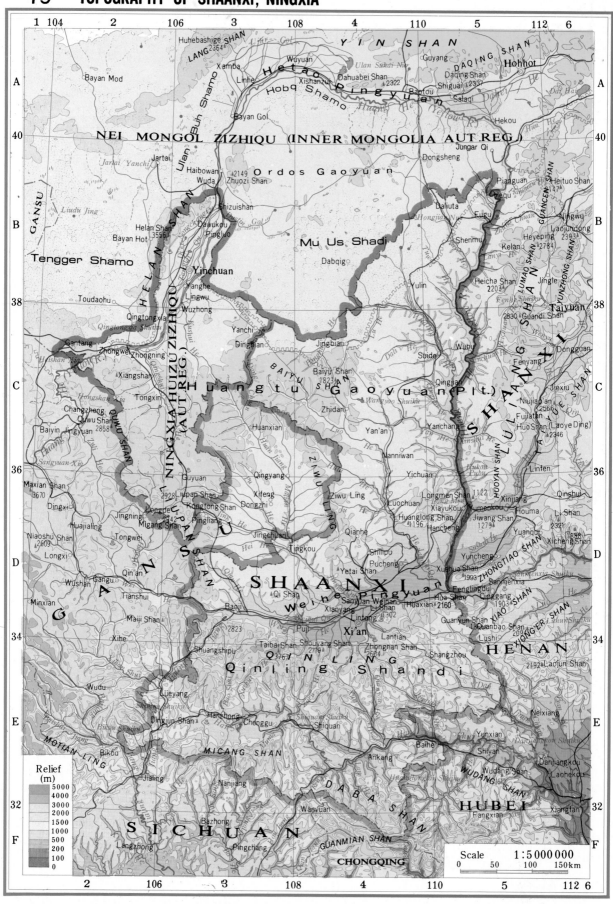

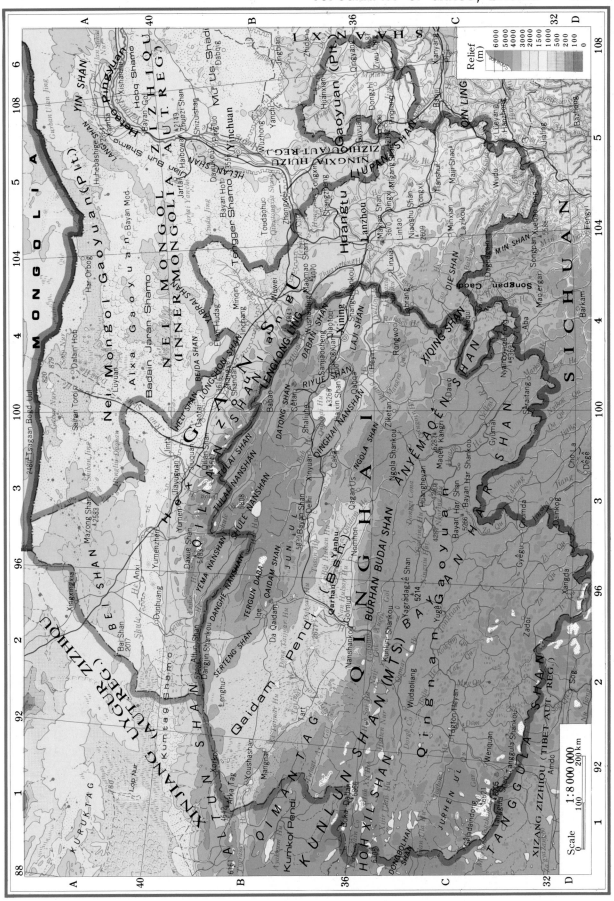

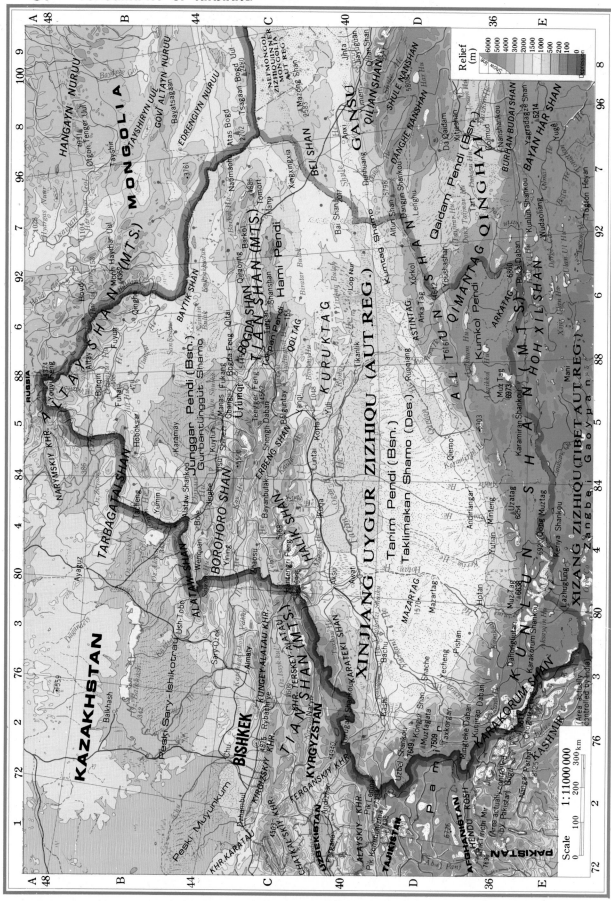

APPENDIX

Pronunciation of Chinese Phonetic Alphabet
Noted with Approximate English Equivalents

Following is a Chinese phonetic alphabet table showing the alphabet pronunciation with approximate English equivalents. Spelling in the Wade system is in brackets for reference.

"a"(a),a vowel,as in far;

"b"(p),a consonant,as in be;

"c"(ts), a consonant, as "ts" in its; and "ch" (ch), a consonant, as "ch" in church, strongly aspirated;

"d"(t),a consonant,as in do;

"e"(e), a vowel, as "er" in her, the "r" being silent;but"ie", a diphthong, as in yes;and"ei", a diphthong, as in way;

"f"(f),a consonant,as in foot;

"g"(k),a consonant,as in go;

"h"(h),a consonant,as in her,strongly aspirated;

"i"(i),a vowel,two pronunciations:

1)as in eat;

2)as in sir in syllables beginning with the consonants c,ch,r,s,sh,z,and zh;

"j"(ch),a consonant,as in jeep;

"k"(k),a consonant,as in kind,strongly aspirated;

"l"(l),a consonant,as in land;

"m"(m),a consonant,as in me;

"n"(n),a consonant,as in no;

"o"(o),a vowel,as "aw" in law;

"p"(p),a consonant,as in par,strongly aspirated;

"q"(ch),a consonant,as"ch"in cheek;

"r"(j),a consonant pronounced as"r"but not rolled,or like"z"in azure;

"s"(s,ss,sz), a consonant, as in sister; and "sh"(sh),a consonant,as"sh"in shore;

"t"(t),a consonant as in top,strongly,aspirated;

"u"(u),a vowel,as in too,also as in the French "u" in "tu" or the German umlauten "u" in "Muenchen",

"v"(v),is used only to produce foreign and national minority words,and local dialects;

"w"(w),used as a semi-vowel in syllables beginning with"u"when not preceded by consonants,pronounced as in want;

"x"(hs),a consonant ,as"sh"in she;

"y",used as a semi-vowel in syllables beginning with "i" or "u" when not preceded by consonants,pronounced as in yet;

"z"(ts,tz),a consonant,as in zero;and"zh" (ch),a consonant,as"j"in "jump".

Pronunciation of Chinese Phonetic Alphabet
Noted with International Phonetic Symbols

a〔a〕	b〔p〕	c〔ts'〕	ch〔ʂ'〕	chi〔tʂ'ʅ〕
ci〔ts'ɿ〕	d〔t〕	e〔ə〕	er〔ər〕	f〔f〕
g〔k〕	h〔x〕	i〔i〕	-ie〔iɛ〕	j〔tɕ〕
ju〔tɕy〕	jue〔tɕyɛ〕	k〔k'〕	l〔l〕	m〔m〕
n〔n〕	ng〔ŋ〕	o〔o〕	p〔p'〕	q〔tɕ'〕
qu〔tɕ'y〕	que〔tɕ'yɛ〕	r〔ʐ〕〔r〕	ri〔ʐʅ〕	s〔s〕
sh〔ʂ〕	shi〔ʂʅ〕	si〔sʅ〕	t〔t'〕	u〔u〕
ü〔y〕	-üe〔yɛ〕	v〔v〕	w〔w〕	x〔ɕ〕
xu〔ɕy〕	xue〔ɕyɛ〕	y〔j〕	ye〔je〕	yu〔y〕
yue〔yɛ〕	z〔ts〕	zh〔tʂ〕	zhi〔tʂʅ〕	zi〔tsʅ〕

GLOSSARY in pinyin（Chinese phonetic alphabet）and English

Pinyin/English

Ansha/Shoal,Reef
Arxan/Hot spring
Bandao/Peninsula(Pen.)
Bao(Bu,Pu)/Village
Bei/North(N)
Bulag/Spring
Changcheng/The Great Wall
Chuan/River(R.)
Co/Lake(L.)
Cunzhuang/Village
Chi/Lake(L.)
Da/Greater,Grand,Big
Daban/Ridge,Pass
Dalai/Sea,Lake
Dao/Island(I.)
Dian/Shallow lake
Ding/Peak,Top
Dong/East(E)
Feng/Peak,Mount
Fenhongqu/Flood diversion area
Gang/Harbour,Port
Gaoyuan/Plateau(Plt.)
Gobi/Gobi,Semidesert
Gol/River(R.)
Gonglu/Highway(Hwy.)
Gou/River(R.),Ditch
Guan/Pass
Hai/Sea
Haixia/Strait(Str.),Channel(Chan.)
He/River(R.)
Hot/City,Town
Hou/Rear,Back
Hu/Lake(L.)
Hudag/Well
Ji/Market
Jiang/River(R.)
Jianhe/Distributary
Jiao/Reef
Jiao/Cape
Jie/Street(St.),Avenue(Ave.)

Jing/Well
Jiu/Old
Ju/Temple
Kou/Mouth
La/Pass,Mountain
Liedao/Islands(Is.),Archipelago
Ling/Mountains(Mts.),Ridge
Linqu/Forest region
Lu/Road(Rd.)
Meng/League(Lea.)
Moron/River
Muchang/Pasture
Nan/South(S)
Nei/Inner
Nongchang/Farm
Nur/Lake(L.)
Obo/Heap of stones
Pao/Lake(L.)
Pendi/Basin(Bsn.)
Pingyuan/Plain(Pln.)
Po/Lake(L.)
Pubu/Waterfall
Qi/Banner(B.)
Qian/Front
Qiao/Bridge
Qiuling/Hills
Qu/River(R.)
Qu/Irrigation canal
Quan/Spring
Qudao/Islands(Is.),Archipelago
Qunjiao/Reefs
Sanjiaozhou/Delta
Shadi/Sandy land,Desert
Shamo/Desert(Des.)
Shan/Mountain(Mt.),Mountains(Mts.)
Shandi/Mountain land
Shang/Upper
Shankou/Pass
Shanmai/Mountains(Mts.)
Sheng/Province(Prov.)
Shi/City(C.)
Shui/River(R.)

Shuidao/Channel(Chan.)
Shuiku/Reservoir(Res.)
Si/Temple
Tag/Mountain
Tan/Beach,Bank
Tan/Pool
Tequ/Special district
Tielu/Railway(Rwy.)
Tun/Village
Ul/Mountain
Wai/Outer
Wan/Gulf(G.),Bay
Xi/West(W)
Xi/Stream,Brook
Xia/Gorge,Valley
Xia/Lower
Xian/County (Co.)
Xiao/Little,Lesser,Small
Xin/New
Xueshan/Snowberg
Xuhongqu/Flood storage area

Yan/Rock,Crag
Arxan/Hot spring
Yang/Ocean,Water,Sea
Yanhu/Salt lake
Yiji/Relics
You/Right
Yu/Island(I.)
Yunhe/Canal
Zangbo/River
Zhan/Station,Post
Zhaoze/Swamp,Marsh
Zhen/Town
Zhixiashi/Municipality(M.)
Zhong/Central,Middle
Zizhiqi/Autononous banner(Aut. B.)
Zizhiqu/Autonomous region(Aut. Reg.)
Zizhixian/Autonomous county(Aut. Co.)
Zizhizhou/Autonomous prefecture(Aut. Pr.)
Zu/Nationality,Ethnic group
Zuo/Left

ABBREVIATIONS

AH/Anhui
BJ/Beijing
FJ/Fujian
GD/Guangdong
GS/Gansu
GX/Guangxi
GZ/Guizhou
HB/Hubei
HEB/Hebei
HEN/Henan
HK/Hongkong
HI/Hainan
HL/Heilongjiang
HN/Hunan
JL/Jilin
JS/Jiangsu
JX/Jiangxi

LN/Liaoning
MC/Macau
NM/Nei Mongol
NX/Ningxia
QH/Qinghai
SC/Sichuan
SD/Shandong
SH/Shanghai
SN/Shaanxi
SX/Shanxi
TJ/Tianjin
TW/Taiwan
XJ/Xinjiang
XZ/Xizang
YN/Yunnan
ZJ/Zhejiang

ATLAS
OF
CHINA

INDEX

INDEX

An Xian SC45/46C5
Anxiang Xian HN37/38B5
Anxing HL15/16E7
Anxin Xian(Xin'an) HEB5/6E3
Anxi Xian GS57/58B2
Anxi Xian FJ25/26E4
Anyang HEB3/4D2
(Anyang)Du'an Yaozu Zizhixian
　GX43/44D6
Anyang Shi HEN33/34A6
Anyang Xian HEN33/34A6
A'nyêmaqên Shan GS57/58E5-F5
　　　　　　　QH50/60C6-D8
Anyi SX7/8F3
Anyi Xian(Longjin) JX29/30C3
Anyou HI42C2
Anyuan JX29/30D1
Anyuan FJ25/26D2
Anyuan Xian JX29/30F3
Anyue Xian SC45/46C5
Anze Xian SX7/8E4
Anzhao Xinhe HL15/16D3
Anzhen JS17/18E6
Anzhou HEB5/6E3
Aocheng JX29/30E2
Aohan Qi(Xinhui) NM9/10F12
Aohuan ZJ21/22D6
Ao Jiang ZJ21/22E5
Aojiang ZJ21/22E5
Aoping SC47/48A1
Aoquanxu HN37/38F5
Aoshang HN37/38E2
Aoshang HN37/38F6
Aoshanwei SD31/32C7
Aoshi GZ49/50D8
Aoti TW27/28B3
Aotou GD39/40D7
Aotou GD39/40C6
Aotou GD39/40D7
Aotou GD41A4
Aoxi GZ49/50C6
(Aoxi)Le'an Xian JX29/30D3
Aoyang Jiang GD39/40D4
(Aoyang)Shanggao Xian JX29/30C2
Aoyuzhou GX43/44B8
Aozai GD39/40C5
Ap Chau HK41A3
Aqal XJ63/64E5
Aqqan XJ63/64G6
Aqqan XJ63/64G8
Aqqikkol Hu XJ63/64G10
Aral QH59/60A2
Aral XJ63/64E6
Araltobe XJ63/64B11
Argan XJ63/64E10
Ar Horqin Qi(Tianshan) NM9/10F13
Arkatag XJ63/64G10-11
Arka Tag QH80B1 XJ81D6
Artux Xian XJ63/64F4
Aru Co XZ53/54C4
Arun He HL15/16C2-D2
Arun Qi(Naji) NM9/10C14
Arxan XJ63/64D8

Arxan Shi NM9/10D12
Arxat XJ63/64D7
Arxiang LN11/12B6
Asar NM9/10D11
Astintag XJ81D6
Atatkan He XJ59/60B1-2
Audi GZ49/50C5
Awat Xian XJ63/64E6
Awuni NM9/10B14
Ayakkum Hu XJ63/64G10
Aydingkol Hu XJ63/64D10
Ayila Ri'gyü XZ78B1-C2

B

Babaihu NX61/62D3
Babailiqiao JS17/18D4
Babao YN51/52D6
Babao GZ49/50E4
(Babao)Qilian Xian QH59/60A7
Babian Jiang YN51/52D4
Babu GZ49/50D4
(Babu)He Xian GX43/44C9
Bacang QH59/60C7
Bacha HL15/16C7
Bacheng JS17/18E6
Bachi GD39/40B8
Bachi Jiang GX43/44E6
Bachu(Maralwexi)Xian XJ63/64F5
Bacun HI42C2
Bacun GD41A1
Badahe YN49/50F3
Badain Jaran Shamo NM9/10G3
Badai Oroi NM9/10E12
Badajia JS17/18C6
Bada Ling BJ3/4B3
Badaogou JL13/14D10
Badaogou HEB5/6B2
Badaohao LN11/12C3
Badaohe BJ3/4B3
Badaohe HEB5/6C6
Badaohezi JL13/14D7
Badong Xian HB35/36C3
Badou GX43/44B7
Badou NX61/62D2
Badouling AH23/24D4
Badu ZJ21/22E3
Badu FJ25/26D5
Badu JX29/30C6
Badu JX29/30D3
Badu GX43/44C3
Badu GZ49/50F4
Bagang GD41A3
Bagar XZ53/54D9
Bag Nur NM55/56A5
Bagong SX7/8F4
Bagong GX43/44C5
Bag Onggon NM9/10J21
(Bagong)Sansui Xian GZ49/50D7
Bagong Shan AH23/24D3
Bagou QH59/60C7
Bag Tal NM11/12A6
Bagui GX43/44C4
Bahao JL13/14B7

Bahaolazi HL15/16E5
Ba He SC45/46C6
Ba He SN55/56H5
Bahuang GZ49/50C8
Baibao GX43/44E5
Baibaozhai HB35/36D4
Baibei JX29/30D3
Baibi SX7/8D4
Baibu SD31/32C6
Baibu GD39/40C7
Baicao HEB5/6B4
Baicaogou JL13/14D10
Baicao Ling YN51/52B4
Baiceng GZ49/50E4
Baicha JX29/30B3
Baicheng(Bay) Xian XJ63/64E6
Baicheng Shi JL13/14B3
Baichengzi SN55/56B4
Baichi HEN33/34D6
Baichihe SD31/32C6
Baicun SC47/48C1
Baidafan AH23/24E3
Baidanghu AH23/24F4
Baidaokou HEN33/34B6
Baidian AH23/24F6
Baidicheng SC45/46C7
Baidishi HN37/38E4
Baidu GD39/40B9
Baidun HB35/36E7
Baidunzi GS57/58B2
Baidunzi GS57/58D7
Baiduqiao AH23/24E5
Bai'e JX29/30F3
Baifang HN37/38E5
Baifusi HB35/36E2
Baigezhuang HEB5/6D6
Baigou HEB5/6D4
Baigou He HEB3/4C3
Baiguantun HEB3/4C4
Baigui SX7/8D4
Baiguishan Shuiku HEN33/34D5
Baiguo HB35/36C7
Baiguo HN37/38D5
Baiguo GZ49/50D3
Baiguoba HB35/36E2
Baiguoshi HN37/38E5
Baihanchang YN51/52B4
Baihao GD41B2
Baihe HEB5/6E2
Baihe SC47/48C3

Baihe HB35/36C3
Bai He BJ3/4B3
Bai He HEN33/34E4
Bai He SC45/46B4
Baihe HEN33/34C4
Baihe GX43/44E7
Baihebu BJ3/4B3
Baihedian ZJ21/22C5
Baihegang SH19/20B4
Baiheqiao YN51/52D5
Baihe Xian SN55/56H6
Baihou GD39/40B9

Baihu AH23/24E4
Baihua SC47/48C2
Baihua GD39/40D7
Baihuadong GD41A2
Baihuapai NM15/16B3
Baihua Shan BJ3/4C2
Baihua Shuiku GZ49/50D5
Baihugou HEB5/6B5
Baihuyao SX7/8E4
Baiji GX43/44E6
Baijia JX29/30E2
Baijian HEB5/6D3
Baijiang ZJ21/22C4
Baijiantan XJ63/64C8
Baijiaping HN37/38E4
Baijiazhuang SX7/8E2
Baijie SC47/48C4
Baijieshen ZJ19/20C5
Baijigou NX61/62A3
Baijiji NM9/10H3
Baijin JL13/14E10
Baijin GZ49/50D5
Baiji Shan ZJ21/22C3 AH23/24G5
Baiju JS17/8C6
Baijuanzi NX61/62C2
Bailakan GZ49/50C5
Baile HEB3/4C1
Baile GX43/44C4
Baili JL13/14E9
Bailian HI42B3
Bailian FJ25/26D3
Bailiang SN55/56E6
Bailianhe HB35/36D8
Bailianhe Shuiku HB35/36D8
Bailicun GX43/44B8
Baili Dao GD41C2
Bailin FJ25/26C6
Bailin HN31/38E6
(Bailingmiao)Darhan Muminggan Lianheqi
  NM9/10G8
Bailong SN55/56G3
Bailong Jiang GS57/58F7
Bailu He HEN33/34E7-F7
Bailuoji HB35/36E6
Bailuqiao HN37/38C5
Bailutang ZJ21/22B5
Baima SC47/48C5
Baima GX43/44E8
Baima SC47/48C1
Baima SC47/48C2
Baima NX61/62C2
(Baima)Baxoi Xian XZ53/54D11
Baimachang SC47/48B3
Baimahu JS17/18C5
Baima Jian AH23/24E3
Baimajing HI42B2
Baimamiao SC47/48C2
Baimang GD39/40B5
Baimang GZ49/50D6
Baimang GD41A2
Baimangshen SX7/8B5
Baimangying HN37/38G4
Baimao JS17/18E6

Baimaokou JS19/20B4
Baimaoping HN37/38E3
Baimao Tang JS19/20B3-4
Baimaqiao JS19/20B2
Baimashi JX21/22C3
Baimasi HN37/38C5
Baimasi HEN33/34C4
Baimatan SN55/56E6
Baima Xian(Sêraitang) QH59/60D7
Baimayi HEN33/34D7
Baimiao HEN33/34C7
Baimiaozi LN11/12D4
Baina GZ49/50C4
Bainang Xian XZ53/54E7
Baingoin Xian XZ53/54D8
Bainijing NM9/10K20
Bainiqiao HB35/36E7
Bainiu HEN33/34E4
(Baini)Yuqing Xian GZ49/50C6
Bainyai SC45/46B4
Baipeng GX43/44C7
Baipenyao BJ3/4C3
Baipu JS17/18D6
Baiqên QH59/60D7
Baiqi HEB5/6C5
Baiqiu HEN33/34E4
Baiquan ZJ21/22B7
Baiquan HEN33/34B5
(Baiquan)Dongliao Xian JL13/14E5
Baiquan Xian HL15/16D4
Baiquesi SN55/56G2
Baiqueyuan HEN33/34F7
Bairab Co XZ53/54B4
Bairin Qiao NM9/10F12
Bairin Youqi(Daban) NM9/10F12
Bairin Zuoqi(Lindong) NM9/10F12
Bairuopu HN37/38C5
Baisang HB35/36B3
Baisha HN37/38C7
Baisha SC45/46D6
Baisha SC47/48C4
Baisha FJ25/26E3
Baisha SC47/48D3
Baisha HI42B2
Baisha GZ49/50C7
Baisha JX29/30E3
Baisha HEN33/34C4
Baisha HEN33/34C5
Baisha GX43/44F7
Baisha GD39/40D5
Baisha GX43/44C8
Baisha GX43/44D7
Baisha HN37/38E5
Baisha GD39/40B6
Baisha FJ25/26E5
Baisha FJ25/26E2
Baishaguan JX29/30B6
Baishaling JX29/30B2
Baisha Lizu Zizhixian HI42B2
Baishan GX43/44C7
Bai Shan ZJ19/20C4
Bai Shan GS75/58B1
Baishan HEN33/34B5

Baishan AH23/24C3
Baishan Shi JL13/14F7
Baishanzhen JL13/14E8
Baishanzu ZJ21/22E4
Baishapu HB35/36E8
Baisha Shan ZJ19/20D5
Baisha Shuiku HEN33/34C5
Baishatan SD31/32C8
Baishawan GD41A3
Baishazhen FJ25/26D5
Baishe JX29/30D4
Baishi ZJ21/22D5
Baishidu HN37/38F6
Baishi Feng FJ25/26D2
Baishilazi HL15/16B4
Baishishan JL13/14D8
Baishishan AH23/24E4
Baishi Shan HEB5/6D2
Baishiyi SC45/46D6
Baishizhou GD41A2
Baishui ZJ21/22B4
Baishui FJ25/26F3
Baishui JX29/30D3
Baishui HN37/38E4
Baishui SC45/46B5
Baishui SC45/46B6
Baishuifan HB35/36D8
Baishuijiang SN55/56G2
Baishui Jiang SC45/46B5 GS57/58F7
Baishuijing LN11/12E5
Baishui Xian SN55/56E5
Baishuyang ZJ21/22D5
Baisikou NX61/62B2
Baisong Gaun FJ25/26F3 GD39/40B9
Baisuo GZ49/50E5
Baita ZJ21/22D5
Baitabu JS17/18B4
Baita He JX29/30C4-5
Baitang QH59/60D5
Baitang GD39/40C7
Baitao SC47/48C5
Baitapu HEB3/4C2
Baitashui NX61/62C3
Baitazi NM11/12B4
Baitiao He SC47/48B1-2

Baitu GX43/44C6
Baitu JS17/18E5
Baitugang NX61/62C3
Baitugang HEN69/70D4
Baiwan GD39/40B5
Baiwan SC45/46C3
Baiwang GX43/44C6
Baiwanzi SN55/56C3
Baiwen SX7/8C3
Baiwujie YN51/52B5
Baixi ZJ21/22D6
Baixi AH23/24G4
Baixian ZJ19/20B2
Baixiang HEN33/34B4
Baixiang Xian HEB5/6F2
Baixing GZ49/50D4
Baixingt NM11/12A5

(Baixi)Yibin Xian SC45/46D5
Baixu GX43/44D6
Baiya NX61/62D2
Baiya BJ3/4B4
Baiyan ZJ21/22D5
Baiyang HB35/36D4
Baiyang HEN33/34C4
Baiyang FJ25/26C5
Baiyangba HB35/36D1
Baiyang Dian HEB5/6E4
Baiyanggou LN11/12D6
Baiyanghe XJ63/64D10
Baiyangping HB35/36D2
Baiyangqiao HEB3/4D3
Baiyangtang HB35/36D1
Baiyangtian HN37/38B6
Baiyan Shan FJ25/26D4
(Baiyashi)Dong'an Xian HN37/38E4
Baiyi SC47/48A5
Baiyin Shi GS57/58D7
Baiyin Shi GS57/58D7
Baiyügoinba QH59/60D7
Baiyun FJ25/26D4
Baiyunkou GX43/44B7
Baiyun Shan GD75C5
Baiyun Shan JX29/30E3
Baiyunshan Shuiku JX29/30E3
Baiyu Shan SN55/56C4
Baiyutan Shuiku HN37/38E5
Baiyü Xian SC45/46C2
Baizaogou JS17/18B5
Baizhang ZJ19/20C2
Baizhang SC45/46C4
Baizhangji ZJ21/22E5
Baizhangkou ZJ21/22E4
Baizhao HB35/36C6
Baizhitai HN37/38B4
Baizhong FJ25/26D4
Baizi SX7/8E4
Baizi SC45/46C5
Baizi SC47/48B3
Bajia GD39/40E4
Bajiao SC47/48A3
Bajiao SX7/8B3
Bajiao HB35/36D2
Bajiaolou SC45/46C3
Bajiaomiao HB35/36D3
Bajiazi JL13/14E10
Bajiazi LN11/12B5
Bajie GZ49/50F4
Bajilei JL13/14C5
Bajing JX29/30C3
Bakai GZ49/50E7
Bakeshiying HEB5/6C5
Bakeshu LN11/12B8
Bala GX43/44B4
Balang JL13/14B5
Balguntay XJ63/64D9
Balhai NM9/10K17
Baliang NM9/10J19
Balidianzi LN11/128
Baliguan SN55/56G3

Balihan NM11/12C2
Balin NM9/10C14
Baling GZ49/50E4
Baliying HEN33/34B6
Balougou SX7/8C3
Bamao GZ49/50E5
Bamao ZJ21/22C5
Bama Yaozu Zizhixian GX43/44C5
Bam Co XZ53/54D8
Bamda XZ53/54D11
Bamencheng TJ3/4C4
Bamian GX43/44B6
Bamiancheng LN11/12A8
Bamian Shan HN37/38E6
Bamianshanzhao JL13/14B4
Banbar Xian(Domartang) XZ53/54D10
Banbishan HEB5/6C5
Bancheng JS17/18C4
Banfangzi SN55/56G4
Banfu GD39/40D6
Banfu GD41B1
Bangchui Shan NM11/12C2
Bangdag Co XZ53/54B3
Bangdong GZ49/50D8
Bangong Co XZ53/54C2
Bangjun TJ3/4C4
Bangluo GS57/58E7
Bangma Shan YN51/52D3
Bangong Co XJ53/54C2
Bangtou FJ25/26E4
Bangun GX43/44F5
Bangxi HI42B2
Bangxu GX43/44D5
Bangzha GZ49/50F3
Bangzhen SH19/20B4
Banhong YN51/52D3
Banhu JS17/18C5
Banjiegou XJ63/64D10
Banjieta HEB5/6B5
Banjin JS17/18D6
Bankengting FJ25/26D4
Banlamen LN11/12C6
Banlan GX43/44B7
Banli GX43/44E5
Banliao HB35/36E2
Banling GX43/44C5
Banmian FJ25/26D4
Banpu JS17/18B5
Banqiao HEN33/34D5
Banqiao HN37/38E5
Banqiao HI42C1
Banqiao GS57/58C5
Banqiao HB35/36C4
Banqiao JS17/18E4
Banqiao AH19/20C1
Banqiao BJ3/4C2
Banqiao AH23/24D4
Banqiao YN51/52C5
Banqiao YN51/52C6
Banqiao AH23/24C3
Banqiao GS57/58E8
Banqiao SC47/48C2
Banqiao GZ49/50C5

Banqiao YN43/44C2
Banqiao YN51/52B6
Banqiao YN51/52C3
Banqiaochang SC47/48C3
Banqiaoji AH23/24D3
Banqiao Shuiku HEN33/34E5
Banquan SD31/32D5
Banshan ZJ19/20C3
Banshanping HEN33/34D4
Banshanpu HN37/38D6
Banshi JX29/30E3
Banshigou JL13/14E7
Banshu AH23/24E5
Bantaji AH23/24D5
Bantao GX43/44C3
Bantian GD41A3
Banxi GZ49/50B7
Banyanzhen SN55/56G5
Banyao GX43/44C5
Bao'an GX43/44C5
Bao'an GX43/44D7
Bao'an HB35/36D7
Bao'an HEN33/34D5
Bao'an SN55/56F5
Bao'an ZJ21/22D3
(Bao'an)Zhidan Xian SN55/56D4
Baoban HI42B1
Baochang JS19/20A4
(Baochang)Taibus Qi NM9/10G10
Baocheng SN55/56G2
Baode Xian SX7/8B3
Baodian SD31/32B3
Baodian SX7/8E4
Bao Ding SC47/48B4
Baoding Shi HEB5/6E3
Baodi Xian TJ3/4C4
Baodong HJ15/16E7
Baodugu SD31/32E4
Baofang HI42B3
Baofei SC47/48C2
Baofeng HB35/36B2
Baofeng NX61/62A3
Baofeng Xian HEN33/34D5
Baofu ZJ21/22B4
Baogang HI42C2
Baoguolao LN11/12B4
Bao He HEN33/34D7-8
Baohe SC47/48B2
Bao He HEB5/6C6
Bao He HEB3/4C2
Baohu Jiao HI42A3
Baoji JS17/18C4
Baoji AH23/24C4
Baojia JL13/14C6
Baojialou SC45/46D7
Baojing Xian(Qianling) HN37/38C2
Baojishan GS61/62D1
Baoji Shi SN55/56F3
Baoji Xian(Guozhen) SN55/56F3
(Baokang)Horqin Zuoyi Zhongqi
  NM9/10E14
Baokang Xian HB35/36C4
Baokou GD39/40C8

Baoliansi HEN33/34A6
Baolin HL15/16E5
Baolinchang SC47/48B3
Baolizhen LN11/12B7
Baolongshan NM9/10E14
Baoluan SC47/48C5
Baolun SC45/46B5
Baoluo HI42B3
Baonian JS17/18E5
Baoping GX43/44C5
Baoping HI42B1
Baoqing Xian HL15/16D7
Baoquan HL15/16C4
Baoquan SD31/32C6
Baoquanling HL15/16D6
Baoshan HL15/16C2
Baoshan SH17/18E7
Baoshan YN51/52B6
Baoshan Diqu YN51/52C3
Baoshan Shi YN51/52C3
Baoshansi BJ3/4B3
Baoshi HEB3/4C1
Baoshou JL13/14C7
Baoshui HB35/36D2
Bao Shui SN55/56G3
Baoshui HEB5/6E2
Baota NX61/62B3
Baotian GZ49/50E3
Baoting Lizu Miaozu Zizhixian HI42C2
Baotou Shi NM9/10G7
Baoxia HB35/36B3
Baoxing HL15/16C6
Baoxing Xian SC45/46C4
Baoxinji HEN33/34E6
Baoxiu YN51/52D5
Baoxu GD39/40D3
Baoyi AH23/24D3
Baoying Xian JS17/18C5
(Baoyou)Ledong Lizu Zizhixian HI42C1
Bapocun SX7/8F3
Baqên XZ53/54C9
Baqên Xian(Yêtatang) XZ53/54D10
Baqi HEN33/34C5
Baqi JS19/20B3
Baqiao JS17/18D5
Baqiao SN55/56F5
Baqiaozhen JS17/18D5
Baqiu JX29/30D3
Barga XZ53/54D3
Barkam Xian SC45/46C4
Barkol Hu XJ63/64D12
Barkol Kazak Zizhixian XJ63/64D12
Barong SC45/46C2
Bart NM9/10D12
Bart NM9/10E12
Barun QH59/60B5
Barun QH59/60C5
Basalt Island HK41B3
Bashan SC45/46C6
(Bashan)Chongren Xian JX29/30D4
Bashan Shuiku SD31/32D5
Bashimu ZJ21/22E5
Bashiqiao JS17/18E6

Ba Shui HB35/36D8
(Basuo)Dongfang Lizu Zizhixian HI42B1
Basuo Gang HI42B1
Batan JS17/18B6
Batang SC47/48C4
Batang GX43/44D7
Batang HN37/38C5
Batang Xian(Bazhong) SC45/46D2
Batou GX43/44D4
Batou ZJ21/22C3
Batu SD31/32C4
Batuyingzi LN11/12C4
Bawan YN51/52C3
Bawang SC45/46C3
Bawangjie AH23/24C4
Bawangling HI42B2
Baweigang JS17/18E6
Bawolung SC45/46D3
Baxi SC45/46B4
Baxi JX29/30E3
Baxian SN55/56H5
Baxianzhuozi TJ3/4B4
Baxin YN51/52D5
Baxkorgan XJ63/64F11
Baxoi Xian(Baima) XZ53/54D11
Baxu GX43/44C5
Bayan QH59/60C5
Bayan NM9/10F7
Bayan QH59/60B7
Bayan Bulag NM9/10E10
Bayan Bulag NM910E11
Bayanbulak XJ63/64D8
Bayan Delger NM9/10F10
Bayanggin Sum NM9/10F10
Bayan Gol NM9/10F10
Bayan Gol QH59/60B5
(Bayan Gol)Dengkou Xian NM9/10K16
Bayangolin Mongol Zizhizhou XJ63/64F8-12
Bayan Har Shan QH59/60C4-D7
Bayan Har Shankou QH59/60C5
Bayan Hatai NM9/10J19
(Bayan Hot)Alxa Zuoqi NM9/10H5
Bayan Hua NM9/10G7
Bayan Hua NM11/12B5
Bayan Hua NM9/10F8
(Bayan)Hualong Huizu Zizhixian QH59/60B8
Bayan Hudag NM9/10J18
(Bayan Hure)Chen Barag Qi NM9/10C12
(Bayan Huxu)Horqin Youyi Zhongqi NM9/10E13
Bayan Kele NM61/62B1
Bayan Mod NM9/10G5
Bayan Moron NM9/10H6
Bayannuur Meng NM9/10G6-7
Bayan NM9/10G7
Bayan Qagan HL15/16D3
(Bayan Qagan)Qahar Youyi Houqi NM9/10G9
Bayan Shan QH80B3
Bayan Tal NM9/10E13

Bayan Tal NM9/10D4
Bayan Tal NM11/12A4
Bayan Tohoi NM61/62A3
Bayan Tohoi NM57/58C8
Bayan Tohoi NM11/12A4
Bayan Tohoi Nongchang NM9/10K16
Bayan Toroi Nongchang NM9/10G3
Bayan Tug NM9/10E10
Bayan Ul NM9/10E9
(Bayan Ul Hot)Xi Ujimqin Qi NM9/10E11
Bayan Us NM9/10G7
Bayan Xian HL15/16D4
Bayiji JS17/18B3
Bayi Nongchang XJ63/64C9
Bayizhen XZ53/54E10
Bayuquan LN11/12D6
Bazhai HEB3/4B5
Bazhai YN51/52D6
Bazhai GZ49/50D7
Bazhan HL15/16B3
(Bazhong)Batang Xian SC45/46D2
Bazhong Diqu SC45/46B6-C6
Bazhong Shi SC45/46C6
Bazhou Shi HEB5/6D4
Bazi GD39/40B7
Bazilu HN37/38C4
Baziyang ZJ21/22C4
Beaufort Island HK41B3
Bêca QH59/60D5
Behleg QH59/60B2
Bei'anfeng JS17/18C6
Bei'an Shi HL15/16C4
(Bei'ao)Dongtou Xian ZJ21/22E6
Beiba SN55/56H3
Beibei SC45/46D6
Beibu Gulf 39/40F1-2

Beicang TJ3/4C4
Beichangshan Dao SD31/32B7
Beichangtan NX61/62C1
Beicheng SX7/8E4
Beicheng YN51/52C5
Beichuan He QH59/60B7
Beichuan Xian SC45/46C5
Beicuo FJ25/26E5
Beida HI42C3
Beidabei HEB3/4D1
Beida Chi NM61/62C4

Beidagang Shuiku TJ3/4D4
Beida He GS57/58C3
Beidaihe HEB5/6D7
Beidaihehaibin HEB5/6D7
Beidao GS57/58E8
Beidaoqiao XJ63/64C10
Beidaqiao GS57/58B2
Beida Shan NM9/10H3
Beidian LN11/12C8
Beidianzi SD31/32B8
Beidou GD39/40E5
Beidou SC47/48B2
Beidu HEN33/34D5

Beifei He　AH23/24C3
Beifeng Ding　SD73B6
Beigang　JL13/14E8
Beigang　HB35/36E6
Beigao　HEB5/6G2
Beigou　HL15/16C5
Beigou　SD31/32B7
Beiguan Dao　ZJ21/22E5
Beiguantao　SD31/32C2
Beiguo　JS17/18E6
Beihai Shi　GX43/44F7
Beihan　HEB3/4D3
Bei Har Huxu　NM13/14C2
Beihe　GD39/40F2
Beihedian　HEB5/6D3
Beihuaidian　TJ3/4C4
Beihuangcheng Dao　SD31/32A7
Bei Hulsan Hu　QH59/60B4
Beiji　SN55/56E4
Beiji　GD39/40B9
Beijiadian　HEB5/6D6
Beijiang　HN37/38G4
Bei Jiang　GD39/40B6-C5
Beijiao　FJ25/26D5
Beijing　SX7/8F2
Beijin Gang　GD39/40E5
Beijinggang　HN37/38B5
Beijing Shi　BJ3/4C3
Beijingzi　LN11/12E7
Beijipo　SD31/32C4
Beijishan Liedao　ZJ21/22E6
Beijuma He　BJ3/4C2-3
Beikan　JS17/18D7
Beikuo　SD31/32D6
Beilian　HL15/16C3
Beiling　GD39/40B8
Beiliu Jiang　GX43/44D8-F8
Beiliutang He　JS17/18C4-B5
Beiliu Shi　GX43/44E8
Beilongshan　ZJ21/22E5
Beilu　LN11/12C3
Beilu He　QH9/10C3
Beiluheyan　QH59/60C3
Beilun　ZJ21/22C6
Beilun He　GX43/44F5
Beima　SD31/32B7
Beimajuanzi　HEB3/4B4
Beimianhe　NX61/62E3
Beimuzhen　SC45/46D5
Beining Shi　LN11/12C5
Beipai He　HEB3/4D4
Beipan Jiang　GZ49/50E4
Beipiao Shi　LN11/12C4
Beiping　SX7/8E4
Beipo　GD39/40E2
Beipo　HI42C3
Beiqiao　SH19/20B4
Beirong　HN37/38C3
Beiru He　HEN33/34C4-D5
Beisanjia　LN111/12B8
Bei Shan　GS57/58B3
Beishan　GX43/44C6
Bei Shan　ZJ21/22C4

Beishan　GD41B2
Beishe　SX7/8E5
Beishengcang　HN37/38C6
Beishicheng　BJ3/4B3
Beishidian　SD31/32D4
Beishidian　SX7/8F4
Beishuang Dao　FJ25/26D6
Beishuangdong　HEB3/4B4
Beishuiquan　HEB5/6C2
Beisi　SD31/32B5
Beitai　GD41B1
Beitai Ding　SX7/8B5
Beitaishang Shuiku　BJ3/4B3
Beitang　TJ3/4C4
Beitaolaizhao　JL13/14C6
Beita Shan　XJ63/64C11
Beitian　SX7/8D4
Beitou　JX29/30F2
Beitou　GD39/40B7
Beitun　XJ63/64B9
Beiwancun　SX7/8E3
Beiwang　HEB3/4C3
Beiwei Tan　GD39/40E9
Beiwenquan　SC47/48C4
Beiwudu　HEN33/34D5
Beixi　HN37/38F6
Bei Xi　FJ25/26C3
Beixiaochuan　BJ3/4B3
Beixiaodian　SX7/8C4
Beixing　HJ15/16C3
Beixinzhuang　HEB3/4D3
Beiya　YN51/52B4
Beiya　GX43/44C6
Beiyan　SD31/32C5
Beiyandang Shan　ZJ21/22D6
Beiye　HEB5/6E1
Beiying　SX7/8D4
Beiyuan　SD31/32C4
Bei Yunhe　TJ3/4C3-4
(Beizhen)Binzhou Shi　SD31/32B5
Beizhengzhen　JL13/14C4
Beizhou　GD41A1
Beizhouzhuang　SX7/8B4
Beizhuang　BJ3/4B4
Beizifu　NM11/12B4
Beizijie　HEN33/34D4
Bencha　JS17/18D6
Bencha Yunhe　JS19/20A3
(Bencheng)Luannan Xian　HEB5/6D6
Bengbu Shi　AH23/24D4
Beng He　SD31/32D5
Beng He　LN11/12B3
Benhao　HI42C2
Benjing　NM9/10H5
Benniu　JS17/18E5
Benxi Manzu Zizhixian　LN11/12C8
Benxi Shi　LN11/12C7
Benzhuang　GZ49/50C6
Benzilan　YN51/52A3
Biandan Gang　JS17/18B6
Biangou　LN11/12D8
Bianlinzhen　SD31/32B3
Bianqiao　SD31/32D4

Biantang　JS17/18B3
Bianya　GX43/44C3
Bianyang　GZ49/50E5
Bianzhangzi　LN11/12C4
Bianzhao　JL13/14C4
Bianzhuang　AH23/24D5
(Bianzhuang)Cangshan Xian　SD31/32E5
Bibei　GD39/40A6
Bidian　HEN33/34E5
Bieguzhuang　HEB3/4C3
Bieqiao　JS17/18E5
Bi'er　HN37/38C2
Bieshan　TJ3/4C4
Biguo　SD31/32B7
Bihenying　GZ49/50E4
Bihu　ZJ21/22D4
Bi Jiang　YN77B2-C2
Bijiaquan　HEB5/6D6
Bijia Shan　FJ25/26C3
Bijie Diqu　GZ49/50C3-4
Bijie Shi　GZ49/50C4
Bijiguan　YN51/52C5
Bikeqi　NM9/10K21
Bikou　GS57/58F7
Bikou Shuiku　GS57/58F7
Bila He　NM15/16C2
Bilian　ZJ21/22D5
Bilingwei　GD41A3
Biliu He　LN11/12E6
Biluo Xueshan　YN51/52B3
Bin'an　HL15/16E4
Bincheng　SD31/32B4
Binchuan Xian(Niujing)　YN51/52C4
Bingcaowan　GS57/58D6
Bingcun　GD39/40B9
Bingfang　JS19/20A4
Bingfangjie　SN55/56H5
(Bingmei)Congjiang Xian　GZ49/50E7
Bingzhongluo　YN51/52A3
Binhai Xian(Dongkan)　JS17/18B5
Binhuai　JS17/18B6
Bin Jiang　GD39/40B5-C5
Binjiang　GX29/30D2
Binkeng　GD41A1
Binxi　HL15/16E4
Bin Xian　HL15/16E4
Bin Xian　SN55/56E4
Binyang Xian　GX43/44D6
Binzhou Diqu　SD31/32B4-C4
Binzhou Shi　SD31/32B5
Bipu　ZJ21/22C4
Biqiao　AH19/20B2
Bi Qu　QH59/60D3
Biratar Bulak　XJ63/64E11
Biru Xian　XZ53/54D9
Bisezhai　YN51/52D5
Bishan　JX29/30B4
Bishan Xian　SC45/46D6
Bishi　HN37/38C6
Bishui　HL15/16A2
Bixi　JX29/30E2
Biyang He　HEN33/34E5
Biyang Xian　HEN3/34E5

Biyong HN37/38D2
Biyu GS57/58E7
Bizhou HL15/16B3
Bjiaogou SC45/46D4
Bluff Island HK41B3
Bo'ai YN51/52D7
Bo'ai Xian HEN33/34B5
Bo'ao HI42B3
Bobai Xian GX43/44E7
Bobi HEN33/34B5
Bobso SC45/46B4
Bodu JL13/14B5
Bogcang Zangbo XZ53/54D6
Bogda Fang XJ63/64D10
Bogda Shan XJ63/64D10-11
Bohai SD31/32B5
Bohai ZJ21/22D4
Bohai HL15/16E5
Bo Hai 5/6E6-7
Bohai Haixia 11/12F5
Bohai Wan 3/4D4-5
Bohe GD39/40E4
Bohou HI42B2
Bohu(Bagrax)Xian XJ63/64E9
Boin Sum NM9/10F9
Bolan HI42B2
Bolao GX43/44E7
Bole(Bortal)Shi XJ63/64C7
Bolishan JL13/14D4
Boli Xian HL15/16E6
Boluntay QH59/60B3
Boluobu SN55/56B5
Boluochi LN11/12C3
Boluokeng GD39/40B6
Boluonuo HEB5/6B5
Boluopao JL13/14C5
Boluo Xian GD39/40C7
Bomai SC45/46D2
Bomei GD39/40D8
Bomi(Bowo)Xian(Zhamo) XZ53/54E10
Boming SX7/8C4
Bonihe JL13/14D6
Boping SD31/32C3
Boping Ling FJ25/26E3-F3
Boqê XZ53/54D8
Boqiang SX7/8B5
Borohoro Shan XJ63/64C7-D8
Bor Ondor JL13/14C3
Bortal Mongol Zizhizhou XJ63/64C6-7
Bose Diqu GX43/44C4-D5
Bose Shi GX43/44D4
Boshan SD31/32C4
Boshang YN51/52D4
Boshan Shuiku HEN33/34E5
Bostan XJ63/64G8
Bosten(Bagrax)Hu XJ63/64E9
Botou SD31/32A4
Botou SD31/32B5
Botou Shi HEB 5/6E4
Bowang HEN33/34D4
Bowang AH23/24E5
Boxing Xian SD31/32B5
Boxodoi NM9/10F10

Boyang GS57/58E8
Boyang GD39/40D3
Boyang HN37/38E2
Boyang Xian JX29/30B4
Boyao GZ49/50E6
Boye Xian HEB5/6E3
Bozhai GX43/44C7
Bozhou HN37/38D2
Bozhou Shi AH23/24C2
Bucun SD31/32C4
Budongquan QH59/60C3
Bugt NM9/10F13
Bugt NM9/10C13
Bugugou HEB5/6B5
Buhai JL13/14C6
Buhe HB35/36D5
Buh He QH59/60B6
Buir Nur NM9/10D11
Buji GD41A3
Buka Daban QH59/60B2 XJ63/64G11
Bukou HB35/36B5
Bulang GZ49/50D4
Bulanggin Nur NM9/10K17
Bulanggin Sum NM9/10H6
Bulaotun BJ3/4B3
Buliu SD31/32B9
Buliu He GX43/44C4
Bulongji GS57/58B3
Bulu ZJ21/22D5
Bulungkol XJ63/64F3
Bumbat NM9/10G5
Bumdirla XZ53/54F9
Bungona'og XZ53/54C8
Bünsum XZ53/54D4
Buqian GD39/40C7
Burang Xian XZ53/54D3
Burd NM9/10F10
Burhan Budai Shan QH59/60B4-C5
Burjay XJ63/64D10
Burqin He XJ63/64A9
But Nur NM9/10E12
Butou GX43/44C9
Butuo Xian SC45/46E4
Buyant NM9/10G6
Buyiqiao JS17/18E5
Buyuan Jiang YN51/52D4
Buyun Shan LN11/12D6
Buze SX7/8E5
Buzhen SH17/18E7
Buzi JS17/18C4
Buzidian HEB3/4B4

C

Cada QH59/60B6
Caicunba AH23/24F5
Caidian HB35/36D7
Caigongzhuang TJ3/4D4
Caigou HEN33/34D6
Caihua HB35/36D3
Caijia JL13/14D5
Caijia SC47/48C4
Caijiagang AH23/24D3
Caijiagang SC45/46D6

Caijiagou JL13/14B7
Caijiahe HB35/36D8
Caijialiang NX61/62B3
Caijiapo SN55/56F3
Caijiaya SX7/8C3
Caijiazhuang SD31/32C6
Cainnyigoin SC45/46B4
Caishen GZ49/50C3
Caishi AH23/24E5
Caishi HN37/38E4
Caitingqiao HEB5/6D5
Caiwan GX43/44B8
Caixi FJ25/26E2
Cai Xi ZJ21/22D3
Caiyu BJ3/4C3
Caiyuan HEN33/34B6
(Caiyuanzhen)Shengsi Xian ZJ21/22B7
Caizhai SD31/32B5
Caizhuang HEN33/34C6
Caizhuang HEN31/32B7
Caizi Hu AH23/24F4
Caka Yanhu QH59/60B6
Caluo SC45/46D4
Cangbu HB35/36D7
Cangcheng GD39/40D5
Cang'erhui SX7/8D3
Cangfang HEN33/34E3
Canggang HN37/38C4
Canggeng GZ49/50F3

Cangnan Xian (Lingxi) ZJ21/22E5
Cangoubu HEB5/6D2
Cangqian ZJ19/20C2
Cangqing HL15/16C5
Cangshan HL15/16B2
Cangshan Xian (Bianzhuang) SD31/32E5
Cangshanzhen SC45/46C5
Cangshi LN11/12C8
Cangshuipu HN37/38C5
Cangtou AH23/24E4
Cangtou He SX7/8A4
Cangwu Xian (Langxu) GX43/44D9
Cang Xian HEB5/6E4
Cangxi Xian SC45/46C5
Cangyuan Vazu Zizhixian YN51/52D3
Cangzhou Shi HEB5/6E4
Cao'an AH23/24D4
Caoba SC45/46D4
Caoba YN51/52D5
Caoban JS17/18D6
Caobi SN55/56F3
Caobo HN37/38D6
Caobu GD41A3
Caochi SC47/48B2
Caocun AH23/24B4
Cao Daban QH59/60A7
Caodian HB35/36B4
Caodian JS17/18C5
Caodu He GZ49/50E6
Cao'e ZJ21/22C5
Cao'e Jiang ZJ21/22C5
Caofeidian HEB5/6E6
Caogang HEN33/34C6

Caogou AH23/24C4
Cao Hai GZ49/50D3
Caohe HEB5/6E3
Cao He HEB3/4D2
(Caohe)Jinchun Xian HB35/36D8
Caohekou LN11/12D7
Caohezhang LN11/12C8
Caohu XJ63/64E8
Caojiachuan SX7/8G3
Caojiaji AH23/24D2
Caojialu BJ3/4B4
Caojian YN51/52C3
Caojiawa NX61/62D2
Caojiawan SN55/56F2
Caojiawu HEB3/4C3
Caolaoji AH23/24C4
Caomaji SD31/32E3
Caomiao NX61/62D3
Caomiao JS17/18C6
Caonian JS17/18D6
Caopandi HB35/36D8
Caoping SN55/56G5
Caopingjie SN55/56G5
Cao Po HEB3/4C5
Caopu JS17/18B4
Caoqiao JS17/18E5
Caoshi AH23/24C3
Caoshi HN37/38E6
Caoshi HB35/36D5
Caoshi LN11/12B9
Caosi HEB3/4D3
Caota ZJ21/22C5
Caotan GD39/40E2
Caotang JS19/20B2
Caotang(Houchang) GZ49/50C6
Caowei HN37/38B5
Caoxi JX29/30C5
Cao Xian SD31/32E2
Caoxizhuang HEB5/6D7
Caoyankou JS17/18C5
Cao Yu FJ25/26E5
Caoyuan HEB5/6B4
(Caozhou)Heze Shi SD31/32D2
Caozhuang HEB5/6E3
Caozhuang SD31/32E5
Ceheng Xian (Zhelou) GZ49/50E4
Celing GX43/44C5
Cengang ZJ21/22B7
Cengong Xian(Siyang) GZ49/50C7
Cengshan SD31/32E5
Cenhe HB35/36D5
Cen Shui HN37/38B4
Centianhe Shuiku HN37/38F4
Cenwang Laoshan GX43/44C4
Cenxi Shi GX43/44E8
Cêri XZ53/54D5
Ceshi SX7/8D5
Cêtar QH59/60B7
Cetian Shuiku SX7/8B5
Ceyang GZ49/50E4
Ceyu HEB5/6F3
Cezishan ZJ21/22B6
Cha'anpu HN37/38C4

Chabu FJ25/26C3
Chabyêr Caka XZ53/54D4-5
Chadao HEB5/6C3
Chadian SC47/48B3
Chadian GZ49/50C8
Chadian TJ3/4C4
Chadianzi HB35/36D3
Chado Kangri XZ53/54B5
Chadong HN37/38C2
Cha'enshi HN37/38D5
Chafang SN55/56D5
Chafang SC47/48C1
Chagan GD39/40B8
Chagannao JL13/14B4
Chaggur QH59/60C4
Chahayang HL15/16C3
Chahe HI42B1
Chahe GZ49/50D2
Chahe JS17/18D6
Chahe JS17/18C5
Chaheji AH23/24D5
Chaheze SN55/56B5
Chahua AH23/24C2
Chahuaping GZ49/50B6
Chaichangtun BJ3/4C3
Chaigou SD31/32C6
(Chaigoubu)Huai'an Xian HEB5/6C2
Chaihe HL15/16E5
Chai He LN11/12B8
Chaihe NM9/10D13
Chaihepu LN11/12B8
Chaihe Shuiku LN11/12B7
Chaihudian SD31/32B3
Chaiji AH23/24D2
Chaiqiao ZJ21/22C6
Chaiwan JS19/20A3
Chaiwopu XJ63/64D9
Chajian AH23/24D5
Chajianling HEB5/6D2
Chakou AH19/20D1
Chakou SX7/8C5
Chakou SX7/8D3
Chalaxung QH59/60C5
Chalengkou QH59/60A3
Chaling Xian HN37/38E6
Chaluhe JL13/14D6
Chalukou JL13/14C7
Chalukou AH23/24D3
Chamda XZ53/54E8
Chamo Co QH59/60C2
Chang'an GX43/44C7
Chang'an HI42B3
Chang'an GD39/40C4
(Chang'an)Rong'an Xian GX43/44B7
Chang'an Xian SN55/56F4
Chang'anzhen ZJ21/22B5
Changba SC47/48C5
Changbai Chaoxianzu Zizhixian
　JL13/14F9
Changbaishan ZJ45/46B7
Changbai Shan JL 13/14E9 – F8
Changbai Shandi JL69C5 – A8
　　　　　　　　HL70G3 – E5
Changbaishan Tianchi JL13/14E8

Changbiao Dao FJ25/26D6
Changbu GD39/40C8
Changcao BJ3/4C2
Changcaogou GS57/58C2
Changcheng SX7/8A5
Changcheng SX7/8D5
Changcheng SD31/32E5
Changcheng HI42C2
Changcheng HI42B1
Changchi SC45/46B6
Changchi SX7/8C5
Changchuanba ZJ19/20C3
Changchun HL15/16D3
Changchunling JL13/14B6
Changchunpu GZ49/50C4
Changchun Shi JL13/14D6
Changcun HEN33/34D5
Changcun SX7/8E4
Changdang Hu JS17/18E5
Changdao Xian SD31/32B7
Changde Shi HN37/38B4
Changdi HEB3/4B2
Changdian LN11/12D8
Changdianhekou LN11/12D8
Changfa GX43/44D9
Changfatun HL15/16D6
Changfeng HEB3/4D3
Changfeng Xian(Shuijiahu) AH23/24D4
Changgang JX29/30E3
Changgang GD39/40C4
Changgang GZ49/50C5
Changgangdian AH23/24E4
Changgao LN11/12C5
Changge Shi HEN33/34C5
Changgou AH23/24C4
Changgou BJ3/4C2
Changgouyu BJ3/4C2
Changhai Xian(Sikuaishi) LN11/12E6
Changhao HI42C2
Changhe ZJ21/22B5
Changheshi ZJ21/22B6
Chang Hu HB35/36D5
Changhua HI42B1
Changhua ZJ21/22B4
Changhua Hsien TW27/28C2
Changhua Jiang HI42B1-C2
(Changhua)Mengjin Xian HEN33/34C4
Changjia HL15/16C5
Chang jiang JX29/30B4-5
Changjiangbu HB35/36D6
Changjiang Kou SH17/18E7
Changjiang Lizu Zizhixian HI42B2
Changjiang Sanjiaozhou JS71C3-4
Changjiang Shuiku GD41B1
Chang Jiang(Yangtze R.) SH17/18E6-7
　　　　　　　　　　　AH23/24E5
　　　　　　　　　　　JS17/18E6-7
　　　　　　　　　　　JX29/30B4
　　　　　　　　　　　HB35/36E8
　　　　　　　　　　　SC45/46D6
　　　　　　　　　　　HN37/38B5
Changjiang Zhongxiayou Pingyuan
　JS71C2-3 AH71C2-3

Changjie ZJ21/22C6
Changji Huizu Zizhixian XJ63/64C9-11
Changji Shi XJ63/64C9
Changkai JX29/30C4
Changkou ZJ21/22C4
Changlao GX43/44C5
Changle HN37/38C6
Changle ZJ21/22C5
Changle AH23/24E4
Changle GX43/44C5
Changle SC45/46C6
Changle GX43/44F7
(Changleng)Xinjian Xian JX29/30C3
Changleping HB35/36D3
Changlepu NX61/62C2
Changle Shi FJ25/26E5
Changle Xian SD31/32C5
Changlezhen JS19/20B4
Changli SD31/32C6
Changlianggou SX7/8C4
Changliangzi HB35/36D2
Changling JL13/14D6
Changling SN55/56H3
Changling GD41A3
Changlinggang HB35/36C6
Changlingji HEN33/34E7
Changlingjie YN51/52D6
Changling(Ming Tombs) BJ3/4B3
Changlingpi GD41A3
Changlingpu AH23/24F3
Changling Xian JL13/14C4
Changlingzi LN11/12E5
Changlingzi LN11/12E6
Changlingzi LN11/12F5
Changlinhe AH23/24E4
Changliushui NM61/62B2
Changliushui NX61/62C1
Changli Xian HEB5/6D7
Changlong JL13/14C5
Changlong SX7/8E4
Changlu SD31/32D4
Changma GS57/58C3
Changma HEB5/6G3
Changmao Shuiku HI42C2
Changmar XZ53/54B2
Changmen Yan SD31/32C7
Changming GZ49/50D6
Changning GD39/40C7
Changning HEB5/6D6
Changning SX7/8D4
Changning SN55/56F4
Changningpu GS57/58C6
Changning Xian SC45/46D5
Changning Xian YN51/52C3
Changning Shi HN37/38E5
Changpianqiao SC45/46C4
Changpin TW27/28D3
Changping GD39/40D6
Changping Xian BJ3/4B3
Changpo HI42B2
Changpo HI42B3
Changqiao FJ25/26D4
Changqiao FJ25/26F3

Changqing Xian SD31/32C3
Changsa HI42B3
Changshaba Shuiku SC47/48C2
Changshageng SC47/48B2
Changshan SD31/32C4
Changshan SC47/48C2
Changshan JL13/14D7
Changshan FJ25/26G3
Changshan Qundao LN11/12E6-7
Changshantou NX61/62C2
Changshantou Shuiku NX61/62C2
Changshan Xian ZJ21/22D3
Changshanyu HEB5/6C5
Changshaoying BJ3/4B3
Changshapu SD31/32B8
Changsha Shi HN37/38C5
Changsha Xian HN37/38C5
Changshaxu GD41B2
Changshazhen JS19/20A4
Changsheng JX29/30E4
Changsheng JL13/14E6
Changsheng SC47/48C4
Changshi GZ49/50C4
Changshoudian HB35/36C5
Changshoujie HN37/38C6
Changshou Xian SC45/46D6
Changshui HEN33/34C3
Changshun Xian GZ49/50D5
Changshu Shi JS17/18E6
Changtai ZJ21/22D3
Changtaiguan HEN33/34E6
Changtai Xian FJ25/26F3
Changtan ZJ21/22D6
Changtan HB35/36C5
Changtan GX43/44C8
Changtang GX43/44E6
Changtan Shuiku ZJ21/22D6
Changting HL15/16E5
Changting Xian(Tingzhou) FJ25/26E2
Changtu ZJ19/20C5
Changtuan HEB3/4B2
Changtu Xian LN11/12B8
Changweiliang QH59/60A3
Changwu HL15/16D3
Changwu Xian SN55/56E3
Changxindian BJ3/4C3
Changxing SC47/48D3
Changxing SN55/56F3
Changxing SX7/8F5
Changxing Dao LN11/12E5
Changxing Dao SH17/18E7
Changxingdian LN11/12C5
Changxing Xian(Zhicheng) ZJ21/22A4
Changxuanling HB35/36C7
Changyan HB35/36C7
Changyang BJ3/4C3
Changyangsha JS19/20B3
Changyang Tujiazu Zizhixian HB35/36D4
Changying HEN33/34C6
Changyi Shi SD31/32C6
Changyoulian GD41B2
Changyuan He SX7/8D4
Changyuan Xian HEN33/34B6

Changzhen SX7/8B3
Changzhen GD41A2
Changzheng HI42C2
Changzheng GS57/58D7
Changzhi Shi SX7/8E5
Changzhi Xian(Handian) SX7/8E5
Changzhou Shi JS17/18E5
Changzhuang HEB3/4C5
Changzhuang SD31/32C4
Changzhuang SD31/32D3
Changzhuyuan HEN33/34F7
Chankeng FJ25/26E3
Chankou GS57/58E7
Chanping HB35/36C4
(Chanpu)Suining Xian HN37/38E3
Chansha GD39/40B9
Chantai SC45/46C2
Chanxi GZ49/50C7
Chanxinpu NX61/62B3
Chanzhi Shuiku SD31/32C7
Chao'an Xian(Anbu) GD39/40C9
Chaobai He BJ3/4B3
Chaobai Xinhe TJ3/4C4
Chaobei HEN33/34D4
Chaochou TW27/28E2
Chaodi GZ49/50B7
Chaodong GX43/44B9
Chaohan Shan NM9/10C14
Chao He HEB5/6C5
Chaohe SD31/32D6
Chao Hu AH23/24E4
Chaohua HEN33/34C5
Chaohu Diqu AH23/24E4-5
Chaohu Nongchang NX61/62B3
Chaohupu NX61/62A3
Chaohu Shi AH23/24E4
Chaolian Dao SD31/32D7
Chaoliangzi HEB3/4B5
Chaoshui SD31/32B7
Chaotian SC45/46B5
Chaoyang JL13/14C7
Chaoyang HB35/36C4
Chaoyang HI42B3
Chaoyang GZ49/50E6
Chaoyangchuan JL13/14E10
Chaoyangcun NM9/10B15
Chaoyanggou HEN33/34C5
Chaoyang Hu XZ53/54B6
(Chaoyang)Huinan Xian JL13/14E7
Chaoyangji AH23/24C4
(Chaoyang)Jiayin Xian HL15/16C6
Chaoyang Shi LN11/12C4
Chaoyang Shi GD39/40C9
Chaoyangwanzi HEB5/6A5
Chaoyang Xian LN11/12C4
Chaoyi SN55/56F6
Chaozhong NM9/10B13
Chaozhou Shi GD39/40C9
Chaozhuang HEN33/34C6
Chaping Shan SC76C5-6
Charbaqi NM15/16C2
Chashan'ao HN37/38E5
(Chatang)Zhanang Xian XZ53/54E8

Chatian ZJ21/22E3
Chating JX29/30D5
Chating JS17/18E5
Chawan AH23/24E5
Chawu BJ3/4B3
Chaxi HN37/38C3
Chayang GD39/40B9
Chayashan HEN33/34D5
Chayuan HN37/38D5
Chayuan ZJ21/22C6
Chayuanpu HN37/38D5
Chazhen SN55/56G4
Checheng TW27/28E2
Checheng TW27/28D2
Checun HEN33/34D4
Chedao SD31/32C8
Chefang JS17/18E6
Chegang GD39/40D5
Chehe GX43/44C5
Chejiang HN37/38E5
Chek Chue HK41B3
Chek Lap Kok HK41B2
Chekou ZJ21/22D6
Chelu HL15/16C5
Cheluo JS17/18D5
Chen Barag Qi(Bayan Hure)
  NM9/10C12
Chencai ZJ21/22C5
Chencheng FJ25/26G3
Chencun AH23/24F5
Chencun SN55/56F3
Chencun Shuiku AH23/24F5
Chendai FJ25/26G3
Chendong FJ25/26F4
Chen'erpu HN37/38B4
Chenfan JX29/30C5
Cheng'an AH23/24F4
Cheng'an Xian HEB5/6G2
Chengbihe Shuiku GX43/44D4
Chengbu Miaozu Zizhixian(Rulin)
  HN37/38E3
Chengcheng Xian SN55/56E5
Chengchuan NM9/10I7
Chengcun GD39/40E4
Chengde Shi HEB5/6C5
Chengde Xian(Xiabancheng) HEB5/6C6
Chengdong HEB3/4D2
Chengdong Hu AH23/24D3
Chengdongqiao YN51/52C5
Chengdu Shi SC45/46C5
Chenggang JX29/30E3
Chenggezhuang SD31/32C6
Chenggong Xian YN51/52C5
Chenggu Xian SN55/56G3
Cheng Hai YN51/52B4
Chenghai Shi GD39/40C9
Cheng Hu JS17/18E6
Chenghuang GX43/44E7
Chengji JS17/18C5
Chengjia SX7/8D5
Chengjia GD39/40B5
Chengjiachang SC47/48C2
Chengjiadian SD31/32D3

Chengjiang JX29/30F3
(Chengjiang)Taihe Xian JX29/30E2
Chengjiang Xian YN51/52C5
Chengjiangzhen SC47/48C4
Chengjiaqiao JS17/18D4
Chengjiashi AH23/24E5
Chengkou SD31/32A4
Chengkou FJ25/26E3
Chengkou GD39/40A6
Chengkou Xian SC45/46C7
Chengkung TW27/28D3
Chenglingji HN37/38B6
Chengliu HEN33/34B4
Chenglong JX29/30G2
Chengmai Xian(Jinjiang) HI42B2
Chengnanzhuang HEB5/6E2
Chengping HN37/38E6
Chengqian SD31/32D4
(Chengqiao)Chongming Xian SH19/20B4
Chengshan Jiao SD31/32B9
Chengtan ZJ21/22C5
Chengtou JS17/18B4
Chengtoujiao GD41A3
Chenguantun TJ3/4D3
Chenguanzhuang HEN33/34C8
Chengwu Xian SD31/32E2
Chengxi FJ25/26F3
Chengxi SC47/48B5
Cheng Xian GS57/58F7
Chengxiangzhen SC47/48B2
Chengxiangzhen JX29/30C4
Chengxi Hu AH23/24D3
Chengyang NX61/62E3
Chengyang SD31/32C7
Chengyuan FJ25/26C5
Chengyue GD39/40E3
Chengzhaichang GZ49/50B5
Chengzhuang SX7/8C3
Chengzhuangzhai HEN33/34C7
Chengzi HEB5/6B5
Chengzi BJ3/4C3
Chengzihe HL15/16E6
Chengzi Hu JS17/18C4
Chengzitan LN11/12E6
Cheniu Shan 31/32E6
Chenji JS17/18C5
Chenji JS17/18D5
Chenji JS17/18B5
Chenji HEN33/34E7
Chenjiagang JS17/18B5
Chenjiang GD39/40C7
Chenjiaqian AH19/20A1
Chenjiaqiao SC47/48C4
Chenjiatuan SD31/32B8
Chenjiawan SX7/8D3
Chenjiazhen SH17/18E7
Chenjiazhuang SD31/32B5
Chenjiazhuang SX7/8C5
Chenliu HEN33/34C6
Chenlu SN55/56E5
Chenming HL15/16D5
Chenmu JS17/18E6
Chenpo SD31/32D2

Chenqing HL15/16C4
Chenshi HEB5/6E3
Chenshu JS19/20B3
Chen Shui HN37/38D2-3
Chentang GX43/44D8
Chentuan SD31/32D6
Chenwanggetan NM9/10J18
Chenwu JS19/20A2
Chenxiangtun LN11/12C7
Chenxi Xian HN37/38C3
Chenyang JS17/18C6
Chenye JX29/30E3
Chenying AH23/24D5
(Chenying)Wannian Xian JX29/30C5
Chenyu ZJ21/22D6
Chenzhai AH23/24B3
Chenzhou Shi HN37/38F6
Chenzhuang SD31/32D4
Chenzhuang HEB5/6E2
Chepan SC47/48C5
Chepan JX29/30D5
Cheqiao JS17/18C5
Chetian GX43/44A8
Chetou JX29/30F3
Chetou ZJ21/22C5
Cheung Chau HK41B3
Cheung Chau HK41B3
Cheung Sha HK41B2
Chexu FJ25/26F3
Chezhen SD31/32B4
Chia-i Hsien TW27/28D2
Chia-i Shih TW27/28D2
Chiahsien TW27/28D2
Chiali TW27/28D2
Chi'an ZJ21/22C5
Chian TW27/28D3
Chiangchunao Yu TW27/28D1
Chiaohsi TW27/28C3
Chiaopanshan TW27/28C3
(Chiapaotai)Pahsien TW27/28C3
Chiating TW27/28E2
Chibakou HB35/36E6
Chibi HB35/36E6
Chicheng Xian HEB5/6C3
Chichi TW27/28D2
Chichin TW27/28E2
Chidong GD39/40D3
Chienshih TW27/28C3
Chifeng Shi NM9/10F12
Chigan SN55/56F4
Chigang JX29/30C4
Chigu Co XZ53/54E8
Chi He AH23/24D4
Chihe AH23/24D4
Chihpen TW27/28E3
Chihshang TW27/28D3
Chihsing Yen TW27/28F2
Chihu FJ25/26F3
Chihwei Yu TW27/28G6
Chijiang JX29/30F2
Chijinpu GS57/58B3
Chikang GD39/40E3
Chikang GD39/40D5

Chikeng GD41A1
Chik Nai Ping HK41B3
Chilai Chushan TW27/28C3
Chilan TW27/28C3
Chilung Kang TW27/28B3
Chilung (keelung) Shih TW27/28B3
Chilung Tao TW27/28B3
Chimei HEN33/34D3
Chimei Yu TW27/28D1
Chindu Xian(Chuqung) QH59/60D5
Ching Chau HK41B3
Chingpu TW27/28D3
Chingshan TW27/28C3
Chingshang TW27/28C3
Chingshui TW27/28C2
Chingshui TW27/28C3
Chingtsadhu TW27/28C2
Chingtung TW27/28B3
Chini GD41A2
Chiniwa SX7/8C4
Chinkuashih TW27/28B3
Chinmen Hsien FJ25/26F4
Chinmen Tao FJ25/26F4
Chinshan TW27/28B3
Chinshui TW27/28C2
Chipei Yu TW27/28D1
Chiping Xian SD31/32C3
Chishan TW27/28E2
Chishan Hsi TW27/28D2
Chishanji SD31/32C9
Chishi FJ25/26C4
Chishi ZJ21/22D4
Chishui JX29/30E4
Chishui FJ25/26E4
Chishui SN55/56F5
Chishui GX43/44D9
Chishui GD39/40D5
Chishui He SC45/46E5 GZ49/50B4-5
Chishui Shi GZ49/50B4
Chitan Dao GD41B2
Chitanzhen AH19/20C1
Chitou Shan ZJ21/22E5
Chitu JX29/30F2
Chiukang TW27/28C2
Chiwan GD41B2
Chiwei GD39/40C9
Chixi JX29/30C4
Chixi GD39/40E5
Chixi FJ25/26E4
Chiyuan FJ25/26D4
Chizhen AH23/24E5
Chizhou AH23/24F4
Chizhou Shi AH23/24F4
Chogori Feng XJ63/64H4
Cho La SC45/46C2
Cholan TW27/28C2
Chola Shan SC45/46B2-C2
Chong'anjiang GZ49/50D6
Chong'an Jiang GZ49/50D6
Chongde HL15/16D3
(Chongde)Chongfu ZJ19/20C3
Chongfang SD31/32E5
Chongfu ZJ21/22B5
Chonggangpu NX61/62B3

Chonggou SD31/32E5
Chonggu SH19/20B4
Chonghe HL15/16E4
Chongkan SC47/48B3
Chongkü XZ53/54D11
Chongling Shui HN37/38E5
Chongli Xian(Xiwanzi) HEB5/6C3
Chonglou GD39/40D5
Chongming Dao SH17/18E7
Chongming Xian SH17/18E7
Chongpo HI42C1
Chongqing Shi SC45/46D6
Chongqing Shuiku BJ3/4C3
Chongren ZJ21/22C5
Chongren He JX29/30D4
Chongren Xian(Bashan) JX29/30D4
Chongshan JL13/14E9
Chongshi JX29/30F3
Chongwu FJ25/26F4
Chongxian JX29/30E3
Chongxin GZ49/50C5
Chongxin GZ49/50B6
Chongxing GS57/58C6
Chongxing HI42B3
Chongxingzhai NX61/62B3
Chongxin Xian GS57/58E8
Chongyain Qu XZ76D2
Chongyangdian HEN33/34D3
Chongyang Xi FJ25/26C4
Chongyang Xian HB35/36E7
Chongyi HEN33/34B4
Chongyicun NX61/62E3
Chongyi Xian(Hengshui) JX29/30F2
Chongzhou Shi SC45/46C4
Chongzuo Xian(Taiping) GX43/44E5
Choshui Hsi TW27/28D2-3
Choushui JL13/14E8
Choushui He NX61/62D2
Chuaigutuan HEB5/6C2
Chuanbu GD39/40D4
Chuanchang FJ25/26F3
Chuanchang He JS17/18C6
Chuancheng JS17/18C4
Chuandong GZ49/50C8
Chuangang JS17/18E7
Chuangang GD39/40D5
Chuanjie YN51/52C5
Chuankeng JX29/30C6
Chuankou SN55/56D4
Chuankou HEN33/34C2
Chuankou NX61/62E3
Chuanliao ZJ21/22D5
Chuanliudian HEN33/34E7
Chuansha SH17/18E7
Chuanshan ZJ21/22C6
Chuanshan GX43/44C7
Chuanshanping HN37/38C6
Chuanshan Qundao GD39/40E5
Chuanshi FJ25/26C4
Chuantan JX29/30B2
Chuantang GD39/40B7
Chuanxi Gaoyuan SC76C3-4
Chuanxindian HB35/36D5

Chuanyao Gang JS17/18D7
Chubalung SC45/46D2
Chubxi QH59/60C6
Chucha JX29/30C4
Chuchi TW27/28D2
Chucun AH23/24C3
Chudianji AH23/24C3
Chuen Lung HK41B3
(Chugqênsumdo)Jigzhi Xian QH59/60D7
Chu He AH19/20B1-A1 JS19/20A1
(Chuimatan)Jishishan Bonanzu Dong-
   xiangzu Salarzu Zizhixian GS57/58E6
Chujia SD31/32B8
Chujiang SC47/48B1
Chuka XZ53/54E12
Chukou HN37/38F6
Chukuang Liehtao FJ25/26E5
Chulan AH23/24B4
Chumda QH59/60D5
Chumen ZJ21/22D6
Chunan TW27/28C2
Chun'an Xian(Pailing) ZJ21/22C4
Chunchi FJ25/26C5
Chungli TW27/28C3
Chungyang Shan TW27/28C3-D2
Chunheji HEN33/34E7
Chunhu ZJ21/22C6
Chunhua JL13/14D12
Chunhua JS17/18E4
Chunhua Xian SN55/56F4
Chunhuazhen SD31/32B5
Chunkou HN37/38C6
Chunmuying HB35/36D2
Chunshui HEN33/34D5
Chunshui GD39/40C5
Chunwan GD39/40D4
(Chunxi)Gaochun Xian JS17/18E4
Chunyang JL13/14D10
Chun Zhou GD41A4
(Chuosijia)Guanyinqiao SC45/46C3
(Chuqung)Chidu Xian SC59/60D5
Chushan TW27/28D2
Chutan JX29/30F2
Chutoulang NM5/6A6
Chutung TW27/28C3
Chuwang HEN33/34A6
Chuwei TW27/28B3
Chuxiong Shi YN51/52C4
Chuxiong Yizu Zizhizhou YN51/52C4-5
Chuzhou Qu JS17/18C4
Chuzhou Shi AH23/24D5
Chuzhuangji Ah23/24C4
Cicheng AJ21/22C6
Ci'eryingzi HEB3/4B3
Cigou HEN33/34D5
Ci He AH23/24C2
Cihe HB35/36B4
Ci He HEB5/6E2
Cihu AH23/24E5
Cihua JX29/30C2
Cihua HB35/36D4
Cihuai Xinhe AH23/24D3
Cijian HEN33/34C4
Cijiawu BJ3/4C2

Cikou HB35/36E7
Cili Xian HN37/38B4
Cilucun LN11/12A8
Ciqiu SD31/32D3
Cishan HEB5/6G2
Cishangang AH19/20C2
Citang GD41A3
Ci Xian HEB5/6G2
Cixifei He AH23/24D3
Cixi Shi ZJ21/22B6
Ciyao SD31/32D4
Ciyaopu NX61/62B3
Ciyu HEB5/6E2
Ciyutuo LN11/12C6
Cizao FJ25/26F4
Cizhu SC47/48C4
Cogsum SC45/46D3
Coka XZ53/54D10
Coloane Island MC41B2
Comai Xian(Damxoi) XZ53/54E8
Co Nag XZ53/54C8
Cona Xian XZ53/54F8
(Condü)Nyalam Xian XZ53/54E5
Co'nga XZ53/54D12
Conghua Shi GD39/40C6
Congjiang Xian(Bingmei) GZ49/50E7
Congluoyu SX7/8D2
Congru FJ25/26D5
Coqên XZ53/54D5
Coqên Xian(Maindong) XZ53/54D5
Crescent Island HK41A3
Crooked Island HK41A3
Cuangshunchang SC45/46D5
Cuifeng NM15/16B3
Cuigang HL15/16A3
Cuihengcun GD41B2
Cuihuangkou TJ3/4C4
Cuijia'ao ZJ21/22C6
Cuijiaba HB35/36D2
Cuijiaji SD31/32C6
Cuijiamiao HEB5/6F4
Cuijiayu SD31/32D5
Cuiling HL15/16B3
Cuiluan HL15/16D5
Cuimiao HEN33/34C5
Cuimu SN55/56F3
Cuiqiao HEN33/34C6
Cuiyang HEB5/6F3
Culai Shan SD31/32C4
Cunqian JX29/30C3
Cuocheng HEN33/34D8
Cuoyang HEN33/34C8
Cuozhen AH23/24E4

D

Da'a JX29/30F2
Da'an ZJ21/22E4
Da'an FJ25/26C3
Da'an GD39/40C8
Da'an GX43/44D8
Da'an HI42C2
Da'an SN55/56G2
Da'an HI42B2

Da'anbei JL13/14B5
Da'anchang SC47/48C4
Da'anping HN37/38B2
Da'anshan BJ3/4C2
Da'an Shi JL13/14B5
Da'ao ZJ19/20C5
Da'ao ZJ21/22C7
Daba NX61/62C3
Daba GZ49/50B5
Daba LN11/12B6
Daba SC45/46D5
Daba GD39/40B9
Daba NM9/10C11
Daba XZ53/54D2
Dabachang GZ49/50C7
Dabai'an ZJ21/22D4
Dabaichi HEB3/4D2
Dabaidi JX29/30E4
Dabailou BJ3/4C3
Dabaimi JS17/18D6
Dabaiyang HEB3/4B2
Dabaizhuang TJ3/4C4
(Daban)Bairin Youqi NM9/10F12
Dabancheng XJ63/64D10
Dabangdian HB35/36C6
Dabang He GZ49-50E4
Dabanqiao YN51/52C5
Daban Shan QH59/60B7-8
Daban Shankou QH59-60B7
Dabao SC45/46D4
Dabao SC47/48A1
Dabaocun AH23/24F5
Daba Shan SC45/46C7 SN55/56H4-I5
Dabazhan NX61/62B2
Dabeibu AH23/24G4
Dabiegai GS57/58C2
Dabie Shan AH23/24E2-F3
             HB35/36C8
             HEN33/34F6-7
Dabin GZ49/50F5
Dabizhuang TJ3/4C4
Daboji JL13/14E7
(Dabqig)Uxin Qi NM9/10H7
Dabsan QH59/60B4
Dabsan Hu QH59/60B4
Dabs Nur JL13/14C4
Dabu JX29/30F3
Dabu SD31/32E5
Dabu HEB3/4B2
Dabu GD41B1
Dabugang FJ25/26C3
(Dabu)Liucheng Xian GX43/44C7
Dabu Xian(Huliao) GD39/40B9
Dacang YN51/52C4
Dacêgoin SC45/46B4
Dachaigou GS57/58D6
Dachan Dao GD41A2
Dachang SC45/46C7
Dachang SH17/18E7
Dachang JS17/18D4
Dachang GX43/44C5
Dachang Huizu Zizhixian HEB5/6D4
Dachangshan Dao LN11/12E6
(Dachangshandao) Changhai LN11/12E6

Dachangtu Shan ZJ21/22B7
Dachechang NM9/10H3
Dachen ZJ21/22C5
Dacheng JX29/30C3
Dacheng HI42B2
Dachengwei HEB5/6E3
Dachengzi BJ3/4B4
(Dachengzi)Harqin Zuoyi Mongolzu Zizhi-
   xian LN11/12C3
Dachenzhuang HEB5/6F2
Dachi FJ25/26E2
Dachong GD41B2
Dachuan JL13/14D8

Daciyao SX7/8B5
Dacun SC45/46D6
Dacun BJ3/4B2
Dacundian HN37/38E4
Dade LN11/12B6
Dadenggou NX61/62A3
Dadi HN37/38E7
Dadian SD31/32D5
Dadianji AH23/24C4
Dadianzi LN11/12B8
Dadong GX43/44E6
Daduan JX29/30C2
Dadu He SC45/46C4-D4
Dadui GD41A4
Dadukou SC47/48C4
Dadukou AH23/24F4
Daduo JS17/18D6
Daduzhuang HEB3/4D3
Da'erhao HEB5/6B4
Dafan HB35/36E7
Dafang GD39/40D4
Dafangshen LN11/12E6
Dafangshen JL13/14C6
Dafang Xian GZ49/50C4
Dafanpu NM7/8B3
Dafen JX29/30E2
Dafeng SC45/46C6
Dafengman JL13/14D7
(Dafeng)Shanglin Xian GX43/44D6
Dafeng Shi (Dazhong) JS17/18C6
Dafo SC47/48B2
Dafu FJ25/26E5
Dafu AH23/24G5
Dafu Shui HB35/36C6
Dagai SC45/46C3
Dagan FJ25/26D3
Dagan GZ49/50B6
Dagang JS17/18C6
Dagang JX29/30C4
Dagang TJ3/4D4
Dagang JS17/18D5
Dagang JS19/20B2
Dagangtou ZJ21/22D4
(Dagcagoin)Zoigê Xian SC45/46B4
Dagcanglhamo GS57/58E6
(Dage)Fengning Manzn Zizhixian
   HEB5/6B4
Daglung XZ53/54E8

Dagma   XZ53/54D9
Dagmala Shan   XZ53/54D11
Dagong Dao   SD31/32D7
Dagou   GS61/62E2
Dagou He   GX43/44B5-C5
　GZ49/50E6-F6
Dagt   NM9/10J17
Dagtog   QH59/60D6
Dagu   TJ3/4D4
Daguan   SC47/48C4
Daguan   SC45/46D5
Daguan   GZ49/50D5
Daguanchong   GZ49/50D5
Daguangdingzi Shan   NM9/10C13
Daguan Hu   AH23/24F3
Daguantou   BJ3/4B3
Daguan Xian   YN51/52B5
Dagudian   AH23/24E3
Dagu He   SD31/32C7
Dagui Shan   GX75B4
Dagujia He   SD31/32B8
Dagujiazi   LN11/12B7
Daguokui Shan   HL15/16E5
Dagur   QH59/60B4
Dagushan   JL13/14D6
Dagushan   LN11/12C7
Dagzê Co   XZ53/54D6
Dagzê Xian(Dêqên)   XZ53/54E8
Dagzhuka   XZ53/54E7
Dahaibei   TJ3/4C4
Dahaituo Shan   BJ3/4B2
　HEB5/6C3
Dahe   FJ25/26E2
Daheba   QH59/60C6
Daheba   GZ49/50B5
Daheba   HB35/36E2
Daheiding Shan   HL15/16D5
Dahei He   NM9/10K21
Dahei Shan   JL13/14D5-6
Dahei Shan   JL13/14D6
Daheishan Dao   SD31/32B7
Daheiting Shuiku   HEB5/6C6
Dahekou   NM5/6A4
Dahekou   SN55/56H4
Dahenan   HEB5/6D3
Daheng   FJ25/26E3
Dahetun   HEN33/34E5
Dahezhen   HL15/16D7
Da Hinggan Diqu   HL15/16A2-B4
　　　　HL15/16B2
Da Hinggan Ling   NM9/10B14-D13
Dahongcheng   NM9/10K21
Dahonghe Shuiku   SC45/46C6
Dahongliutan   XJ63/64H5
Dahongluo Shan   LN11/12D4
Dahongmen   BJ3/4C3
Dahongqi   LN11/12C6
Dahongqiao   HEN33/34B5
Dahong Shan   HB35/36C5
Dahong Shan   HB35/36C5-6
Dahu   FJ25/26D3
Dahu   HN37/38C6
Dahuabei Shan   NM9/10K19

Dahuai   GD39/40D5
Dahuanggou   JL13/14D11
Dahuanglong Shan   ZJ21/22B7
Dahuangshan   JS17/18B3
Dahuan Jiang   GX43/44B6
Dahuashan   BJ3/4B4
Dahua Yaozu Zizhixian   GX43/44D5
Dahugou Shan   JL11/12C10
Dahuichang   BJ3/4C3
Dahujiang   JX29/30E2
Dahulun   HEB5/6B3
Dahuofang Shuiku   LN11/12C8
Da Hure   NM5/6B1
Dahushan   LN11/12C6
Daibu   YN51/52B5
Daibu   JS17/18E5
Daicheng Xian   HEB5/6E4
Daifang   JX29/30D3
Dai Hai   NM7/8A4
Daihua   GZ49/50E5
Daiji   HEN33/34D7
Daiji   AH23/24D4
Daijiaba   SN55/56G2
Daijiagou Shuiku   SC47/48B1
Dai Jiang   FJ25/26D5
Daijiapu   JX29/30E2
Đaijiayao   JS17/18D6
Dailing   HL15/16D5
Daimao Shan   FJ25/26E2
Dainan   JS17/18D6
Dainkog   SC45/46B1
Dainkognubma   XZ53/54C11
Daiqin Tal   NM9/10E13
Daiqu Yang   ZJ19/20C5
Dai Shan   ZJ21/22B7
Daishan Xian(Gaoting)   ZJ21/22B7
Daishi   SC45/46C6
Daisi   SC47/48C3
Daitou   FJ25/26E5
Daiwan   SC47/48C1
Daiwang   HEN33/34B5
Daiwangcheng   HEB5/6D2
Daixi   ZJ21/22B5
Daixi   FJ25/26D5
Dai Xian   SX7/8B4
(Daiyue)Shanyin Xian   SX7/8B4
Daiyun Shan   FJ25/26D4-E5
Daji   ZJ21/22E4
Dajiagou   JL13/14C6
Dajiang   GD41B1
Dajiang   GX43/44B7
Dajiangkou   HN37/38D2
Dajiao   SX7/8F3
Dajiawa   SD31/32B5
Dajichang   HB35/36E2
Dajieshi   SD31/32B8
Dajin Chuan   SC45/46C4-3
Dajindian   HEN33/34C4
Dajing   JX29/30E2
Dajing   GD39/40D3
Dajing   GS57/58D6
Dajing   NM61/62C1
Dajing   ZJ21/22D6

Dajingshan Shuiku   GD41B1
Dajinpu   HB35/36D8
Dajin Shan   SH19/20C4
Dajinzhu   JX29/30D3
Dajishan   JX29/30G2
Daji Shan   ZJ21/22B7
Dajiuba   XJ63/64G11
Dajiu Zhou   GD41B2
Daji Yang   SH21/22B7
Da Juh   QH59/60B4
Dakai Shuiku   GX43/44D7
Dakeng   JX29/30E3
Dakengkou   GD39/40B6
Dakou   SX7/8F4
Dakoutun   TJ3/4C4
Dakuang   SD31/32C7
Dakui   GD41A1
Dakunlun   SD31/32C4
Dala   GS57/58F6
Dalabin   NM15/16C3
Dalachi   GS57/58D7
Dalad Qi(Shulinzhao)   NM9/10G8
Dalai   JL69A5
(Dalain Hob)Ejin Qi   NM9/10G3
Dalai Nur   NM9/10F11
Dalan   GD39/40C7
Dalan   HN37/38C2
Dalang   GD39/40B5
Dalang Shan   NM9/10J17
Dalan Turu   NM9/10G5
Dalaoba   XJ63/64E7
Dalaozi   SD31/32C5
Daleng   GX43/44D4
Dali   HI42C2
Dali   YN51/52C4
Dali   GX43/44D8
Dalian Dao   LN11/12E6
Daliang   TJ3/4C4
Daliang   GX43/44C7
Daliang   QH59/60B7
Daliang Shan   SC45/46D4
Daliang Zhuang   TJ3/4C4
Dalianhe   HL15/16D4
Dalian Shi   LN11/12F5
Dalian Wan   LN11/12F5
Dali Baizu Zizhizhou   YN51/52C3-4
Dalie Dao   GD41B2
Dali He   SN55/56C5
Daliji   JS17/18C3
Daliji   AH23/24D4
Dalijia   SD31/32B3
Dalikou   FJ25/26D4
Dalin   NM13/14D3
Dalinchi   SD31/32C4
Daling   GX43/44E5
Daling   JL13/14B7
Dalinggong   HEB3/4C5
Daling He   LN11/12C4-5
(Dalinghe)Jin Xian   LN11/12C5
Dalinghe Kou   LN11/12D5
Dalinhe   SX7/8B5
Dalinzi   JL13/14B6
Dali Shi   YN51/52C4

Daliudian HEN33/34D5
Daliuhe HEB3/4D3
Daliuta SN55/56A6
Daliutun LN11/12B6
Daliuzhen HEB3/4D3
Daliuzhuang HEN33/34D6
Dali Xian SN55/56F5
Daliyuan AH23/24C4
Dalizhuang HEN33/34D5
Dalizi JL13/14F7
Dalong JX29/30E2
Dalongdong Shuiku GX43/44D6
Dalongdong Shuiku GD41C1
Dalonghua HEB3/4C2
Dalongkou AH19/20B1
Dalongwan TJ3/4C4
Dalou Shan GZ49/50B6-C5
Dalu GS57/58D7
Dalü GX43/44F6
Dalu SC47/48C4
Dalu HI42B3
Dalu JL13/14F6
Dalubian GD39/40A5
Dalu Dao LN11/12E7
Dalu Dao GD41B2
Daluhao NM9/10J23
Dalun JS19/20A3
Daluo YN51/52E4
Daluomi HL15/16E5
Daluozhen HL15/16D4
Damachang AH23/24D5
Damafang HEB3/4D2
Dama He YN51/52D6
Damaijiao SX7/8D3
Damaliu Zhou GD41B1
Damanzhuang HEB5/6E4
Damao HI42C3
Damao Feng JS17/18E5
Damao Shan JX29/30C5
Damaqun Shan HEB5/6B3
Damaying HN37/38F5
Dameisha GD41A3
Damen Dao ZJ21/22E6
Dameng'e YN51/52D3
Damian SC47/48B2
Damiao NM5/6A6
Damiao GS61/62C1
Damiao HEB5/6B5
Damiao NM9/10J20
Damiao JS17/18B3
Damiao JX29/30C2
Damiao NM9/10H6
Damiaokou HN37/38E4
Damiaoqiao NX61/62C3
Daming Xian HEB5/6G3
Damingzhen LN11/12B7
Damintun LN11/12C6
Dam Qu QH59/60D3
Damuchang HB35/36B3
Damu Yang ZJ21/22C7
(Damxoi)Comai Xian XZ53/54E8
Damxung Xian(Gongtang) XZ53/54D8
Danan JL13/14D6

Danan SC47/48D1
Dananhu XJ63/64D12
Dananqiao JX29/30C6
Danba(Rongzhag)Xian SC45/46C3
Danbazhai SN55/56D4
Dancheng Xian HEN33/34D7
(Dancheng)Xiangshan Xian ZJ21/22C6
Dancun SN55/56F5
Dandai JL13/14A4
Dandian HB35/36D8
Dandong SC45/46C3
Dandong Shi LN11/12D8
Danfeng Xian SN55/56G6
Dangan Dao GD41B3
Dangan Liedao GD39/40D7
Dangba HEB5/6C6
Dangbizhen HL15/16E6
Dangchang Xian GS57/58E7
Dangcheng HEB5/6E2
(Dangchengwan)Subei Mongolzu Zizhixian
    GS57/58C2
Dangchuan GS57/58E8
Dang He GS57/58C2
Danghe Nanshan GS57/58C2-3
    QH59/60A4-5
Dangjiang QH59/60D4
Dangjiaxian GS61/62E2
Dangjiazhuang SD31/32C3
Dangjin Shankou GS57/58C2
    QH59/60A4
Dangkou JS17/18E6
Dangmu SN55/56F5
Dangqên XZ53/54D8
Dangshan Xian AH23/24B3
Dangtu Xian AH23/24E5
Dangui YN51/52C5
Dangyang Shi HB35/36D4
Dangyu HEB3/4C5
Dan He SX7/8F4-5
Danhu JS19/20B1
Daning GX43/44C9
Daningchang SC45/46C7
Daning He SC45/46C7
Daning Xian SX7/8E2
Daniudian SX7/8C4
Danjiang HN37/38F4
Dan Jiang HEN33/34D2-3
    SN55/56G6-7
Danjiangkou Shi HB35/36B4
Danjiangkou Shuiku HEN33/34E3
               HB35/36B4
(Danjiang)Leishan Xian GZ49/50D7
Danjinli Caohe JS19/20B2
Danling Xian SC45/46C4
Danshui GD39/40F3
Danshui HEN33/34D3
(Danshui)Huiyang Xian GD39/40D7
Dantu Xian JS17/18D5
Dantuzhen JS17/18D5
Danxia Shan GD39/40A6
Danyang FJ25/26D5
Danyang Shi JS17/18D5
Danzhai Xian(Longquan) GZ49/50D6

Danzhou GX43/44B7
Danzhou Shi HI42B2
Danzhu GX43/44D8
Danzi AH23/24D5
Daobashui GZ49/50C5
Daocheng(Dabba)Xian SC45/46D3
Daodi HEB3/4C5
Daodou'ao ZJ21/22B7
Daoguanhe Shuiku HB35/36D7-8
Daohe HL33-34E6
Daojiang GX43/44C7
(Daojiang)Dao Xian HN37/38F4
(Daokou)Hua Xian HEN33/34B6
Daolang SD31/32C3
Daolazui HEB5/6C3
Daomaguan HEB5/6D2
Daoping GZ49/50D6
Daordeng LN11/12D3
Daoshiwu ZJ21/22B3
Dao Shui HB35/36C7-D7
Daoshui GX43/44D9
Daoshuqiao JS19/20B2
Daotaiqiao HL15/16D5
Daotanghe QH59/60B7
Daotian SD31/32C5
Daotiandi HL15/16C6
Daotou SD31/32B7
Daotuo SD31/32D5
Dao Xian(Daojiang) HN37/38F4
Daozhen Gelaozu Miaozu Zizhixian(Yuxi)
    GZ49/50B6
Daozhuang SD31/32B5
Daozuobu SN55/56D5
Dapa GX43/44C8
Dapaisha GD41B1
Dapeng GD39/40D7
Dapeng GX43/44D8
Dapeng Shan ZJ19/20C4
Dapeng Wan(Mirs Bay) HK41B3-4
Daping NX61/62E2
Daping GX43/44C9
Daping FJ25/26D5
Daping HN37/38B3
Daping SC47/48A3
Daping GZ49/50C7
Daping SN55/56G5
Daping GD39/40C8
Daping GX43/44E9
Dapingfang LN11/12C4
Dapo GX43/44B7
Dapo HI42B3
Dapu JS19/20B2
Dapu LN11/12D8
Dapuchaihe JL13/14E9
Dapujie HN37/38E5
Dapuzi HN37/38E2
Da Qaidam Hu QH59/60B4
Da Qaidam Zhen QH59/60B4
Daqian ZJ19/20C3
Daqianshan Zongganqu AH23/24E3
Daqiao YN51/52B5
Daqiao GX43/44E8
Daqiao SC45/46D4

Daqiao   JS17/18D5
Daqiao   SC45/46E4
Daqiao   AH23/24E5
Daqiao   SC47/48A3
Daqiao   JX29/30C5
Daqiao   JL13/14D9
Daqiao   JS17/18D6
Daqiao   FJ25/26D4
Daqiao   GD39/40A6
Daqiao   SC47/48D3
Daqiao   GS57/58F7
Daqiao   GD39/40E3
Daqiaobian   HB35/36D4
Daqiaowan   HN37/38D5
Daqigezhuang   HEB3/4C5
Daqin Dao   SD31/32A7
Daqing   LN11/12B7
Daqinggou   HEB5/6B2
Daqinghe   HEB5/6D6
Daqing He   TJ3/4C3   HEB5/6D4
Daqing He   SD31/32D3
Daqing He   LN11/12D6
Daqingliu He   SC47/48C3
Daqing Shan   LN11/12D3
Daqing Shan   HL13/14B8-9
Daqing Shan   NM9/10K20-J22
Daqing Shi(Sartu)   HL15/16D3
Daqingzui   JL13/14C6
(Daqin Tal)Naiman Qi   NM9/10F13
Daqiu   FJ25/26E5
Daqiutian   JX29/30G2
Daqiuzhuang   TJ3/4D4
Da Qu   SC45/46B2-C3
Daquan   GS57/58B2
Daquanshan   SX7/8A5
Daquanwan   XJ63/64D12
Daquanyuan   JL13/14F6
Daqu Shan   ZJ21/22B7
Darhan Muminggan Lianheqi(Bailingmiao)
   NM9/10G8
Darhan Ul   NM9/10E9
Ďarlag Xian(Gyümai)   QH59/60D6
Darongjiang   GX43/44B8
Darong Shan   GX43/44D8-E8
Daru Co   XZ59/60E2
Darzhao   XZ53-54C7
Dasanchakou   HEB3/4B4
Dasanguan   SN55/56F3
Dasanyanjing   HEB5/6B3
Dasha   GD39/40D5
Dasha   GD39/40C5
Dashahe   JL13/14E9
Dasha He   HEB5/6E2
Dashan   SD31/32A4
Dashan   SD31/32C7
Dashan   GZ49/50E4
Dashan   SC47/48B2
Dashan Dao   LN11/12F5
Dashan Dao   31/32D6
Dashangtun   HEB3/4D3
Dashanpu   SC47/48C2
Dashanshao   GZ49/50D4
Dashanzui   JL13/14D9

Dashaping   HB35/36E6
Dashen   FJ25/26E3
Dashenggedan   NM9/10J18
Dashetai   NM9/10G7
Dashetou   SX7/8C3
Dashi   GD41A2
Dashi   ZJ21/22C3
Dashi   LN11/12C5
Dashiju   ZJ21/22C6
Dashimiao   HEB3/4B4
Dashiqiao   SC47/48B3
Dashiqiao   HEB5/6F2
Dashiqiao Shi   LN11/12D6
Dashitou   JL13/14D9
Dashitou   XJ63/64D11
Dashizhai   NM9/10D13
Dashu   SD31/32D4
Dashu   SC45/46D6
Dashu   SC47/48B5
Dashuijing   YN51/52B5
Dashuikeng   NX61/62C3
Dashuipo   SD31/32B9
Dashuiqiao   QH59/60B6
Dashuiquan   HEB3/4B4
Dashuitou   GS61/62D1
Dashujie   AH23/24D4
Dashun   ZJ21/22D4
Dashun   SC47/48C5
Dasi   GX43/44E6
Dasigezhuang   HEB5/6D3
Dasiji   AH23/24C2
Dasizhuang   JS19/20A2
Dasong   ZJ21/22C6
Dasongshu   YN51/52B6
Dasuifen He   JL13/14D11
Dasuihe   HL15/16F6
Dasuzhuang   TJ3/4D4
Datai   BJ3/4C2
Datan   NM9/10J22
Datan   HEB5/6B4
Datang   GZ49/50D7
Datang   GX43/44E6
Datang   JX29/30F2
Datang   HN37/38F6
Datang   GD41A1
Datang   GX43/44C6
Datangba   SC45/46B2
Datangpu   SC47/48B1
Dateng Xia   GX43/44D7
Datian   HI42B1
Datian   ZJ21/22D6
Datian   AH23/24D2
Datian   JX29/30F3
Datian   GD39/40C8
Datian   GD39/40D5
Datian Ding   GD39/40D4
Datian Xian   FJ25/26E3
Datong   YN51/52C6
Datong   HL15/16D3
Datong   ZJ19/20D3
Datong   ZJ21/22C4
Datong   HI42B3
Datong   SC47/48B3

Datong   AH23/24F4
Datong   JL13/14B3
Datong He   QH59/60B8
Datong Hu   HN37/38B5
Datong Huizu Tuzu Zizhixian
   QH59/60B7
Datong Jiang   SC45/46B6   SN55/56H3
Datongjie   AH23/24D5
Datong Shan   QH59/60B6-7
Datong Shi   SX7/8A5
Datong Xian(Xiping)   SX7/8A5
Datongzhen   JS17/18D7
Datongzhuang   HEB3/4C5
Datoushan   HL15/16B4
Datou Zhou   GD41B2
Datuan   SH17/18F7
Datudingzi Shan   JL13/14C9
Datun   JL13/14D6
Datun   JL13/14B4
Datuopu   HN37/38C5
Datushan   JL13/14D4
Dawa   LN11/12A7
Dawa   JL13/14B5
Dawan   NX61/62E3
Dawan   GX43/44D7
Dawan   GD39/40B5
Dawan   GD39/40D4
Dawan   GZ49/50D3
Dawan   YN51/52B6
Dawang   SD31/32C5
Dawang   SN55/56F4
Dawang   SX7/8G2
Dawangdian   HEB5/6D3
Dawangji   SD31/32E2
Dawangjia Dao   LN11/12E7
Dawangqian   GD41A4
Dawang Shan   JX29/30D4
Dawangtan Shuiku   GX43/44E6
Dawangzhuang   HEB3/4D2
Dawanshan Dao   GD41C2
Dawa Xian   LN11/12D6
Dawaxung   XZ53/54D5
Dawê   SC45/46B3
Dawê   SC45/46C4
Dawei   HEB3/4D2
Dawei   GD41B3
Daweizhen   HEN33/34C5
Dawen He   SD31/32D3-4
Dawenkou   SD31/32D4
(Dawo)Maqên Xian   QH59/60C7
Dawoping   HN37/38C3
Dawu   SX7/8D3
Dawu   SD31/32D3
Dawujiang   GZ49/50C6
(Dawukou)Shizuishan Shi   NX61/62A3
Dawulan   LN11/12C5
Dawulan   HEB5/6C7
Dawusi   QH59/60B2
Dawusu   HL15/16B3
Dawu Xian   SC45/46C3
Dawu Xian   HB35/36C7
Daxi   ZJ21/22D6
Daxi   GZ49/50C4

Daxia He   GS57/58E6
Daxiakou   HB35/36C3
Da Xian   SC45/46C6
Daxiang Ling   SC45/46D4
Daxidu   JX29/30C4
Daxihaizi Shuiku   XJ63/64E9
Daxijiang   HL15/16C3
Daxin   JS17/18C4
Daxin   GX43/44D8
Daxin   GD41A3
Daxindian   HEN33/34D5
Daxindian   SD31/32B7
Daxing   JL13/14E6
Daxing   YN51/52B5
Daxing   GZ49/50C8
Daxing   NM9/10F13
Daxing   JL13/14C4
Daxing   SC47/48C4
Daxing   SC47/48B1
Daxingdao   HL15/16D7
Daxinggou   JL13/14D10
(Daxing)Ninglang Yizu Zizhixian
   YN51/52B4
Daxing Xian(Huangcun)   BJ3/4C3
Daxingzhen   SD31/32E5
Daxin Xian(Taocheng)   GX43/44E5
Daxinzhuang   HEB3/4C5
Daxi Shuiku   JS17/18E5
Daxizhai Dao   ZJ19/20C5
Daxu   HN37/38G4
Daxu   GX43/44B8
Daxu   GX43/44D7
Daxucun   JX29/30C6
Daxue Shan   YN77C2
Daxue Shan   GS57/58C3
Daxue Shan   SC45/46C3-D3
(Daxue)Wencheng Xian   ZJ21/22E5
Daxujia   JS17/18B3
Daxu Shan   JX29/30D4
Dayan   HB35/36B3
Dayan   ZJ21/22C6
Dayandang   HN37/38B4
Dayang   JL13/14E6
Dayang   AH23/24C2
Dayang   SD31/32C3
Dayang   SX7/8E3
Dayang   SX7/8F4
Dayang   GX43/44D8
Dayang   FJ25/26E4
Dayang He   LN11/12D7
Dayangqi   NM9/10B15
Dayang Shan   ZJ21/22B9
Dayangshu   NM9/10C15
Dayangzhuang   HEB3/4D2
(Dayan)Lijiang Naxizu Zizhixian
   YN51/52B4
Dayanyang   FJ25/26D4
Dayao   HN37/38D6
Dayao Shan   GX43/44C8-D8
Dayao Xian(Jinbi)   YN51/52C4
Daya Wan   GD39/40D7
Daye Shi   HB35/36D7
Dayi   SD31/32D3

Dayi   GZ49/50E5
Dayiji   SD31/32E2
Dayiji   JS17/18D5
Dayin   ZJ21/22C6
Dayin   HEB3/4D2
Daying   HEB3/4C3
Daying   SX7/8C4
Daying   JL13/14E8
Daying   HEN33/34D5
Daying   HEN33/34D4
Daying   HEB5/6F3
Daying   SX7/8B5
Daying   HEN33/34C3
Dayingji   AH19/20A1
Dayingji   AH23/24C3
Dayingji   AH23/24C4
Daying Jiang   YN51/52C2-3
Dayingpan   HEB5/6B2
Dayingpan   HEB3/4B4
Dayingzi   LN11/12D7
Dayiqiao   JS19/20B3
Dayi Xian   SC45/46C4
Dayong   GZ49/50D4
Dayou   JS17/18B5
Dayou   SC47/48D5
Dayou   JX29/30E4
Dayu   SX7/8C4
Dayuan   GD39/40A6
Dayuan   JX29/30C5
Dayuan   ZJ21/22B5
Dayuan   SD31/32B6
Dayuan   HN37/38E7
Dayuan   ZJ21/22D5
Dayudu   SX7/8G2
Dayukou   GD39/40C4
Dayu Ling   JX29/30F2   GD39/40A7
Dayunsi   ZJ19/20C2
Dayunwu Shan   GD39/40D4
Dayu Shan   ZJ19/20C4
Dayu Shan   FJ25/26D6
Dayushu   HL15/16D2
Dayushu   NM9/10F13
Dayushupu   LN11/12C5
Dayu Xian(Nan'an)   JX29/30F2
Daze Shan   SD31/32C7
Dazhai   SX7/8D5
Dazhai   YN51/52B5
Dazhang   HEN33/34C3
Dazhang   GX43/44D7
Dazhang Xi   FJ25/26E4-5
Dazhangzi   HEB5/6C6
Dazhaoying   HEN33/34B5
Dazhe   ZJ21/22D4
Dazhengjiatun   LN11/12E6
(Dazhe)Pingyuan Xian   GD39/40B8
Dazhi   GX43/44F6
Dazhipo   HI42B3
Dazhi Zhou   GD41B2
(Dazhong)Dafeng Xian   JS17/18C6
Dazhongqiao   HN37/38E4
Dazhongzhuang   TJ3/4C4
Dazhou   ZJ21/22D3
Dazhou   SC45/46C6
Dazhou Dao   HI42C3

Dazhou Shi   SC 45/46C6
Dazhuang   AH23/24C4
Dazhuangke   BJ3/4B3
Dazhuangtou   HEN33/34C6
Dazhu Xian   SC45/46C6
Dazigou   XJ63/64D12
Daziwen   HEB5/6E3
Daziying   LN11/12E7
Dazong Hu   JS71B3
Dazou   JS17/18C5
Dazui   HB35/36D7
Dazuo   FJ25/26F4
Dazu Xian   SC45/46D5
De'an Xian   JX29/30B3
Debao Xian   GX43/44D4
Dechang Xian   SC45/46E4
(Dedang)Yongde Xian   YN51/52C3
Daying Xian   SC45/46C5
(Defeng)Liping Xian   GZ49/50D8
Degan   SC47/48C4
Dêgê Xian   SC45/46C2
Dê'gyi   XZ53/54E6
(Dêgyiling)Rinbung Xian   XZ53/54E7
Dehong Daizu Jingpozu Zizhizhou
   YN51/52C2-3
Dehua Xian   FJ25/26E4
Dehui Shi   JL13/14C6
Dehui Xinhe   SD31/32B4-3
Dêjiang Xian   GZ49/50B7
Dêlêg   XZ53/54E6
Delhi Nongchang   QH59/60B5
Delhi Shi   QH59/60B5
Dêmqog   XZ53/54C2
Dengbu Dao   ZJ19/20D5
Dengcheng   HEN33/34D6
Dengchuan   YN51/52C4
Dengfeng Shi   HEN33/34C5
Dengguanzhen   SC45/46D5
(Dengjiabu)Yujiang Xian   JX29/30C4
Dengjiapu   HN37/38E3
Dengjiatang   HN37/38F6
(Dêngka)Têwo Xian   GS57/58E6
Dengkou Xian   NM9/10G6
Denglonghe   NM9/10F11
Denglong Shan   GD41A2
Denglou Jiao   GD75D3
Dengmingsi   HEB5/6F4
Dêngqên Xian   XZ53/54D10
Dengta   NX61/62E3
Dengta   GD39/40B7
Dengta Shi   LN11/12C7
Dengyoufang   HEB5/6B2
Dengzhou Shi   HEN33/34E4
Deping   SD31/32B3
Dêqên   XZ53/54D8
(Dêqên)Dagzê Xian   XZ53/54E8
Dêqên Xian   YN51/52A3
Dêqên Zangzu Zizhizhou   YN51152B3-4
Deqing Xian   ZJ21/22B5
Derbur   NM9/10B13
Dêrlagsumdo   QH59/60D5
Dêrnang   QH59/60D7
Dêrong Xian   SC45/46D2
Dêr Qu   QH59/60C5

Derst NM9/10F9
Desheng GX43/44C6
Deshengbu SX7/8A5
Deshengguan JX29/30D4
Deshengpu HB35/36B2
Deshengtai LN11/12B7
Detuo SC45/46D4
Dewang GZ49/50C7
Dewu GZ49/50D3
Dēxing XZ53/54E10
Dexing Shi JX29/30C5
Dexingtai JL13/14C3
Deyang Shi SC45/46C5
Deyueguan SC45/46D5
Dezhou Shi SD31/32B3
Dianbai Xian(Shuidong) GD39/40E3
Dianbei JX29/30E2
(Dianbu)Feidong Xian AH23/24E4
Diancang Shan YN51/52C6
Diancheng GD39/40E4
Dian Chi YN51/52C5
Dian He YN49/50F2
Dianji SD31/32C7
Dianjiang Xian SC45/46C6
Dianlanba SC47/48D1
Dianmen HN37/38D5
Dianqian ZJ21/22D5
Dianqian AH23/24F3
Dianshang SX7/8F5
Dianshan Hu JS17/18E6
Diantou FJ25/26C6
Diantou SN57/58E5
Dianwei YN51/52C5
Dianxia JX29/30D3
Dianzegou SN55/56C6
Dianzi NM5/6B6
Dianziwa Shuiku NX61/62E3
Diaocha Hu HB35/36D6
Diao'e HEB5/6C3
Diao He HEN33/34E3-4
Diao Jiang GX43/44C5-6
Diaokou SD31/32A5
Diaoling HL15/16E6
Diaolou HI42B2
Diaoluo Shan HI42C2
Diaopu JS17/18D5
Diaowo HEB3/4C3
Dibabu SX7/8C2
Didao HL15/16E6
Didianzhen NX61/62E3
Didou GD39/40C5
Diduo JS17/18D6
Di'er Nongchang Qu NX61/62B3
Die Shan GS59/60C8
Difang SD31/32D4
Digang AH23/24E5
Dige HEN33/34C6
Diguojiadang QH59/60A5
Dijiatai GS57/58D7
Dikou FJ25/26D4
Dilicheng AH23/24D2
Dima YN51/52D4
Ding'an GX43/44C3

Ding'an Xian HI42B3
Dingba Qu XZ53/54E10
Dingbian Xian SN55/56C3
Dingbu AH19/20B2
Dingbujie AH23/24E2
Dingcun SX7/8F3
Dingdang GX43/44D5
Dinggo XZ53/54C5
Dinggou JS17/18D5
Dinggyê Xian(Gyangkar) XZ53/54E6
Dinghai ZJ71C5
Dinghe HEN33/34D3
Dinghu GD39/40C5
Dingji AH23/24D3
Dingji HEN33/34D6
Dingjia SC47/48C4
Dingjiafan ZJ21/22C6
Dingjiafang LN11/12B7
Dingjiang JX29/30D3
Dingjiasuo JS17/18D6
Dingjiatang NX61/62C2
Dingjun Shan SN55/56G2
Dingluan HEN33/34B6
Dingmugou SC47/48B1
Dingnan Shui GD29/30G3
Dingnan Xian(Lishi) JX29/30G3
Dingnian JS17/18D6
Dingqiao ZJ19/20C3
Ding Qu SC45/46D2
Dingshan XJ63/64B9
Dingshui SC47/48A3
Dingshuzhen JS17/18E5
Dingtang ZJ21/22C6
Dingtao Xian SD31/32D2
Dingwei GZ49/50E7
Dingxi GD41B1
Dingxiang AH23/24F4
Dingxiang Xian SX7/8C4
Dingxiao GZ49/50E3
Dingxi Diqu GS57/58D7-E7
Dingxin GZ49/50C5
Dingxin GS57/58B4
Dingxing Xian HEB5/6D3
Dingxi Xian GS57/58E7
Dingying HEN33/34D5
Dingyu SX7/8D6
Dingyuan Xian AH23/24D4
Dingzhai HB35/36E2
Dingzhou Shi HEB5/6E2
Dingzi Gang SD31/32C8
Dingzikou QH59/60A3
Dipai GD39/40C7
(Dipu)Anji Xian ZJ21/22B4
Dirangzong XZ53/54F9
Discovery Bay HK41B3
Dixu YN51/52C6
Diyingou JL13/14D11
Dizhuang HN37/38C3
Dobdain QH59/60C7
Dobzêbo XZ78C3
Dobzha XZ53/54E7
Dodê XZ53/54D7
Dogai Coring XZ53/54B7

Dogaicoring Qangco XZ53/54B7
Dogxung Zangbo XZ53/54E6
Doijang XZ53/54D7
Doilungdêqên Xian(Namka) XZ53/54E8
Dokog He SC45/46B3
Dolod NM13/14C2
Dolon Hudag NM9/10J22
(Domartang)Banbar Xian XZ53/54D10
Dom Qu QH59/60C6
Dong'an HL15/16D8
Dong'an JS19/20B2
Dong'an AH23/24F5
Dong'anji HEN33/34D6
Dong'an Xian(Baiyashi) HN37/38E4
Dong'anzhen JS19/20B4
Dong'ao HI42C3
Dong'ao GD41B2
Dong'ao Dao GD41B2
Dongba BJ3/4C3
Dongba JS17/18E5
Dongba SC47/48A4
Dongba QH59/60B7
Dongba QH59/60D4
Dongbanchuan SX7/8B4
Dongbatu GS57/58B2
Dongbei GD39/40A5
Dongbei JX29/30D4
Dongbei Pingyuan NM68C9-D8
LN、JL69A5-B4
HL70D3-F2
Dongbeiwang BJ3/4B3
Dongbianjing HL15/16D4
Dongbolhai Shan XZ78B4 QH80C1
Dongchan SC45/46B3
Dongchang SC47/48B1
Dongchangjie JS17/18D5
Dngchen JS17/18D6
Dongcheng HI42B2
Dongcheng HEB5/6C2
Dongcheng JL13/14E10
Dongcheng ZJ21/22D6
Dongchong FJ25/26D5
Dongchuan SN55/56G4
Dong Chuan GS55/56D3
Dongchuan Shi(Xincun) YN51/52B5
(Dongchuan)Yao'an Xian YN51/52C4
Dongco XZ53/54C5
Dong Co XZ53/54C5
Dongcun SX7/8C4
Dongcun SX7/8G2
(Dongcun)Haiyang Xian SD31/32C8
(Dongcun)Lan Xian SX7/8C3
Dongdadao LN11/12C4
Dongdagu TJ5/6E5
Dongdai FJ25/26D5
Dong Dian HEB3/4C3
Dongding Dao FJ25/26F4
Dongdongting Shan JS17/18E6
Dongdu SD31/32D4
Dong'e Xian(Tongcheng) SD31/32C3
Dong'ezhen SD31/32C3
Dongfang Shi HI42B1
Dongfanghong HL15/16D7

Dongfang Lizu Zizhixian(Basuo) HI42B1
Dongfeng HL15/16D3
Dongfeng FJ25/26C4
Dongfeng SX7/8F4
Dongfenggang SD31/32A5
Dongfeng Qu SC47/48B2
Dongfeng Shuiku SC47/48B2
Dongfeng Xian JL13/14E6
Dongfu Shan FJ19/20C5
Donggan YN51/52D6
Donggang JL13/14E8
Donggang SD31/32D6
Donggang YN51/52D3
Donggang JX29/30B5
Donggang Shi LN11/12E8
Dong Ganqu NX61/62C3
Donggaodi BJ3/4C3
Donggaoying HEN33/34E4
Dongge HI42B3
Dongge JS19/20A1
Donggi Conag QH59/60C6
Donggong HB35/36C4
Donggong Shan FJ25/26C5
Donggou SX7/8F4
Donggou JS17/18C5
Donggou JS17/18D4
Donggou QH59/60C7
Dongguan SC47/48B4
Dongguan JX29/30D4
Dongguan HEB5/6E5
Dongguan AH23/24E4
Dongguan SX7/8D4
Dongguang Xian HEB5/6F4
Dongguan Shi GD39/40C6
Dongguanyingzi LN11/12C4
Dongguanzhen ZJ21/22B5
Donggu(Gonglüe) JX29/30E3
Dongguo SD31/32D4
Donghaiba NX61/62D2
Donghai Dao GD39/40E3
Donghai Xian(Niushan) JS17/18B4
Dong He SC45/46C6
Dong He GS55/56D3
Donghe NM9/10K20
Donghe HB35/36E4
Dong He SC47/48B5
Donghe SN55/56H4
(Donghe)Jinting JS19/20B3
Donghenan SX7/8B6
Dong He(Narin He) NM9/10F3-G3
Donghong HEN33/34D6
Donghongsheng NM9/10J20
Donghu HN37/38E6
Donghu ZJ19/20C3
Donghuachi GS57/58D9
Donghuangdian HB35/36C7
Donghuangshui SX7/8C4
(Donghuang)Xishui Xian GZ49/50B5
Donghuayuan HEB5/6C3
Donghui ZJ19/20D2
Donghuishe HEB5/6E2
Donghuo Shan ZJ19/20C4
Dongji JS17/18B5
Dongjia GZ49/50E5

Dongjia JX29/30C3
Dongjiachang SC47/48C2
Dongjiafang HEB5/6C3
Dongjiang JS19/20B3
Dongjiang GX43/44B7
Dongjiang GX43/44C6
Dong Jiang HN37/38F6
Dong Jiang GD39/40C7
Dongjiang HI42B2
Dongjiangkou SN55/56G4
Dongjiao HI42B3
Dongjiaying NM9/10K21
Dongjie HEN33/34D4
Dongji Liedao ZJ21/22D6
Dongjin GX43/44D7
Dongjingcheng HL15/16E5
Dongjing He HB35/36D6
Dongjingji HEB5/6C2
Dongjingling LN11/12C7
Dongjin He AH19/20C2
Dongjin Shui JX29/30C2
Dongjinwan HB35/36B5
Dongji Shan ZJ21/22D6
Dongjiugou HEB5/6F3
Dongjug XZ53/54E10
(Dongkan)Binhai Xian JS17/18B5
Dongkar XZ53/54E8
Dongkeng GD39/40C8
Dongkeng ZJ21/22E4
Dongkeng JX29/30D2
Dongkeng JX29/30G2
Dongkengkou ZJ21/22C3
Dongkor SC45/46C3
Dongkou SN55/56F2
Dongkou SD31/32D2
Dongkou Xian HN37/38D3
Donglai NM11/12A5
Donglang HB35/36B3
Donglan Xian GX43/44C5
Dongli GD39/40F3
Dongliang LN11/12C5
Dongliang SX7/8C5
Dongliang Shan AH19/20B1
Dongliangzhuang SD31/32D4
Dongliangzhu He HL69A7
Dongliao He LN11/12A7
            JL13/14E5
Dongliao Xian(Baiquan) JL13/14E5
Donglicun GD41A2
Donglidian SD31/32C5
Dongling SX7/8C3
Dongling GX43/44D4
Dongling LN11/12C7
Donglingjing SX7/8C4
Dongling Shan BJ3/4B2
Dongliu SC47/48B5
Dongliu FJ25/26E1
Dongliu JX29/30B5
Dongliu AH23/24F3
Dongliuji AH23/24C4
Donglong GD39/40C9
Donglou SX7/8C4
Donglü HEB3/4D2

Donglühua Shan ZJ19/20C5
Donglük XJ63/64F10
Dongluo GX43/44E5
Dongmajuan TJ3/4C3
Dongmao HEB5/6C4
Dongmen HN37/38C7
Dongmen GX43/44E5
Dongmiaohe HEB3/4B4
Dongming NM9/10F13
Dongmingji SD31/32D2
Dongming Xian SD31/32D2
Dongning Xian HL15/16E6
Dongping FJ25/26C4
Dongping GD39/40E5
Dongping GX43/44F7
Dongping JL13/14A4
(Dongping)Anhua Xian HN37/38C4
Dongping Hu SD31/32C3
Dongping Xian SD31/32D3
Dongpu ZJ21/22B5
Dongpu Shuiku AH23/24E4
Dongqian ZJ19/20C3
Dongqian Hu ZJ21/22C6
Dongqiao JX29/30D1
Dongqiao HB35/36C5
Dongqiao XZ53/54D8
Dongqing He JS19/20B3
Dongqinghu NM9/10I5
Dong Qu QH59/60D3
Dongquan SX7/8D4
Dongquan GX43/44C7
Dongquan XJ63/64C12
Dongren SX7/8G2
Dongsanjia JL13/14C5
Dongsha ZJ21/22B7
Dongsha Dao GD39/40F9
Dongsha He HEN33/34C7-D8
Dongshan GD39/40E3
Dongshan FJ25/26G3
Dongshan HI42B3
Dongshan HN37/38E2
Dongshan JS19/20B3
Dongshan Dao FJ25/26G3
(Dongshan)Jiangning Xian JS17/18E4
Dongshanmiao HEB3/4B2
Dongshan Nei'ao FJ25/26G3
Dongshanqiao JS19/20B1
(Dongshan)Shangyou Xian JX29/30F2
Dongshan Xian(Xibu) FJ25/26G3
Dongshao JX29/30E3
Dongsha Qundao GD39/40F8-9
Dongshe SX7/8D4
Dongshe SX7/8C5
Dongsheng SC47/48C5
Dongsheng JL13/14B2
Dongshengmiao NM9/10J17
Dongsheng Shi NM9/10H7
Dongshengyong JL13/14E10
Dongshi FJ25/26F4
Dongshi GD39/40B8
Dongshi HN37/38C4
Dongshi HB35/36D4
Dongshiqiao HEB3/4D2

Dongshuanggou JS17/18C4
Dongshuanghe HEN33/34E6
Dongshuangtang TJ3/4D3
Dongshui GD39/40B8
Dongsunba SC47/48C4
Dongtai He JS17/18D6
Dong Taijnar Hu QH59/60B3
Dongtai Shi JS17/18D6
Dongtang GD39/40A6
Dongtangchi AH23/24E4
Dongtiangezhuang BJ3/4B4
Dongtianmu Shan ZJ21/22B4
Dongtiao Xi ZJ21/22B5
Dongting HEB5/6E3
Dongting Hu HN37/38B5
Dongtingxi HN37/38C3
Dongtou GX43/44B6
Dongtou Dao ZJ21/22E6
Dongtou Xian(Bei'ao) ZJ21/22E6
Dongtou Yang ZJ21/22E6
Dongtuanbu HEB3/4C1
Dong Ujimqin Qi(Uliastai) NM9/10E11
Dongwan GS57/58D7
Dongwang HEB5/6F3
Dongwangzhuang HEB5/6E2
Dongwankou HEB5/6C4
Dongwu Yang FJ25/26D5
Dong Xi ZJ25/26C5 FJ25/26G3
Dongxi ZJ21/22C6
Dongxi SC45/46D6
Dongxi SC45/46B6
Dong Xi FJ25/26C5
Dongxia AH23/24E6
Dongxiang GX43/44D7
Dongxiang Dao FJ25/26E5
Dongxiang Xian(Xiaogang) JX29/30C4
Dongxiangzu Zizhixian GS57/58E6
Dongxiao FJ25/26E3
(Dongxiaotun)Handan Xian HEB5/6G2
Dongxiating HEN33/34D6
Dongxi Liandao JS17/18B5
Dongxin JL13/14D10
Dongxing JS19/20A4
Dongxing Shi GX43/44 F6
Dongxing NM9/10K20
Dongxing HL15/16D4
Dongxing GX43/44B6
Dongxingzheng JS19/20B3
Dongxinzhuang LN11/12D4
Dong Xire NM11/12A3
Dongxiuzhuang SX7/8C3
Dongyang SX7/8F3
Dongyang SX7/8D4
Dongyang HL15/16C3
Dongyang SD31/32D4
Dongyangdu HN37/38F5
Dongyangguan SX7/8E5
Dongyang He HEB5/6C1-2
Dongyang Jiang ZJ21/22C4-5
Dongyang Shi ZJ21/22C5
Dongyanzhuang JS19/20A3
Dongyao HEN33/34B5
Dongye SX7/8C5

Dongye SX7/8F4
Dongyetou SX7/8D5
Dongyi SC45/46D3
Dongying HEB3/4B4
Dongying HI42A3
Dongying Shi SD31/32B5
Dongying. SD31/32B6
Dongyou FJ25/26C4
Dongyu SX7/8E4
Dongyu SX7/8B4
Dongyuan FJ25/26F4
Dongyuan GD39/40C9
Dongyuan Xian GD39/40C7
Dongyueguan HN37/38B4
Dongzha ZJ19/20C3
Dongzhai SX7/8C4
Dongzhang HEN33/34C6
Dongzhang FJ25/26E5
Dongzhang Shuiku FJ25/26E5
Dongzhaobao HEN33/34C4
Dongzhen GS57/58C6
Dongzhen SX7/8F3
Dongzhen Shuiku FJ25/26E4
(Dongzhen)Xinyi Xian GD39/40D3
Dongzhi GS57/58E8
Dongzhi Xian(Yaodu) AH23/24F4
Dongzhong SD31/32C6
Dongzhuang HEN33/34B6
Dongzhugou SD31/32C6
Dongzicun GS57/58D6
Dongziling HEN33/34B4
Dongziya TJ3/4D3
Doqên Co XZ78C4
Doqoi XZ53/54E8
Do Qu QH59/60C5
Doramarkog QH59/60D5
Dorbod Mongolzu Zizhixian(Taikang) HL15/16D3
Dorgê Co QH59/60C3
Dorsoidong Co XZ53/54C7
Double Island HK41A3
Doucun SX7/8C5
Doudian BJ3/4C3
Douge YN51/52D4
Dougong HEN33/34A6
Dougou HEN33/34E6
Dou He HEB3/4C5
Douhe Shuiku HEB5/6D6
Douhutun SD31/32C2
Doujiang GX43/44B7
Doujiazhuang HEB3/4C3
Doukou SC45/46B5
Doulishan HN37/38D4
Doulong Gang JS17/18C6
Doulonggang Kou JS17/18C6
Douluo SX7/8C4
Doumen HEN33/34C6
Doumen Xian(Jin'an) GD39/40D6
Doumenzhen SN55/56F4
Doumuhu HN37/38C4
Doushaguan YN51/52A6
Doushan Shuiku SD31/32D5
Doushui JX29/30F2

Doushui Shuiku JX29/30F2
Douyu HEB5/6F2
Douzhangcun TJ3/4C3
Dowa QH59/60B7
Doxong XZ53/54E10
Du'an GX43/44D4
Duancun SX7/8D4
Duancun HEB3/4D2
Duandian HB35/36D7
Duanji HEN33/34F7
Duanjiagou NX61/62D2
Duanjialing HEB3/4C4
Duanqiaopu HN37/38E4
Duanshan GZ49/50E5
Duanshi SX7/8F4
Duanting SX7/8D4
Duanxin JX29/30B6
Du'an Yaozu Zizhixian(Anyang) GX43/44D6
Duchang Xian JX29/30B4
(Ducheng)Yunan Xian GD39/40C4
Ducun SD31/32C6
Ducun JS19/20B3
Dudang HEB5/6G2
Duguan HEN33/34C2
Dugui Qarag NM9/10H7
Dugui Tal NM9/10K18
Du He HB35/36B3
Duhu GD39/40D5
Duihekou Shuiku ZJ21/22B4
Duiqingshan HL15/16E4
Duiyingzi BJ3/4B3
Duizhen SX7/8D3
Duiziliang SN55/56C4
Duiziqian JX29/30E2
Duji SD31/32B3
Duji AH23/24C3
Dujia SC47/48C2
Dujiang GZ49/50E7
Dujiang Yan SC45/46C4
Dujiangyan Shi SC45/46C4
Dujiatai HB35/36D6
Dujie GX43/44D5
Dujing ZJ21/22C3
Dukou NM9/10K17
Dukou JX29/30C6
Dukou HEB5/6G2
Dukou GX43/44B4
Dukou SC76E3
Dulansi QH59/60B6
Dulan Xian(Qagan Us) QH59/60B6
Dulaying GZ49/50D5
Dule HEB3/4C2
Dulin HEB5/6E4
Duliu TJ3/4C3
Duliu Jiang GZ49/50E7 GX37/38F2
Duliu Jianhe TJ3/4D4
Dulong YN51/52D6
Dulou AH23/24B3
Dumen ZJ21/22C5
Dumo GX43/44C8
Dumuhe HL15/16D7
(Dund Hot)Zhenglan(Xulun Hoh)Qi

NM9/10F11
Dunfangdian HEN33/34B6
Dung Co XZ59/60E2
(Dunhou)Ji'an Xian JX29/30D2
Dunhuang Shi GS57/58B2
Dunhua Shi JL13/14D9
Dunkou HB35/36D7
Dunshang JS17/18B5
Duntou ZJ21/22C4
Duntouwei GD41A2
Duobaowan HB35/36D5
Duobukur He NM15/16B3
Duodaoshi HB35/36D5
Duoding GZ49/50C6
Duofu SC47/48B3
Duohuo SX7/8F5
Duojing GX43/44D4
Duolun(Dolonnur)Xian NM9/10F11
Duomula XZ53/54B4
Duoque GZ49/50D4
Duowen HI42B2
Duoyue SC47/48B1
Duozhu GD39/40C7
Duozhuang SD31/32D5
Dupang Ling HN37/38F4 GX43/44B9
Duping GD39/40C4
Duqu SN55/56F5
Düre XZ63/64B10
(Duru)Wuchuan Gelaozu Miaozu Zizhixian
    GZ49/50B6
Dushan AH23/24E3
Du Shan HEB5/6C6
Dushan Hu SD31/32D3
Dushanji SD31/32D3
Dushan Xian GZ49/50E6
Dushanzi XJ63/64C8
Dusheng HEB5/6E4
Dushi SC47/48C4
Dushi SC47/48A5
Dushikou HEB5/6B3
Dushu HEN33/34D5
Dushtou SD31/32D5
Dustin Gol NM9/10H6
Dusuo GD41A3
Dutang Shuiku FJ25/26G3
Dutou HN37/38F6
Duwei FJ25/26E4
Düxanbibazar XJ63/64G6
Duxiaqiao ZJ21/22D6
Duxun FJ25/26G3
Duya HEB3/4C2
Duyang GX43/44D5
Duyang Shan GX43/44C5
Duyi GZ49/50E5
Duyun Shi GZ49/50D6
Duze ZJ21/22C3
Duzhenwan HB35/36D3
Duzhou SC47/48C5
Duzhuang SX7/8D5
Duzhuang SX7/8B5

E

East China Sea 21/22C8-D7

East Lamma Channel HK41B3
Ebian Yizu Zizhixian SC45/46D4
Ebinur Hu XJ63/64C7
Ebu GD39/40D7
Echeng SD31/32C3
Egong JX29/30G3
Egong GD41B2
Egongling GD41A2
(Ehen Hudag)Alxa Youqi NM9/10H3
Ehu JX29/30B5
Ejia YN51/52C4
Ejin Horo Qi (Altan Xiret) NM9/10H7
Ejin Qi (Dalain Hob) NM9/10G3
Ekou SX7/8B5
Elixku XJ63/64F4
Eman HI42B2
Emei Feng FJ25/26C3
Emei Shan SC45/46D4
Emeishan Shi SC45/46D4
Emin(Dorbiljin) Xian XJ63/64B7
Emin He XJ63/64B7
Emu JL13/14D9
Emur He HL15/16A2
Emur Shan HL15/16A2
Encha HEB5/6F3
Encheng SD31/32B3
Engger Us NM9/10G4
Engh Had NM9/10A13
Enhepu NX61/62C2
En Jiang JX29/30D3
(Enjiang)Yongfeng Xian JX29/30D3
Enle YN51/52D4
Enping Shi GD39/40D5
Enshi Shi HB35/36D2
Enshi Tujiazu Miaozu Zizhizhou
    HB35/36D1-3
Enyangzhen SC45/46C6
Eqiao AH23/24E5
Er'an JS17/18D6
Erba AH23/24E5
Erbeng Shan XJ81C5
Erdao Baihe JL13/14E9
Erdaochuan NM61/62C4
Erdaodianzi JL13/14D8
Erdaogou QH59/60C3
Erdaohezi HL15/16E5
Erdaohu NM61/62B1
Erdao Jiang JL13/14E8
Erdaoqiao SC45/46C3
Erden Bulag NM9/10K18
Erdu JX29/30D4
Eren Gobi NM9/10D12
Erenhot Shi NM9/10F9
Eren Nur NM9/10F8
Erfengshan SX7/8F3
Erfenzi NM9/10J20
Ergexun NM9/10K20
Ergouwan NM9/10K19
Ergu HL15/16D5
Ergun He NM9/10A13-B12
Ergun Shi NM9/10B13
Er Hai YN51/52C4
Erhlin TW27/28D2

Erhshui TW27/28D2
Erhulai LN11/12C9
Erjiazhen JS17/18D7
Erkou JX29/30D5
Erlang GZ49/50B5
Erlanghe AH23/24F3
Erlangmiao HEN33/34D4
Erlangping HEN33/34D3
Erlang Shan SC45/46D4
Erling JS17/18E5
Erlong JL13/14B4
Erlongshan JL13/14D3
Erlongshan HL15/16D7
Erlong Shan JL13/14D9
Erlongshan Shuiku JL13/14D5
Erlongshantun HL15/16C4
Ermao Dao GD41A2
Ermi JL13/14F6
Erpengdianzi LN11/12C9
Erpu GZ49/50D5
Erpu XJ63/64D12
Ershengqiao JS19/20B2
Ershijiazi LN11/12C4
Ershilipu AH23/24E4
Ershilipu SD31/32C6
Ershilipu SD31/32D3
Ershilitai LN11/12E5
Ershiwuzhan HL15/16A2
Ershiyizhan HL15/16A3
Ertai HEB5/6B2
Ertai XJ63/64C11
Ertang GX43/44D7
Ertang GX43/44C8
Ertix He XJ63/64B8-9
Eryuan Xian YN51/52B3
Erzhan HL15/16C4
Erzhan HL15/16E3
Erzhou Dao GD41B3
Eshan Yizu Zizhixian YN51/52C5
Eshi HN37/38E6
Ewenkizu Zizhiqi NM9/10C12
Ewirgol XJ63/64D9
Eyang FJ25/26D4
Ezhou Shi HB35/36D7
Ezhuang SD31/32D5

F

Facheng SD31/32B7
Faku Xian LN11/12B7
Famensi SN55/56F3
Fanchang Xian AH23/24E5
Fancheng HEN33/34D5
Fanchuan JS17/18D5
Fancun SX7/8D4
Fangbian JS19/20B2
Fangcheng Gang GX43/44F6
Fangchenggang GX43/44F6
Fangchenggang Shi GX43/44F6
Fangcheng Xian HEN33/34D4
Fangcun ZJ21/22C3
Fangcun AH19/20B1
Fangcun FJ25/26D4
Fangcun JS17/18B3

Fangdao FJ25/26C4
Fangdou Shan SC35/36D1
Fanggaoping HB35/36D7
Fangguan HEB3/4C2
Fangji HB35/36C5
Fangji AH23/24D2
Fangjia SC47/48B2
Fangjiatun LN11/12B7
Fangli HEN33/34B6
Fangliao TW27/28E2
Fanglou JX29/30D1
Fangmutun LN11/12B8
Fangqian SD31/32D5
Fangqiao JS19/20B2
Fangshan JS17/18B4
Fangshan SX7/8C3
Fangshan BJ3/4C2
Fangshan TW27/28E2
Fangshan Xian(Gedong) SX7/8D3
Fangshanzhen LN11/12C6
Fangshen LN11/12B4
Fangshunqiao HEB5/6E3
Fangsi SD31/32C3
Fangtang JX29/30C6
Fangtou JX29/30C5
Fangxi JX29/30C2
Fangxia SD31/32C4
Fang Xian HB35/36B3
Fangxianzhen JS19/20B2
Fangyang FJ25/26F3
Fangyuan TW27/28D2
Fangyuanxu HN37/38F5
Fangzhen SN55/56E6
Fangzheng Xian HL15/16E5
Fangzhuang HEN33/34B5
Fangzi SD31/32C6
Fanjia HI42B2
Fanjiachuan GS61/62D4
Fanjiagang AH23/24D4
Fanjiaji JS19/20A2
Fanjiang HN37/38D5
Fanjiapu JX29/30B3
Fanjiashan HN37/38D4
Fanjiatun JL13/14D6
Fanjiaya HB35/36C3
Fanjing Shan GZ49/50C7
Fankou GD39/40A6
Fankou HB35/36D7
Fankuai SC45/46C7
Fan Lau HK41B2
Fanli HEN33/34C3
Fanling HK41B3
Fanshan HEB5/6C3
Fanshan ZJ21/22E5
Fanshan AH23/24E4
Fanshi ZJ21/22B6
Fanshi Xian SX7/8B5
Fanshui JS17/18C5
Fanxiang HEN33/34B6
Fan Xian(Yingtaoyuan) HEN33/34B7
Fanyang HI42C2
Fanzhen SD31/32C4
Fanzipai BJ3/4B3

Fate JL13/14C7
Fatou ZJ21/22B4
Fazhong SX7/8E4
Feicheng Shi SD31/32C3
Feidong Xian(Dianbu) AH23/24E4
Feiheji AH23/24C2
Feihuang He JS17/18C5-B6
        SD31/32E3
Feihuanghe Kou JS17/18B6
Feijiantan Shuiku JX29/30D2
Feilong SC47/48B4
Feiluan FJ25/26D5
Feima SC47/48A2
Feishuiyan HN37/38D4
Feitian HN37/38E5
Fei Xian SD31/32D4
Feixiang Xian HEB5/6G2
Feixianqiao HN37/38F5
Feixi Xian AH23/24E4
Feiyun Ding GD39/40C7
Fencheng SX7/8F3
Fenchihu TW27/28D2
Feng'an GD39/40C7
Fengcheng ZJ21/22B4
Fengcheng SD31/32C5
Fengcheng SD31/32C8
Fengcheng SH17/18F7
Fengchengpu GS57/58C5
Fengcheng Shi LN11/12D8
Fengcheng Shi JX29/30C3
Fengchuan GD39/40C4
(Fengchuan)Fengxin Xian JX29/30C3
Fengchunling YN51/52D5
Fengcun HEB5/6F2
Fengdeng NX61/62B3
Fengdengwu HEB3/4C4
Fengdian SC47/48B2
Fengdong GZ49/50E6
Fengdu FJ25/26D4
Fengdu Xian SC45/46D6
Fengfeng HEB5/6G2
Fenggang JX29/30F2
Fenggang GD39/40C5
Fenggang GD41A2
Fenggang Xian(Longguan) GZ49/50C6
(Fenggang)Yihuang Xian JX29/30D4
Fenggaopu SC47/48C3
Fenggeling SN55/56F2
Fenggezhuang SD31/32C7
Fenggu SC45/46C5
Fengguang JL13/14C7
Fenghe SC47/48B5
Feng He BJ3/4C3
Fengheying BJ3/4C3
Fenghuang GD39/40C9
Fenghuang GX43/44D7
Fenghuang SH17/18E7
Fenghuang GX43/44C5
Fenghuangcun HN37/38E5
Fenghuang Shan GX43/44B5-C5
Fenghuang Xian(Tuojiang) HN37/38D2
Fenghuangzui SN55/56G5
Fenghua Shi ZJ21/22C6

Fenghui ZJ21/22C5
Fengjia SD31/32B8
Fengjia LN11/12B6
Fengjiakou HEB5/6E4
Fengjiang JX29/30D2
Fengjiangkou Shuiku HB35/36B6
Fengjiapu HEB5/6E5
Fengjiashan Shuiku SN55/56F2
Fengjiayu BJ3/4B3
Fengjie Xian SC45/46C7
Fengjigou NX61/62C3
Fengjing SH17/18F7
Fengkai Xian(Jiangkou) HB39/40C4
Fengkang TW27/28E2
Fengkou HB35/36D6
Fengku JL13/14C4
Fengle HL15/16E3
Fengle FJ25/26C4
Fengle HB35/36C5
Fengle GZ49/50B6
Fengle He AH23/24E3-4
Fenglezhen HEN33/34A6
Fengli JS17/18D7
Fengli HEN33/34C4
Fengliang GD39/40C9
Fenglin TW27/28D3
Fenglin ZJ21/22D5
Fenglingdu SX7/8G2
Fengling Guan FJ25/26B4
Fenglingtou JX29/30C5
Fengma GD41A2
Fengman JL13/14D7
Fengmiaoji AH23/24C4
Fengming Dao LN11/12E5
Fengmu HI42B2
Fengnan Shi HEB5/6D6
Fengning Manzu Zizhixian(Dage)
        HEB5/6B4
Fengpin TW27/28D3
Fengpo HI42B3
Fengqiao ZJ21/22C5
Fengqing Xian(Fengshan) YN51/52C3
Fengqiu Xian HEN33/34B6
Fengren FJ25/26F2
Fengren GD39/40B8
Fengrun SX7/8C3
Fengrun Xian HEB5/6D6
Fengshan JX29/30E4
Fengshan GX43/44C7
Fengshan GX43/44E8
Fengshan HL15/16D5
Fengshan HEB5/6B5
(Fengshan)Fengqing Xian YN51/52C3
(Fengshan)Kaohsiung Hsien
        TW27/28E2
Fengshan Linchang HL15/16D5
Fengshan Xian GX43/44C5
Fengshi FJ25/26F2
Fengshiyan HN37/38E5
Fengshuba Shuiku GD39/40B8
Fengshui SD31/32C5
Fengshui Shan HL15/16A2
Fengshun Xian(Tangkeng) GD39/40C9

Fengtai BJ3/4C3
Fengtai Xian AH23/24D3
Fengtaizhen TJ3/4C4
Fengtan Shuiku HN37/38C2
Fengtian JX29/30C2
Fengtian JX29/30F3
Fengtian GD39/40B6
Fengtian JX29/30D2
Fengting FJ25/26E4
Fengxi HB35/36C2
Fengxi FJ25/26D2
Feng Xian JS17/18B2
Fengxiangba GZ49/50C5
Fengxiangdun AH19/20B1
(Fengxiang)Luobei Xian HL15/16D6
Fengxiang Xian SN55/56F3
Feng Xian(Shuangshipu) SN55/56G2
Fengxian Xian(Nanqiao) SH17/18F7
Fengxin Xian(Fengchuan) JX29/30C3
Fengyan GZ49/50C6
Fengyang Xian AH23/24D4
Fengyi SX7/8E4
Fengyi YN51/52C4
(Fengyi)Mao Xian SC45/46C4
(Fengyi)Zheng'an Xian GZ49/50B6
Fengyu SC47/48B2
Fengyuan SN55/56E5
(Fengyuan)Taichung Hsien TW27/28C2
Fengzhou FJ25/26F4
Fengzhou JX29/30F1
Fengzhou SN55/56G2
Fengzhuang NX61/62D3
Fen He SX7/8F3
Fen He HEN33/34D6
Fenhe Shuiku SX7/8C3
Fenjie GD39/40D4
Fenkou ZJ21/22C3
Fenqing He HB35/36C3
Fenshi HN37/38F5
Fenshouling NX61/62C2
Fenshui SC47/48D3
Fenshui JX29/30G5
Fenshui LN11/12D6
Fenshui ZJ21/22C4
Fenshui SD31/32D6
Fenshuichang SC45/46C7
Fenshui Guan FJ25/26G3
Fenshui Guan FJ25/26C3
Fenshuiguan ZJ21/22E5
Fenshui Jiang ZJ21/22C4
Fenshuijie SC45/46E5
Fenshuiling SC45/46C5
Fentai AH23/24C2
Fenxiang HB35/36D4
Fenxi Xian SX7/8E3
Fenyang Shi SX7/8D3
Fenyi Xian JX29/30D2
Foding Shan GZ49/50C7-6
Fogang Xian(Shijiao) GD39/40C6
Foluo HI42C1
Fong Ma Po HK41B3
Foping Xian SN55/56G3

Foshan Shi GD39/40C6
Fotan FJ25/26F3
Fotang ZJ21/22C5
Foziling AH23/24E3
Foziling Shuiku AH23/24E3
Fu'an JS17/18D6
Fu'an Shi FJ25/26C5
Fubao HI42C2
Fubao SC45/46D6
Fubian SC45/46C4
Fubin GD39/40C9
Fuchang HB35/36D6
Fucheng SX7/8F5
Fucheng GX43/44D6
Fucheng Xian HEB5/6F4
Fuchikou HB35/36E8
Fuchong GD41B1
Fuchuan Yaozu Zizhixian GX43/44C9
Fuchun JX29/30B5
Fuchun Jiang ZJ21/22C4-B5
Fuchunjiang ZJ21/22C4
Fucun SN55/56D5
Fucun YN51/52C6
(Fuda)Mei Xian GD39/40B9
Fude FJ25/26E3
Fudian HEN33/34C4
Fuding Shi FJ25/26C6
Fudong JL13/14E10
Fu'e AH19/20D1
Fufang JX29/30E4
Fufeng Xian SN55/56F3
Fugong FJ25/26F3
Fugong Xian YN51/52B3
Fugou Xian HEN33/34C6
(Fuguo)Zhanhua Xian SD31/32B5
Fugu Xian SN55/56A7
Fuhai HL15/16D3
Fuhai(Burultokay)Xian XJ63/64B9
Fuhai Linchang XJ63/64B10
Fuhai Shuiku XJ63/64B9
Fuhe GD39/40D4
Fu He JX29/30C4
Fuhongcun GZ49/50D6
Fuhuchang SC47/48A3
Fuji HEN33/34C6-9
Fuji SC45/46D5
Fujia SC45/46D5
Fujiabu HEB3/4B1
Fu Jiang SC76C5
Fujiang SC45/46D5
Fujiaqiao HN37/38E4
Fujiatan SX7/8E3
Fujiatun LN11/12A7
Fujiayan HB35/36D3
Fujiazuo HEB5/6E3
Fujin Shi HL15/16D7
Fukang Shi XJ63/64C9
Fuke HI42B2
Fukeshan HL15/16A1
Fukou HN37/38D4
Fukou FJ25/26D3
Fukuei Chiao TW27/28B3
Fule YN51/52C6

Fule HL15/16A3
Fuli TW27/28D3
Fuli GX43/44C8
Fuli GX43/44C9
Fuliangpeng YN51/52C5
Fuliang Xian JX29/30B5
Fuliji AH23/24C3
Fuling FJ25/26C4
Fuling Shi SC45/46D6
Fulingxia AH23/24F5
(Fulin)Hanyuan Xian SC45/46D4
Fulinpu HN37/38C6
Fulong HI42B2
Fulong SC47/48B1
Fulongquan JL13/14C5
Fulu GX43/44B7
Fulu HL15/16D3
Fulu SC47/48C1
Fulu GX43/44D4
Fuluo HN37/38D2
Fuluo GX43/44C9
Fumeng Xinhe AH23/24C3
Fumian GX43/44E8
Fumintun JL13/14E7
Fumin Xian YN51/52C5
Funan Xian AH23/24D2
Fung Kat Heung HK41B3
Funing Wan FJ25/26D6
Funing Xian HEB5/6D7
Funing Xian JS17/18C5
Funing Xian YN51/52D6
Funiu Shan HEN33/34D3-4
Fuping Xian HEB5/6E2
Fuping Xian SN55/56F5
Fuqiang HL15/16D3
Fuqiao JS17/18E7
Fuqingpu HN37/38C4
Fuqing Xian FJ25/26E5
Fuquan Shi GZ49/50D6
Furao HL15/16D3
Furao HL15/16C5
Fur He JL13/14E8
Furong ZJ21/22D6
Furong Jiang GZ49/50B6
Furongzhang Shuiku GD41A2
Fusha GD41A1
Fushan AH23/24C5
Fushan GD39/40C9
Fushan SD31/32B8
Fushan HI42B2
Fushan JS17/18E6
Fushan Xian SX7/8F3
Fushi FJ25/26F2
Fushi GX43/44B7
Fushi Shuiku ZJ21/22B4
Fushu GX43/44E5
Fu Shui HB35/36E7-8
Fushui SN55/56G6
Fushuigang HB35/36C6
Fushui Shuiku HB35/36E7
Fushuling JX29/30D5
Fushun SC47/48A3
Fushuncheng LN11/12C7

Fushun Shi LN11/12C7
Fushun Xian LN11/12C7
Fushun Xian SC45/46D5
Fusong Xian JL13/14E8
Fusui Xian GX43/44E5
Futai JL13/14E7
Futang GD39/40B5
Futian JX29/30B2
Futian JX29/30D2
Futian JX29/30E2
Futian GD39/40C6
Futian HI42B3
Futianhe HB35/36C8
Futianpu HN37/38D5
Futou Hu HB35/36D7-E7
Futou Wan FJ25/26G3
Futun Xi FJ25/26C3
Fuwang GX43/44E7
Fuwen HI42B3
Fuwen FJ25/26D3
Fuwen ZJ21/22C4
Fuxi GD39/40A6
Fuxi FJ25/26C5
Fuxian JL13/14D4
Fu Xian SN55/56D5
Fuxian Hu YN51/52C5
Fuxi He SC47/48C2
Fuxing JL13/14D11
Fuxing NM9/10G6
Fuxing SC47/48A3
Fuxing SC45/46C6
Fuxing HL15/16E5
Fuxing SC47/48C3
Fuxing AH23/24G3
Fuxing SC47/48A1
Fuxing SC47/48B2
Fuxingchang HN37/38C2
Fuxingchang GZ49/50B4
Fuxingdi LN11/12B5
Fuxingji AH23/24D4
Fuxingpo NX61/62C2
(Fuxing)Wangmo Xian GZ49/50E5
Fuxin Mongolzu Zizhixian LN11/12B5
Fuxin Shi LN11/12B5
Fuyang GD39/40C9
Fuyang GZ49/50B6
Fuyangba SC45/46B6

Fuyang He HEB5/6E3-F4
Fuyang Shi AH23/24D2
Fuyang Shi ZJ21/22B4
Fuyang Xinhe HEB5/6F3
Fuyangzhan AH23/24D2
Fuyi SC45/46C5
Fuying Dao FJ25/26D6
Fuyi Shui HN37/38E3
Fuyong YN51/52D3
Fuyuan TW27/28D3
Fuyuan LN11/12B8
Fuyuan Xian HL15/16C8
Fuyuan Xian(Zhong'an) YN51/52C6
Fuyun(Koktokay)Xian XJ63/64B10
Fuyu Xian HL15/16D3

Fuyu Xian JL13/14C7
Fuzhoucheng LN11/12E5
Fuzhou JX29/30D4
Fuzhou He LN11/12E5
Fuzhou Shi FJ25/26D5
Fuzhou Wan LN11/12E5
Fuzhuang SD31/32E5
Fuzhuang TJ3/4C4
Fuzhuangyi HEB5/6E4

G

Gadê Xian QH59/60D6
Gahai GS57/58E6
Gahai QH59/60B5
Ga Hai QH59/60B7
Gaiyang FJ25/26D3
Gaizhou Shi LN11/12D6
Gala XZ53/54E7
Galanba YN51/52D4
Gamba Xian XZ53/54E7
Gamtog XZ53/54D12
Gana SC45/46B3
Ganbashao GZ49/50D6
Gancaodian GS57/58E7
Gancaohu XJ63/64E10
Ganchang SC45/46B6
Ganchazi HL15/16C5
Gancheng HI42C1
Ganchengzi NX61/62D3
Ganchong HI42B2
Ganda XZ53/54D10
Gandu QH59/60C8
Ganfang JX29/30C2
Gangbei GD39/40B8
Gangbei HI42C3
Gangbei Gang HI42C3
Gangca Xian(Shaliuhe) QH59/60B7
Gangca Zhan QH59/60B7
Gangcheng SD31/32D3
Gangdisê Shan XZ53/54D3-E6
Gang'erkou HN37/38C4
Gangfang YN51/52B3
Gangji AH23/24E4
Gangkou AH23/24F5
Gangkou GD41A1
Gangkou JS37/38D5
Gangkou JS19/20B3
Gangkou JX29/30C5
Gangkou HN37/38B6
Gangmei GD39/40D4
Gangnan HEB5/6E2
Gangnan Shuikn HEB5/6E1
Gangou JL13/14F6
Gangou HEB5/6C7
Gangou NX61/62C3
Gangou GS61/62E2
Gangoumen HEB5/6B4
Gangouyi GS57/58E7
Gangshang SD31/32F5
Gangshangji JX29/30C4
Gangtou FJ25/26E5
Gangtou ZJ21/22D5
Gangtun LN11/12D4

Gangu Xian GS57/58E7
Ganguyi SN55/56D5
Gangwei FJ25/26F4
Gangxia GD41A3
Gangyao JL13/14C7
Gangziji AH23/24D4
Gangziyao HEN33/34A6
Gangziyao HEB5/6G2
Ganhe NM9/10B14
Gan He NM9/10B15-C15
Ganhezi XJ63/64C10
Ganjia Ai FJ25/26D2 JX29/30E4
Ganjiagou LN11/12D4
Ganjiang SC47/48C1
Gan Jiang JX29/30C3-D3
Ganjiapan NX61/62C4
(Ganjig)Horqin Zuoyi Houqi NM9/10F14
Ganjing SN55/56E6
Ganjingzi LN11/12F5
Ganlin ZJ21/22C5
Ganlu SC47/48C2
Ganluo Xian SC45/46D4
Gannan Xian HL15/16D2
Gannan Zangzu Zizhizhou GS57/58E6
Ganpu ZJ21/22B5
Ganq QH59/60B3
Ganq Ger JL13/14A4
Ganquanshan JS19/20A2
Ganquan Xian SN55/56D5
Ganshui SC45/46D6
Gantang NX61/62C1

Gantang FJ25/26D4
Gantang FJ25/26D5
Gantang HN37/38E2
Gantang GX43/44E6
Gantang AH71C3
(Gantang)Lingchuan Xian GX43/44B8
Gantao He HEB5/6F2
Gantian GX43/44C4
Gantian HN37/38D6
Ganting SX7/8E3
Ganxi ZJ21/22C6
Ganxi JX29/30C6
Ganxi GZ49/50B7
Ganxi GZ49/50C7
Gan Xian(Meilin) JX29/30F3
Ganxitan HN37/38B4
Ganxitang HN37/38F2
Ganxu GX43/44E6
Ganyanchi NX61/62D2
Ganyu Xian(Qingkou) JS17/18B5
Ganzhao LN11/12C3
(Ganzhe)Minhou Xian FJ25/26D5
Ganzhou JX29/30C3
Ganzhou Diqu JX29/30F2-3
Ganzhou Shi JX29/30F2
Ganzhu JX29/30E4
Ganzi SC47/48B5
Ganziyuan HN37/38F4
Gao'an SC47/48B5
Gao'an FJ25/26F3
Gao'an Shi JX29/30C3

Gaoba GS57/58D6
Gaobadian SN55/56G6
Gaobai SX7/8D4
Gaoban SC47/48B2
Gaobei GD39/40B9
Gaobei JX29/30E2
Gaobeidian BJ3/4C3
Gaobeidian Shi HEB5/6D3
Gaobu ZJ21/22B5
Gaochang SC47/48D2
Gaochang City Site XJ63/64D10
Gaochangdian HEB3/4D2
Gaocheng JS19/20B2
Gaocheng SD31/32B4
Gaocheng JX29/30C2
Gaocheng HB35/36C6
Gaocheng Shi HEB5/6E2
Gaochun Xian(Chunxi) JS17/18E4
Gaocun SD31/32B9
Gaocun JX29/30C2
Gaocun SX7/8C4
Gaocun ZJ21/22B4
Gaocunqiao HEN33/34B6
Gao Dao ZJ21/22D6
Gaodeng Shan SC47/48B4
Gaodu SX7/8F4
Gaofeng HI42C2
Gaofeng GD39/40D4
Gaofu JX29/30D5
Gaogang JX17/18D5
Gaogongmiao AH23/24C2
Gaogou JS17/18B5
Gaohe SX7/8E5
(Gaohe) Huaining AH23/24F3
Gaohu JX29/30C3
Gaoji SD31/32C3
Gaojiabu SX7/8B4
Gaojiabu SN55/56B6
Gaojiacun NM9/10K19
Gaojiadian LN11/12B8
Gaojiadian JL13/14C6
Gaojiafang HN37/38C5
Gaojialiugou SD31/32D5
Gaojian ZJ21/22C6
Gaojiawan SN55/56D4
Gaojiayan HB35/36D4
Gaojiaying HEB3/4B1
Gaojiazhen SC45/46C6
Gaojingzhuang TJ3/4C4
Gaokan LN11/12D6
Gaokeng JX29/30D1
Gaolan JX29/30C2
Gaolan Dao GD39/40E6
Gaolan Xian GS57/58D6
Gaoleng HL15/16D5
Gaoli HEB3/4C2
Gaoliang SC47/48C3
Gaoliang GD39/40C4
Gaoliangji AH23/24D4
(Gaoliangjian)Hongze Xian JX17/18C4
Gaoligong Shan YN51/52B3
Gaolincun HEB3/4C2
Gaoling SD31/32B8

Gaoling BJ3/4B4
Gaoling GX43/44C6
Gaolingjiao AH23/24G4
Gaoling Xian SN55/56F5
Gaolingzi HL15/16E5
Gaolintun NM13/14D3
Gaoliu JS17/18B4
Gaoliying BJ3/4B3
Gaolong HN37/38E6
Gaolou HEB3/4C3
Gaolou ZJ21/22E5
Gaolu AH23/24C3
Gaoluo SX7/8D5
Gaoluo SX7/8F3
Gaoluo HB35/36E2
Gaomiao SC47/48C1
Gaomiao QH59/60B8
Gaoming Shi GD39/40D5
Gaomi Shi SD31/32C6
Gaomutang HN37/38E4
Gaoniang GZ49/50D8
Gaopai JX29/30F3
Gaopian SC47/48A2
Gaoping HB35/36D3
Gaoping HN37/38C6
Gaoping GZ49/50C5
Gaoping Shi SX7/8F4
Gaopo GD39/40D3
Gaopoling Shuiku HI42B1
Gaoqi FJ25/26F4
Gaoqiao GD39/40E2
Gaoqiao SH17/18E7
Gaoqiao JS19/20A2
Gaoqiao FJ25/26D3
Gaoqiao SD31/32D5
Gaoqiao HN37/38E3
Gaoqiao GZ49/50B5
Gaoqiaozhen LN11/12D4
Gaoqing Xian(Tianzhen) SD31/32B4
Gaoqitou HN37/38C3
Gaoquan XJ63/63C8
Gaorenzhen NX61/62B3
Gaosha HN37/38E3
Gaosha FJ25/26D3
Gaoshan FJ25/26E5
Gaoshan SX7/8A4
Gaoshangtian GX43/44B8
Gaoshanzi LN11/12C6
Gaoshawo NX61/62B4
Gaoshi SC47/48C2
Gaositai HEB5/6B5
Gaotai GZ49/50C6
Gaotaishan LN11/12B6
Gaotai Xian GS57/58C4
Gaotan SN55/56H4
Gaotan GD39/40C8
Gaotan SC47/48B4
Gaotan AH23/24F4
Gaotang FJ25/26D3
Gaotang SN55/56F5
Gaotangji AH23/24D3
(Gaotangling)Wangcheng Xian
 HN37/38C5

Gaotangpu AH23/24D4
Gaotang Xian SD31/32C3
Gaotan He SC47/48B5
Gaotian JX29/30E4
(Gaoting)Daishan Xian ZJ21/22B7
Gaotingsi HN37/38E5
Gaowan HEB5/6E5
Gaowang JS19/20A1
Gaowei JX29/30F3
Gaowuwei GD41A2
Gao Xian SC45/46D5
Gaoxian SX7/8F3
Gaoxianji HEN33/34C6
Gaoxing SC47/48B4
Gaoxing SD31/32D6
Gaoxingxu JX29/30E3
Gaoxinji HEN33/34C7
Gaoxishi HN37/38E4
Gaoya SN55/56F3
Gaoya SD31/32C5
Gaoya NX61/62D2
Gaoyakou BJ3/4B2
Gaoyan JS17/18C4
Gaoyang HB35/36C3
Gaoyang Xian HEB5/6E3
Gaoyi HEN33/34E5
Gaoyi Xian HEB5/6F2
Gaoyou Hu JS17/18D5
Gaoyou Shi JS17/18D5
Gaoyu HEB5/6G2
Gaoyu ZJ19/20C2
Gaoze SD31/32D6
Gaozeng GZ49/50E7
Gaozha NX61/62C3
Gaozhen SN55/56C5
Gaozhou Shi GD39/40E3
Gaozhuang HEB3/4B2
Gaozi JS17/18D5
Gaozuo JS17/18C4
Gaozuo JS17/18C5
Gaqung XZ53/54E6
Garang QH59/60B7
(Garbo)Lhozhag Xian XZ53/54E8
Gar Qu QH59/60D3-2
Garqu Yan QH59/60D3
(Gartog)Markam Xian XZ53/54E12
Gar Xian(Shiquanhe) XZ53/54C3
Gar Xincun XZ53/54C2
Garyarsa XZ53/54D3
Garyi SC45/46C2
Gar Zangbo XZ53/54C3-D3
Garzê Xian SC45/46C2
Garzê Zangzu Zizhizhou SC45/46C2-3
Gase XZ53/54D6
Gas Hure Hu QH59/60A2
Gaxun Gou QH59/60B6
Gaxun Nur NM9/10F2
Gaya He JL13/14D10
Gayao Shi GD39/40C5
Gebu GX43/44C3
Gedi SX7/8E2
Gedian HB35/36D7
Geding NM61/62B1

Gedong GZ49/50D7
(Gedong) Fangshan Xian SX7/8D3
Gefan ZJ21/22D4
Gegen Sum NM13/14B3
Gegong AH23/24F4
Gegou SD31/32D5
Gegu YN51/52D5
Gegu TJ3/4D4
Gêg'yai Xian (Napug) XZ53/54C3
Ge Hu JS17/18E5
Gejia SD31/32B8
Gejiu Shi YN51/52D5
Gekeng FJ25/26E4
Gêladaindong QH59/60D2
Gelanchang SC45/46C6
Geleshan SC47/48C4
Gelin GZ49/50B6
Geling FJ25/26E5
Gelinqiao AH19/20C1
Geliping SC45/46E3
Gengche JS17/18C4
Gengda SC47/48A1
Gengle HEB5/6G1
Genglou GD39/40D5
Gengma Daizu Vazu Zizhixian
    YN51/52D3
Gengpeng AH23/24D3
Gengxin GX43/44C4
Gengzhen SX7/8C5
Gengzhuang LN11/12D6
Gen He NM9/10B12-13
Genhe Shi NM9/10B13
Geni He NM70C2
Gensi JS17/18D6
Gepai SN55/56G5
Gepu HB35/36D6
Ger Qulu NM9/10E13
Gerseng NM11/12A4
Gêrzê Xian (Luring) XZ53/54C5
Geshan ZJ21/22C5
Getai SN55/56E6
Getu He GZ49/50E5
Gexiang He YN51/52B6
Gexiang He GZ49/50D3
(Gexianzhuang) Qinghe Xian HEB5/6F3
Geyitou YN51/52C6
Geyuan JX29/30C5
Geyucheng HEB3/4C3
Gezhentan SN55/56D6
Gezhouba HB35/36D4
Gezidong QH59/60A7
Gobi QH59/60B5
Goicangmai XZ53/54C3
Goincang QH59/60D7
Goinsargoin XZ53/54D12
Golin Baixing NM9/10E13
(Golingka) Gongbo'gyamda Xian
    XZ53/54E9
Golmud He QH59/60B4
Golmud Shi QH59/60B4
Golmud Shuiku QH59/60B4
Golog Shan (Nyainbo Yuzê) QH59/60D7
Golog Zangzu Zizhizhou QH59/60C5-D7

Gomang Co XZ53/54D7
Gomo XZ53/54C5
Gomo Co XZ53/54C5
Gong'ai HI42C1
Gong'ai Nongchang HI42C1
Gong'an GX43/44F5
Gong'an GX43/44C9
Gong'an Xian HB35/36D5
Gongbei GD41B2
Gongbo'gyamda Xian (Golingka) XZ53/
54E9
Gongchakou GS57/58C3
Gongchangling LN11/12C7
Gongcheng Yaozu Zizhixian GX43/44C8
Gongchuan GX43/44D5
Gongchuan FJ25/26D3
Gongcun HEB5/6D4
Gongfang JX29/30D3
Gonggar Xian (Gyixong) XZ53/54E8
Gongguan GX43/44F7
Gongguan GD39/40E3
Gongguoqiao YN51/52C3
Gonghe HL15/16D4
Gonghe Xian (Qabqa) QH59/60B7
Gonghui HEB5/6B2
Gonghui GX43/44C9
Gongjiapeng HEN33/34F6
Gongjing SC45/46D5
Gongkala Shan SC76C3
Gonglama NM9/10K21
Gonglang YN51/52C4
Gongli SD31/32D4
Gongliu (Tokkuztara) Xian XJ63/63D7
(Gonglüe) Donggu JX29/30E3
Gongmiaozi NM9/10K18
Gongpeng JL13/14C7
Gongpengzi JL13/14B6
Gongping GX43/44B8
Gongping GD39/40C8
Gongpingxu HN37/38E5
Gongpo HI42B3
Gongpoquan GS57/58B3
Gongqian HEN33/34C3
Gongqiao AH19/20B1
Gongqingtuan Nongchang XJ63/64C9
Gongshan YN51/52C5
Gongshan Derungzu Nuzu Zizhixian
    YN51/52B3
Gong Shui JX29/30F3
Gongtan SC45/46D7
(Gongtang) Damxung Xian XZ53/54D8
Gongtian HN37/38B6
Gongwangling SN55/56F5
Gongwang Shan YN77B4-C4
Gongxi JX29/30D3
Gong Xian SC45/46D5
Gongxing SC47/48B1
Gongyi GD39/40D5
Gongyibu NX61/62E2
Gongyingzi LN11/12C3
Gongyi Shi HEN33/34C4
Gongzheng GX43/44E6
Gongzhuling Shi JL13/14D5

Gongzhutun LN11/12B6
Gongzui Shuiku SC45/46D4
Gonjo Xian XZ53/54E8
Goqên XZ53/54E11
Gora SC45/46C3
Gorhon NM9/10E12
Gorhon Gol NM69A2
Gosu SC45/46B2
Goubangzi LN11/12C5
Gouchang GZ49/50E5
Gou Chi SN55/56C3
Goudun JS17/18C5
Gougezhuang HEB3/4D3
Goujiaochang SC47/48B4
Goujiaya HB35/36C4
Goujie YN51/52D5
Goujiezi YN51/52C5
Goukou NX61/62E3
Goukou NM9/10C14
Goulin HEN33/34E4
Goumenzi LN11/12D3
Gouqi Shan ZJ21/22B7
Goushi HEN33/34C4
Goutai NX61/62C3
Gouxi NX61/62D3
Gouyadong HEN37/38F5
Gowaqungo XZ53/54D6
Gozha Co XZ53/54B3
Grass Island HK41B3
Green Island HK41B3
Guabu JS17/18D4
Guai'er SX7/8D5
Guaihe HEN33/34D5
Guaimozi LN11/12C9
Guaizihu NM9/10G4
Guala GZ49/50D3
Gualanyu HEB5/6C5
Guali ZJ21/22B5
Guanbei FJ25/26F3
Guanbei JX29/30D1
Guanbuqiao HB35/36E7
Guanbuqiao AH23/24F4
Guancen Shan SX7/8B4
Guanchang GD39/40F3
Guanchao JX29/30E2
Guancheng HEB3/4D2
Guancheng SX7/8C4
Guancheng SD31/32D2
Guancheng ZJ21/22B6
Guandang HN37/38B5
Guandaokou HEN33/34C3
Guandi HEB5/6B4
Guandi JL13/14D5
Guandian GZ49/50B5
Guandian AH23/24D5
Guandian GD41B1
Guandiankou HB35/36D3
Guandiping HN37/38B3
Guandi Shan SX7/8D3
Guandong GZ49/50E8
Guandu HB35/36C3
Guandu HN37/38C6
Guandu GD39/40B6

Guandu   SC45/46C7
Guandu   SC47/48B4
Guandu   GZ49/50B5
Guandu He   HB35/36B3-C3
Guandukou   HB35/36C3
Guan'er   SX7/8B5
Guanfangpu   HB35/36A2
Guanfenghai   GZ49/50C2
Guang'an Diqu   SC45/46C6
Guangang   TJ3/4D4
Guangang   AH23/24G3
Guang'an Xian   SC45/46C6
Guangba   HI42B1
Guangchang Xian   JX29/30E4
Guangcun   HI42B2
Guangdegong   NM9/10F12
Guangde Xian   AH23/24F6
Guangdian   HEN33/34D4
Guange   SC47/48B4
Guangfaxu   HN37/38F5
Guangfeng Xian(Yongfeng)   JX29/30C6
Guangfu   SC45/46C5
Guangfu   JS17/18E6
Guangfulin   SH19/20B4
Guanghai   GD39/40E5
Guanghan Shi   SC45/46C5
Guanghe Xian   GS57/58E6
Guanghua   SX7/8F2
Guanghua   JL13/14F6
Guanghua   SX7/8E3
Guanghuasi   HB35/36D5
Guangli   GD39/40C5
Guangling Xian   SX7/8B6
Guanglingzhen   JS7/8D6
Guanglu Dao   LN11/12E6
Gongqingcheng   JX29/30 B3
Guangnan Xian   YN51/52C6
Guangning Xian (Nanjie)   GD39/40C5
Guangou   AH23/24D6
Guangping   HN37/38E2
Guangping   FJ25/26D3
Guangping   JL13/14E9
Guangpinghe   SN55/56H1
Guangping Xian   HEB5/6G2
Guangpo   HI42C3
Guangrao Xian   SD31/32B5
Guangshan   GZ49/50D5
Guangshan Xian   HEN33/34E6
Guangshui   HB35/36C6
Guangshui Shi   HB35/36C6
Guangwu   NX61/62C2
Guangwu   HEN33/34C5
Guangwu   AH23/24C2
Guangxinyuan   NM9/10F11
Guangxingzhou   HN37/38B5
Guangya   HI42B2
Guangyuan Shi   SC45/46B5
Guangze Xian   FJ25/26C3
Guangzhou Shi   GD39/40C6
Guangzong Xian   HEB5/6F3
Guan He   HEN33/34E7
Guan He   JS17/18B5
Guanhe Kou   JS17/18B5

Guanhu   JS17/18B3
Guanhu   GD41A3
Guanji   AH23/24C2
Guanjian   SC47/48C3
Guan Jiang   GX43/44B9
Guanjian He   SC47/48B3
Guanjiaqiao   HN37/38C6
Guanjiashan   YN51/52D5
Guanjiawu   HEB3/4D3
Guanjiazui   HN37/38E4
Guanjing   FJ25/26E5
Guankou   HB35/36D8
Guankou   FJ25/26F3
Guanlan   GD41A3
Guanli   SD31/32B7
Guanlin   JS17/18E5
Guanling   HN37/38E5
Guanling Buyeizu Miaozu Zizhixian
    (Guansuo)   GZ49/50E4
Guanlu   ZJ21/22D5
Guanmenshan   NX61/62D2
Guanmian Shan   SC76C7
Guannan Xian (Xin'an)   JS17/18B5
Guanpo   HEN33/34D2
Guanputou   TJ3/4D4
Guanqian   JX29/30C2
Guanqian   FJ25/26C4
Guanqian   FJ25/26E2
Guanqian   FJ25/26D3
Guanqiao   FJ25/26E4
Guanqiao   SD31/32E4
Guanqiao   FJ25/26F4
Guanqiaobu   NX61/62D2
Guanshan   JX29/30D3
Guanshan Dao   ZJ21/22E5
Guanshang   SX7/8D3
Guanshi   HN37/38E5
Guanshuai   SD31/32D6
Guanshui   LN11/12D8
Guansongzheng   HL15/16D5
(Guansuo)Guanling Buyeizu Miaozu
    Zizhixian   GZ45/50E4
Guantang   SC47/48B4
Guantangyi   HB35/36E7
Guantao Xian   HEB5/6G3
Guantian   JX29/30F2
Guantian   JX29/30D2
Guantianba   SC47/48D1
Guanting   NX61/62D3
Guanting   HEB5/6C3
Guanting   AH23/24E3
Guanting   HEN33/34C5
Guanting   GS57/58F7
Guanting   QH59/60C8
Guanting Shuiku   HEB5/6C3
Guantingzhan   HEB3/4B2
Guantou   FJ25/26D5
Guantou   SX7/8E2
Guantunbu   NM7/8A5
Guanwangmiao   SX7/8F3
Guanwang Shuiku   AH71B2
Guan Xian   HEB5/6D4
Guan Xian   SD31/32C2

Guanxian   SC76C4
Guanxu   GD39/40C4
Guanyang   FJ25/26C6
Guanyang Xian   GX43/44B9
Guanyin   SC47/48B1
Guanyin   GX43/44B8
Guanyin   SC47/48B4
Guanyin   SC47/48C2
Guanyinge   HN37/38D3
Guanyinqiao(Chuosijia)   SC45/46C3
Guanyinshan   SN55/56F2
Guanyintan   HN37/38E4
Guanyintang   HEN33/34C5
Guanyintang   HEN55/56H4
Guanyintang   HEN33/34C3
Guanyin Xia   SC47/48C4
Guanyinzhen   SC45/46D5
Guanyuemiao   AH23/24E2
Guanyun Shan   HEN33/34C2
Guanyun Xian   JS17/18B5
Guanzhai   GZ49/50D4
Guanzhangpu   HEN33/34D3
Guanzhen   JS17/18C4
Guanzhou   GZ49/50B7
Guanzhu   GD39/40E4
Guanzhuang   NX61/62E3
Guanzhuang   TJ3/4B4
Guanzhuang   HEN33/34E5
Guanzhuang   HEB5/6F2
Guanzhuang   SD31/32C6
Guanzhuang   SN55/56F4
Guanzhuang   HN37/38C3
Guanzhuang   HB35/36C5
Guanzhuang   HEN33/34E6
Guanzhuang Shuiku   HN37/38D6
Guanziyao   GZ49/50E3
Guazhou   GS5/15DB2
Guazhou   JS17/18D5
Gubai   SC45/46D5
Gubazhen   JS19/20A3
Gubei   JX29/30F3
Gubei   AH23/24E2
Gubeikou   BJ3/4B4
Gubu   JX29/30C4
Gucheng   HEB5/6F4
Gucheng   SX7/8A5
Gucheng   SX7/8F3
Gucheng   SX7/8F2
Gucheng   JS17/18D4
Gucheng   AH23/24C2
Gucheng   AH23/24D4
Gucheng   FJ25/26E2
Gucheng   JX29/30E2
Gucheng   SD31/32D2
Gucheng   GX43/44C9
Gucheng   SC45/46B5
Gucheng   SN55/56G3
Gucheng   HL15/16C3
Gucheng   GS57/58D6
Gucheng   NX61/62B3
Gucheng   NX61/62E3
Gucheng   GS57/58B4
Gucheng   HEN33/34D6

Gucheng   HEB5/6D3
Gucheng   HEB5/6F4
Gucheng   SX7/8E4
Guchenggedan   NM9/10J17
Gucheng Hu   JS17/18E4
Gucheng Xian   HB35/36B4
Gucheng Xian(Zhengjiakou)   HEB5/6F3
Guchuan   SN55/56F2
Gucun   JX29/30D3
Gucun   JX29/30E4
Gudatun   SX7/8A6
Gudi   SD31/32C6
Gudian   SX7/8A5
Gudianzi   JL13/14D7
Guding   GD39/40D4
Gudingqiao   SX7/8B5
Gudong   GZ49/50D6
Gudong   YN51/52C3
Gudong He   JL13/14E9
Gufang   ZJ21/22C4
Gugancheng   HEN33/34B7
Gugang   HN37/38C6
Guguan   SN55/56F2
Guguantun   SD31/32C3
Guhe   AH23/24E4
Guhou   JX29/30E4
Guhuai   FJ25/26E5

Guide   SD31/32C3
Guidebu   SN55/56B5
Guidexiang   SC47/48C2
Guide Xian(Heyin)   QH59/60B7
Guiding Xian   GZ49/50D6
Guidong Xian   HN37/38E6
Guifu   SC47/48A4
Guigang Shi   GX43/44D7
Guiguo   GZ49/50D4
(Guihua)Mingxi Xian   FJ25/26D3
Guihuayuan   SC45/46C5
Guiji   AH23/24D3
Guijiaba   AH23/24F4
Gui Jiang   GX43/44C8-D8
Guiji Shan   ZJ21/22C5
Guiler   NM13/14A2
Guiler Gol   NM13/14A2
Guilin Diqu   GX43/44B8-C8
Guiling   GX43/44C9
Guilin Shi   GX43/44B8
Guimen   ZJ21/22C5
Guimeng Ding   SD31/32D4
Guinan Xian(Mangra)   QH59/60C7
Guiping Shi   GX43/44D8
Guiren   JS17/18C4
Guishan   YN51/52C5
Guishan   ZJ19/20C2
Guishan   GD41B2
Guishan Dao   GD41B2
Guishi Shuiku   GX43/44C9
Guitai   GX43/4E6
Guitou   GD39/40B6
Guiwu   JS17/18D4
Guixi   YN51/52A5
Guixi Shi (Xiongshi)   JX29/30C5

Guiyang   HN7/38E5
Guiyangnan   GZ49/50D5
Guiyang Shi   GZ49/50D5
Guiyang Xian   HN37/38F5
Guizi   GD39/40D4
Gujiang   JX29/30D2
Gujiao   SX7/8F5
Gujiao   SX7/8F3
Gujiao   GZ49/50D5
Gujiao Shi   SX7/8D4
Gujiazi   JL13/14D5
Gujun   SC45/46C7
Gukai   GZ49/50C4
Gula   GX43/44D6
Gulaben   NM61/62A3
Gula He   YN43/44D4-3
Gulai   ZJ21/22C5
Gulang   YN51/52B3
Gulang Xian   GS57/58D6
Gulangyu   FJ25/26F4
Gulaobei   HB35/36D4
Guleitou   FJ25/26G3
Guli   JS19/20B3
Guli   SD31/32D4
Guli   GZ49/50D7
Gulian   HL15/16A2
Guling   GX43/44D6
Guling   JX29/30B3
Gulingtuo   SC45/46C7
Gulin Xian   SC45/46D5
Guliushu   SD31/32C2
Guliya Shan   NM9/10C14
Gulong   HL15/16E3
Gulong   GX43/44D8
Gulong   GZ49/50D7
Gulonggang   JX29/30E3
Gulou   HN37/38C4
Gulou   HN37/38F5
Gulougang   AN23/24D4
Gulung   SC45/46C2
Gumei   GX43/44D4
Gumiao   HEN33/34E5
Gumu   YN51/52D6
Gunan   JX29/30B4
Gunbei   GX43/44B6
Güncang   XZ53/54E10
Gun He   HB35/36B5-C5
Guobei   SC47/48C3
Guoche   FJ25/26E2
Guochengyi   GS57/58D7
Guochuangang   JS19/20A2
Guocun   SX7/8E4
Guocun   JS19/20A2
Guocun   AH23/24F4
Guocun   HEB5/6C3
Guodao   SX7/8E4
Guodian   SD31/32C4
Guodian   HEN33/34C5
Guodiantun   SD31/32C2
Guodu   SD31/32D4
Guofu   SC47/48D4
Guo He   HNE33/34C6   AH23/24C3
Guohua   GX43/44D5

Guoji   JS17/18B5
Guoji   HEN33/34E5
Guojia   GS57/58E7
Guojia   JL13/14C6
Guojiaba   HB35/36D3
Guojiadian   SD31/32B7
Guojiadian   JL13/14D5
Guojiaqiao   JX29/30B4
Guojiatun   HEB5/6B5
Guojiayangwa   NX61/62D3
Guojiazhai   SD31/32C7
Guoju   ZJ21/22C7
Guokeng   FJ25/26F3
Guokui Shan   HL13/14B10
Guoleizhuang   HEB5/6C2
Guoliji   SD31/32D3
Guolutan   HEN53/54E7
Guoma   GX43/44C4
Guomaying   QH59/60C7
Guosong   JL13/14F7
Guotan   HEN33/34E4
Guoxianyao   NM9/10K22
Guoyang Xian   AH23/24C3
Guoyangzhen   SX7/8C4
Guozhen   SN55/56G1
Guozhen   HN37/38B6
(Guozhen) Baoji Xian   SN55/56F3
Guozhuang   HEB5/6E2
Guozhuang   AH23/24B3
Guozhuang   HEN33/34C7
Guozhuangmiao   JS17/18E5
Guozhuangzi   NX61/62C3
Gupei   AH23/24D4
Gupeitang   HN37/38C6
Gupeng   GX43/44D6
Gupi   JS17/18B3
Guqiang   HEN33/34D6
Guqiao   AH23/24D3
Guraoji   AH23/24C3
Gurban Obo   NM9/10F9
Gurbantünggüt Shamo   XJ63/64C9-10
Gurban Ulan Jing   NM9/10F6
Gurt   XJ63/64C7
Gushan   ZJ21/22D5
Gushan   SX7/8A5
Gu Shan   FJ25/26D5
Gushan   AH19/20B1
Gushan   LN11/12D6
Gushan   SN55/56A6
Gushan   JS19/20A3
Gushan   LN11/12E7
Gushan   SD31/32C3
Gushanzi   JL13/14E7
Gushi   ZJ21/22D4
Gushi   JX29/30B2
Gushi   GD39/40A7
Gushi   SN55/56F5
Gushitan Shuiku   HEN33/34D5
Gushi Xian   HEN33/34E7
Gushu   HEB3/4C4
Gushu   GD41A2
Gushui   GD39/40C5
Gushui   HEN33/34C4

Gushui HEN37/38D5
Gushuji HEN33/34C7
Gutan JX29/30B5

Gutian FJ25/26E2
Gutian FJ25/26E2
Gutian Shuiku FJ25/26D4
Gutian Xian FJ25/26D4
Guting JX29/30F2
(Guting) Yutai Xian SD31/32D3
Guxi SC47/48B3
Guxian SX7/8E4
Guxian JX29/30D3
Guxian SD31/32C7
Guxian SD31/32B8
Guxian HEN33/34E5
Guxian HEN33/34C3
Guxian HEN33/34C2
Guxian JX29/30C3
Guxian SD31/32D4
Guxianchang SC47/48B4
Guxiansi AH23/24D3
Gu Xian (Yueyang) SX7/8E3
Guyang HEN33/34C6
Guyang Xian NM9/10G8
Guye HEB5/6D6
Guye GD39/40B9
Guyi SC47/48B1
(Guyi) Sanjiang Dongzu Zizhixian
　GX43/44B7
Guyong YN51/52C3
Guyuan NM15/16B3
Guyuan Diqu NX61/62D2-3
Guyuan Xian NX61/62D3
Guyuan Xian (Pingdingbu) HEB5/6B3
Guyushu LN11/12A7
Guzhai GX43/44C7
Guzhang GX43/44C2
Guzhang Xian HN37/38C2
Guzhen Xian AH23/24C4
(Guzhou) Rongjiang Xian GZ49/50E7
Guzhu GD39/40C7
Guzhu JX29/30E4
Gyaca Xian (Ngarrab) XZ53/54E9
Gyaco XZ53/54E6
Gyaco XZ53/54C4
(Gya'gya) Saga Xian XZ53/54E5
(Gyaijêpozhanggê) Zhidoi Xian
　QH59/60D4
Gyairong QH59/60D5
Gya La XZ53/54E5

(Gyangkar) Dinggyê Xian XZ53/54E6
Gyangrang XZ53/54D5
Gyangzê Xian XZ53/54E7
Gyaring QH59/60C5
Gyaring Co XZ53/54D7
Gyaring Hu QH59/60C5
Gyatoisangxung QH59/60C4
Gyawa SC45/46D3
(Gyêgu) Yushu Xian QH59/60D5
Gyêmdong XZ53/54E9

(Gyigang) Zayü Xian XZ523/54E11
Gyimda XZ53/54D9
Gyimkar QH59/60D7
Gyipug XZ53/54C3
Gyirong XZ53/54E5
Gyirong Xian (Zongga) XZ53/54E5
Gyitang XZ53/54D11
(Gyixong) Gonggar Xian XZ53/54E8
Gyiza QH59/60D4
Gyobrag QH59/60D5
(Gyümai) Darlag Xian QH59/60D6
Gyumgo QH59/60C7

H

Habahe (Kaba) Xian XJ63/64A9
Habirag NM9/10F10
Hadamen JL13/14E11
Hadapu GS57/58E7
Hadat NM9/10C12
Hadatin Sum NM11/12A3
Hadayang NM9/10C15
Hadilik XJ63/64G9
Hafu JL13/14D5
Haǧin Gol NM61/62B2
Hai'an GD39/40F3
Haian Shan TW27/28D3
Hai'an Xian JS17/18D6
Haibei HL15/16D4
Haibei Zangzu Zizhizhou QH59/60A6-B7
(Haibowan) Wuhai Shi NM9/10H6
Haicang FJ25/26F3
Haicheng GX43/44D5
Haicheng FJ25/26F3
Haicheng Shi LN11/12D6
Haidian BJ3/4C3
Haiding Hu QH59/60C3
Haidong Diqu QH59/60B8
Haifeng Xian GD39/40D8
Haifuzhen JS17/18E7
Hai He TJH3/4C4
Haihe Pingyuan TJ67C4-5 HEB67C4-5
Haihu QH59/60B7
Haihui JX29/30B4
Haijiang HL15/16C3
Hai Jiao ZJ21/22B8
Haikou ZJ21/22D5
Haikou FJ25/26E5
Haikou TW27/28E2
Haikou JX29/30B5
Haikou Shi HI42A3
Hailang He HL13/14C9-10
Hailar He NM9/10C12-13
Hailar Shi NM9/10C12
Hailing GD39/40E4
Hailing Dao GD39/40E4
Hailin Shi HL15/16E5
Hailong JL13/14E6
Hailong Shuiku JL13/14E6
Hails NM11/12A3
Hailü Dao SD31/32B9
Hailun Shi HL15/16D4
Haimen GD39/40C9
Haimen Wan GD39/40C9

Haimen Shi JS17/18E7
Hainan Dao HI42B2-3
Hainan Jiao HI42A3
Hainan Zangzu Zizhizhou QH59/60C6-7
Haining Shi ZJ21/22B5
Haiqing HL15/16D8
Hairag QH59/60B7
Haisgai NM11/12A6
Haitan Dao FJ25/26E5
Haitan Xia FJ25/26E5
Haitou JS17/18B5
Haitou HI42B1
Haituo JL13/14B4
Haiwei HI42B1
Haixi Mongolzu Zangzu Zizhizhou
　QH59/60B2-6 C1-D3
Haixing HL15/16D4
Haixing Xian HEB5/6E5
Haixi Shan QH59/60B7
Haixiu HI42A3
Haiyan GD39/40E5
Haiyang GX43/44B8
Haiyang HEB5/6D7
Haiyang Dao LN11/12E7
Haiyang He GX37/38F3
Haiyang Shan GX43/44B8
Haiyangsuo SD31/32C8
Haiyang Shi (Dongcun) SD31/32C8
(Haiyang) Xiuning Xian AH23/24G5
Haiyan Xian QH59/60B7
Haiyan Xian (Wuyuan) ZJ21/22B5
Haiyin Shan HL15/16D7
(Haiyou) Sanmen Xian ZJ21/22C6
Haiyuan GX43/44E5
Haiyuan Xian NX61/62D2
Haizhou JS17/18B5
Haizhou Wan JS17/18B5
Haizijie GZ49/50C4
Haizijing NX61/62C3
Haiziliang SN55/56C3
Haizi Shuiku BJ3/4B4
Haju NM9/10F2
Haladaokou NM11/12B3
Halagang HEB3/4C3
Halaha JL13/14C6
Halahai JL13/14C6
Halahei NM13/14A2
Halawu NM61/62B2
Hale NM9/10G8
Halhin Gol NM9/10D12
Halik Shan XJ63/64D6-7
(Haliut) Urad Zhongqi NM9/10G7
Haltang He QH59/60A4-5
Hamatang JL63/64D10
Ha Mei Tsui HK41B3
Ham Hang Mei HK41A3
Hami (Kumul) Diqu XJ63/64D12-13
Hami (Kumul) Shi XJ63/64D12
Hami Pendi XJ81C6-7
Hanbei He HB35/36D6
Hancha SN55/56C5
Hancheng HEB5/6D6
Hancheng HEN33/34C3

Hancheng Shi   SN55/56E6
Hanchuan Shi   HB35/36D6
Hancun   HEN33/34B7
Hancun   HEB5/6D4
Handan Shi   HEB5/6G2
Handan Xian(Dongxiaotun)   HEB5/6G2
Handaokou   HEN33/34C8
Handaqi   HL15/16B4
Handian   HL15/16E3
(Handian)Changzhi Xian   SX7/8E5
Hanfang   JX29/30F3
Hanfuwan   NX61/62D3
Hangang   HEN33/34C5
Hangbu   ZJ21/22D3
Hangbu He   AH23/24E3-4
Hangcun   JS19/20B2
Hangdong   GX43/44C4
Hanggai   ZJ21/22B4
Hanggai Gobi   NM9/10J17
Hanggin Nur   NM9/10G7
Hanggin Qi(Xin)   NM9/10H7
Hangkou   JX29/30B2
Hangkouping   ZJ21/22C4
Hangou   TJ3/4C4
Hangtou   SH19/20B4
Hangu   TJ3/4C4
Hanguang   GD39/40B6
Hangu Nongchang   TJ3/4C4
Hangya   QH59/60B5
Hangzhou Shi   ZJ21/22B5
Hangzho Wan   ZJ21/22B5-6
Hanhong   SX7/8E4
Hanji   SD31/32E2
Hanjiacun   HEB5/6B2
Hanjiadian   LN11/12C5
Hanjialing   SX7/8B5
Hanjialou   SX7/8B3
Han Jiang   GD39/40B9-C9
Hanjiang   FJ25/26E5
Hanjiang Qu   JS17/18D5
Hanjiaoshui   NX61/62C2
(Hanjia)Pengshui Miaozu Tujiazu Zizhixian
    SC45/46D7
Hanjiawa   HEB5/6E2
Hanjiayuanzi   HL15/16A3
Hanjing   SN55/56E5
Hankou   HB35/36D7
Hanlin   HI42B3
Hanling   LN11/12C7
Hanmaying   HEB5/6B5
Han Qu   NX61/62C3
Hanshan Xian(Huanfeng)   AH23/24E5
Hanshou Xian   HN37/38C4
Han Shui   HB35/36D5-6
        SN55/56H5-6
Han Sum   NM9/10E12
Hantai   HEBC5/6E2
Hantan   JX29/30C5
Hantang   JX29/30C2
Hantengri Feng   XJ63/64D6
Hanting   SD31/32C6
Hanting   AH23/24F5
Han Ul   NM69A2

Han Ul   NM9/10E12
Hanwang   SC45/46C5
Hanwang   SD31/32D5
Hanwang   SX7/8D5
Hanwangcheng   SN55/56H4
Hanxia   GS57/58C3
Hanyang   SC47/48C1
Hanyang   HB35/36D7
Hanyang Feng   JX29/30B3
Hanyangping   SN55/56H4
Hanyangzhen   SX7/8G2
Hanyan Qu   NX61/62B3
Hanyin Xian   SN55/56H4
Hanyuan Xian(Fulin)   SC45/46D4
Hanyue   SX7/8F2
Hanzhang Diqu   SN55/56G2-3
Hanzhong Shi   SN55/56G3
Hanzhuang   SD31/32E4
Hanzhuang   BJ3/4B4
Haobei   SX7/8E4
Haocheng   AH23/24C4
Haocun   FJ25/26C4
Haocun   HEB5/6E4
Haocungoumen   HEB5/6B4
Haodian   NX61/62E3
Haogou   AH23/24C4
Haojiadian   HB35/36C6
Haojiaji   NX61/62D2
Haojiapo   SX7/8C3
Haojiaqiao   NX61/62B3
Haojiatai   NX61/62C4
Haokou   HEB3/4D2
Haokou   FJ25/26E4
Haolianghe   HL15/16D5
(Haomen)Menyuan Huizu Zizhixian
    QH59/60B7
Haoqiao   HEB5/6F2
Haoshanhe   HL15/16D7
Haotou   GD41A1
Hao Xi   ZJ21/22D5

Haozhai   JS17/18B2
Haozhigang Kou   JS19/20A4
Hao Zhou   GD41B2
Haozhuang   HEB5/6F2
Haozhuang   HEN33/34D5
Haozichuan   NX61/62D2
Haozikou   HB45/46D5
Harba Ling   JL13/14D10
Harbin Shi   HL15/16E4
Hargant   NM9/10C12
Har Hu   QH59/60A5
Har Huxu   NM9/10K20
Harleg   QH59/60B5
Har Mod   JL13/14C6
Har Orbag   NM9/10G4
Harqin Qi (Jinshan)   NM9/10G12
Harqin Zuoyi Mongolzu Zizhixian
    (Dachengzi)   LN11/12C3
Hartao   LN11/12B6
Har Us   NM9/10C14
Hasalbag   XJ63/64G4
Haxaklik He   XJ53/54A7-8

Haxat   QH59/60B3
Haxian   GS61/62D1
Hebachang   SC47/48B1
Hebei   SX7/8F4
Hebei   BJ3/4C2
Hebei   HL15/16D6
Hebeitun   TJ3/4C4
Hebian   SX7/8C5
Hebian   SC47/48B3
Hebian   SC47/48C4

Hebi Shi   HEN33/34B6
Hebu   JX29/30D3
Hecheng   GD39/40D5
(Hecheng)Qingtian Xian   ZJ21/22D5
(Hecheng)Zixi Xian   JX29/30D5
Hechi   GX43/44C5
Hechi Diqu   GX43/44C5-6
Hechi Shi   GX43/44C6
Hechuan   SX7/8E4
Hechuan   NX61/62E3
Hechuan Shi   SC45/46C6
Hechun   GD39/40E3
Hecun   ZJ19/20D2
Hecun   ZJ21/22D3
(Hede)Sheyang Xian   JS17/18C6
Hedi   SX7/8C5
Hedi   SX7/8E3
Hedi   ZJ21/22E4
Hedi He   YN51/52D5
Hediling   HEN33/34C7
Hedi Shuiku   GD39/40E3
Hedong   SD31/32D5
Hedongdian   SN55/56G2
Hefei Shi   AH23/24D4
Hefengchang   SC47/48B2
Hefengqiao   HEN33/34F7
Hefeng Xian   HB35/36E3
Hefu   HN37/38B4
Hegang Shi   HL15/16D6
Hegeng   SC47/48C3
Hegumiao   HEB5/6G3
Hehe   GD39/40D5
Hehe   SX7/8E2

Heicha Shan   SX7/8C3
Heicheng   NM9/10K21
Heicheng   NM7/8A3
Heichengzhen   NX61/62D3
Heidashan   NM5/6A4
Hei He   SN79D3   GS70D3
Hei He   QH59/60A6   GS57/58C5
Hei He   SN55/56G2
Hei He   GS45/46B4   SC45/46B4
Hei He   HEB5/6B4-C4
Heihe Shi   HL15/16B4
Heihumiao   SD31/32D2
Heijing   YN51/52C4
Heilangkou   TJ3/4C4
Heilaoyao   NM7/8A4
Heilin   JS17/18A4
Hei Ling Chau   HK41B3
Heilinzi   JL13/14D5
Heilinzi   JL13/14C7

Heilongguan SN55/56D6
Heilongguan SX7/8E3
Heilong Jiang HL15/16D6-C8
Heilongkou SN55/56F5
Heilongtan Shuiku SC45/46C5
Heilongzhen HEN33/34E4
Heimahe QH59/60B6
Heiping SC47/48A3
Heiquan GS57/58C4
Hei Shan LN11/12D3 HEB11/12D3
Heishan SN55/56G5
Heishanke LN11/12D3
Heishansi HEB3/4B2
Heishantou NM9/10B12
Heishan Xia GS57/58D7
Heishan Xian LN11/12C6
Heishanzui HEB5/6B4
Heishenmiao GZ49/50C5
Heishi JL13/14D9
Heishi JL13/14E7
Heishitou GZ49/50D3
Heishui JL13/14B3
Heishui LN11/12B3
Heishui SC45/46D7
Heishui He SC45/46E4
Heishui He GX43/44E4-5
Heishui He SC45/46B4-C4
Heishuisi SN55/56D4
Heishui Xian(Luhua) SC45/46B4
Heitai HL15/16E6
Heituhe GZ49/50C2
Heituo Shan SX7/8B4
Heiwuwan Shuiku HB35/36C6
Heiyanzhen HEN33/34D3
Heiyukou SX7/8C2
Heiyupao JL13/14B4
Hei Zhou GD41B2
Hejia SC47/48C2
Hejia JX29/30C4
Hejia ZJ21/22C3
Hejiachuan SN55/56B6
Hejian HEN33/34B5
Hejiang GD39/40E3
He Jiang GX43/44C9-D9
Hejiang Xian SC45/46D5
Hejian Shi HEB5/6E4
Hejiaping HB35/36D3
Hejiayan SN55/56G2
Hejiazhuang SX7/8F3
Hejicun GX43/44D7
Hejie GX43/44C9
Hejing Xian XJ63/64D9
Hejin Shi SX7/8F2
Heka QH59/60C7
Hekou FJ25/26D2
Hekou HN37/38B4
Hekou NM7/8A3
Hekou SX7/8C3
Hekou SX7/8D4
Hekou NM9/10K21
Hekou JS17/18D5
Hekou HB35/36C4 C7
Hekou SD31/32B5

Hekou HN37/38B4
Hekou HN37/38E3
Hekou GD39/40A6
Hekou GD39/40C5
Hekou GD39/40C8
Hekou GD39/40E4
Hekou SC45/46C6
(Hekou)Yanshan Xian JX29/30C5
Hekou Yaozu Zizhixian YN51/52D5
Helan LN11/12D7
Helan Shan NM9/10H5 NX61/62A3
Helan Xian(Xigang) NX61/62B3
Hele HI42C3
Heli GX43/44D6
Heli HL15/16D6
Helin SC47/48B5
Heli Shan GS57/58C4-5
Heliu SC45/46C6
Heliuji AH23/24C3
Helixi AH23/24F6
Helong LN11/12B8
Helong JL13/14C6
Helong Shi JL13/14E10
Helukou HN37/38G4
Hemianshi Shuiku GX43/44C9
Hemu GX43/44C7
Henan Mongolzu Zizhixian(Yêgainnyin)
    QH59/60C7
Hengchuandu AH23/24F4
Hengchun TW27/28E2
Hengcun ZJ19/20D2
Hengdan GS57/58F7
Hengdang GD41A1
Hengdaohe LN11/12D6
Hengdaohezi HL15/16E5
Hengdaohezi LN11/12B7
Hengdaozi JL13/14D8
Hengdi GZ49/50C3
Hengdian HB35/36D7
Hengdong Xian HN37/38D5
Hengduan Shan YN51/52A3-B3
            XZ53/54E12-F12
Hengfan ZJ21/22B4
Hengfeng Xian JX29/30C5
Henggang GD41A3
Henggang JX29/30B3
Henggang AH23/24F4
Henggang Dao GD41B3
Henggouqiao HB35/36E7
Henggouzi LN11/12A8
Henghe ZJ19/20C4
Henghu ZJ21/22B4
Hengjian SX7/8D3
Hengjian JS19/20B2
Hengjian HEN33/34D3
Hengjiang JX29/30E4
Hengjiang SC45/46D5
Heng Jiang YN51/52A6
Hengjiangdu JX29/30E2
Hengjiangqiao HN37/38E2
Hengjing JS17/18E6
Hengjin Shuiku ZJ21/22C5
Hengkou SN55/56H4

Henglang GD41A2
Hengli GD39/40C7
Hengli GD41A1
Hengliangdian JS19/20A1
Hengli Dao GD41B1
Henglin JS17/18E6
Hengling HEB3/4B2
Hengling SX7/8D5
Henglingguan SX7/8F3
Hengling Hu HN37/38C5
Henglongqiao HN37/38C5
Henglu JX29/30B5
Henglutou ZJ21/22B4
Hengmei GD41B1
Heng Men GD39/40D6
Hengmen Dao GD41A2
Hengmian SH19/20B4
Hengnan Xian HN37/38E5
Hengqin Dao GD41B2
Hengqu SN55/56F3
Heng Sha SH17/18E7
Heng Shan SX7/8B5
Hengshan HL15/16E6
Hengshan AH23/24E5
Hengshan GD39/40E3
Hengshan JS19/20B3
Hengshan SC47/48B3
Heng Shan HN37/38D5
Hengshanling Shuiku HEB5/6E2
Hengshanpu NX61/62B3
Hengshanqiao JS19/20B3
Hengshan Shuiku SX7/8B5
Hengshan Shuiku JS19/20B2
Hengshan Shuiku JX29/30C4
Hengshan Shuiku ZJ21/22C6
Hengshan Xian SN55/56C5
Hengsha Xian HN37/38D5
Hengsheng HB35/36D8
Hengshi HB35/36E7
Hengshi JX29/30E2
Hengshui SX7/8F3
Hengshui SX7/8F5
Hengshui HEN33/34C4
Hengshui SN55/56F3
(Hengshui)Chongyi Xian JX29/30F2
Hezhou Diqu GX43/44.C9
Hengshui Hu HEB5/6F3
Hengshui Shi HEB5/6F3
Hengtang JS19/20B2
Hengtang JS19/20B3
Hengxi ZJ21/22C4
Hengxi JS19/20B1
Hengxi ZJ21/22C6
Hengxi ZJ21/22D5
Heng Xian GX43/44E7
Hengxiang JS19/20A3
Hengyang Shi HN37/38E5
Hengyang Xian(Xidu) HN37/38E5
Heng Zhou GD41B2
Hepeng HN37/38C3
Hepeng AH23/24E3
Heping SX7/8E3
Heping FJ25/26C3

Heping FJ25/26E3
Heping GD39/40C9
Heping HI42C2
Heping ZJ21/22B4
Heping Xian(Yangming) GD39/40B7
Hepingyingzi JL13/14E9
Hepingzhen HN37/38D2
(Hepo)Jiexi Xian GD39/40C8
Hepu HB35/36D8
Hepu ZJ21/22C6
Hepu Xian(Lianzhou) GX43/44F7
Heqiao JS17/18E5
Heqiao JS17/18D4
Heqiao ZJ21/22B4
Heqiaoyi GS57/58D6
Heqing HI42B2
Heqing SC47/48A2
Heqing Xian YN51/52B4
Hequ Xian SX7/8B3
Herlen NM9/10C10
Herlen He NM9/10D10-C10
Herong HB35/36D4
Heshan HN33/34B6
Heshan GX43/44D6
Heshan GD39/40E5
Heshan HL15/16C3
Heshangfangzi LN11/12D3
Heshangzhen ZJ21/22C5
Heshan Shi GX43/44D6
Heshan Shi GD39/40D5
Heshe HI42B2
Hesheng GS57/58E8
Hesheng ZJ21/22D5
Heshengqiao HB35/36D7
Heshi JX29/30C2
Heshi SC47/48C2
Heshi FJ25/26E4
Heshi SC47/48A5
Heshu SC47/48B4
He Shui JX29/30D2-E2
Heshui GX43/44B7
Heshui GD39/40D4
Heshuilangcheng GS57/58D9
Heshui Xian(Xihuachi) GS57/58E9
Heshun FJ25/26C3
Heshun HEN33/34A5
Heshun Xian SX7/8D5
Hetanbu JX29/30C5
Hetang FJ25/26D5
Hetao Pingyuan NM68D4-5
Hetian FJ25/26E2
(Hetian)Luhe Xian GD39/40C8
Hetou GD39/40E2
Hetou GD39/40B6
Hetou ZJ21/22C6
Hetoudian SD31/32B7
Hetupu AH23/24F3
Hexi SC47/48D5
Hexi FJ25/26F3
Hexi HN37/38C2
Hexi SX7/8F4
Hexi SC45/46E4
Hexi SC45/46B5
Hexia JX29/30D2

Hezhou Shi GX43/44C9
Hexiangqiao HN37/38D3
He Xian(Liyang) AH23/24E5
Hexigten Qi(Jingpeng) NM9/10F11
Hexing SH19/20B4
Hexipu GS57/58C6
Hexiwu TJ3/4C3
Hexi Zoulang GS80A3-B4
Heyang SD31/32D5
Heyang Xian SN55/56E6
Heyeping SX7/8C3
(Heyin)Guide Xian QH59/60B7
Heyu HEN33/34D3
Heyuan Shi GD39/40C7
Heyun GD39/40C5
Heze Diqu SD31/32D2
Heze Shi(Caozhou) SD31/32D2
Hezhang Xian GZ49/50C3
Hezheng Xian GS57/58E6
Hezhi SX7/8B3
Hezhou GD41A2
Hezixu JX29/30G3
Hezuo Shi GS57/58E6
High Island Reservoir HK41B3
Himalayas XZ53/54D2-E4
Hingganling Pinggang NM9/10D13
Hinggan Meng NM9/10D13-14
Hoboksar Mongol Zizhixian XJ63/64B8
(Hobor)Qahar Youyi Zhongqi
    NM9/10J22
Hobq Shamo NM9/10K17-18
Ho Chung HK41B3
(Hoh Ereg)Wuchuan Xian NM9/10J21
Hohhot Shi NM9/10G8
Hoh Sai Hu QH59/60C3
Hoh Xil Hu QH59/60C2
Hoh Xil Shan QH59/60C1-3
              XZ53/54B7-8
Hoh Yanhu QH59/60B5
Hoi Ha HK41B3
Hoit Taria QH59/60B5
Hok Tsui Village HK41B3
Holoin Gun NM9/10F4
Homei TW27/28C2
Hondlon NM13/14D2
Hondlon Ju NM9/10K19
Hong'ao GD41A2
Hong'an Xian HB35/36C7
Hongbai SC47/48A2
Hongchang HEN33/34C5
Hongchengshui NX61/62C3
Hongchengzi GS57/58D6
Hongcibu SX7/8A5
Hongcun JX29/30D4
Hongda HL15/16D4
Hongdao HI42B2
Hongdao SX7/8C5
Hongde GS57/58D8
Hongdong GD41B1
Hongdu GX43/44D6
Hongdu GZ49/50B7
Hongdu He GZ49/50B7-6
Hongdunzi NX61/62B3

Hongfeng Hu GZ49/50D5
Honggolj NM9/10C12
Honggong GD39/40B6
Honggor NM9/10E9
Honggor NM9/10F10
Honggou SD31/32C5
Hongguan JX29/30B5
Hongguang SC47/48B1
Hongguangying NX61/62B3
Hogguo GZ49/50E3
Hongguozi NX61/62A3
Honghai Wan GD39/40D8
Honghe QH59/60B6
Honghe NX61/62E3
Hong He AH23/24D2 HEN33/34E6-7
Hong He GS61/62E4 NX61/62E3
Honghe Hanizu Yizu Zizhizhou
    YN51/52D5
Honghe Xian YN51/52D5
Honghu SC47/48C4
Hong Hu HB35/36E6
Honghuabu SD31/32E5
Honghuapu SN55/56F2
Honghuatang SC47/48B2
Honghuatao HB35/36D4
Honghuayuan GZ49/50B5
Honghu Shi HB35/36E6
Hongjiabu HEN33/34E7
Hongjiaguan HN37/38B3
Hongjiang Shi HN37/38D2
Hongjian Nur NM9/10H7 SN55/56A5
Hongjing SX7/8E5
Hongjingzi NX61/62C4
Hongkeli HL15/16D5
Hongkong HK41B3
Hongkou SC47/48A1
Hongkou SC45/46B6
Honglai FJ25/26E4
Honglan JS17/18E4
Honglingjin Shuiku NM9/10K21
Honglinqiao AH23/24F5
Hongliu Daquan NM9/10G2
Hongliugou SN55/56C3
Hongliuhe GS57/58B2
Hongliu He NM55/56C4
Hongliuqiu Jing GS57/58A3
Hongliuquan QH59/60A2
Hongliuyuan GS57/58B2
Hongliuyuan GS57/58C5
Hongliuyuan GS57/58C6
Honglu SC47/48C3
Honglu FJ25/26E5
Hongluoxian LN11/12C4
Hongmao HI42B2
Hongmen ZJ21/22C5
Hongmen JX29/30D4
Hongmen AH19/20C1
Hongmen Shuiku JX29/30D4
Hongmiao HEN33/34C6
Hongmiaochang SC47/48B1
Hongmiaotang SN55/56H2
(Hongning)Wulian Xian SD31/32D6
Hongnong Jian HEN33/34C2

Hongqi HI42B3
Hongqi LN11/12D7
Hongqi JL13/14C7
Hongqi GD41B2
Hongqiao SC45/46D5
Hongqiao HEB5/6D5
Hongqiao HN37/38C6
Hongqiao ZJ21/22D6
Hongqicun XJ63/64D12
Hongqikang XJ63/64D11
Hongqiling JL13/14E7
Hongqi Qu HEN33/34A5
Hongqiying HEB3/4A2
Hongquan NX61/62C2
Hongsha HI42C2
Hongshan YN51/52A3
Hongshan NM9/10F12
Hongshan HL15/16D5
Hongshan GD39/40A6
Hongshan HI42C2
Hongshan SX7/8D4
Hongshan SD31/32C4
Hongshanqiao FJ25/26D5
Hongshan Shuiku NM11/12B3
Hongshansi NM61/62B1
Hongshan Xia GS57/58D7
Hongshanzi NM9/10J21
Hongshi JL13/14E8
Hongshila HEB3/4B4
Hongshila HEB5/6B4
Hongshilazi LN11/12D9
Hongshiya HEN33/34D5
Hongshui SX7/8E5
Hongshui QH59/60B8
Hongshui He GX43/44D6-7
Hongshuizhuang TJ3/4B4
Hongsipu NX61/62C3
Hongta AH23/24C5
Hongtai XJ63/64D11
Hongtangsi HEB5/6B4
Hongtangxiang ZJ21/22C6
Hongtao Shan SX7/8B4
Hongtian FJ25/26E3
Hongtong Xian SX7/8E3
Hongtoushan LN11/12B8
Hongtulu NX61/62E3
Hongtumiao LN11/12B8
Hongtupo NX61/62C3
Hongtuxi HB35/36D2
Hongwei He SD31/32E2
Hongweihe Beizhi SD31/32D2
Hongxi GZ49/50C7
Hongxi SC45/46D4
Hongxin AH23/24D4
Hongxing BJ3/4C3
Hongxing HL15/16C5
Hongxing JL13/14C4
Hongxingqiao ZJ21/22B4
Hongya Chi SN61/62C4
Hongyan HN37/38E6
Hongyan NM9/10C15
Hongyancun SC47/48C4
Hongyang GD39/40C9

Hongyangfang NX61/62D2
Hongyangshu AH19/20B1
Hongyansi HB35/36D2
Hongyao NX61/62D2
Hongyashan Shuiku GS57/58C6
Hongya Xian SC45/46D4
Hongyazi NX61/62A3
Hongyazi QH59/60A4
Hongyuan JX29/30B5
Hongyuan Xian SC45/46B4
Hongze Hu JS17/18C4
Hongze Xian(Gaoliangjian) JS17/18C4
Hongzhen AH23/24F3
Hongzhuang NX61/62D3
Hongzhuang JS17/18B4
Hopai TW27/28C2
Ho Pui HK41B3
Hor QH59/60C7
Horinger Xian NM9/10G8
Horqin Shadi NM9/10F13-14
Horqin Youyi Qianqi NM9/10D14
Horqin Youyi Zhongqi(Bayan Huxu)
　NM9/10E13
Horqin Zuoyi Houqi(Ganjig)
　NM9/10F14
Horqin Zuoyi Zhongqi(Baokang)
　NM9/10E14
Hotan He XJ63/64F6
Hotan Shi XJ63/64G5
Hotan Xian XJ63/64G5
Hotong Qagan Nur NM9/10H7
Hou'an HI42C3
Houbachang GZ49/50C5
Houbaishu JS17/18E5
Houchang GZ49/50E5
(Houchang)Caotang GZ49/50C6
Houcheng HEB5/6C4
Houcheng JS17/18E6
Hougang HB35/36D5
Hou Hai GD41A2
Houji HEN33/34E4
Houjiagang JX29/30B4
Houjiahe NX61/62C4
Hou Jiang SC45/46C6
Houjiaying TJ3/4C4
Houjiazhuang HEB5/6F2
Houjie GD39/40D6
Houliangzhuang HEN33/34D5
Houlingshan ZJ21/22C5
Houlung TW27/28C2
Houma Shi SX7/8F3
Houmen GD39/40D8
Houpi TW27/28D2
Houping HB35/36C4
Houping HN37/38B3
Houpo HEN33/34E3
Houri QH59/60B6
Houshi JL13/14E6
Houshui Wan HI42B2
Housuo SX7/8B4
Houwa NX61/62C4
Houxia XJ63/64D9
Houxian Ling HI42C2

Houxijie ZJ21/22D3
Houxinqiu LN11/12B6
Houyi HEB3/4C3
Houyingzi LN11/12D7
Houzhai ZJ21/22C5
(Houzhai)Nan'ao Xian GD39/40C10
Houzhen SD31/32C5
Houzhenzi SN55/56G3
Houzihe QH59/60B7

Hoxtolgay XJ63/64B9
Hoxud Xian XJ63/64D9
Hoygyan HN37/38B2
Hoyor Amt NM9/10G5
Hsiaokang TW27/28E2
Hsiaolan Yu TW27/28F3
Hsiatahsi TW27/28E2
Hsichih TW27/28B3
Hsichi Yu TW27/28D1
Hsichuan Tao FJ25/26E5
Hsienhsi TW27/28C2
Hsihu TW27/28D2
Hsikou TW27/28D3
Hsilo TW27/28D2
Hsincheng TW27/28C3
Hsinchuang TW27/28B3
Hsinchu Hsien TW27/28C3
Hsinchu Shih TW27/28C2
Hsinhua TW27/28D2
Hsin-i TW27/28D2
(Hsinkang)Chengkungtsun TW27/28D3
(Hsinkang)Kanghsitsun TW27/28D2
Hsinkang Shan TW27/28D3
Hsinpi TW27/28E2
Hsinpu TW27/28C3
Hsinshih TW27/28D2
Hsintien TW27/28C3
Hsinwu TW27/28C3
(Hsinying)Tainan Hsien TW27/28D2
Hsiochinmen Tao FJ25/26F4
Hsiukuluan Hsi TW27/28D3
Hsiukuluan Shan TW27/28D3
Hsiyin Tao FJ25/26D6
Hsi Yu TW27/28D1
Hsuehchia TW27/28D2
Hsueh Shan TW27/28C3
Hua'an Xian FJ25/26E3
Huabei Pingyuan HEB67C5-E5
　　　　　　SD73B4-C4
　　　　　　HEN73B4-C4
Huabu ZJ21/22C3
Huacheng GD39/40B8
Huachi Xian GS57/58D8
Huachongji JS17/18B4
Huachu GZ49/50D4
Huachuan Xian(Yuelai) HL15/16D6
Huade Xian NM9/10G9
Huadian Shi JL13/14E7
Huadianzi JL13/14F6
Huading Shan ZJ21/22C6
Huadu Shi GD39/40C6
Huafang JX29/30B3
Huafeng SX7/8F3

Huafeng SD31/32D4
Huagang AH23/24E4
Huagbaiyuan SN55/56G3
Huagmeiqiao JS19/20A2
Huagu AH19/20C2
Huagu SC47/48D2
Huagushan JX29/30D2
Huahai GS57/58B3
Huahaizi QH59/60A4
Huai'ancheng HEB5/6C2
Huai'an Shi JS17/18C5
Huai'an Xian(Chaigoubu) HEB5/6C2
Huaibai SN55/56E5
Huaibei Shi AH23/24C3
Huaibin Xian HEN33/34E7
Huaide SC47/48C3
Huaidezhen JL13/14D5
(Huaidian)Shenqiu Xian HEN33/34D7
Huaifengji HEN33/34E7
Huai He HEN3/34E6
Huai He AH23/24C4

Huaihua Shi HN37/38D2
Huaiji Xian GD39/40C5
Huaikouzhen SC45/46C5
Huailai Xian(Shacheng) HEB5/6C3
Huailin AH23/24E4
Huainan FJ25/26E3
Huainan Shi AH23/24D3
Huaining Xian AH23/24F3
Huaiqun GX43/44C6
Huairen SD31/32B4
Huairen Xian SX7/8B5
Huairou Shuiku BJ3/4B3
Huairou Xian BJ3/4B3
Huaisha He HEB5/6F2
Huaishu SC47/48A3
Huaishu Xinhe JS17/18B4-C4
Huaishuzhang SN55/56E4
Huaisiqiao JS19/20A2
Huaiya SN55/56F3
Huaiyang Xian HEN33/34D6
Huai'an Shi JS17/18C4
Huaiyin Qu (Wangyin) JS17/18C5
Huaiyuan SC45/46C4
Huaiyuan Xian AH23/24D4
Huaiyu Shan JX29/30C5
Huaizhen HEB5/6E4
Huaizhong JX29/30D2
Huaji AH23/24D2
Huajia JL13/14C6
Huajialing GS57/58E7
Huajiang GZ49/50E4
Huajiang HN37/38F4
Huajianzi LN11/12C9
Huajiaoping HB35/36D2
Huajing GX43/44B8
Hualandian SD31/32C3
Huale SX7/8E3
Huali SN55/56H5
Huali GZ49/50C6
Hualiangting AH23/24F3
Hualiangting Shuiku AH23/24F3

Hualien Hsi TW27/28D3
Hualien Hsien TW27/28D3
Hualien Kang TW27/28D3
Hualin HL15/16E5
Hualong Huizu Zizhixian(Bayan)
  QH59/60B8
Huama HL15/16D6
Huamenlou HN37/38D5
Huaminglou HN37/38C5
Huanan Xian HL15/16D6
Huancheng SD31/32C4
Huancheng SD31/32E4
Huandun JS17/18B4
(Huanfeng)Hanshan Xian AH23/24E5
Huang'an SD31/32D2
Huangang JS17/18D7
Huang'ao JX29/30E2
Huangbai JX29/30C5
Huangbai JL13/14F7
Huangbai He HB35/36C4-D4
Huangban GZ49/50B8
Huangbanqiao Shuiku SC47/48B2
Huangbayi SN55/56H2
Huangbei JX29/30E3
Huangbei JX29/30D4
Huangbeijiao HEN33/34B4
Huangbizhuang Shuiku HEB5/6E2
Huangcai HN37/38C5
Huangcai Shuiku HN37/38C5
Huangcaoling YN51/52D5
Huangcao Shan SC47/48B5-C5
Huangcaoxia SC47/48C5
Huangcheng GS57/58D5
Huangchengji SD31/32B7
Huangchi AH19/20B1
Huangchong GD41B2
Huangchuan Xian HEN33/34E7
Huangcun GD39/40C8
Huangcun GX43/44C8
Huangcun ZJ21/22D5
Huangcun AH19/20C1
(Huangcun)Daxing Xian BJ3/4C3
Huangdao HEN33/34C5
Huang Dao SD31/32C7
Huangda Yang ZJ21/22B7
Huangdi LN11/12D4
Huangdizhen JS17/18E6
Huangdu AH19/20C1
Huangdu SH19/20B4
Huangdun SD31/32D6
Huangdunmiao AH23/24C4
Huangduobu NX61/62D3
Huangfengqiao HN37/38D6
Huanggai Hu HB35/36E6
Huanggang GD39/40B6
Huanggang GD39/40C5
Huanggang AH23/24D2
Huanggang JX29/30B4
Huanggangji SD31/32E3
Huanggangkou JX29/30C2
Huanggangliang NM9/10F11
Huanggangmiao HB35/36D8
(Huanggang)Raoping Xian GD39/40C10

Huanggang Shan JX29/30D5
Huanggang Shan FJ25/26C3
Huanggang Shi HB35/36D7
Huanggang Shuiku FJ25/26E2
Huanggu JX29/30C5
Huangguan GX43/44B9
Huangguoshu Pubu GZ49/50E4
Huangguzha AH23/24E4
Huanghe QH59/60C6
Huang He HEN33/34E7
Huanghe Kou SD31/32B5-6
Huangheya SD31/32B3
Huangheyan QH59/60C6
Huang He(Yellow R.) SD31/32B4-5
  HEN33/34C5-6
  SN55/56B6-C6
  QH59/60C7
  GS59/60B8-9
  NX61/62A3-B3
  SX7/8E2-F2
  NM9/10G7-8
Huang Hu AH23/24F3
Huanghua HB35/36C4
Huanghuacheng BJ3/4B3
Huanghuadian SD31/32D6
Huanghuadian LN11/12D7
Huanghuadian TJ3/4C3
Huanghua He GX43/44E8-9
Huanghuai Pingyuan HEN73D3-5
  AH71A1-3
  JS71A1-3
Huanghua Shi HEB5/6E5
Huanghuashi HN37/38C6
Huanghunyu HEB3/4B5
Huangji JS17/18B3
Huangji JS17/18C4
Huangji HB35/36B5
Huangjia SD31/32B4
Huangjiaba GZ49/50C6
Huangjiadu HN37/38E5
Huangjiajian JS17/18C6
Huangjian AH23/24G5
Huangjiao Shan ZJ21/22D6
Huangjin GX43/44C6
Huangjin'ao HN37/38D2
Huangjinbu JX29/30C4
Huangjindong HB35/36E2
Huangjindong HN37/38C7
Huangjing JS17/18E7
Huangjinggou SC45/46D5
Huangjinjing HN37/38D3
Huangjiuguan HEB3/4B4
Huangjuezhen JS17/18D5
Huangkan BJ3/4B3
Huangkeng FJ25/26C3
Huangkeng GD39/40A7
Huangkou AH23/24B3
Huanglaomen GX29/30B3
Huangli SN55/56F3
Huangli JS17/18E5
Huangliangmeng HEB5/6G2
Huangliangping HB35/36C3
Huanglianguan SC45/46E4

Huanglianyu FJ25/26E2
Huangling HEN23/24B6
Huangling AH23/24C2
Huangling HI42B3
Huanglingji HB35/36D7
Huanglingmiao HB35/36D4
Huangling Xian SN55/56E5
Huanglishu Shuiku AH23/24D5
Huangliu HI42C1
Huanglongang FJ25/26D4
Huanglongchi SX7/8B3
Huanglongdai Shuiku GD41A2
Huanglongdang HB35/36C5
Huanglonghu GD41A3
Huanglong Shan SN79D4
(Huanglongsi)Kaifeng Xian
  HEN33/34C6
Huanglongtan HB35/36B3
Huanglongtan Shuiku HB35/36B3
Huanglong Xian SN55/56E5
Huanglu SC47/48A2
Huangludian HNE33/34D4
Huangluohe AH23/24E4
Huangma TW27/28D3
Huangmabu GD41A2
Huangmao GX43/44D7
Huangmao JX29/30C2
Huangmao Dao GD41B2
Huangmao Hai GD41C2
Huangmao Jian ZJ21/22E4
Huangmaoyuan HN37/38D3
Huangmei Xian HB35/36D8
Huangmian GX43/44C7
Huangmudu AH23/24E5
Huangnan Zangzu Zizhizhou
  QH59/60C7-8
Huangnian SX7/8E5
Huangniba JS19/20A1
Huangnihe JL13/14D9
Huangnihe YN51/52C6
Huangni He GZ49/50E3-F3
          YN51/52C6
Huangnihe AH23/24E4
Huangnitang HN37/38E5
Huangniupu SN55/56F2
Huangniushi JX29/30G2
Huangnizhen AH23/24F3
Huangping Xian GZ49/50D6
Huangpi Xian HB35/36D7
Huangpo GD39/40E3
Huangpu GD39/40C6
Huangpu SN55/56E5
Huangpu GD41A1
Huangpu Jiang SH17/18E7-F7
Huangqi FJ25/26D5
Huangqi SC47/48C5
Huangqiao JS17/18D6
Huangqiao HN37/38D3
Huangqiao He JS19/20A3
Huangqi Hai NM9/10G9
Huangquhe HB35/36B5
Huangquqiao NX61/62A3
Huangsha GX43/44B7

Huangshagang JX29/30C3
Huangshahe GX43/44A9
Huangshajie HN37/38B6
Huangshan SD31/32C9
Huangshan AH23/24F5
Huang Shan AH23/24F4-5
Huangshan ZJ21/22C5
Huangshanguan SD31/32B7
Huangshanpo HEN33/34E6
Huangshan Shi(Tunxi) AH23/24G5
Huangshantou HB35/36E5
Huangshapu HN37/38F5
Huangshaqiao JX29/30C2
Huangshatuo LN11/12C6
Huangshayao ZJ21/22D3
Huangshengguan SC45/46B4
Huangshi JX29/30D4
Huangshi GD39/40B8
Huangshiguan JX29/30E3
Huangshikou HEB5/6D2
Huangshi Shi HB35/36D8
Huangshi Shuiku HN37/38B4
Huang Shui QH59/60B8
Huangsi HEB5/6F2
Huangsi SD31/32E3
Huangsongdian JL13/14D8
Huangtan JX29/30B5
Huangtan ZJ21/22C6
Huangtan FJ25/26D4
Huangtang GD39/40C7
Huangtankou ZJ21/22D3
Huangtankou Shuiku ZJ21/22D3
Huangtian ZJ21/22D5
Huangtian GD39/40C7
Huangtiangang JS19/20B3
Huangtianpu HN37/38E4
Huangtingshi HN37/38E4
Huangtong HI42B2
Huangtong JS17/18E5
Huangtong JX29/30D4
Huangtu JS19/20B3
Huangtudian HN37/38C4
Huangtugang JX29/30D3
Huangtugang HB35/36C8
Huangtu Gaoyuan NX79C2-5
                SN79C2-5
                GS80B4-6
Huangtujing GX43/44A9
Huangtukan LN11/12E7
Huangtukeng HN37/38E3
Huangtuliangzi HEB5/6B6
Huangtuling HN37/38D6
Huangtupo BJ3/4C3
Huangtupu HN37/38E4
Huangwan ZJ21/22B5
Huangweihe AH23/24E3
Huangwei Yu TW27/28G5
Huangwutun GX43/44F6
Huangxi JX29/30C3
Huang Xian SD31/32B7
Huangxikou FJ25/26C3
Huangxing Dao ZJ19/20C5
Huangxuzhen SC45/46C5
Huangyadong SX7/8E5

Huangyaguan TJ3/4B4
Huangyang ZJ21/22E4
Huangyangjie JX29/30E2
Huangyangsi HN37/38E4
Huangyangtan NX61/62B3
Huangyangwan NX61/62C2
Huangyangzhen GS57/58D6
Huangyan ZJ21/22D6
Huangyao GX43/44C9
Huangying JS17/18C5
Huangyuan Xian QH59/60B7
Huangyuchong GD41A4
Huangyunpu HB35/36A3
Huangze Yang ZJ21/22B7
Huangzhai ZJ21/22C5
(Huangzhai)Yangqu Xian SX7/8C4
Huangzhan HB35/36C7
Huangzhong Xian(Lushar) QH59/60B7
Huangzhu HI42B3
Huangzhuang HEB3/4C4
Huangzhuang SD31/32C4
Huangzhuang TJ3/4C4
Huangzhulin YN51/52D4
Huangzi Sha JS17/18C7
Huaniao Shan ZJ21/22B7
Huaning Xian YN51/52C5
Huaniushan GS57/58B2
Huan Jiang GS57/58D8
Huanjiang Maonanzu Zizhixian
  GX43/44C6
Huankou JS17/18B2
Huanren Manzu Zizhixian LN11/12C9
Huanren Shuiku LN11/12C9
                JL13/14F6
(Huanshan)Yuhuan Xian ZJ21/22D6
Huan Shui HB35/36C6
Huantai Xian(Suozhen) SD31/32C5
Huantan HB35/36C6
Huantuling LN11/12D6
Huanxi HN37/38E6
Huan Xian GS57/58D8
Huanxiang He HEB3/4C4
Huanxintian HL15/16D7
Huanze ZJ21/22C5
Huanze Shan ZJ21/22B7
Huapen BJ3/4B3
Huapichang JL13/14D7
Huapi Ling HEB5/6B3
Huaping HB35/36D3
Huaping Xian(Zhongxin) YN51/52B4
Huaping Yu TW27/28B3
Huaqi GZ49/50D5
Huaqiao FJ25/26C3
Huaqiao FJ25/26C4
Huaqiao JX29/30C5
Huaqiao ZJ21/22D6
Huaqiao JX29/30D5
Huaqiao SC47/48B1
Huaqiao HN37/38D4
Huaqiao SC45/46C6
Huaqiao HN37/38E6
Huaqiao HN37/38D3
Huaqiao HN37/38E4

Huaqiu GZ49/50B5
Huarong Xian HN37/38B5
Hua Shan SN55/56F6
Huashan JS17/18B2
Huashan JL13/14F7
Huashaoying HEB5/6C2
Huashi GX43/44F6
Huashi JS17/18E6
Huashi HN37/38D5
Huashi Shan GD39/40B6
Huashixia (Zogainrawar) QH59/60C6
Huashulinzi JL13/14D8
Huasuo GS61/62E4
Huatan SC45/46D4
Huatangpu HN37/38F5
Huating FJ25/26E4
Huating Xian GS57/58E8
Huatong LN11/12D5
Huatou SC47/48C1
Huaxi ZJ21/22C5
Huaxi GZ49/50D5
Huaxi JX29/30D2
Hua Xian SN55/56F5
Hua Xian (Daokou) HEN33/34B6
Huaxi Shuiku GZ49/50D5
Huayang SN55/56G3
Huayang AH23/24F3
Huayang GD39/40C8
Huayang ZJ21/22C5
Huayanghe Shuiku HB35/36B5
(Huayang) Jixi Xian AH23/24F5
Huaying Shan SC45/46C6-D6
Huaying Shi SC45/46C6
Huayin Shi SN55/56F6
Huayu TW27/28D1
Huayuan HN37/38E3
Huayuan He GZ49/50B8 HN37/38C2
Huayuankou HEN33/34C5
Huayuankou JL13/14E8
Huayauan Xian HN37/38C2
(Huayuan) Xiaochang HB35/36C6
Huayuanzui JS17/18D4
Huazangsi GS57/58D6
Huazhaizi GS57/58C5
Huazhou Shi GD39/40E3
Huazhuang HEN33/34E7
Huazi LN11/12C7
Huazikou JS19/20A1
Huaziping SN55/56C5
Hubei Kou HB35/36A2 SN55/56G5
Hubin HN37/38B6
Huchao GZ49/50D5
Hucun SX7/8D4
Hucun FJ25/26D2
Hudai JS19/20B3
Hudian SN55/56F2
Hudong GS61/62D3
Hudu He HB35/36E5
Hufang FJ25/26D3
Hufang JX29/30D5
Hufang JX29/30C5
Hufengchang SC47/48C4
Hufu JS19/20B2

Hugezhuang HEB5/6D6
Hugou AH23/24C4
Huguan Xian SX7/8E5
Huguochang SC45/46D5
Huguozhuang HEB3/4C2
Huhebashige NM9/10G6
Huhsi TW27/28D1
Huhur He NM68C7-8
Hui'anpu NX61/62C3
Hui'an Xian FJ25/26E4
Huibaoling Shuiku SD31/32E4
Huibie Yang ZJ21/22B6
Huibu JX29/30C3
Huibu JX29/30C3
Huichang Xian JX29/30F3
(Huicheng) She Xian AH23/24G5
Huichuan GS57/58E6
Huicun HEN33/34D8
Huidong Xian SC45/46E4
Huidong Xian (Pingshan) GD39/40D7
Huidun JS17/18B5
Huifa HL15/16E5
Huifa He JL13/14E7
Huifengzhen JS17/18E7
Huiguozhen HEN33/34C4
Huihe SD31/32C4
Hui He AH23/24C3-4
Hui He SX7/8B4
Huihe NM9/10C12
Huijiatai NX61/62E3
Huiji He HEN33/34C6-7
Huikoujie AH23/24G3
Huilai Xian GD39/40C9
Huilan SC47/48B3
Huili SD31/32B8
Huili SX7/8D3
Huiliuji AH23/24D2
Huili Xian SC45/46E4
Huilong GD39/40B6
Huilong FJ25/26C4
Huilong SC47/48B5
Huilong SC47/48B4
Huilong HEB5/6G2
Huilongchang SC47/48A4
Huilongshan Shuiku LN11/12C9
Huilongsi HN37/38E4
Huimin Xian SD31/32B4
Huiminxiang NX61/62B3
Huinan JL13/14E7
(Huinan) Nanhui Xian SH17/18E7
Huinan Xian (Chaoyang) JL13/14E7
Huingong Xian NX61/62A3
Huining Xian GS57/58E7
Huinong Qu NX61/62B3
Hui Shan JS17/18E6
Huishan ZJ21/22C5
Huishan HI42B3
Huishangang HN37/38C5
Hui Shui AH23/24F5
Huishuiwan SN55/56H4
Huishui Xian GZ49/50D5
Huitang HN37/38C5
Huiten Nur QH59/60C2

Huiting HEN33/34C8
Huitingshan Shuiku HB35/36C6
Huitong JX29/30E4
Huitongqiao YN51/52C3
Huiton Xian HN37/38E2
Huiwan He HB35/36B2
Huiwen HI42B3
Hui Xian GS57/58F8
Huixian Shi HEN33/34B5
Huiyang Shi GD39/40D7
Huize Xian YN51/52 B5
Huizhou AH23/24 G5
Huizhou Shi GD39/40 C7
Huji HB35/36 C5
Huji SD31/32 D3
Huji AH23/24C2
Huji JS17/18C4
Hujiachang SC45/46C6
Hujiadun AH23/24E5
Hujiatuo HEB5/6D7
Hujiaxiaojing NX61/62C3
Hujiaying HB35/36B3
Hujiayu SX7/8F3
Hujiayuan SN55/56G5
Hujie YN51/52C5
Hujigou NM9/10K20
Hujirt NM9/10J19
Hukeng FJ25/26F2
Hukou HN37/38E6
Hukou TW27/28C3
Hukou Pubu SX7/8E2 SN55/56D6
Hukou Xian (Shuangzhong) JX29/30B4
Hulan JL13/14D7
Hulan Ergi HL15/16D2
Hulan He JL13/14C8
Hulan He HL15/16D4
Hulan Xian HL15/16D4
Hulei FJ25/26F2
Hulesi AH23/24F5
(Huliao) Dabu Xian GD39/40B9
Huling ZJ21/22E5
Hulin Gol NM9/10E13-14
           JL13/14B3-4
Hulingol Shi NM9/10E12
Hulin Shi HL15/16E7
Huliu He HEB5/6C2-D2
Hulstai NM61/62A3
Huludao Shi LN11/12D4
Hulu He GS57/58D9 SN55/56D4-E4
Hulu He GS57/58E7 NX61/62E2
Hulu Hu QH59/60C2
Hulun Buir Gaoyuan NM68B7
Hulun Buir Meng NM9/10C12-14
Hulun Buir Shadi NM68B7
Hulun Nur NM9/10C11
Hulushan FJ25/26D4
Huluzhai HN37/38C2
Huma He HL15/16B4
Huma He HL15/16A3
Hu Men GD39/40D6
Humu HEB3/4C2
Hunan ZJ21/22D3
Hunanzhen Shuiku ZJ21/22D3
Hunchun He JL13/14D11-E11

Hunchun Shi   JL13/14E11
Hung Shui Kiu   HK41B2
Hunhe   LN11/12C7
Hun He   NM7/8A3
Hun He   SX7/8B5
Hun He   LN11/12C7-6
Hun Jiang   LN11/12C9   JL13/14F6
Hunshandake Shadi   NM9/10F10-11
Hunt   NM9/10E12
Hunyuan Xian   SX7/8B5
Hunyuanyao   NM3/4C1
Huocheng Xian (Suiding)   XJ63/64C6
Huodao   GD41B1
Huodifangzi   HL15/16D3
Huoditang   SN55/56G4
Huodoushan   HEB3/4B4
Huohong   GZ49/50E5
Huojia Xian   HEN33/34B5
Huojing   SC47/48B1
Huokou   FJ25/26D5
Huolianzhai   LN11/12C7
Huolongmen   HL15/16C3
Huolongping   HB35/36E1
Huolu   SC45/46D6
Huoqiu Xian   AH23/24D3
Huorqi   NM15/16C2
Huoshan   GD39/40B6
Huo Shan   AH71C2
Huo Shan   SX7/8E3
Huoshaoliao   TW27/28C3
Huoshaoping   HB35/36D3
(Huoshao Tao)Lu Tao   TW27/28E3
Huosha Xian   AH23/24E3
Huoshishan   HL15/16D3
Huoshiying   HEB3/4C5
Huoshizhai   NX61/62D2
Huotian   HN37/38E6
Huotian   FJ25/26F3
Huotong   FJ25/26D5
Huotong Xi   FJ25/26D5
Huoxian   BJ3/4C3
Huoyan Shan   SX7/8E3-F2
Huozhou Shi   SX7/8E3
Huping   JX29/30D3
Hupu   JS17/18E6
Huqiao   JS19/20B2
Huqid Wanggin Sum   NM9/10E11
Huqiu   JS19/20B3
Hure Qi   NM9/10F13
Huret   NM9/10J21
Huretin Sum   NM9/10G4
Hurleg Hu   QH59/60B5
Hurt   XJ63/64A9
Hushan   HL15/16E6
Hushan   ZJ21/22D3
Hushan   FJ25/26F2
Hushan   HI42B3
Hushan   JX29/30C2
(Hushan)Wuyi Xian   ZJ21/22D4
Hushi   JL13/14C6
Hushi   SC47/48D3
Hushi   FJ25/26E5
Hushiha   HEB5/6C4

Hushi He   SC47/48C3
Hushitai   LN11/12C7
Hushu   JS17/18E4
Hutian   HN37/38D5
Hutiao   SC45/46C5
Hutiao Xia   YN51/52B4
Hutongzhen   HL15/16B4
Hutou   HL15/16E7
Hutou   FJ25/26D4
Hutou   FJ25/26E4
Hutoushan Shuiku   XZ78C4
Hutouya   SD31/32B6
Hutuanji   AH23/24D3
Hutubi Xian   XJ63/64C9
Hutun   SD31/32C3
Hutuo He   SX7/8C5   HEB5/6E3
Hut Yanchi   NM9/10H5
Huwan   JX29/30D4
Huwan   HEN33/34F6
Huwei   TW27/28D2
Huxi   SC47/48B3
Huxi   ZJ21/22C5
Hu Xian   SN55/56F4
Huxiang   HEN33/34C7
Huxin   HI42A3
Huxun Sun   NM9/10E12
Huyang   FJ25/26E4
Huyangzhen   HEN33/34E4
Huyu   FJ25/26E5
Huyuan   HL15/16B2
Huyuan   FJ25/26D3
Huzhaikou   HEB5/6F2
Huzhang   SX7/8F3
Huzhen   ZJ21/22D5
Huzhen   ZJ21/22C4
Huzhong   HL15/16A2
Huzhou Shi   ZJ21/22B5
Huzhu Tuzu Zizhixian   QH59/60B7

I

Ichu   TW27/28D2
Ih Dabs   NM9/10J20
Ih Hurgalj   NM9/10C11
Ih Ju Meng   NM9/10H6-8
Ih Suj   NM9/10J21
Ih Tal   NM11/12A6
Ikkisu   XJ63/64F4
Ilan Hsien   TW27/28C3
Ili Diqu   XJ63/64D6-7
Ili He   XJ63/64D5-6
Ili Kazak Zizhizhou   XJ63/64D7-B10
(Inder)Jalaid Qi   NM9/10D14
Indirakoli Shankou   XJ63/64H4
Inggen   NM9/10G5
Ingget   NM61/62B1
Injigan Gol   NM69A2
Iqe   QH59/60A4
Iqe He   QH59/60A4

J

Jagdaqi   NM9/10B15
Jaggaiqiao   SC45/46D3
Jaggang   XZ53/54C2

Jaggoi   YN51/52A3
Jagt   NM61/62B1
Jainca Xian(Magitang)   QH59/60C7
Jalaid Qi(Inder)   NM9/10D14
Jalai Nur   NM9/10C11
Jalat   JL13/14B5
Jamati   XJ63/64C7
Jamt   NM13/14C3
Jamtai   XJ63/64E6
Jangco   XZ53/54D8
Jaramtai   NM9/10C13
Jargalang   NM9/10F14
Jargalangt   NM9/10K17
Jargalangt   NM9/10E10
Jartai   NM9/10H5
Jartai Yanchi   NM9/10H5
Jarud Qi(Lubei)   NM9/10E13
Jeminay   XJ63/64B8
Jeminay Xian   XJ63/64B8
Jenai   TW27/28C3
Jênlung   XZ53/54E7
Jergentei   QH59/60B5
Jia'ao   GZ49/50C7
Jiachuan   SC45/46B6
Jiading   SH17/18E7
(Jiading)Xinfeng Xian   JX29/30F2
Jiadou   SX7/8B6
Jiafang   GX43/44D6
Jiafu   FJ25/26E3
Jiagou   AH23/24C4
Jiagui   GX43/44C6
Jiahe   HB35/36B3
Jiahe Xian(Zhuquan)   HN37/38F5
Jiahezhai   JS17/18B3
Jiahui   GX43/44C8
Jiajia   SC47/48C3
Jiajiachang   SC45/46C5
Jiajiang Xian   SC45/46D4
Jiajiatun   SX7/8A6
Jiajiaying   HEB3/4B2
Jiajin Shan   SC45/46C4
Jiajiu   GZ49/50E7
Jiakou   JS17/18B3
Jiakou   ZJ21/22B4
Jialai   HI42B2
Jiale   HI42B2
Jialequan   SX7/8C4
Jialiang   GZ49/50E6
Jialing   SX7/8D4
Jialing   SC76B5
Jialing Jiang   SC45/46C5-6
Jialou   HEN33/34E5
Jialu   AH23/24F5
Jialu He   HEN33/34C6-D6
Jiamao   HI42C2
Jiamaying   SD31/32B2
Jiaming   SC47/48C3
Jiamusi Shi   HL15/16D6
Ji'an   SC47/48B4
Ji'an   SC47/48C3
Jian'an   JL13/14D6
Jianba   GZ49/50B6
Jianbi   JS17/18D5

Jianchang LN11/12C8
Jianchang Xian LN11/12D3
Jianchapu HEB3/4C3
Jianchaxi GZ49/50B6
Jianchipu SN55/56H4
Jianchuan Xian YN51/52B3
Jiande Shi ZJ21/22C4
Ji'an Diqu JX29/30E2-3
Jiandou FJ25/26E3
Jianfeng HI42C1
Jianfeng Nongchang NM9/10J18
Jiang'an HB35/36D7
Jiangan He TJ3/4C4
Jiang'an Xian SC45/46D5
Jiangao Shan YN51/52C3
Jiangba JSD17/18C4
Jiangbei HN37/38C6
Jiangbei SC47/48C4
Jiangbeixu JX29/30E3
Jiangbian HI42C1
Jiangbiancun JX29/30D3
Jiangchangying HEB5/6C6
Jiangcheng GD39/40C4
Jiangcheng HEB5/6E3
Jiangcheng Hanizu Yizu Zizhixian
    (Mengliejie) YN51/52D4
Jiangchuan Xian YN51/52C5
Jiangcun JX29/30B5
Jiangcun JX29/30C5
Jiangcun HN37/38F4
Jiangcun SX7/8C5
Jiangdi YN51/52B5
Jiangdian AH23/24E3
Jiangdong HN37/38D3
Jiangduo JS17/18D6
Jiangdu Shi JS17/18D5
Jiange Xian SC45/46B5
Jianggang JS17/18D6
Jianggezhuang HEB5/6D7
Jiangguantun SD31/32C3
Jianghong GD39/40E2
Jianghu GD39/40E3
Jianghuaqiao JS17/18D6
Jianghua Yaozu Zizhixian HN37/38F4
Jiangji AH23/24C3
Jiangji HEN33/34E7
Jiangjiabu JX29/30C4
Jiangjiachang SC47/48C4
Jiangjiadian JL13/14E7
Jiangjiadian HEB5/6A5
Jiangjiajie JL13/14E6
Jiangjiapo SD31/32C7
Jiangjiayingzi NM5/6A6
Jiangjiehe GZ49/50C6
Jiangjin Shi SC45/46D6
Jiangjunguan BJ3/4B4
Jiangjunhe HB35/36B3
Jiangjunmiao AH23/24F4
Jiangjunmiao XJ63/64C10
Jiangjunmu HEB5/6F2
Jiangjunshi LN11/12E5
Jiangjuntai GS57/58B3
Jiangkou ZJ21/22C6

Jiangkou HB35/36D4
Jiangkou JX29/30F3
Jiangkou JX29/30D3
Jiangkou SC45/46D6
Jiangkou FJ25/26E5
Jiangkou JX29/30D2
Jiangkou SC47/48B1
Jiangkou GX43/44D8
Jiangkou GX43/44C8
Jiangkou HB35/36E3
Jiangkou HN37/38D2
Jiangkou HN37/38D3
Jiangkou GX43/44C7
Jiangkou SN55/56G3
Jiangkou FJ25/26C4
(Jiangkou) Fengkai Xian GD39/40C4
Jiangkouji AH23/24D3
Jiangkoù Shuiku JX29/30D2
Jiangkou Xian GZ49/50C7
Jiangkouzhen SC45/46C7
Jiangle Xian FJ25/26D3
Jiangling HB35/36D5
Jianglong GZ49/50E4
Jiangluozhen GS57/58F7
Jiangmen Shi GD39/40D6
Jiangmifeng JL13/14D7
Jiangnan HN37/38C4
Jiangnan SC47/48C4
Jiangnan Qiuling JX72C2-B3
                HN74E2-D4
                AH71E1-C3
Jiangnan Yunhe(Grand Canal)
    JS17/18E5
(Jiangna) Yanshan Xian ZJ21/22B5
                        YN51/52D6
Jiangning GX43/44E7
Jiangning Xian(Dongshan) JS17/18E4
Jiangningzhen JS17/18E4
Jiangoushan NX61/62C2
Jiangpu Xian JS17/18D4
Jiangqiao HL15/16D2
Jiangshan FJ25/26E2
Jiangshan GX43/44F6
Jiangshan ZJ21/22C6
Jiangshan SD31/32C7
Jiangshan Gang ZJ21/22D3
Jiangshan Shi ZJ21/22D3
Jiangshe HN37/38D5
Jiangshijie HN37/38D5
Jiangshui HEB5/6F1
Jiangtaibu NX61/62E2
Jiangtang SX7/8D5
Jiangtian FJ25/26E5
Jiangtou GD39/40A7
Jiangtuanji AH23/24C3
Jiangtun LN11/12C6
Jiangui NM9/10H6
Jianguo HEB5/6F3
Jiangwan SH19/20B4
Jiangwan JX29/30B6
Jiangwan GD39/40B6
Jiangwei GD39/40B7
Jiangwei GD41A2
Jiangxi YN51/52D4

Jiangxia HB35/36D7
Jiangxiadian AH23/24E3
Jiang Xian SX7/8F3
Jiangxiang AH23/24D4
Jiangxiang JX29/30C4
Jiangxigou QH59/60B7
Jiangxin JS19/20A2
Jiangya HN37/38B3
Jiangyan Shi JS17/18D6
Jiangyi JX29/30B3
Jiangyi YN51/52B4
Jiangyin Dao FJ25/26E5
Jiangyin Shi JS17/18E6
Jiangyong HN37/38F4
Jiangyou Shi SC45/46C5
Jiangyu SD31/32C5
Jiangyuan Xian JL13/14F7
Jiangyugou HB35/36C4
Jiangzaogang JS19/20B4
Jiangzhang SN55/56F3
Jiangzhen SH19/20B4
Jiangzhou GZ49/50D6
Jiangzhou SC45/46E4
Jiangzhuang SD31/32C6
Jianhe HE3/4C5
Jianhe Xian(Liuchuan) GZ49/50D7
Jianhu ZJ19/20C3
Jianhu Xian JS17/18C5
Jian Jiang GD39/40E3
Jianjiang FJ25/26D5
Jianjiaxi HN37/38C4
(Jianjun)Yongshou Xian SN55/56F4
Jiankang SC45/46E3
Jianling HEN33/34E5
Jianli Xian HB35/36E5
Jianmenguan SC45/46B5
Jianming (Xipucun) HEB3/4B5
Jiannan HB35/36D1
Jianning Xian FJ25/26D2
Jian'ou Shi FJ25/26C4
Jianping LN11/12C3
Jianping Xian(Yebaishou) LN11/12C3
Jianqiao HEB5/6F4
Jianqiao ZJ21/22B5
Jiansanjiang HL15/16D7
Jianshan HB35/36E1
Jianshan ZJ21/22C5
Jianshan JX29/30C3
Jianshanzi HL15/16D7
Jianshe QH59/60D6
Jianshe FJ25/26E3
Jianshe SC45/46B5
Ji'an Shi JX29/30D2
Ji'an Shi JL13/14F7
Jianshi Xian HB35/36D2
Jianshui Xian YN51/52D5
Jiantian HB35/36D2
Jiantian JX29/30B4
Jiantiao ZJ21/22C6
Jiantou HEN33/34E7
Jiantou SD31/32E4
Jianxi AH23/24D5
Jianxi FJ25/26D3

Jian Xi FJ25/26D4
Ji'an Xian(Dunhou) JX29/30D2
Jianxing SC45/46C5
Jianyang JS17/18C5
Jianyang Shi FJ25/26C4
Jianyang Shi SC45/46C5
Jianyangyi HB35/36D5
Jianzhong HEB5/6G3
Jiaoba GZ49/50B7
Jiaobei Zhou GD41A2
Jiaochang SC45/46B4
Jiaochangba HB35/36C3
Jiaocheng Xian SX7/8D4
Jiaocun HEN33/34C2
Jiaocun AH23/24F5
Jiaodao BJ3/4C3
Jiaodao SN55/56E5
Jiaodi HEN33/34C3
Jiaodi SX7/8F3
Jiaodong SD31/32C7
Jiaohai Dao GD41B1
Jiao He SD31/32C6
Jiaohe Shi JL13/14D8
Jiaohuji HEN33/34B6
Jiaojiehe BJ3/4B3
Jiaokou SX7/8E4
Jiaokou SN55/56D6
Jiaokou Shuiku ZJ21/22C6
Jiaokou Xian SX7/8E3
(Jiaokui)Yiliang Xian YN51/52B6
Jiaolai He SD31/32C6
Jiaolai He NM11/12A5-B4
Jiaoling Xian GD39/40B9
Jiaoliu He JL13/14B2-3
Jiaomei FJ25/26F3
Jiaomiao SD31/32C3
Jiaonan Shi SD31/32D6
Jiaoping SN55/56E4
Jiaopingdu YN51/52 B5
Jiaoqu SX7/8 D5
Jiaoshi SC47/48 C5
Jiaotan JX29/30 B5
Jiaotang GD39/40D5
Jiaotang JX29/30B3
Jiaotou ZJ45/46C7
Jiaowei FJ25/26E4
Jiaoxi FJ25/26C3
Jiaoxi JS19/20B3
Jiao Xi FJ25/26C5-D5
Jiaoxi GZ49/50C7
Jiaoxie JS17/18D6
Jiaoyang FJ25/26E2
Jiaoyuan HB35/36D2
Jiaoyuan SD31/32D1
Jiaozhou Shi SD31/32C6
Jiaozhou Wan SD31/32C7
Jiaozhuang HEN33/34D6
Jiaozhuanghu BJ3/4B3
Jiaoziya HN37/38B3
Jiaozuo Shi HEN33/34B5
Jiapigou LN11/12D8
Jiapigou JL13/14E8
Jiapu ZJ21/22A4
Jiarsu QH59/60B4

Jiashan Xian(Weitang) ZJ21/22B5
Jiashi HN37/38C2
Jiashi(Payzawat)Xian XJ63/64F4
Jiashizhuang HEB5/6F2
Jiasi SC47/48C4
Jiasong HNE33/34E4
Jiatan HEN33/34D7
Jiatang NX61/62D2
Jiawang JS17/18B3
Jia Xian HEN33/34D5
Jiaxiang Xian SD31/32D3
Jia Xian (Jialu) SN55/56B6
Jiaxing Shi ZJ21/22B5
Jiaxinzi LN11/12E6
Jiaxinzi HL15/16E5
Jiayi HN37/38C6
Jiayin Xian(Chaoyang) HL15/16C6
Jiayou GX43/44C4
Jiayue SD31/32C6
Jiayuguan GS57/58C4
Jiayuguan Shi GS57/58C4
Jiayu Xian HB35/36E6
Jiazhai HEN33/34C7
Jiazhen SD31/32C2
Jiazhou Dao GD41B2
Jiazhuan GX43/44C5
Jiazi GD39/40D9
Jiazi HI42B3
Jiazi Gang GD39/40D8-9
Jicai Ling HN37/38F4
Jichang JL13/14D6
Jichang GZ49/50D5
Jichang GZ49/50C4
Jichang GZ49/50E6
Jichangping GZ49/50E3
Jichangzhuang HEB5/6F3
Jicun AH23/24F4
Jicun HN37/38F5
Jicun SX7/8D3
Jidoi QH59/60D4
Jidongping HN37/38C2
Jidong Xian HL15/16E6
Jiebu JX29/30C3
Jiebu JX29/30D3
Jiedi HEB5/6E4
Jiedi Jianhe HEB5/6E5
Jiedong Xian GD39/40C9
Jiedu SX7/8D5
Jiedunji AH23/24E4
Jiefang Muchang XJ63/64G8
Jiefang Qu SC47/48B1-C1
Jiehe SD31/32D4
Jiehedian HEB5/6G2
Jiehekou SX7/8C3
Jieheshi HB35/36D4
Jiehualong JX29/30D1
(Jiehu)Yinan Xian SD31/32D5
Jieji JS17/18C4
Jieji HL15/16D2
Jiejinkou HL15/16D7
Jiekou AH23/24G5
Jiekou ZJ21/22C3
Jieliqiao HN37/38E4

Jielongchang SC47/48C4
Jiemian FJ25/26E4
Jiepai SD31/32D5
Jiepai AH23/24F6
Jiepaidian HB35/36C6
Jiepaiji AH23/24D4
Jieshan SD31/32D3
Jieshang HB35/36E6
Jiesheng GD39/40D8
Jieshi SC47/48C3
Jieshi HEB5/6D7
Jieshi GD39/40D8
Jieshipu GS57/58E7
Jieshi Shan HEB5/6D7
Jieshi Wan GD39/40D8
Jieshou SD31/32C3
Jieshou FJ25/26C3
Jieshou JS17/18C5
Jieshou GX43/44B8
Jieshou HN37/38E6
Jieshou Shi AH23/24C2
Jieshouzhen AH23/24D5
Jieshui JX29/30D2
Jieting GX43/44C3
Jietou JX29/30C4
Jietou ZJ21/22C5
Jiexiu Shi SX7/8D3
Jiexi Xian (Hepo) GD39/40C8
Jieyang Shi GD39/40C9
Jiezhenxi GZ49/50B5
Jiezhongdian HEN33/34E4
Jiezhudu JX29/30C5
Jiezi He SN55/56E5
Jifeng SC47/48A2
Jigong Shan HB35/36C7 HEN33/34F6
Jiguan JL13/14D10
Jiguang SC47/48B2
Jiguanshan LN11/12B8
Jiguanshan LN11/12D7
Jigzhi Xian(Chugênsumdo) QH59/60D7
Jihyueh Tan TW27/28D2
Jijadianzi SD31/32D5
Jijia GD39/40F2
Jijiashi JS17/18D6
Jijiazhuang HEB5/6C2
Jijiazhuang NX61/62C2
Jijie YN51/52D5
Jijihu NM61/62C1
Jijiling GS57/58C5
Jijitai GS57/58B4
Jijü SC45/46D3
Jili HEN33/34 C4
Jili YN51/52 B5
Jiliaojie HEN33/34 C4
Jili Hu XJ63/64 B9
Jilin Hada Ling JL13/14E5-D7
          LN11/12B8-9
Jilin Shi JL13/14D7
Jiliu He NM9/10A13-B14
(Jiliyüzi)Yining (Gulja) Xian XJ63/64C6
Jilong GD39/40D7
Jilongjie HN37/38E5
Jimei FJ25/26F4
Jiming SC45/46C7

Jiming HB35/36D8
Jimo Shi SD31/32C7
Jimsar Xian XJ63/64D10
Jin'an ZJ21/22D4
Jinan City Site HB35/36D5
Jinan Shi SD31/32C4
(Jin'an) Songpan (Sungqu) Xian
  SC45/46B4
Jinbao GX43/44C8
Jinbaotun NM11/12A7
Jinbiao GD41A2
(Jinbi) Dayao Xian YN51/52C4
Jinbo HI42B2
Jinchai GX43/44C6
Jinchang HEB3/4B4
Jinchang Shi (Jinchuan) GS57/58C6
Jincheng LN11/12C5
Jincheng YN51/52C5
Jinchengjiang GX75B3
Jincheng Jiang GX49/50F7
Jinchengshi HN37/38E4
Jincheng Shi SX7/8F4
(Jincheng) Wuding Xian JX51/52C5
Jinchuan JL13/14E7
Jinchuan Xian SC45/46C4
Jinchuanxia Shuiku GS57/58C6
Jinci SX7/8D4
Jincun ZJ21/22A4
Jindian HB35/36C6
Jindi He HEN33/34B7
Jinding SN55/56D4
(Jinding) Lanping Baizu Primizu Zizhixian
  YN51/52B3
Jindong GD39/40D3
Jindou FJ25/26E4
Jindu GD41A1
Jinduhe BJ3/4B3
Jinduicheng SN55/56F5
Jinfeng SC47/48B3
Jinfeng FJ25/26E5
Jinfo Shan SC45/46D6
Jinfosi GS57/58C4
Jing'an GS57/58C5
(Jing'an) Doumen Xian GD39/40D6
Jingangtou HN37/38D6
Jingangtou SC47/48C4
Jing'anji JS17/18B2
Jing'an Xian (Shuangxi) JX29/30C3
Jingbian SC47/48A4
Jingbian Xian SN55/56C4
Jingcheng FJ25/26F3
Jingchuan Xian GS57/58E8
Jingcun SN55/56F6
Jingde Xian (Jingyang) AH23/24F5
Jingdezhen Shi JX29/30B5
Jingdian HEN33/34B6
Jingdong Yizu Zizhixian YN51/52C4
Jing'ertou JS17/18B4
Jingfeng NM69A5
Jingfuyuan SC47/48B3
Jinggang HN57/58C5
Jinggang Shan JX29/30E2
Jinggangshan Shi JX29/30E2

Jinggongqiao JX29/30B5
Jinggu GS57/58E6
Jingguanchang SC47/48C4
Jinggu Daizu Yizu Zizhixian YN51/52D4
Jinghai GD39/40C9
Jinghaiwei SD31/32C9
Jinghai Xian TJ3/4D3
Jinghe JS17/18C5
Jing He SN55/56F4
Jing He GS57/58E8-9
Jinghe HEB5/6E4
Jinghe (Jing) Xian XJ63/64C7
Jinghong Shi YN51/52D4
Jinghui Qu SN55/56F4
Jingjiang ZJ19/20C3
Jingjiang Fenhongqu HB35/36D5
Jingjiang Shi JS17/18D6
Jingjiazhuang BJ3/4B3
Jingjiazhuang SD31/32B4
Jingjukou ZJ21/22D4
Jingkou GD41A1
Jingkou JS17/18C5
Jingle Xian SX7/8C3
Jinglonggong HEN33/34C6
Jingmen Shi HB35/36C5
Jingmi Yinshuiqu BJ3/4B3
Jingnan GX43/44D9
Jingnan GZ49/50F3
Jingning Shezu Zizhixian ZJ21/22E4
Jingoutun HEB5/6B5
Jingouzi LN11/12B8
(Jingpeng) Hexigten Qi NM9/10F11

Jingpo HN37/38F6
Jingpo HL15/16F5
Jingpo Hu HL15/16F5
Jingqiao JS19/20B2
Jing Shan HB35/36C4
Jingshan JL13/14E7
Jingshan Xian HB35/36C6
Jingzhou Shi HB35/36D5
Jingshuizi NM61/62C2
Jingtai Xian GS57/58D7
Jingtanggang HEB5/6D7
Jingtieshan GS57/58C3
Jingtoujiang HN37/38E5
Jingtouxu HN37/38E4
Jingu FJ25/26E4
Jinguan YN51/52B4
Jingui NX61/62B3
Jingxi SC47/48B4
Jingxi FJ25/26D3
Jing Xian AH23/24F5
Jing Xian HEB5/6F4
Jingxing HEB5/6E2
Jingxing HL15/16D2
Jingxing Xian (Weishui) HEB5/6E2
(Jingxin) Yongshan Xian YN51/52A5
Jingxi Xian GX43/44D4
(Jingyang) Jingde Xian AH23/24F5
Jingyang Xian SN55/56F4
Jingyan Xian SC45/46D5
Jingyou SX7/8C3

Jingyuan Xian NX61/62E3
Jingyuan Xian GS57/58D7
Jingyu Xian JL13/14E7
Jingzhi SD31/32C6
Jingzhou GD39/40C9
Jingzhou HB35/36D5
Jingzhou Miaozu Dongzu Zizhixian
  (Quyang) HN37/38E2
Jingzhupu HN37/38E3
Jingzichang SC47/48D2
Jingziguan HEN33/34D3
Jinhe NM9/10B13
Jinhe HL15/16D4
Jinhe HN37/38D2
Jinhua SC47/48B1
Jinhua Shi ZJ21/22C4
Jindong Qu ZJ21/22C4
Jinhuazhen SC47/48B3
Jinhu Xian (Licheng) JS17/18C7
Jining Shi SD31/32D3
Jining Shi NM9/10G9
Jinji GX43/44D8
Jinji NX61/62C3
Jinji AH23/24D6
Jinji GD39/40D5
Jinjia HN37/38D5
Jinjia JX29/30B5
Jinjiabu BJ3/4B2
Jinjiang HN37/38F5
Jinjiang YN51/52B4
Jin Jiang FJ25/26F4
Jinjiang JX29/30C4
Jin Jiang GZ49/50C8
Jin Jiang JX29/30C2-3
(Jinjiang) Chengmai Xian HI42B3
Jinjiang Shi FJ25/26F4
Jinjiang Shuiku GD39/40D5
Jinjiataizi NM9/10K17
Jinjiazhen LN11/12B7
Jinjicun GX43/44E6
Jinjie GX43/44D5
Jinjing FJ25/26F4
Jinjing HN37/38C6
Jinkong SC47/48A3
Jinkou SD31/32C7
Jinkou HB35/36D7
Jinkouhe SC47/48C1
Jinkouhe SC45/46D4
Jinlansi HN37/38D5
Jinlijing SC47/48C2
Jinlingsi LN11/12C4
Jinlingzhen SD31/32C5
Jinlong GX43/44E4
Jinlun SC47/48A2
Jinluo SX7/8D3
Jinmian YN51/52B4
Jinnan TJ3/4D4
Jinning YN51/52C5
Jinniu AH23/24E4
Jinniu HB35/36D7
Jinping SC45/46C6
Jinping Miaozu Yaozu Daizu Zizhixian
  YN51/52D5
Jinping Shan SC45/46D3-E3

Jinping Xian(Sanjiang) GZ49/50D8
Jinpu HB35/36D8
Jinqian He HB35/36A2-3 SN55/56G5
Jinqiao AH23/24E3
Jinqiao JX29/30C6
Jinqing ZJ21/22D6
Jinrui JX29/30D2
Jinsha JL13/14D7
Jinsha AH23/24F5
Jinsha FJ25/26E4
Jinsha Jiang SC45/46E4-D4
         YN51/52A5-B5
         XZ53/54C12-E12
Jinshan SC47/48A2
Jinshan JL13/14C4
Jinshan HL15/16B4
Jinshan FJ25/26F3
Jinshan SC47/48C1
Jinshan HI42A3
(Jinshan)Harqin Qi NM9/10G12
(Jinshan)Lufeng Xian YN51/52C5
Jinshantun HL15/16D5
Jinshan SH17/18F7

Jinshanzui SH19/20C4
Jinshatan SX7/8B4
Jinshawan SC45/46D5
Jinsha Xian GZ49/50C5
Jinshendun AH23/24F3
Jinshi SC47/48A2
Jinshiqiao HN37/38D3
Jinshi Shi HN37/38B4
(Jinshi) Xinning Xian HN37/38E3
Jinshui SN55/56G3
Jinshuikou HEB3/4C2
Jinsiniangqiao ZJ21/22B6
Jinsu SC47/48C1
Jinsuoguan SN55/56E5
Jintai SD31/32C6
Jintan JX29/30D3
Jintan GD39/40B5
Jintang SN55/56D4
Jintang ZJ19/20C4
Jintang HB35/36E7
Jintang Shan ZJ21/22B6
Jintang Xian(Zhaozhen) SC45/46C5
Jintan Shi JS17/18E5
Jintanzhen HEB5/6G3
Jintao FJ25/26E4
Jinta Xian GS57/58C4
Jintian JX29/30D2
Jintiancun GX43/44D8
Jintian Shuiku GX43/44D8
Jinting JS17/18E6
Jinuoluoke YN51/52D4
Jin Xi FJ25/26D3
Jinxi SC47/48A4
Jinxiang ZJ21/22E5
Jinxiang Xian SD31/32D3
Jinxing Gang GD41B2
Jinxiu Yaozu Zizhixian GX43/44C8
Jinxi Xian JX29/30D4

Jinya GX43/44C4
Jinyangkou HB35/36D4
Jinyang Xian SC45/46E4
Jinyinshan GZ49/50C4
Jinyuan SX7/8D4
Jinyun Xian(Wuyun) ZJ21/22D5
Jinze SH19/20B2
Jinzhai Xian(Meishan) AH23/24E2
Jinzhangzi LN11/12D3
Jinzhen JS17/18C4
Jinzhong GZ49/50D3
Jinzhong SX7/8D4
Jinzhong Shi SX7/8D5
Jinzhong He TJ3/4C4
Jinzhong Shan GX43/44C2
Jinzhou LN11/12E5
Jinzhou Shi HEB5/6E3
Jinzhou Shi LN11/12C5
Jinzhou Wan LN11/12E5
Jinzhou Wan LN11/12D5
Jinzhu GX43/44E9
(Jinzhu)Daocheng(Dabba) Xian
     SC45/46D3
Jinzhushan HN37/38D4
Jinzipai AH23/24G4
Jiqing HN37/38D4
Jiqing SC47/48B2
Jiqinhe HL15/16D2
Ji Qu QH59/60D4

Jirmeng QH59/60B6
Jishan SD31/32D2
Jishan GD41B2
Jishan Xian SX7/8F2
Jisha Xi JX29/30C6
Jishengtai NM9/10J21
Jishi SX7/8E4
Jishishan Bonanzu Dongxiangzu Salarzu
     Zizhixian (Chuimatan) GS57/58E6
Jishi Xia QH59/60C8
(Jishi)Xunhua Salarzu Zizhixian
     QH59/60C7
Jishou Shi HN37/38C2
Jishu JL13/14C7
Jishui HEN33/34D7
Jishui Xian(Wenfeng) JX29/30D3
Jishuji SD31/32E3
Jitan JX29/30G3
Jitian SC45/46C5
(Jitian)lianshan Zhuangzu Yaozu Zizhixian
     GD39/40B5
Jiubingtai LN11/12C8
Jiubujiang HN37/38D6
Jiubujiang Shuiku HN37/38D6
              GX43/44B9
Jiucaiping GZ49/50D3
Jiucaitai LN11/12C6
Jiuchang GZ49/50D5
Jiuchangge HEN33/34C5
Jiucheng HEB5/6E3
Jiucheng SD31/32D2
Jiucheng GX43/44E5
Jiucheng GZ49/50B6
Jiucheng YN51/52C3

Jiucheng HEB5/6E5
Jiuchong HEN33/34E3
Jiudaoling LN11/12C5
Jiudaoyaoxian NX61/62D2
Jiudian HEB5/6G2
Jiudian SC47/48C5
Jiuding Shan SC45/46C4
Jiudu JX21/22C2
Jiufang YN51/52D3
Jiufeng FJ25/26F3
Jiufeng GD39/40A6
Jiufeng Shan FJ25/26C4-D4
Jiugongqiao HN37/38D4
Jiugong Shan JX29/30B2 HB35/36E7
Jiugongxian HEN33/34C5
Jiuguan ZJ19/20C3
Jiuguan SD31/32B8
Jiuguling AH23/24F3
Jiuhe GD39/40C8
Jiuhu SD31/32B4
Jiuhuajie AH23/24F4
Jiuhua Shan AH23/24F4
Jiuhuaxian HEN33/34B6
Jiujiang GD39/40D6
Jiujiang Shi JX29/30B3
Jiujiang Xian JX29/30B3
Jiujing HL15/6C3
Jiujing AH23/24E3
Jiukou HB35/36D5
Jiuli SC45/46D4
Jiulian GD39/40B7
(Jiulian)Mojiang Hanizu Zizhixian
     YN51/52D4
Jiulianshan JX29/30G2
Jiulian Shan GD39/40B7
Jiuling Shan JX29/30C2-B3
Jiulinzi SD3/32C5
Jiulizhe JS19/20B2
Jiulong ZJ21/22D4
Jiulong JX29/30C4
Jiulong GD39/40B5
Jiulong SC47/48B4
Jiulonggang AH23/24D4
Jiulong Jiang FJ25/26F3
Jiulongpo SC47/48C4
Jiulong Shan ZJ21/22D3
Jiulong Xi FJ25/26D2
Jiulong Xian SC45/46D3
Jiulongzhen JS17/18E7
Jiumengjin HEN33/34C4
Jiumiao LN11/12B5
Jiumu FJ25/26B4
Jiuningshan SN55/56G4
Jiupu JS17/18D4
Jiuqian GZ49/50E7
Jiuqihe SD31/32C3

Jiuquan Diqu GS57/58B2-3
Jiuquan Shi GS57/58C4
Jiuqujiang HI42B3
Jiurongcheng SD31/32B9
Jiushan SD31/32C5
Jiushan Liedao ZJ21/22C7

Jiushixia GD41A3
Jiusi HB35/36E2
Jiusuo HI42C1
Jiutai Shi JL13/14C6
Jiutang GX43/44D6
Jiutiaoling GS57/58D6
Jiuwan Dashan GX43/44B6-7
　　　　　GZ49/50E7
Jiuwuqing TJ3/4C3
Jiuxi HN37/38B4
Jiuxian ZJ21/22C4
Jiuxian AH23/24D5
Jiuxian SC47/48C4
Jiuxian SN55/56E5
Jiuxian HEN33/34D5
Jiuxian HEN33/34C3
Jiuxian HB35/36C4
Jiuxian SD31/32C4
Jiuxian HEB5/6F5
Jiuxian FJ25/26C4
Jiuxian BJ3/4B3
Jiuxian SX7/8B3
Jiuxiangcheng HEN33/34D6
Jiuxiangling GD41A2
Jiuxiangzhen SC45/46D4
Jiuxianji AH23/24C2
Jiuxiantang JX29/30C2
Jiuxu GX43/44C5
Jiuyi HN37/38F4
Jiuyi Shan HN37/38F4-5 GD75B5
Jiuyongshou SN55/56F4
Jiuzhai LN11/12D6
Jiuzhai GZ49/50D8
Jiuzhaigou Xian SC 45/46 B5
Jiuzhan JL13/14D7
Jiuzhan HL15/16B3
Jiuzhan LN11/12C7
Jiuzhangqiu SD31/32C4
Jiuzhen FJ25/26F3
Jiuzhou GZ49/50C6
Jiuzhou GX43/44E6
Jiuzhou GX43/44C3
Jiuzhou HEB3/4C3
Jiuzhou HI42B3
Jiuzhou Jiang GD43/44F8-7
Jiuzhuang GZ49/50C5
Jiuzhuangwo HEB3/4B2
Jiuzihe HB35/36C8
Jiwang Shan SX7/8F3
Jiwen NM15/16B2
Ji Xian SX7/8E2
Jizhou Shi HEB5/6F3
Jixian HL15/16D6
Ji Xian TJ3/4B4
Jixiang FJ25/26D4
Jixian Xian HL15/16D6
Jixin HN37/38C2
Jixi Shi HL15/16E6
Jixi Xian(Huayang) AH23/24F5
Jiyang FJ25/26C4
Jiyang HEN33/34C7
Jiyang Xian SD31/32C4
Jiyi SN55/56E6

Jiyuan SN55/56C3
Jiyuan Shi HEN33/34B4
Jiyun He TJ3/4C4
Jize Xian HEB5/6G2
Jizhen SN55/56C6
Jizu Shan YN51/52B4
Jomda Xian XZ53/54D12
Jonê Xian GS57/58E6
Jos He NM67A6
Juancheng Xian SD31/32D2
Juan Shui HN37/38D5
Jubaoshan JL13/14C5
Jucun ZJ21/22D4
Judian YN51/52B3
Juding HI42B3
(Juegang)Rudong Xian JS17/18D7
Juexi ZJ21/22C6
Juexizhen SC45/46D5
Jufeng SD31/32D6
(Jugar)Sêrxü SC45/46B2
Jugezhuang BJ3/4B3
Juh NM9/10I7
Ju He SN55/56E4
Ju He TJ3/4C4 HEB5/6C5-D5
Juhongtu QH59/60B5
Juhua Dao LN11/12D4
Juifang TW27/28B3
Juisui TW27/28D3
Jukou FJ25/26C3
Jukoupu HN37/38D4
Julebu SX7/8A5
Juliuhe LN11/12B6
Julong Shan HB35/36C4
Julu Xian HEB5/6F3
Juma He HEB5/6D3
Jumanggoin SC45/46B2
Junan Xian(Shizilu) SD31/32D5
Jun Bel NM61/62A3
Juncheng HEB5/6E2
Junchuan HB35/36C6
Juncun JX29/30E3
Jundaping HN37/38C3
Jundian HB35/36B3
Jundu SX7/8D2
Jundu Shan BJ3/4B3
Jungar Qi (Shagedu) NM9/10H8
Junggar Pendi XJ63/64C8-10
Junji Guan HEB5/6F1 SX7/8D5
Junkou FJ25/26D2
Junliangcheng TJ3/4C4
Junlian Xian SC45/46D5
Junling JX29/30C4
Jun Mahai Hu QH59/60A4
Junmenling JX29/30F3
Junpu AH23/24E4
Jun Shan HN37/38B5
Junshanpu HN37/38C5
Jun Ul QH80B3
Junxiang BJ3/4C2
(Junyang)Gao'an Xian JX29/30C3
Junzhao HEN33/34C4
Jurh NM9/10E13
Jurh NM9/10F9

Jurong Shi JS17/18E5
Jusheng HL15/16C4
Jushi GX43/44D7
Jushui ZJ21/22E3
Ju Shui HB35/36C7-D7
Jushui ZJ21/22E4
Ju Shui HB35/36C4-D4
Juting SN55/56G2
Ju Ud Gaoyuan NM68D7
Juxi FJ25/26E2
Ju Xian SD31/32D5
Juyangzhen JS19/20B4
Juye Xian SD31/32D3
Juyongguan BJ3/4B3
Juzhang He HB35/36D4
Juzhen JS17/18D7

K

Kagang QH59/60C7
Ka-ho MC41B2
Kai'an JL13/14C6
Kaibamardang QH59/60A5
Kaiben GZ49/50C7
Kaicheng NX61/62E3
Kaichengqiao AH23/24E4
Kaidu(Karaxahar)He XJ63/64D8
Kaifeng HB35/36C4
Kaifeng Shi HEN33/34C6
Kaifeng Xian(Huanglongsi)
　　HEN33/34C6
Kaihe SD31/32D3
Kaihua Xian ZJ21/22C3
Kaihui HN37/38C6
Kai Jiang SC47/48A2
Kaijiang Xian SC45/46C6
Kaikou GZ49/50D6
Kaikukang HL15/16A3
Kaili Shi GZ49/50D6
Kailu Xian NM9/10F13
Kaimar QH59/60D4
Kaiping HEB5/6D6
Kaiping Shi GD39/40D5
Kaishantun JL13/14E10
(Kaitong)Tongyu Xian JL13/14C4
Kai Xian SC45/46C7
Kaiyang Xian GZ49/50C5
Kai Yet Kok HK41B2
Kaiyuan JL13/14C8
Kaiyuan Shi YN51/52D5
Kaiyuan Shi LN11/12B8
Kaizha SX7/8D4
Kakpakkuduk XJ63/64C12
Kalaqin LN11/12C3
Kalmakkuduk XJ63/64G7
Kalpin Xian XJ63/64E5
Kalun JL13/14C6
Kamen He XZ53/54F9
Kangbao Xian HEB5/6B2
Kangcheng SX7/8E3
Kangcun HEN33/34B5
Kangding(Dardo)Xian SC45/46C3
Kanggar SC45/46D3

Kanggardo Rizê   XZ78D5
Kanggar Shan   SC45/46D3
Kanghsitsun   TW27/28D2
Kangjiahui   SX7/8C4
Kangjiazhuang   SD31/32C6
Kangjinjing   HL15/16D4
(Kangle)Wanzai Xian   JX29/30C2
Kangle Xian   GS57/58E6
Kangmar Xian   XZ53/54E7
Kangning   SX7/8C3
Kangping Xian   LN11/12B7
Kangrigarbo Qu   XZ51/52A2
Kangrinboqê Feng   XZ53/54D3
Kangro   XZ53/54C5
Kangshan   TW27/28E2
Kangshan   JX29/30C4
Kangtan   NX61/62C2
Kangtog   XZ53/54C5
Kangtzu   TW27/28E2
Kang Xian(Zuitai)   GS57/58F7
Kangxiwar   XJ63/64G5
Kangzhuang   BJ3/4B2
Kangzhuang   SD31/32C2
Kangzhuangyi   SD31/32D3
Kanmen   ZJ21/22D6
Kanshan   ZJ19/20C3
Kanshi   FJ25/26F2
Kansu   XJ63/64F3
Kantou   AH23/24F5
Kantuanji   AH23/24C3
Kanzi   LN11/12E6
Kaohsiung Hsien(Fengshan)
   TW27/28E2
Kaohsiung Kang   TW27/28E2
Kaohsiung Shih   TW27/28E2
Kaolao   SX7/8G2
Kaoping Hsi   TW27/28E2
Kaoshan   JL13/14D6
Kaoshan   JL13/14C6
Kaoshanji   BJ3/4B4
Kaoshanpu   HB35/36D7
Kaoshantun   JL13/14E7
Kaoshu   TW27/28E2
Kaotai Shih   TW27/28F3
Kapu   GZ49/50E6
Kaqung   XJ63/64G4
(Karabura)Yumin Xian   XJ63/64B7
Karajül   XJ63/64E4
Karakax He   XJ63/64G5
Karaki   XJ63/64G6
Karakorum Shan   XJ63/64G3-H4
Karakorum Shankou   XJ63/64H4
Karamay Shi   XJ63/64C8
Karamiran He   XJ63/64G8
Karamiran Shankou   XZ53/54A6
                  XJ63/64G9
Karasay   XJ63/64G5
Karasay   XJ63/64G7
Karatax Shan   XJ78A2
Karateki Shan   XJ81C3
Karatünggü   XJ63/64B10
Karayulgun   XJ63/64E6
Kar Qu   QH59/60C5

Kashi(Kaxgar)Diqu   XJ63/64F4-G4
Kashi(Kaxgar)Shi   XJ63/64F3
Kat Hing Wai   HK41B3
Kau Lung Hang   HK41B3
Kau Sai   HK41B3
Kau To   HK41B3
Kau Wa Keng   HK41B3
Kau Yi Chau   HK41B3
Kaxgar He   XJ63/64F4-5
Kax He   XJ63/64D7
Kaxong Co   XZ53/54B5
Kebailamuga   NM61/62B2
Kebaocun   YN51/52C5
Kecheng   SX7/8E3
Kecheng   QH59/60B5
Kedian   HB45/46C5
Kedong Xian   HL15/16C4
Kedu   GZ49/50E5
Kedu He   GZ49/50D3   YN49/50D3
Kejing   HEN33/34B4
Kekou   GS57/58D6
Kekou   GX43/44B7
Kekouji   AH23/24D3
Kekou Shuiku   SN55/56B5
Kelan Xian   SX7/8C3
Kele   GZ49/50C3
Kelegou   HEB5/6B6
Kelu   GD39/40E2
Keluo He   HL15/16C3-4
Keluotun   HL15/16C3
Keng Hau   HK41B3
Kengkou   JX29/30C5
Kengkou   FJ25/26C4
Kengkouxu   GD39/40C5
Kengxi   JX29/30D2
Kenli Xian   SD31/32B5
Keqiao   ZJ21/22B5
Kequan   HEN33/34A6
Keriya He   XJ63/64G6   XJ63/64H6
Keriya Shankou   XZ53/54B3
Kesha   HN37/38B2
Keshan Xian   HL15/16C3
Ketian   QH59/60D2
Keyi   XJ63/64D7
Keyihe   NM9/10B14
Kirkoxak   XJ63/63B8
Kizilawat   XJ63/64F4
Kizilsu Kirgiz Zizhizhou   XJ63/64F3-E5
Kocê   GS57/58E6
Kogbo   SC45/46B3
Koikyim Qu   QH59/60C4
Koktokay   XJ63/64B4
Kokyar   XJ63/64G4
Kongcheng   AH23/24E4
Kongdian   AH23/24D4
Kongjiawan   HB35/36C5
(Kongjiazhuang)Wanquan Xian
   HEB5/6C2
Konglong   HB35/36E8
Kongtan   SC45/46D5
Kongtian   JX29/30G3
Kongtong Dao   SD31/32B8
Kongtong Shan   GS57/58E8

Kongur Shan   XJ63/64F3
Kongzhen   JS17/18E4
Konqi He   XJ63/64E9-10
Koramlik   XJ63/64G8
Korgas   XJ63/64C6
Korla Shi   XJ63/64E9
Korlondo   SC45/46B2
Korqag   XZ53/54D3
Korra   XZ53/54D11
Kosrap   XJ63/64G4
Ko Tong   HK41B3

Koubu   SD31/32C5
Kou He   LN11/12B8
Kouhezi   NM13/14E2
Kouhu   TW27/28D2
Koumenzi   XJ63/64D12
(Kouqian)Yongji Xian   JL13/14D7
Kouquan   SX7/8A5
Koushang Shuiku   HEB5/6G1
Koutou   HEB5/6E2
Koutou Shuiku   HEB5/6E2
Kouzhen   SD31/32C4
Kouzhen   SN55/56F4
Kouzhuang   HEB5/6C6
Kouzigou   NX61/62C3
Kouziji   AH23/24D3
Kowloon   HK41B3
Kox Kuduk   XJ63/64E12
Koxlax   XJ63/64F6
Koxtag   XJ63/64G4
(Kuaidamao)Tonghua Xian   JL13/14F6
Kuai He   SX7/8F3
Kuaitanggou   AH23/24C4
Kuaize He   YN51/52C6
Kuanao   FJ25/26F4
Kuanbang   LN11/12D4
Kuancheng Manzu Zizhixian   HEB5/6C6
Kuandian Manzu Zizhixian   LN11/12D8
Kuangjiahe   HB35/36D8
Kuangqu   SX7/8A5
Kuangshancun   HEB5/6G2
Kuangshanzhen   YN51/52B5
Kuanhsi   TW27/28C3
Kuankuoba   GZ49/50B6
Kuanmiao   TW27/28E2
Kuanshan   TW27/28D3
Kuantian   JX29/30F3
Kuantzuling   TW27/28D2
Kuanyin   TW27/28B3
Kuder   NM9/10B13
Kueiluan Tao   TW27/28C3
Kueishan   TW27/28C3
Kueishan Tao   TW27/28C3
Kugqa   SC45/46C3
Kugri   QH59/60C6
Kuichong   GD41B3
Kuidesu   LN11/12C3
Kuidou   FJ25/26E4
Kuile He   NM15/16B2-C3
Kuishan Ding   GX43/44E7
Kuitan   GD39/40C8
Kuitang   GX43/44E4
Kuixiang   YN51/52B6

Kuixu GX43/44D4
Kuizhuang HEB5/6C6
Kuke He YN51/52C3
Kukuan TW27/28C2
Kumkol Pendi XJ81D6
Kum Kuduk XJ63/64E11
Kumtag Shamo XJ63/64F11-12
Kümüx XJ63/64D10
Kundu He NM67B6
Künes Chang XJ63/64D8
(Kunggar) Maizhokunggar Xian
    XZ53/54E8
Kunggü Co XZ53/54D4
Kungssuliao TW27/28C2
Kunjirap Daban XJ63/64G3
Kunlun Guan GX43/44D6
Kunlunqi HL15/16D5
Kunlun Shan XJ63/64G4-H7
    QH59/60B2-C4
Kunlun Shankou QH59/60C4
Kunming Shi YN51/52C5
Kunshan Shi JS17/18E6
Kunyu Shan SD31/32C8-B9
Kuocang Shan ZJ21/22D5
Kuohsing TW27/28C2
Kuqa He XJ81C4
Kuqa Xian XJ63/64E7
Kuqiao JX29/30C5
Kurbin He HL15/16C5
Kuruktag XJ63/64E9-10
Kushuigoumen NM61/62A3
Kushui He NX61/62C3
Kusunlin Jian FJ25/26E3
Kuye He SN55/56B6
Küysu XJ63/64D12
Kuytun He XJ81B5
Kuytun Shi XJ63/64C8
Kwai Chung HK41B3
Kwo Lo Wan HK41B2
Kwu Tung HK41A3
Kyêbxang Co XZ53/54C7
Kyikug QH59/60B7
Kyinzhi QH59/60C7

L

Labagoumen BJ3/4B3
(Labao)Liujiang Xian GX43/44C7
(Labrang)Xiahe Xian GS57/58E6
Ladong GX43/44C7
Lafa JL13/14D8
Lagkor Co XZ53/54C5
Lagushao LN11/12D8
Laha HL15/16C3
Lai'an He AH19/20A1
Lai'an Xian(Xin'an) AH23/24D5
Laibanghe AH23/24F3
Laibin Xian GX43/44D7
Lai Chi Wo HK41A3
Laicun JX29/30E3
Laifeng SC47/48B3
Laifeng Xian HB35/36E2
Laifengyi SC47/48C4
Laiguangying BJ3/4B3

Laimou SC47/48C2
Laishan SD31/32B8
Laishui Xian HEB5/6D3
Laisu SC47/48C3
Laituan GX43/44E5
Laiwudong SD31/32C4
Laiwu Shi SD31/32C4
Laixi He SC47/48C3
Laixi Shi SD31/32C7
Laixizhan SD31/32C7
Laiyang Shi SD31/32C7
Laiyangzhan SD31/32C7
Laiyuan SX7/8D4
Laiyuan FJ25/26E3
Laiyuan Xian HEB5/6D2
Laizhou FJ25/26D4
Laizhou Shi SD31/32B6
Laizhou Wan SD31/32B6
Laji Shan QH59/607-8
Lalang GX43/44C6
Lalie GX43/44C6
Lalin HL15/16E4
Lalin He HL15/16E3-4 JL13/14B7-8
Lamadi YN51/52B3
Lamadian HL15/16D3
Lamadian JL13/14D5
Lamadong LN11/12D3
Lamawan NM9/10G8
Lamma Islands HK41B3
Lanba GZ49/50D4
Lanbian GD41A2
Lancang Jiang YN51/52D4
    XZ53/54D11-E12
Lancang Lahuzu Zizhixian(Menglang)
    YN51/52D3
Lancaodu SC45/46C6
Lancheng SD31/32E4
Lancheng SX7/8C3
Lancun SD31/32C7
Landi SD31/32C6
Landiebu NM9/10J20
La'nga Co XZ53/54D3
Langan AH23/24C4
Langang HL15/16E5
Langao Xian SN55/56H4
Langchuan He AH19/20B2
Langdai GZ49/50D4
Langdong GZ49/50D7
Langfang Shi HEB5/6D4
Langfeng NM9/10C13
Langgangshan Liedao ZJ21/22B7
Langhedian HB35/36B4
Langji Shan ZJ21/22D6
Langju JX29/30D4
Langlishi HN37/38C6
Langnuankou SD31/32C8
Langping GX43/44C4
Langping HB35/36D3
Langqên Zangbo(Xiangquan He)
    XZ53/54D2-3
Langqi FJ25/26D5
Langqiao AH23/24F5
Langru XJ63/64G5

Lang Shan NM9/10G6
Langshan HEB5/6C3
Langshan NM9/10G6
Langshan HN37/38E3
Lang Shan JS17/18E6
Langtang HN37/38C4
Langtian GD39/40A6
Langtou LN11/12D8
Langu FJ25/26C4
Langwang GD41A1
Langwogou HEB5/6B2
Langxiang HL15/16D5
Langxigang JX29/30B4
Langxi Xian AH23/24E6
Langya ZJ21/22C4
Langya SC47/48B4
Langya Shan AH23/24D5
Langya Shan SD31/32D6
Langya Shan HEB5/6D3
Langzhong Shi SC45/46C5
Lan He SX55/56H4-5
Lanhepu HB35/36B2
Lanjia LN11/12C7
Lanjiacun HN37/38E4
Lanjiang SC47/48B3
Lankao Xian HEN33/34C6
Lan Kok Tsui HK41B2
Lankou GD39/40C8
Lanli HN37/38D2
Lanling SD31/32E4
Lanling HL15/16E4
Lanlu Gang SH19/20B4-C4
Lanping Baizu Pumizu Zizhixian(Jinding)
    YN51/52B3
Lanqiyingzi HEB3/4B5
Lanshantou SD31/32D6
Lanshan Xian HN37/38F5
Lanshi HN37/38E6
Lantang GD39/40C7
Lantau Island HK41B2-3
Lantian GZ49/50C8
Lantian GD41A3
Lantianban JX29/30C4
Lantian Xian SN55/56F5
Lantianzhen SC47/48D3
Lanting ZJ21/22C5
Lanxi FJ25/26F2
Lanxi HB35/36D8
Lanxia FJ25/26D3
Lan Xian(Dongcun) SX7/8C3
Lanxi Shi ZJ21/22C4
Lanxi Xian HL15/16D4
Lanxu GX43/44E5
Lanxun HI42B2
Lanyang HEB3/4B5
Lanyang HI42B2
Lanyang Hsi TW27/28C3
Lan Yu TW27/28E3
Lanyu TW27/28E3
Lanzhong GD39/40B4
Lanzhou Shi GS57/58D6
Lanzijing JL13/14C4
Laobatan NX61/62D3

Laobatou AH23/24D3
Laobian LN11/12D6
Laobie Shan YN51/52D3
Laobukou GX43/44B7
Laochang YN51/52C6
Laochang GZ49/50E3
Laocheng JX29/30G2
Laocheng LN11/12B8
Laocheng HEN33/34D3
Laocheng HB35/36D4
Laocheng HI42B3
Laocheng SN55/56G2
Laochengzhen LN11/12B7
Laocun GX29/30F3
Laocun HB35/36D2
Laodaodian HL15/16B4
Laodao He HN37/38C6
Laodaohe HN37/38C5
Laofengkou XJ63/64B7
Laogang SH19/20B4
Laoge JS17/18D5
Laoguan JX29/30D1
Laoguo HEB5/6C6
Laoha He NM9/10F12-G12
           LN11/12C3
Lao He HEN33/34E4
Lao He JX29/30C3
Laohe HEN33/34E4
Laoheishan HL15/16F6
Laohekou Shi GD35/36B4
Laohetou HEB3/4D2
Laohuanghekou SD31/32A5
Laohutun LN11/12E5
Laoji AH23/24D2
Laojie YN51/52C3
Laojieji HL15/16E4
Laojundian SN55/56C5
Laojundong SX7/8C4
Laojunmiao HEN33/34E6
Laojun Shan HEN33/34D3
Laokou GX43/44E6
Laolai HL15/16C3
Laolin SC47/48A4
Laoling JL13/14F7
Lao Ling JL11/12C10
(Laolong)Longchuan Xian GD39/40B8
Laoniugou JL13/14E8
Laonung Hsi TW27/28D2-E2
Laopo SD31/32D5
Laopu HEB3/4C5
Laorencang AH23/24D4
Laosanliuji AH23/24D3
Laoshan SD31/32C7
Lao Shan SD31/32C7
Laoshan SN55/56D5
Laoshan Shuiku SD31/32C7
Laoshan Wan SD31/32C7
Laoshawan XJ63/64C8
Laotie Shan LN11/12F5
Laotieshan Jia LN11/12F5
Laotougou JL13/14E10
Laotuding Shan LN11/12C8
Laotu Dingzi HL70D6

Laowangzhuang HEN3/4C5
Laowei GD41A3
Laowo HEN33/34D6
Laoxian SN55/56H5
Laoximiao NM9/10G3
Laoxinkou HB35/36D5
Laoyacheng QH59/60B8
Laoyanchi NX61/62C3
Laoyanghao NM9/10J19
Laoyan He HEB5/6F3
Laoyatan AH23/24F3
(Laoye Ding)Huo Shan SX67D2
Laoye Ling HL13/14C8-D8
Laoyeling HL13/14D12
Laoye Ling JL13/14C8-D8
Laoyemiao XJ63/64C12
Laoying SX7/8B3
Laoyingpan JX29/30E3
Laoyingyan Shuiku SC47/48B2
Laozhong HEN33/34D6
Laozhu ZJ21/22D4
Laozhuangzi HEB3/4C5
Laozishan JS17/18C4
Laren GX43/44C6
Larshan HN37/38C2
Lasengmiao NM9/10H6
Layi He SX7/8C3
Laysu XJ63/64D7
Lazha SC45/46E3
Lazhuglung XZ53/54B3
Lazikou GS57/58E6
Le'an SC47/48A2
Le'an Jiang JX29/30C5
Le'an Xian(Aoxi) JX29/30D3
Lechang Shi GD39/40A6
Lecheng GD39/40C5
Lede SC47/48C2
Ledong Lizu Zizhixian(Baoyou) HI42C2
Ledu Xian(Nianbai) QH59/60B8
Lehua JX29/30C3
Leibo Xian SC45/46D4
Leidashi HN37/38D6
Leidian ZJ19/20C3
Leifeng FJ25/26E4
Leigong Shan GZ49/50D7
Leiguanji AH23/24D5
Leihe HB35/36C5
Leijiadian HB35/36D8
Leilongwan SN55/56B5
Leiming HI42B3
Leishan Xian(Danjiang) GZ49/50D7
Lei Shui HN37/38E5
Leiya SN55/56E5
Leiyang Shi HN37/38E5
Leiyuan SN55/56E5
Lei Yue Mun HK41B3
Leizhou Bandao GD39/40E2-F3
Leizhou Shi GD39/40F3
Leizhou Wan GD39/40F3
Leizhuang HEB5/6D6
Lelai HI42C3
Leli GZ49/50D7
Leli He GX43/44C4

Leling Shi SD31/32B4
Leluo HI42C1
Lema HEN33/34C7
Lemin GD39/40E2
Lemin GX43/44E7
Lenghuzhen QH59/60A3
Lengji HB35/36B4
Lengkou HEB5/6C6
Lenglong Ling QH57/58D6
              GS57/58D6
Lengqi SC45/46D4
Lengshui SN55/56H5
Lengshui SC47/48C5
Lengshuijiang Shi HN37/38D4
Lengshuipu HN37/38F5
Lengshuipu HB35/36C5
Lengzipu LN11/12C6
Leping Shi JX29/30C5
Leshanchang SC45/46D4
Leshan Shi SC45/46D4
Leshi HN37/38E3
Lesuhe SN55/56G2
Letianxi HB35/36D4
Leting Xian HEB5/6D6
Letupu AH23/24C3
Lewang GZ49/50E5
Leye Xian(Tongle) GX43/44C4
Leyu JS19/20B3
Leyuan GZ49/50E4
Leyue SC45/46E4
Lezhengwu BJ3/4B4
Lezhi Xian SC45/46C5
Lezhu GD39/40D5
Lezi GZ49/50D4
Lhabo SC45/46D3
Lhabuqung Shan XZ78C3
Lhakang SC45/46C3
Lhari Xian XZ53/53D9
Lhasa He(Gyi Qu) XZ53/54E8
Lhasa Shi XZ53/54E8
Lhatog XZ53/54D11
Lhazê Xian(Quxar) XZ53/54E6
Lhomar XZ53/54D8
Lhorong Xian(Zito) XZ53/54D10
Lhozhag Xian(Garbo) XZ53/54E8
Lhünzê Xian(Xingba) XZ53/54E9
Lhünzhub Nongchang XZ53/54E8
Lhünzhub Xian XZ53/54E8
Li'an HI42C3
Liancaipu NX61/62E2
Liancheng AH23/24C6
(Liancheng)Qinglong Xian GZ49/50E4
Liancheng Xian FJ25/26E2
Liandu GD39/40C4
Lianfeng YN51/52B5
Liang'anchang SC47/48B2
Liangbaosi SD31/32D3
Liangbingtai JL13/14D9
Liangbizhou JX29/30E2
Liangcha JS17/18C5
Liangcheng SD31/32D3
Liangcheng SD31/32D6
Liangcheng Xian NM9/10G9

Liangcun HEB5/6E3
Liangcun SD31/32C3
Liangcun GD39/40C5
Liangcun JX29/30E3
Liangcun GZ49/50B5
Liangdang Xian GS57/58F8
Liangdaohe XZ53/54D8
Liangditou SD31/32E2
Liangdong GD39/40E3
Liangdongmiao SC47/48D4
Liangdu SX7/8E3
Liangduo JS17/18D6
Liangfeng GX43/44B8
Liangfengya GZ49/50B5
Lianggang HEB5/6D3
Lianggezhuang HEB5/6D3
Lianghe SC45/46D7
Lianghe SC47/48A3
Lianghe SC47/48D4
Lianghe SN55/56G4
Lianghe HL15/16E5
Lianghekou SC45/46C4
Lianghekou GS57/58F7
Lianghekou HB35/36D2
Lianghekou HB35/36D3
Lianghe Xian YN51/52C3
Lianghua GD39/40C7
Lianghui SC47/48C5
Lianghu Pingyuan HB74C3-D3
Liangjia JL13/14B4
Liangjiadian LN11/12E5
Liangjiadian HEB3/4C4
Liangjiadu JX29/30C4
Liangjiang GX43/44D6
Liangjiang GX43/44B8
Liangjiang GX43/44D7
Liangjiangkou JL13/14E9
Liangkou GX43/44B7
Liangkou GD39/40C6
Liangkou JX29/30E2
Lianglong ZJ21/22C6
Lianglongtan YN51/52C5
Liangma SX7/8E4
Liangmianjing HEB5/6B2
Liangping Xian SC45/46C6
Liangqing GX43/44E6
Liangqiu SD31/32D4
Liangsan HN37/38D1
Liangshan JX29/30D2
Liang Shan SD31/32D3
Liangshan Xian SD31/32D3
Liangshan Yizu Zizhizhou SC45/46D3-4
Liangshe SN55/56F3
(Liangshi)Shaodong Xian HN37/38D4
Liangshui GS57/58F7
Liangshui JL13/14D11
Liangshuihezi JL13/14E7
Liangshuijing HN37/38C3
Liangshuikou HN37/38B3
Liangshuiyuanzi NX61/62C1
Liangshuizhen SD31/32C2
Liangtian GX43/44E8
Liangtian HN37/38F5

Liangtian NX61/62B3
Liangting SN55/56F3
Liangtun LN11/12D6
Liangwa HEN33/34D4
Liangwang Shan YN77C4
Liangwangzhuang TJ3/4C3
Liangwushan HB35/36D1
(Liangxiang)Fangshan BJ3/4 C3
Liangxiongdi Yu ZJ21/22B7
Liangyaping HN37/38D3
Liangyi SN55/56F6
Liangyuan AH23/24E4
Liangzhai JS17/18B2
Liangzhao HEB3/4D3
Liangzhen SN55/56C4
Liangzhu ZJ21/22B5
Liangzi Hu HB35/36D7
Lianhe JL13/14E6
Lianhu QH59/60B5
Lianhua HL15/16D4
Lianhua HL15/16E5
Lianhua GX43/44C8
Lianhua GZ49/50D5
Lianhua GS57/58E7
Lianhuadong Shuiku SC47/48A1
Lianhuajie LN11/12B8
Lianhua Shan GD39/40C8
Lianhuasi SN55/56F5
Lianhua Xian(Qinting) JX29/30D1
Lian Jiang AH19/20D1
Lian Jiang GD39/40B5-6
Lian Jiang GZ49/50D5-E5
Lian Jiang GX39/40E2
Lian Jiang JX29/30F3
Lianjiangkou GD39/40B6
Lianjiangkou HL15/16D6
Lianjiang Shi GD39/40E3
Lianjiang Xian FJ25/26D5
Lianjiechang SC45/46D5
Lianmai GD39/40B5
Liannan Yaozu Zizhixian(Sanjiang)
   GD39/40B5
Lianping SX7/8D5
Lianping Xian(Yuanshan) GD39/40B7
Lianpu AH23/24D4
Lianqiao HN37/38D4
Lianshan SC47/48B2
Lianshan HN37/38E2
Lianshan LN11/12D4
Lianshanguan LN11/12D7
Lianshan Zhuangzu Yaozu Zizhixian(Jitian)
   GD39/40B5
Lianshi ZJ21/22B5
Lianshui Xian JS17/18C5
Liantan GD39/40D4
Liantan AH23/24F4
Liantang JS17/18E6
Liantang SH17/18E7
Liantang JS17/18D4
Liantang FJ25/26C3
Liantang JX29/30E3
Liantang HN37/38E5
Liantang GX43/44E7

Liantang GX43/44C9
Liantang GD41A3
(Liantang)Nanchang Xian JX29/30C3
Liantuo HB35/36D4
Lianxing HL15/16C3
Lianyin HL15/16A2
Lianyuan Shi HN37/38D4
Lianyun JS17/18B5
Lianyungang JS17/18B5
Lianyungang Shi JS17/18B5
Lianyun Shan HN37/38C6
Lianzhen HEB5/6F4
(Lianzhou)Hepu Xian GX43/44F7
Lianzhou Shi GD39/40B5
Lianzhushan HL15/16E6
Lianhua Feng AH23/24 F5
Liaocheng Shi SD31/32C2
Liaodong Bandao LN11/12E5-D7
Liaodong Wan LN11/12D5
Liaodun XJ63/64D12
Liaogou JS17/18D5
Liao He LN11/12C6
Liaohe Kou LN11/12D6
Liaohe Pingyuan LN69B5-C4
Liaoheyuan JL13/14E6
Liaojiangshi HN37/38E6
Liaolan SD31/32C6
Liaoqiao NX61/62C3
Liaoquan GS57/58C5
Liaotun LN11/12C5
Liaoyang Shi LN11/12C7
Liaoyangwopu LN11/12A7
Liaoyang Xian LN11/12C7
Liaoyuan Shi JL13/14E6
Liaozhong Xian LN11/12C6
Liba GZ49/50B6
Libao JS17/18D6
Libazhuang SX7/8B5
Libei JX29/30D4
Libi Xian SC47/48C4
Libo Xian GZ49/50E6
Libu GS61/62E4
Libu GD39/40B5
Libu GX43/44D9
Licang SD31/32C7
Licangji AH23/24C3
Licha SD31/32C6
Licheng SD31/32C4
(Licheng)Jinhu Xian JS17/18C5
Licheng Xian SX7/8E5
Lichuan GS57/58E7
Lichuan SX7/8F4
Lichuan Shi HB35/36D1
Lichuan Xian JX29/30D4
Licun HEB3/4D4
Licun HEN33/34C4
Licun GX43/44E8
Licun JX29/30F3
Lidang FJ25/26C5
Lidao SD31/32B9
Lidesi AH23/24C2
Lidian JS19/20A2
Lidian SC45/46D4
Lidu SC47/48B4
Lidu SC45/46D6

Liebu SX7/8B3
Liejinba SN55/56G2
Liemianzhen SC45/46C6
Lieshan AH23/24C3
Liexi FJ25/26D3
Lifasheng JL13/14C5
Lifu SC47/48B4
Lifuta HN37/38B3
Ligang JX29/30C3
Ligang ZJ21/22B6
Ligangpu NX61/62B3
Ligao GX43/44C7
Ligeta SX7/8F4
Ligou HEB5/6C2
Liguo JS17/18B3
Liguo SD31/32B5
Lihai ZJ21/22B5
Lihe NX61/62A3
Li He HEN33/34D5
Lihen AH23/24G3
Lihu GX43/44B5
Lihu GD39/40C9
Lihuaping NX61/62D2
Liji HB35/36D7
Liji HI42C3
Liji HEN33/34F7
Lijia SD31/32B5
Lijia SC47/48A4
Lijia LN11/12C6
Lijiacha SN55/56C5
Lijiacun SD31/32C6
Lijiadawan Shuiku NX61/62C3
Lijiadu JX29/30C4
Lijiahe HB35/36E2
Lijiajie SC47/48C3
Lijiakou HEB3/4C3
Lijian GX43/44D6
Lijiang JX29/30D3
Li Jiang GX43/44B8-C8
Lijiang Diqu YN51/52B4
Lijiang Naxizu Zizhixian(Dayan)
  YN51/52B4
Lijiaping HN37/38E4
Lijiaqiao JS17/18E6
Lijiaqiao BJ3/4B3
Lijiaquan NX61/62C4
Lijiashi HB35/36D5
Lijiatun LN11/12E6
Lijiaxiang ZJ21/22B4
Lijiaying HEB5/6B6
Lijiayingzi NM11/12B3
Lijiazhai SD31/32D6
Lijiazhai HEN33/34F6
Lijiazhuang SD31/32E5
Lijie GS57/58F7
Lijin LN11/12C5
Lijin Xian SD31/32B5
Lijunbu NX61/62B3
Lijunbu NX61/62D2
Lijushan JX29/30B5
Likang TW27/28E2
Likou AH23/24G4
Likou JS17/18C4

Lili JS17/18F6
Liling Shi HN37/38D6
Limin SX7/8B4
Liming GX43/44D5
Limingcun SD31/32B9
Liminzhen HEN33/34C7
Limu GX43/44C8
Limu GX43/44B8
Limu HI42B2
Limu Ling HI42B2
Lin'an Shi ZJ21/22B4
Linba SC47/48B5
Lincai HEN33/34D6
Lincang Diqu YN51/52C3-D3
Lincang Xian YN51/52D4
Linchang HI42C1
Linchang Jiao HI42B2
Lincheng ZJ21/22B4
(Lincheng)Lingao Xian HI42B2
Lincheng Shuiku HEB5/6F2
Lincheng Xian HEB5/6F2
(Lincheng)Xuecheng SD31/33E4
Linchi JX29/30E3
Linchuan JX29/30C4
Lindai ZJ19/20C4
Lindai GZ49/50D5
Lindian HB35/36C7
Lindian Xian HL15/16D3
(Lindong)Bairin Zuoqi NM9/10F12
Linfen Diqu SX7/8E3
Linfeng GX43/44D5
Linfen Shi SX7/8E3
Ling'an ZJ19/20C3
Lingang JX29/30B5
Ling'ao GD41A4
Lingaojiao HI42A2
Lingao Xian HI42B2
Lingbao Shi HEN33/34C2
Lingbei GD39/40B5
Lingbi Xian AH23/24C4
Lingcheng JS17/18C4
Lingchuan Xian SX7/8F5
Lingchuan Xian(Gantang) GX43/44B8
Lingda AH19/20B2
Lingdi FJ25/26E2
Lingdi JX29/30C6
Lingdianzhen JS17/18E7
Lingding Yang GD41B2
Lingdong Shuiku GX43/44E7
Linghai Shi LN11/12C5
Linghe SD31/32C6
Linghou ZJ21/22C4
Linghu ZJ21/22B5
Lingjiachang SC47/48C2
Lingjiangkou JX29/30C2
Lingjiaopaozi NM11/12B4
Lingjiaqiao AH23/24C4
Lingjiawan AH19/20C1
Lingjing SX7/8C5
Lingjing HEN33/34C5
Lingkou SN55/56F5
Lingkou ZJ21/22C5
Lingkou HI42B3

Lingkou JS17/18E5
Lingli GX43/44E6
Linglongta LN11/12D3
Lingma GX43/44D5
Lingqiao ZJ21/22B5
Lingqiu Xian SX7/8B6
Ling Qu GX43/44B8
Lingshan GD41A2
Lingshan HEB5/6E2
Lingshan HI42B3
Lingshan SD31/32C7
Ling Shan HEB3/4B2
Lingshan Dao SD31/32D7
Lingshan Wan SD31/32D7
Lingshanwei SD31/32D7
Lingshan Xian GX43/44E7
Lingshi Xian SX7/8E3
Lingshou Xian HEB5/6E2
Lingshui Lizu Zizhixan HI42C3
Lingshui Wan HI42C2
Lingtai Xian GS57/58E8
Lingtou FJ25/26E3
Lingtou HI75E3
Lingui Xian GX43/44B8
Lingwu Shi NX61/62B3
Lingxi HEB5/6D3
Lingxi JX29/30C6
Lingxiadian SD31/32D3
Ling Xian HN37/38E6
Ling Xian SD31/32B3
Lingxiang HB35/36D7
Lingxianmiao SC47/48B2
(Lingxi)Cangnan Xian ZJ21/22E5
(Lingxi)Yongshun Xian HN37/38B2
Lingyang AH23/24F4
Lingyang Xia GD39/40C5
Lingyan Shan JS17/18E6
Lingyansi SD31/32C3
Lingyuan Shi LN11/12C3
Lingyun Xian GX43/44C4
Lingza XZ53/54E11
Linhai HL15/16B3
Linhai Shi ZJ21/22D6
Linhe JS17/18C4
Linhe HE33/34E6
Linhepu NX61/62B3
Linhe Shi NM9/10G6
Linhong Kou JS17/18B5
Linhuaiguan AH23/24D4
Linhuan AH23/24C3
Linjiacun SD31/32D6
Linjiang GS57/58F7
Linjiang SC45/46C7
Linjiang FJ25/26C4
Linjiang JX29/30G2
Linjiang GD39/40C7
Linjiangchang SC47/48C3
Linjianghu JX29/30C5
Linjiang Shi JL13/14F7
Linjiangsi SC45/46C5
Linjiangzhen JX29/30C3
Linjiaping SX7/8D2
Linjiatai LN11/12D7

Linjin   SX7/8F2
Linkou   GZ49/50C4
Linkou   HN37/38E2
Linkou Xian   HL15/16E6
Linli Xian   HN37/38B4
(Linmingguan) Yongnian Xian
   HEB5/6G2
Linnancang   HEB5/6D5
Linpa   HEN33/34E3
Linpien   TW27/28E2
Linping   SN55/56F4
Linpu   ZJ21/22B5
Linpuji   SD31/32D2
Linqi   ZJ21/22C4
Linqi   HEN33/34B5
Linqing Shi   SD31/32C2
Linquan   GZ49/50C4
Linquan Xian   AH23/24C2
Linqu Xian   SD31/32C5
Linruzhen   HEN33/34C4
Linshan   ZJ21/22B5
Linshanhe   HB35/36D7
Linshengpu   LN11/12C7
Linshi   SC45/46D6
Linshui   GS57/58C4
Linshui Xian   SC45/46C6
Linshu Xian   SD31/32E5
Lintan   JX29/30F2
Lintan Xian   GS57/58E6
Lintao Xian   GS57/58E6
Lintingkou   TJ3/4C4
Lintong   SN55/56F5
Lintou   AH23/24E4
Linwang   HI42C2
Linwu   GD41A2
Linwu Nongchang   NX61/62B3
Linwu Xian   HN37/38F5
Linxi   HEB5/6D6
Linxi   GX43/44B7
Linxi   AH23/24G5
Linxi   GD41A2
Linxia Huizu Zizhizhou   GS57/58D6-E6
Lin Xian   SX7/8D2
Linxiang Shi   HN37/38B6
Linxianzhan   HEN33/34A5
Linxia Shi   GS57/58E6
Linxia Xian   GS57/58E6
Linxi Xian   NM9/10F12
Linxi Xian   HEB5/6G3
Linying Xian   HEN33/34D5
Linyi Xian   SD31/32B3
Linyi Xian   SD31/32D5
Linyi Xian   SX7/8F2
Linyou Xian   SN55/56F3
Linyuan   TW27/28E2
Linze   JS17/18C5
Linze Xian(Shahepu)   GS57/58C5
Linzhang Xian   HEB5/6G2
Linzhen   SN55/56D5
Linzheyu   SX7/8C2
Linzhou Shi   HEN33/34A5
Linzhuang   SD31/32B3
Linzi   JS19/20A3   SD31/32C5

Linzijie   SD31/32B3
Linzikou   HN37/38C5
Liping Xian(Defeng)   GZ49/50D8
Lipu   ZJ21/22D6
Lipu   ZJ21/22C4
Lipu Xian   GX43/44C8
Liqianhutyn   LN11/12B7
Liqiao   SC47/48C2
Liqiao   GS57/58E8
Liqizhuang   HEB3/4C4
Liqizhuang   TJ3/4C4
Liquan Xian   SN55/56F4
Liren   JS17/18C4
Lirenpo   SX7/8E2
Li Shan   SX7/8F3
Lishan   HB35/36C6
Li Shan   YN77B4
Li Shan   SN55/56F5
Lishan   TW27/28C3
Lishe Jiang   YN51/52C4
Lishi   SC47/48C3
Lishi   SC47/48C4
Lishi   GD39/40B6
(Lishi)Dingnan Xian   JX29/30G3
Lishimen Shuiku   ZJ21/22C5
Lishiwan   HN37/38F4
Lishi Shi   SX7/8D3
Lishizhen   SC47/48C3
Li Shui   HN37/38B4
Lishui Diqu   ZJ21/22D4
Lishui Shi   ZJ21/22D4
Lishui Xian   JS17/18E5
Lishuping   SX7/8B5
Lishu Xian   JL13/14D5
Lishu   HL15/16E6
Lisong   GX43/44C9
Lisui   BJ3/4B3
Lita   JX29/30D4
Litan   HEB5/6E4
Litang   GX43/44D7
Litang Qu   SC45/46D3
Litang Xian   SC45/46C3
Litan He   JX29/30D4
Litian   JX29/30D2
Litouqiao   AH23/24E5
Litun   HEN33/34E6
Liuan   TW27/28C3
Liuba   GS57/58C6
Liubao   JS17/18C5
Liuba Xian   SN55/56G2
Liubinbu   BJ3/4B3
Liubu   GX43/44D9
Liubu   SD31/32C4
Liucan   HEB5/6E3
Liuchang   GZ49/50D5
Liuchang   HEB5/6F3
Liuche   JX29/30G3
Liuchen   GX43/44D8
Liucheng   ZJ21/22D4
Liucheng Xian(Dabu)   GX43/44C7
Liuchiu   TW27/28E2
Liuchiu Yu   TW27/28E2
Liuchong He   GZ49/50C4

(Liuchuan)Jianhe Xian   GZ49/50D7
Liucun   HEB3/4D3
Liucun   SX7/8E3
Liudaogou   JL13/14F7
Liudaogou   JL13/14F8
Liudaohe   JL13/14D8
Liudaohezi   HEB5/6C5
Liudaojiang   JL13/14F7
Liudaokou   TJ3/4C3
Liudingshan   JL13/14D9
Liudongqiao   AH23/24E6
Liudu   GZ49/50B6
Liudu Jing   NM9/10H5
Liuduo   JS17/18B6
Liuduqiao   HN37/38F5
Liuduzhai   HN37/38D3
Liu'erpu   LN11/12C6
Liufang   JX29/30B4
Liufang   JX29/30D3
Liufangling   HB35/36D7
Liufu   AH23/24D4
Liugezhuang   HEB5/6E4
Liugeznuang   SD31/32C8
Liugong   HI42C2
Liugong Dao   SD31/32B9
Liugou   HEB5/6C6
Liugou Shuiku   XJ63/64C8
Liuguang   GZ49/50D5
Liuguang   HEN33/34B6
Liuguantun   GZ49/50E3
Liugu He   LN11/12D4
Liugusi   HEB3/4D3
Liuhang   SH19/20B4
Liuhe   JL13/14C3
Liuhe   HB35/36D8
Liu He   JL13/14E6
Liu He   HEB5/6C5
Liu He   LN11/12B6
Liuhe   HL15/16E5
Liuhe   JS17/18E7
Liuhe   HEB3/4D3
Liuhe Kou   JS19/20B4
Liuheng   ZJ21/22C7
Liuheng Dao   ZJ21/22C7
Liuhe Xian   JL13/14E6
Liuhezhen   HEN33/34C7
Liuhouji   HB35/36C5
Liuhu   NM9/10E13
Liuhu   SD31/32B5
Liuhuang   GD39/40C9
Liuji   HB35/36C4
Liuji   AH23/24D3
Liujia   JS19/20A4
Liujia   GX43/44C5
Liujia   JX29/30C4
Liujia   HB35/36D3
Liujiachang   HB35/36D4
Liujiafan   AH23/24E4
Liujiage   HB35/36D6
Liujiagou   SD31/32B7
Liujiaguan   JL13/14D4
Liujiahe   SC47/48A3
Liujianfang   LN11/12C6

Liujiang SC47/48B1
Liujiang SC47/48C1
Liu Jiang GX43/44C7
Liujiang Xian(Labao) GX43/44C7
Liujiaping HN37/38B3
Liujiata SX7/8B3
Liujiaxia Shuiku GS57/58E6
Liujiayuan SX7/8E3
Liujiazhai GS61/62D2
Liujiazhuang SD31/32D4
Liujiazhuang SD31/32C7
Liujiazi LN11/12C4
Liujing GX43/44E6
Liukesong HL15/16D4
Liukou AH23/24G4
Liuku YN51/52C3
Liukuei TW27/28D2
Liulaozhuang JS17/18C4
Liulihe BJ3/4C3
Liulimiao BJ3/4B3
Liulin HB35/36C6
Liulin HEN33/34F6
Liulincha HN37/38C4
Liulinji SD31/32D2
Liulinshui BJ3/4C2
Liulin Xian SX7/8D2
Liuliping HB35/36B3
Liulisi SD31/32C3
Liuma GX43/44E8
Liuma GZ49/50E4
Liumaoyuan SN61/62C4
(Liupai)Tian'e Xian GX43/44B5
Liupan Shan GS57/58E8 NX61/62E2
Liuqiao JS19/20A3
Liuqiao SD31/32B5
Liuqu SN55/56F5
Liuquan JS17/18B3
Liuquan HEN33/34C4
Liuquan HEB5/6D4
Liurenba HB35/36E7
Liusha Gang GD39/40F2
Liushahe HN37/38C5
Liushan HEN33/34D4
Liushan GX43/44C7
Liushanzhai SD31/32C5
Liushi JX29/30D1
Liushi ZJ21/22D5
Liushi HEB5/6E3
Liushilipu AH23/24D2
Liushouying HEB5/6D7
Liushu SC47/48B3
Liushuhe JL13/14D8
Liushui JL13/14C5
Liushuidian SN55/56H4
Liushuigou HB35/36C5
Liushukou SX7/8F5
Liushuquan XJ63/64D2
Liushuquan HEB3/4C5
Liusiqiao JX29/30B4
Liusong HEB3/4C4
Liutaizhuang HEB5/6D7
Liutang GX43/44C8
Liutao JS17/18B5

Liutuan HL15/16E5
Liutuan SD31/32C6
Liuwan Dashan GX43/44E7
Liuwang GX43/44E8
Liuwei JS17/18D5
Liuxi SC47/48B5
Liuxia ZJ21/22B5
Liuxiandong GD41A2
Liuxi He GD39/40C6
Liuxihe Shuiku GD41A2
Liuxu GX43/44E6
Liuyang He HN37/38C6
Liuyangpu NX61/62C4
Liuyang Shi HN37/38C6
Liuyin SC47/48C4
Liuyu SX7/8D2
Liuyuan HEB5/6G2
Liuyuan GS57/58B2
Liuyuankou HEN33/34C6
Liuzan HEB5/6D6
Liuzhai GX43/44B5
Liuzhan HL15/16B3
Liuzhao Shan GX43/44D3
Liuzhou Diqu GX43/44C7-D7
Liuzhou Shi GX43/44C7
Liuzhuang SD32/32D2
Liuzigang HB35/36D7
Liwangbu NX61/62D3
Liwu Hsi TW27/28C3
Lixi HB35/36C4
Lixi SC47/48B4
Lixi SC45/46E3
Lixi GD39/40C6
Lixi JX29/30D4
Lixi JX29/30B2
Lixian BJ3/4C3
Li Xian GS57/58E7
Li Xian HEB5/6E3
Li Xian HN37/38B4
Li Xian(Zagunao) SC45/46C4
Lixin HN37/38F5
Lixin FJ25/26D2
Lixindian HEN33/34E6
Lixing AH23/24C2
Lixin NX61/62C2
Lixin Xian AH23/24C3
Lixi'oidain Co QH59/60C2
Lixu JX29/30C4
Liyang ZJ21/22C6
Liyang SX7/8D5
(Liyang)He Xian AH23/24E5
Liyang Shi JS17/18E5
Liye HN37/38C2
Liyi SX7/8F5
Liyong GX43/44C7
Liyuan SX7/8F3
Liyuan GD39/40B7
Liyuan HN37/38F5
(Liyuan)Sangzhi Xian HN37/38B3
Liyuantun HEN33/34B6
Liyue GD41B2
Liyujiang HN37/38F6
Li Yunhe JS17/18C5-D5

Lize SC47/48B4
Lizezhen SD31/32B4
Lizhai JS17/18B2
Lizhai JX29/30B5
Lizhen HEN33/34A6
Lizhi HL15/16E3
Lizhigou HI42C2
Lizhou SC45/46D4
Lizhu ZJ21/22C5
Lizhuang SC47/48D2
Lizhuang AH23/24B3
Lizhuang SC45/46D3
Lizhuangzi NX61/62C3
Lizhuangzi HEB3/4C5
Liziping SC45/46D4
Lizui GD39/40B8
Loinbo Kangri XZ53/54E5
Lonchuan Jiang YN51/52C3
Long'an JX29/30D4
Long'an GX43/44B6
Long'anqiao HL15/16D3
Long'an Xian GX43/44D5
Longbo HI42B2
Longbu JX29/30F3
Longchang GZ49/50D3
Longchang GZ49/50D4
Longchang GZ49/50E4
Longchang GZ49/50D6
Longchang LN11/12D7
Longchang Xian SC45/46D5
Longcheng HN37/38E2
Longchi SC47/48C1
Longchi JS19/20A1
Longchuan GX43/44C4
Longchuan Jiang YN77C3
(Longchuan)Nanhua Xian YN51/52C4
Longchuan Xian YN51/52C2
Longchuan Xian(Laolong) GD39/40B8
Longcun GD39/40C8.
Longde Xian NX61/62E3
Longdongping HN37/38B3
Longdu JS17/18E4
Longfang SN55/56E5
Longfeng HL15/16D3
Longfeng SC47/48A1
Longfengba HB35/36D2
Longfengshan Shuiku HL15/16E4
Longgang LN11/12D4
Longgang GD39/40B9
Longgang JS17/18C6
Longgang JX29/30E3
Longgang JX29/30E4
Longgang SD31/32C5
Longgang JL13/14F9
Longgang GD39/40D7
Longgang HB35/36E7
Longgang Shan JL13/14F6-E7
Longgan Hu HB35/36E8-9
Longgong ZJ21/22E3
Longgu JS17/18B2
Longguan HEB5/6C3
Longguang GX43/44D4
Longguang HI42C2
Longgudu JX29/30D4

Longguji   SD31/32D2
Longgun   HI42B3
Longhai Shi   FJ25/26F3
Longhe   GX43/44D3
Longhe   HL15/16A2
Longhe   HL15/16C3
Longhe   JS19/20A2
Longhekou Shuiku   AH23/24E3
Longhu   GX43/44B8
Longhu   JX29/30D4
Longhua   HEB5/6F4
Longhua   FJ25/26E4
Longhua   GD39/40C7
Longhua   SC47/48D2
Longhua   SX7/8F3
Longhua Xian   HEB5/6B5
Longhui   JX29/30F2
Longhui   SC47/48C2
Longhui Xian(Taohong)   HN37/38D4
Longhuo   GX43/44C3
Longji   JS17/18C4
Longji   JS17/18B4
Longjiang   SC47/48C3
Longjiang   GD39/40D6
Longjiang   HI42B2
Long Jiang   GX43/44C6
Long Jiang   JX29/30D3
Longjiang   GD39/40C9
Longjiang Xian   HL15/16D2
Longjiaoshan   HB35/36E7
Longjiapu   JL13/14C6
Longjiazhai   HN37/38B2
Longjie   SC47/48C2
Longjie   YN51/52B6
Longjie   YN51/52C3
Longjie   YN51/52C4
Longjie   GD39/40B7
Longjiezi   GZ49/50C3
(Longjin)Anyi Xian   JX29/30C3
Longjingguan   HEB3/4B5
Longjing Shi   JL13/14E10
Longjing Shuiku   GD39/40C9
Longju   JS17/18B5
Longjuan   FJ25/26F3
Longjuba   SC45/46C7
Longkangji   AH23/24C3
Long Ke   HK41B3
Longkong   SC47/48C2
Longkou   JX29/30E3
Longkou   SD31/32C4
Longkou   HEN33/34E6
Longkou   HB35/36E6
Longkou Gang   SD31/32B7
Longkou Shi   SD31/32B7
Longlin Gezu Zizhixian(Xinzhou)   GX43/44C3
Longling Xian   YN51/52C3
Longli Xian   GZ49/50D5
Longlou   HI42B3
Longma   HI42B3
Longmen   Hl15/16C4
Longmen   AH23/24F5
Longmen   FJ25/26E2

Longmen   FJ25/26F4
Longmen   HEN33/34C4
Longmen   GD39/40F3
Longmen   GX43/44E5
Longmen   GX43/44E7
Longmen   SN55/56E6
Longmen   GX43/44F6
Longmen   SC45/46C6
Longmen   SC47/48B5
Longmen   SC47/48C4
Longmen   HI42B3
Long Men   SX7/8F2
Longmenchang   HN37/38C7
Longmen Shan   SX7/8F2
Longmen Shan   SC45/46B5
Longmen Shuiku   HEB3/4C2
Longmensuo   HEB5/6C3
Longmen Xian   GD39/40C7
Longming   GX43/44E5
Longmu   GD39/40B8
Longnan Diqu   GS57/58E7-F7
Longnan Xian   JX29/30G2
Longnü   SC47/48B4
Longpan   SC47/48B3
Longpeng   YN51/52D5
Longping   HB35/36D3
Longping   HB35/36E8
Longping   GD39/40B5
Longping   GZ49/50C6
Longqiao   HI42B3
Longqiao   SC47/48B2
Longquan   JL13/14E7
Longquan   HL15/16D4
Longquan   SC47/48B3
(Longquan)Danzhai Xian   GZ49/50D6
(Longquan)Fenggang Xian   GZ49/50C6
Longquanguan   HEB5/6E1
Longquan Shan   SC47/48B2
Longquan Shi   ZJ21/22D4
Longquan Xi   ZJ21/22D4
Longquanyi   SC47/48B2
Longriba   SC45/46B4
Longshan   FJ25/26F3
Longshan   ZJ19/20C4
Longshan   SD31/32C4
Longshan   GD39/40C6
Longshan   SC45/46E5
Long Shan   SN55/56F2
Longshanji   AH23/24C3
Longshan Xian(Min'an)   HN37/38B2
Longsheng   GD39/40D5
Longsheng   GX43/44E8
Longsheng   SC47/48B3
Longsheng Gezu Zizhixian   GX43/44B8
Longshengzhuang   NM9/10K23
Longshi   SC47/48B4
(Longshi)Ninggang Xian   JX29/30E1
Longshou Shan   NM9/10H3
                     GS57/58C5
Longshui   GX43/44A8
Longshui   SC47/48C3
Longtai   SC47/48B2
Longtaichang   SC47/48B3

Longtan   HN37/38D3
Longtan   SC47/48C2
Longtan   GX43/44F7
Longtan   SC45/46D6
Longtan   JS17/18D5
Longtang   GZ49/50C7
Longtang   HI42B3
Longtang   HN37/38C4
Longtang   HEN33/34C7
Longtang   JX29/30G3
Longtan He   SC47/48C5
Longtanhe   HN37/38B4
Longtanshan   JL13/14D7
Longtanshui   HN35/36F4
Longtansi   SC47/48B2
Longtansi   AH23/24D2
Longtanxu   HN37/38F5
Longtian   FJ25/26E5
Longtian   HN37/38C4
Longtian   GD39/40B8
Longtian   GZ49/50C7
Longting   SD31/32D4
Longting   SN55/56G3
Longting Shuiku   FJ25/26D4
Longtou   NM9/10C14
Longtou   JX29/30F3
Longtou   GX43/44C6
Longtou   GX43/44C7
Longtou   GX43/44E5
Longtou'an   HN37/38D3
Longtou Jiang   GZ49/50D6
Longtousha   GD39/40E2
Longtou Shan   GX43/44D6
Longwan   ZJ21/22E5
Longwan   AH23/24F3
Longwang   JL13/14C5
Longwangchan   SX7/8E2
Longwangji   HB35/36B4
Longwangmiao   HEB5/6G3
Longwangmiao   LN11/12D7
Longwangmiao   HL15/16E7
Longwangmiao   AH23/24C4
Longwangmiao   SD31/32E3
Longwang Shan   ZJ19/20C2
Longwangtang   AH23/24D2
Longwo   GD39/40C8
Longwu   YN51/52C5
Longxi   SC47/48C5
Longxi   GZ49/50C6
Long Xian   SN55/56F2
(Longxian)Wengyuan Xian   GD39/40B7
Longxi He   SC47/48C5
Longxing   SC47/48C4
Longxing   GZ49/50B6
Longxingshi   HN37/38E6
Longxi Shan   FJ25/26D3
Longxi Xian   GX57/58E7
Longxue Dao   GD41A2
(Longxu)Gangwu Xian   GX43/44D9
Longxu He   GX43/44D4
Longyan   GX43/44D7

Longyang Xia   QH59/60B7
Longyan Shi   FJ25/26E3

Longyao Xian HEB5/6F2
Longyou ZJ21/22C4
Longyuanba JX29/30G2
Longyuankou JX29/30E2
Longzhao HL15/16E6
Longzhao JL13/14B4
Longzhaogou LN11/12D8
Longzhen SC47/48B1
Longzhen SX7/8E5
Longzhen HL15/16C4
Longzhong HB35/36B5
Longzhou Xian GX43/44 E4
Lop Nur XJ63/64 E11
Lop Xian XJ63/64G6
Lo Shue Leng HK41A3
Lo So Shing HK41B3
Lotung TW27/28C3
Loubanzhai SX7/8C4
Loude SD31/32D4
Loudi Diqu HN37/38D4
Loudi Shi HN37/38D4
Loufan Xian SX7/8C3
Lougou SX7/8B3
Loujie JL13/14E7
Loushan Guan GZ49/50B5
Lou Shui HN37/38B3
Loutang SH19/20B4
Louwang JS17/18C5
Louzhuang AH23/24C4
Louzidian NM5/6A7
Luancheng GX43/44E6
Luancheng Xian HEB5/6F2
Luanchuan Xian HEN33/34D3
Lu'an Diqu AH23/24D3-E3
Luanhaizi QH59/60C3
Luanhe HEB5/6C5
Luan He HEB5/6D6
Luanhe Kou HEB5/6D7
Luanjing NM9/10I5
Luannan Xian(Bencheng) HEB5/6D6
Luanping Xian HEB5/6C5
Lu'an Shi AH23/24E3
Luan Xian HEB5/6D6
Luanzhuang SN55/56G6
Luban GZ49/50C5
Lubang Ju NM9/10K17
Lubao GD39/40C5
(Lubei)Jarud Qi NM9/10E13
Lubiao YN51/52C5
Lubu GD39/40C5
Lücaoshan QH59/60B4
Luchang SC45/46E4
Lucheng HN37/38B6
Lücheng JS17/18E5
Lucheng GX43/44C4
Lucheng SX7/8F5
Lucheng Shi SX7/8E5
Luchu TW27/28E2
Luchuan Xian GX43/44E8
Lüchun Xian YN51/52D5
Luci ZJ21/22C4
Lücongpo HB35/36D3
Lucun GX43/44E6

Lucun AH23/24F6
Lucun SD31/32C5
Ludao HL15/16F5
Ludian Xian(Wenping) YN51/52B5
Luding(Jagamka)Xain SC45/46D4
Luduo JS17/18C5
Lüeping SC47/48A2
Lüeyang Xian SN55/56G2
Lufeng FJ25/26F2
Lufeng Shi GD39/40D8
Lufengcun YN51/52C5
Lufeng Xian(Jinshan) YN51/52C5
Lugang AH23/24E5
Lügongbao HEB5/6E4
Lugouqiao BJ3/4C3
Lugu SC45/46D4
Lugu XZ53/54C5
Luguan HN37/38D4
Luguan AH23/24F3
Lugu Hu SC45/46E3 YN51/52B4
Luguo JL13/14E10
Lu He SN55/56C5
Luhe HL15/16D4
Lühe YN51/52C4
Lühedian HEN33/34E6
Lühekou SN55/56H5
Luhe Xian JS17/18D4
Luhe Xian JS17/18D4
Luhe Xian GD39/40C8
Luhezhen JS19/20B4
Luhongshi HN37/38E4
(Luhua)Heishui Xian SC45/46B4
Luhuatai NX61/62B3
Luhun Shuiku HEN33/34C4
Luhuo(Zhaggo)Xian SC45/46C3
Lujiabang JS17/18E7
Lujiabangzhan JS19/20B4
Lujiabu ZJ21/22C6
Lujiagang JS19/20C3
Lujiang Xian AH23/24E4
Lujiashan HB35/36C6
Lujiatun LN11/12D6
Lüjiazhai SD31/32C4
Lujiazhuang SX7/8D5
Lujing GX43/44E8
Lu Jing NM57/58B4
Lujing SN55/56E6
Lüjing GS57/58E7
Lukang TW27/28C2
Lukou JX29/30D2
Lukoupu HN37/38B6
Lukoushe HN37/38C6
(Lukou)Zhuzhou Xian HN37/38D6
Lukouzi AH23/24D3
Lükqün XJ63/64D10
Lüliang Diqu SX7/8C3-D3
Lüliangqiao JS17/18C5
Lüliang Shan SX7/8C4-D3
Luliang Xian YN51/52C5
Luling Guan HEN33/34C2 SN55/56F6
Lulong Xian HEB5/6D6
Lulou JS17/18B2
Luluo HEB5/6F1

Luma HI42C3
Lumadeng YN51/52B3
Lumajangdong XZ53/54C3
Lumu JS17/18E6
Lunan Shan SC45/46E4

Lungchien TW27/28C3
Lunggar XZ53/54D4
Lunggar Shan XZ78C2-3
Lung Kwu Chau HK41B2
Lung Kwu Tan HK41B2
Lungsang XZ53/54E7
Lungsang Qu XZ78B3
Lungtien TW27/28D2
Lungucun GS61/62C1
Lunhe HL15/16D4
Luning SC45/46D3
Lunpei TW27/28D2
Luntai(Bügür)Xian XJ63/64E8
Lunzhen SD31/32C3
Luo'ao JX29/30F3
Luoba SC47/48C1
Luobai GX43/44E5
Luobei Xian(Fengxiang) HL15/16D6
Luobiao SC45/46D5
Luobie GZ49/50D4
Luobu GX43/44C7
Luobuzhuang XJ63/64F10
Luochanghe AH23/24E4
Luocheng GS57/58C4
Luocheng SC47/48C2
Luocheng Mulaozu Zizhixian
   GX43/44C6
Luochuan NX61/62D3
Luochuan Xian SN55/56E5
Luocun SX7/8E2
Luodai HI42B1
Luodai SC47/48B2
Luodian SH17/18E7
Luodian HB35/36C6
Luodian Xian GZ49/50E5
Luoding Jiang GD39/40C4-D4
Luoding Shi GD39/40D4
Luodong GX43/44C6
Luodong Shuiku GX43/44C6
Luodou Sha GD39/40F3
Luoduzhen SC47/48B4
Luofa HEB3/4C3
Luofang FJ25/26E2
Luofang FJ25/26E3
Luofu GD39/40B8
Luofu SN55/56F5
Luofu GX43/44C5
Luofu Shan GD39/40B8-C7
Luogang GD39/40B8
Luogang GD41A2
Luoguhe HL15/16A1
Luohan Jiao GD41A4
Luohe SN55/56H5
Luo He HEN33/34C3 SN55/56F6
Luohe Shi HEN33/34D6
Luoheya SD31/32D5
Luohong HN37/38D4

Luohuang SC47/48C4
Luohui Qu SN55/56F5-6
Luoji AH23/24C3
Luoji AH23/24D4
Luoji HI42B2
Luojia SC47/48B4
Luojiachang SC47/48B4
Luo Jiang SC47/48A2
Luojiang Xian SC45/46 C5
Luojiangkou SC47/48A5
Luojiaqu SX7/8C3
Luojiawa HEB5/6C2
Luojiazhuang SD31/32C5
Luojin GX43/44B8
Luojing SH19/20B4
Luojing GD39/40D4
Luojiu HN37/38D2
Luokan YN51/52B6
Luokou SD31/32C3
Luokou JX29/30E4
Luokun GZ49/50E5
Luoling AH23/24F4
Luolong SC47/48D2
Luolong GZ49/50A6
Luolou SD31/32D2
Luolou GX43/44C4
Luoma Hu JS17/18B4
Luoman GX43/44C7
Luomen GS57/58E7
Luomen ZJ21/22B7
Luonan Xian(Luonan) SN55/56F6
Luoning Xian HEN33/34C3
Luoping SC47/48C1
Luoping Xian(Luoxiong) YN51/52C6
Luoqi SC45/46D6
Luoqiao FJ25/26D5
Luoqiao JX29/30C5
Luoqing Jiang GX43/44B7-C7
Luoquanwan NX61/62C2
Luorong GX43/44C7
Luoshan HB35/36E6
Luoshan Xian HEN33/34E6

Luoshe ZJ19/20C3
Luoshi JX29/30C3
Luoshi SC47/48A4
Luoshuihe SX7/8B6
Luoshuiqian HB35/36D1
Luotang JX29/30D3
Luotang JX29/30E2
Luotian Xian HB35/36D8
Luotun SD31/32D3
Luotuo ZJ21/22C6
Luotuodian HEN33/34E5
Luotuoquan GS57/58B3
Luotuoshan JL13/14D10
Luotuoying LN11/12C4
Luowa NX61/62D3
Luowang HEN33/34C6
Luowenba SC45/46C6
Luowenyu HEB3/4B4
Luowenzao SX7/8A5
Luoxi GX43/44C6

Luoxi JX29/30B2
Luoxiao Shan JX29/30D1-E2
　　　　　　HN37/38D6-E6
(Luoxiong)Luoping Xian YN51/52C6
Luoxiu GX43/44C7
Luoxiu GX43/44D8
Luoxu GX43/44D6
Luoxue YN51/52B5
Luoya GX43/44C6
Luoyang JS19/20B3
Luoyang FJ25/26F4
Luoyang GX43/44C6
Luoyangdian HB35/36C6
Luoyang Shan GX75C3
Luoyang Shi HEN35/36C6
(Luoyang)Taishun Xian ZJ21/22E4
Luoyixi HN37/38C2
Luoyuan Wan FJ25/26D5
Luoyuan Xian FJ25/26D5
Luoyukou SX7/8C2
Luoyun GX43/44D8
Luoze He YN51/52B5-6 GZ49/50C3
Luozhen SD31/32B5
Luozhen SH55/56H3
Luozhou FJ25/26E5
Luozhuang SD31/32E5
Luozigou JL13/14D11
Lupanshui Shi GZ49/50D3
Luping GZ49/50D6
Luqiao AH23/24D4
Luqiao SD31/32D3
Luqiao ZJ21/22D6
Lüqiao HEB5/6E5
Luquan Shi HEB5/6C2
Luquan Yizu Miaozu Zizhixian YN51/52C5
Luqu Xian(Ma'ai) GS57/58E6
(Luring)Gêrzê Xian XZ53/54C5
Lushan TW27/28C3
Lu Shan JX29/30B3
Lushan GZ49/50D6
Lu Shan SD31/32C5
Lushan Xian SC45/46C4
Lushan Xian HEN33/34D4
(Lushar)Huangzhong Xian QH59/60B7
Lushi HB35/36D6
Lushi SC47/48B4
Lushi YN51/52C3
Lushikou ZJ21/22C5
Lushi Xian HEN33/34C3
Lu Shui JX29/30D2
Lu Shui HB35/36E6-7
Lu Shui HN37/38D6
Lushui HN37/38E6
Lushuihe JL13/14E8
Lushui Shuiku HB35/36E7
Lushui Xian YN51/52C3
Lüshun LN11/12F5
Lüsi JS17/18D7
Lüsi Gang JS19/20A4
Lusikou JX29/30C4
Lusi Yu FJ25/26E5
Lutai HEN33/34D7
(Lutai)Ninghe Xian TJ3/4C4

Lutai Nongchang TJ3/4C4
Lütan HEN33/34C6
Lutang HN37/38F5
Lutao TW27/28E3
Lu Tao(Huoshao Tao) TW27/28E3
Lutian JX29/30C4
Lütian GD39/40C6
Luting He JS17/18D5
Lütingyi AH23/24E4
Lutou HB35/36B5
Luwo GX43/44D6
Luwu GX43/44E6
Luxi FJ25/26F3
Luxi Xian JX29/30D2
Luxi SC47/48B4
Luxi SC45/46C5
Lüxia FJ25/26D6
Lüxiang SH19/20C4
Lu Xian(Xiaoshi) SC45/46D5
Luxi Dao ZJ21/22E6
Luxikou HB35/36E6
Luxi Shi (Mangshi) YN51/52C3
Luxi Xian(Wuxu) HN37/38C3
Luxi Xian(Zhongshu) YN51/52C5
Luxu JS17/18E6
Luxu GX43/44D7
Luyang HN37/38D3
Luyang GS57/58D7
Lüyangyi LN11/12C5
Lüyanyi HB35/36B5
Luya Shan SX7/8C3
Luyeh TW27/28E3
Luyimiao HEN33/34D4
Luyi Xian HEN33/34D7
Luyuan JS19/20B3
Lüyuan NM9/10G3
Lu Yunhe SD31/32C2-D3
Luzhai Xian GX43/44C7
Luzhen AH23/24E3
Luzhi JS17/18E6
Luzhi GZ49/50D4
Lüzhi Jiang YN77C3
Luzhi Tequ(Xiayingpan) GZ49/50D4
Luzhou Shi SC45/46D5
Luzhu ZJ19/20D2
Luzui GD41A4

M

(Ma'ai)Luqu Xian GS57/58E6
Ma'an ZJ21/22B5
Ma'an HB35/36B3
Ma'anshan JL13/14D6
Ma'anshan GZ49/50E4
Ma'anshan Shi AH23/24E5
Ma'ao JX29/30B2
Maba JS17/18D4
(Mabai)Maguan Xian YN51/52D6
Mabang GX43/44C2
(Maba)Qujiang Xian GD39/40B6
Mabei GD39/40C7
Mabi FJ25/26D5
Mabi SX7/8F4
Mabian He SC45/46D4

Maḥian Yizu Zizhixian   SC45/46D4
Mabie He   GD49/50E3
Mabu   JX29/30D3
Mabu   ZJ21/22E5
Macao   MC41B2
(Machali)Madoi Xian   QH59/60C6
Machang   HEB5/6E4
Machang   SX7/8E5
Machang   LN11/12B3
Machang   JS17/18B5
Machang   GZ49/50D5
Machang   GZ49/50C5
Machangji   AH23/24C4
Machang Jianhe   TJ3/4D4
Machangping   GZ49/50D6
Machangying   BJ3/4B3
Machebu   ZJ21/22B4
Macheng Shi   HB35/36C8
Machi   SN55/56H4
Machikou   BJ3/4B3
Machong   GD41A2
Machunbu   NX61/62D2
Macun   SX7/8F4
Macun   HI42B3
Madang   JL13/14F6
Madang   JX29/30B4
Madao   SN55/56G2
Madaotou   SN7/8B4
Madeng   YN51/52B3
Madi   GX43/44B8
Madian   HEB5/6E3
Madian   JS17/18D5
Madian   AH23/24C3
Madian   AH23/23D3
Madian   SD31/32C7
Madida   JL13/14E11
Madigou   SN55/56A7
Madihui   SX7/8D3
Madiyi   HN37/38C3
Madoi   QH59/60C5
Madoi Xian(Machali)   QH59/60C6
Madong   GX43/44D8
Madongchuan   SN55/56D5
Maduqiao   HN37/38E4
Ma'erzhuang   NX61/62C3
Mafan   HEN33/34F6
Mafang   BJ3/4B4
Mafang   SX7/8C3
Mafang   SX7/8D5
Mafeng He   JS19/20A4
Mafujiang   HN37/38E6
Mafuxiazi   NM61/62C2
Magezhuang   SD31/32C6
Magezhuang   SD31/32C7
(Magitang)Jainca Xian   QH59/60C7
Magong   GD39/40D8
Magu   GZ49/50D3
Maguan   SC47/48B5
Maguan Xian   YN51/52D6
Magui   GD39/40D4
Magushan   JX29/30D4
Magutian   HEN33/35E5
Mahai   QH59/60A4

Mahao   JL13/14D9
Mahe   GS57/58E7
Mahuanggou   QH59/60B4
Mahuanggou   NM61/62C2
Mahuangshan   NX61/62C4
Mahuiling   JX29/30B3
Maichen   GD39/40F2
Maihao   HI42B3
Maiji Shan   GS57/58F8
Mailing   GX43/44B9
Maima   GS57/58F6
(Maindong)Coqên Xian   XZ53/54D5
Mainkung   XZ53/54E12
Mainling Xian(Tungdor)   XZ53/54E10
Mainri Xueshan   YN51/52A3
Mai Po   HK41B3
Maishi   HB35/36E6
Maiwang   HB35/36D6
Maixie   JX29/30D3
Maiyuan   FJ25/26E3
Maizhokunggar Xian(Kunggar)
    XZ53/54E8
Maji   SD31/32D2
Maji   JS17/18D4
Majia   GZ49/50D3
Majiadazhuang   NX61/62E3
Majiadian   TJ3/4C4
(Majiadian)Zhijiang Shi   HB35/36D4
Majiagang   HL15/16E7
Majiagaozhuang   NX61/62D3
Majiahe   HN37/38D6
Majia He   SD31/32B3-4
Majiahewan   NX61/62C2
Majian   ZJ21/22C4
Majiang   GX43/44D9
Majiang Xian(Xingshan)   GZ49/50D6
Majiaoba   SC45/46B5
Majiaqu   NX61/62C3
Majiatan   NX61/62C3
Majiawan   NX61/62D2
Majiaxi   SC47/48B2
Majiazao   SX7/8A6
Majiazhou   JX29/30E2
Majiazi   LN11/12B3
Majie   YN51/52C5
Majie   YN51/52D6
Majie   SN55/56G5
Majin   ZJ21/22C3
Majing'ao   HN37/38C2
Majin Xi   ZJ21/22C3
Majishan   ZJ19/20C5
Majishan   JS17/18E6
Majitang   HN37/38C4
Majuanzi   LN13/14F5
Majuqiao   BJ3/4C3
Makou   JX29/30C3
Makou   HB35/36D6
Makou   YN51/52B5
(Makung)Penghu Hsien   TW27/28D1
Malan   SD31/32C7
Malanguan   HEB3/4B4
Malanyu   HEB5/6C5
Malanzhen   SN55/56E4

Malian   HL15/16C6
Malianchuan   NX61/62E2
Maliang   HB35/36D5
Maliangji   AH23/24B3
Maliangping   HB35/36C4
Malian He   GS57/58E8
Malianjing   GS57/58C5
Malianjing   GS57/58B2
Maliantan   NX61/62A3
Malianzhuang   SD31/32B7
Malin   HN37/38E3
Maling   JX29/30F3
Maling   GX43/44C8
Maling   GZ49/50E3
Maling   GS57/58D8
Maling Guan   HEB5/6F1   SX7/8D5
Malipo Xian   YN51/52D6
Maliu   SC47/48A5
Malong He   YN77C3
Malong Xian   YN51/52C5
Malu   GS57/58E8
Malu   GX43/44E8
Malu   GS57/58E6
Malukou   HN37/38C4
Malutang   YN51/52B5
Ma Mei Ha   HK41A3
Mamiao   SD31/32D3
Mamingzhen   YN51/52C5
Mamuchi   SD31/32D5
Manas He   XJ63/64C8
Manas Hu   XJ63/64C8
Manas Xian   XJ63/64C9
Mancheng Xian   HEB5/6E3
Manchou   TW27/28E2
Manchuanguan   SN55/56G6
(Mandalt)Sonid Zuoqi   NM9/10F9
Manduhu   LN11/12C6
Mangbu   YN51/52B6
Mangchang   GX43/44B5
Mangdang Shan   HEN33/34C8
Manghe   HEN33/34B4-C4
Mang Kung Uk   HK41B3
Mangnai   QH59/60B2
Mangnai Zhen   QH59/60A2
Mangniu He   HL69A6
Mangniu He   LN11/12B4-C4
(Mangra) Guinan Xian   QH59/60C7
Mangra Qu   QH80C4
(Mangshi)Luxi Xian   YN51/52C3
Mangu   YN51/52D4
Mangui   NM9/10A14
Mangzhangdian   HEN33/34E6
Manhao   YN51/52D5
Man He   HB35/36C5
Mani   XZ53/54B6
Maniao   HI42B2
Maniganggo   SC45/46C2
Mani Qagan Tungge   NM9/10G3
Manjiang   JL13/14F8
Manjing   SC47/48C2
Manshui   HB35/36E2
Manshuihe   AH23/24E2
Mantou Shan   SX7/8B4

Manyunjie   YN51/52C2
Manzhouli Shi   NM9/10C11
Manzhuang   SD31/32C4
Mao'an   HI42C2
Maoba   HB35/36D2
Maoba   HB35/36E2
Maoba   GZ49/50C5
Maobaguan   SN55/56H4
Maocaojie   HN37/38B5
Maocaopu   GZ49/50C5
Maochang   GZ49/50D5
Maochengzi   JL13/14D5
Maocifan   HB35/36C5
Maocun   JS17/18B3
Maocun   FJ25/26E2
Maodao   HI42C2
Maodian   JX29/30F3
Maodianzi   LN11/12D8
Maodongqiao   HN37/38E5
Mao'ergai   SC45/46B4
Mao'er Shan   GX43/44B8
Mao'ershan   HL15/16E4
Mao'ertou   SC47/48C4
Mao'er Xia   SC47/48C4
Maogan   HI42C2
Maogang   HN37/38B3
Maogang   GD39/40D5
Maogong   GZ49/50D7
Maohutang   HB35/36D4
Maoji   HEN33/34E5
Maoji   AH23/24D3
Maojiacun Shuiku   YN51/52B5
Maojiagedu   NM9/10K19
Maojialing   JX29/30C5
Maojianshan Shuiku   AH23/24F3
Maojiaping   NX61/62E2
Maojiazao   SX7/8B5
Maojindu   SX7/8G3
Maojing   GS57/58D8
Maojunxu   HN37/38F5
Maokui Shan   LN11/12D7
Maolan   YN51/52C4
Maolin   JL13/14D4
Maolin   NM15/16F2
Maolin   TW27/28E2
Maolin   AH23/24F5
Maoling   GX43/44F6
Maomaodong   GZ49/50D5
Maomao Shan   GS80B4
Maoming Shi   GD39/40E3
Maoniugou   SC45/46C3
Maoniupo   XZ53/54B6
Maoniushan   QH59/60B5
Maoping   SC47/48C1
Maoping   HB35/36D3
Maoping   JX29/30G3
Maoping   SN55/56H5
Maoping   JX29/30D2
Maoping   JX29/20E2
Maoping   HN37/38B2
Maoping   GZ49/50C6
Maopitou   TW27/28F2
Maoqiao   SC47/48C1

Maoshan   HEB5/6C5
Mao Shan   JS17/18E5
Maoshan   JX29/30G2
Maosheng   GD41A2
Maoshi   HB35/36E6
Maosipu   HN37/38B5
Maotai   GZ49/50C5
Maotanchang   AH23/24E3
Maotian   HB35/36D2
Maotiao He   GZ49/50D5
Maotou Yang   ZJ21/22D6-7
Maotuo Shan   YN51/52C4
Mao Xian(Fengyi)   SC45/46C4
Maoxing   HL15/16E3
Maoyang   ZJ21/22E4
Maòyang   HI42C2
Maoyanma   HEB3/4D3
Maoying   GZ49/50E5
Mao Yu   TW27/28D1
Maozhou   HEB5/6E4
Maozui   HB35/36D6
Mapam Yumco   XZ53/54D3
Mapengwan   JS17/18D5
Maping   HB35/36C6
Maping   GX43/44C7
Mapo   JS17/18B3
Mapo   GX43/44E8
Mapo   SD31/32D3
Mapu   FJ25/26F3
Maqên   XZ53/54D8
Maqên Kangri   QH59/60C6
Maqên Xian(Dawu)   QH59/60C7
Maqiao   HB35/36C3
Maqiao   XJ63/64C9
Maqiaohe   HL15/16E6
Maqiaoji   HEN33/34D8
Maqu   GS57/58E8
Maquan He(Damqog Zangbo)
   XZ53/54D4-E4
Maqu Xian(Nyinma)   GS57/58E6
Margai Caka   XZ53/54B6
Margyang   XZ53/54E7
Markam Shan   XZ53/54D12-E12
Markam Xian(Gartog)   XZ53/54E12
Markit Xian   XJ63/64F4
Markog He   QH59/60D7   SC45/46B3
Marmê   XZ53/54C4
Masanjia   LN11/12C7
Masha   FJ25/26C3
Mashan   ZJ19/20C3
Mashan   HL15/16E6
Mashang   SD31/32C4
Mashankou   HEN33/34D4
Mashan Xian   GX43/44D6
Mashanzhan   LN11/12C4
Mashenqiao   TJ3/4B4
Mashi   GD39/40A7
Mashidian   SD31/32B8
Mashikou   HEB5/6C2
Mashiping   HEN33/34D4
Mashi Shuiku   GX43/44B7
Mashou   SX7/8D5
Mashui   GD39/40D4

Masi   GX43/44C6
Masong   SD31/32C5
Mataian   TW27/28D3
(Mataigou)Taole Xian   NX61/62B3
Matajing   SC45/46D4
Matang   JS17/18D7
Matang   YN51/52D6
Matang   HN37/38B6
Matao   NX61/62D2
Matian   GZ49/50D6
Matian   SX7/8E5
Matian   HN37/38B6
Matianxu   HN37/38E5
Matizi   SC45/46B4
Matou   BJ3/4C3
Matou   HEB5/6G2
Matou   HEB5/6D4
Matou   HEB5/6F4
Matou   JX29/30B3
Matou   SD31/32E5
Matou   TW27/28D2
Matou   FJ25/26E4
Matoucheng   AH23/24D4
Matoucun   HEB3/4C2
Matouji   AH23/24D3
Matouji   SD31/32D2
Matoujie   AH23/24F5
Matouli   HEB5/6F3
(Matou)Pingguo Xian   GX43/44D5
Matoushan   GZ49/50B6
Matouying   HEB5/6D6
Matsu Liehtao   FJ25/26D6
Matsu Tao   FJ25/26D5
Mawan   GD41B4
Ma Wan   HK41B3
Mawang   SC45/46D7
Mawangtang   ZJ19/20C3
Mawei   FJ25/26E5
Mawei   GZ49/50E6
Mawu   SC45/46D7
Mawu   SC47/48C5
Maxi   GD41B1
Maxiang   FJ25/26F4
Maxiang   HEN33/34E6
Maxian Shan   GS80C4
Maxipu   HN37/38C3
Maxu   GD39/40C4
Maya   GS57/58F6
Mayan   HL15/16E5
Mayang   HB35/36D6
Mayang Miaozu Zizhixian   HN37/38D2
Mayanhe   GS57/58E7
Mayaqiao   AH23/24F4
Ma Yau Tong   HK41B3
Mayidui   YN51/52C4
Mayi He   HL15/16E5
Maying   QH59/60B8
Maying   GS57/58E7
Mayu   ZJ21/22E5
Mayu   HEB5/6F3
Mayum La   XZ53/54D4
Mazar   XJ63/64G4
Mazartag   XJ81/D3-4

Mazartag XJ63/64F6
Mazhan ZJ21/22E5
Mazhan SD31/32C5
Mazhangfang LN11/12D4
Mazhaozhen SN55/56F4
Mazhen SN55/56B6
Mazhonghe LN11/12B8
Mazhou JX29/30F3
Ma Zhou GD41A2
Mazhu ZJ21/22B6
Mazhuang HEN33/34E6
Mazhuang SD31/32D5
Mazhuang HEB3/4C3
Mazong Dao GD41B1
Mazong Shan GS57/58B3
Mêdog Xian XZ53/54E10
Mei'an HI42B3
Meichang TJ3/4C4
Meicheng ZJ21/22C4
(Meicheng)Qianshan Xian AH23/24F3
Meichengzhen HN37/38C4
Meichi ZJ21/22C5
Meichuan HB35/36D8
Meichuan GS57/58E7
Meichuan Shuiku HB35/36D8
Meicun AH19/20C2
Meicun JS19/20B3
Meidaizhao NM9/10K20
Meifeng ZJ19/20C2
Meige GD39/40D6
Meigeng AH23/24F4
Meigu Xian SC45/46D4
Meihekou Shi JL13/14E6
Meihua FJ25/26D5
Meihua GD39/40A6
Meihuaxu HN37/38F4
Mei Jiang JX29/30E3
Mei Jiang GD39/40B9
Meijie AH23/24F4
Meikeng GD39/40B7
Meilan GD39/40G5
Meili JS17/18E6
Meilin AH23/24F6
Meilin JX29/30C3
Meilin FJ25/26F3
Meilin ZJ21/22C6
(Meilin)Gan Xian JX29/30F3
Meilisi HL15/16D2
Meilong GD39/40D8
Meinung TW27/28E2
Meipu HB35/36A4
Meiqiao AH23/24C4
Meiren HI42B3
Meishan TW27/28D2
Meishan HI42C2
Meishan FJ25/26E4
Meishan FJ25/26E3
Meishan Diqu SC45/46D4
(Meishan)Jinzhai Xian AH23/24E2
Meishan Shuiku AH23/24E2
Meishan Xian SC45/46C4
Meishuikeng FJ25/26E3
Meitai HI42B2

Meitanba HN37/38C5
Meitan Xian(Yiquan) GZ49/50C6
Meitian HN37/38F5
Meiting HI42B3
Meixi HL15/16D5
Meixi AH23/24F4
Meixi ZJ21/22B4
Meixi GX43/44A8
Meixi GD41B2
Meixia HI42B2
Mei Xian SN55/56F3
Meixian FJ25/26D4
Meixian HN37/38C6
Mei Xian(Fuda) GD39/40B9
(Meixing)Xiaojin(Zainlha)Xian
   SC45/46C4
Meiyao JL13/14B2
Meiyu SC45/56E3
Meiyuan JS19/20B3
Meiyuan ZJ21/22D4
Meiyukou SX7/8A5
Meiyu Yang ZJ21/22C7
Meizhou FJ25/26G3
Meizhou Dao FJ25/26E5
Meizhou Shi GD39/40B8
Meizhou Wan FJ25/26E5-F5
Meizhu AH23/24E6
Meizhuang JX29/30C4
Melhit NM11/12A6
Melmeg JL13/14B4
Mêmar Co XZ53/54B4
Mencun SD31/32C6
Mend NM13/14D4
Meng'a YN51/52D3
Mengba GS57/58E8
Mengban YN51/52D4
Mengcheng NX61/62C3
Mengcheng Xian AH23/24C3
Mengcun GX43/44D7
Mengcun Huizu Zizhixian HEB5/6E5
Mengdingjie YN51/52D3
(Mengdong)Cangyuan Vazu Zizhixian
   YN51/52D3
Mengdong He HN37/38B2
Mengdu GZ49/50B5
Mengfeng SX7/8D4
Menggongshi HN37/38D4
Mengguying HEB5/6B2
Menghai Xian YN51/52E4
Menghe JS17/18D5
Menghun YN51/52E4
Mengji AH23/24D3
Mengjiagang HL15/16D6
Mengjialou HEN33/34E3
Mengjiang GX43/44D8
Meng Jiang GZ49/50E5
Meng Jiang GX43/44D8
Mengjiawan NX61/62C1
Mengjiawan SN55/56B5
Mengjin He JS19/20B2
Mengjin Xian(Changhua) HEN33/34C4
Mengkeshan HL15/16A3
Mengku YN51/52D3

(Menglang)Lancang Lahuzu Zizhixian
   YN51/52D3
Mengla Xian YN51/52E4
Menglian Daizu Lahuzu Vazu Zizhixian
   YN51/52D3
Menglianggu SD31/32D5
(Mengliejie)Jiangcheng Hanizu Yizu
   Zizhixian YN51/52D4
Menglong YN51/52E4
Menglun YN51/52E4
Mengman YN51/52D4
Mengmiao HEN33/34D6
Mengniushao LN11/12A8
Mengpeng YN51/52E4
Mengquan TJ3/4C4
Meng Shan SD31/32D4-5
Mengshan Xian GX43/44C8
Mengsheng YN51/52D3
Mengsi SD31/32B4
Mengtuan SD31/32C6
Mengu HB35/36B3
Mengwang YN51/52D4
Mengxi HN37/38B4
Mengzhou Shi HEN33/34 C4
Mengxi He SC47/48C3-2
Mengxing YN51/52E4
Mengxuan NX61/62E2
Mengyan GZ49/50D7
Mengyang YN51/52D4
Mengyangzhen SC47/48B2
Mengyin Xian SD31/32D4
Mengyong YN51/52D3
Mengyou YN51/52C3
Mengyuan NX61/62E3
Mengyuan SN55/56F6
Mengyuan YN51/52E4
Mengzhe YN51/52D4
Mengzhu Ling HN37/38G4
              GX43/44C9
Mengziling HEB5/6C6
Mengzi Xian YN51/52D5
Menkoutang AH19/20B2
Mentaizi AH23/24D4
Mentougou BJ3/4C3
Menxianshi SX7/8C5
Menyuan Huizu Zizhixian(Haomen)
   QH59/60B7
Mêwa SC45/46B4
Miancaowan QH59/60C6
Miancheng HB35/36D6
Mianchi Xian HEN33/34C3
Miandian YN51/52D5
Mianduhe NM9/10C13
Mianhu GD39/40C9
Mianjin JX29/30E2
Mianmian Shan YN77B3
Mianning Xian SC45/46D4
Mianshan SC45/46D4
Mian Shui JX29/30F4-3
Miansi SC45/46C4
Mian Xian SN55/56G2
Mianyang Shi SC45/46C5
Mianyuan He SC47/48A2

Mianzhu Shi SC45/46C5
Miaobachang SC45/46C6
Miaocheng BJ3/4B3
Miaochuan HB35/36A2
Miao Dao SD31/32B7
Miaodao Liedao SD31/32A7-B7
Miao'ergou XJ63/64C7
Miaofeng Shan BJ3/4B3
(Miaogao)Suicang Xian ZJ21/22D4
Miaogong Shuiku HEB5/6B5
Miaogoumen SN55/56A6
Miaokou HEN33/34B6
Miaoli Hsien TW27/28C2
Miao Ling GZ49/50D5-6
Miaoling JL13/14D10
Miaoping GX43/44B8
Miaoqian JX29/30B3
Miaoqian SX7/8F3
Miaoqian AH23/24F4
Miaoshan SD31/32C4
Miaoshi HN37/38C2
Miaoshou AH23/24F5
Miaotai NX61/62A3
Miaotaizi SN55/56G2
Miaotan HB35/36B4
Miaotang GZ49/50B6
Miaotou GX43/44A9
Miaotou JS17/18B4
Miaowan HEN33/34D6
Miaowan Dao GD41C3
Miaoxi ZJ19/20C2
Miaoxia HEN33/34C4
Miaoyang LN11/12D8
Miaoyu SC45/46C7
Miaozhen SH17/18E7
Miaozigou SC47/48B2
Miaozizhen HEN33/34D3
Micang Shan SN55/56H2-3
            SC45/46B6
Michang GX43/44E8
Midu Xian YN51/52C4
Mienhua Yu TW27/28B4
Migriggyangzham Co XZ53/54C8
            QH59/60D2
Mi He SD31/32C5
Mile Xian YN51/52C5
Miluo Jiang HN37/38C6
Miluo Shi HN37/38C6
Min'an GD39/40C6
(Min'an)Longshan Xian HN37/38B2
Minchuan TW27/28D2
Minfeng SD31/32B5
Minfeng(Niya)Xian XJ63/64G7
Ming'an NM9/10K19
Mingcheng GD39/40D5
Mingcheng JL13/14D7
Mingchien TW27/28D2
Mingfeng JS17/18E5
Minggang HEN33/34E6
Minggao HEN33/34C4
Mingguang Shi AH23/24D4
Ming He HEB5/6G2
Minghechang ZJ19/20C4

Minghua HEB5/6F3
Ming Jiang GX43/44E5
Mingjiang GX43/44E5
Mingjue JS19/20B1
Mingkou JX29/30C5
Minglang YN51/52D3
Mingli SX7/8D4
Minglun GX43/44B6
Mingshan HL15/16D6
Mingshan Shuiku HB35/36C8
Mingshan Xian SC45/46C4
Mingshazhou NX61/62C2
Mingshui GS57/58A3
Mingshui Xian HL15/16D3
Mingteke XJ63/64G3
Mingteke Daban XJ63/64G3
Mingxi Xian(Guihua) FJ25/26D3
Mingyin YN51/52B4
Mingyu SC45/46D6
Mingyue JL13/14D9
Mingyue SC47/48C4
Mingyuechang SC47/48B4
Mingyuechang SC47/48B3
Mingyue Shan SC47/48B5
Mingyue Xia SC47/48C4
Minhang SH17/18E7
Minhe GD41A2
Minhe Huizu Tuzu Zizhixian QH59/60B8
(Minhe)Jinxian Xian JX29/30C4
Minhou Xian(Ganzhe) FJ25/26D5
Minhsiung TW27/28D2
Minjia JL13/14C7
Minjiang SC45/46D4-5
Min Jiang FJ25/26D4
Minjiang Kou FJ25/26D5
Minle HL15/16D4
Minle Xian GS57/58C5
Minqing Xian FJ25/26D4
Minqin Xian GS57/58C6
Minquan Xian HEN33/34C7
Min Shan SC45/46B4
Mintang QH59/60D7
Min Xian GS57/58E7
Minxiao GZ49/50C7
Minzhong GD41A2
Minzhu GZ49/50E3
Miquan Shi XJ63/64D9
Mishan Shi HL15/16E6
Mishazi JL13/14C6
Mi Shui HN37/38D6
Mitangya HEB5/6E1
Mituo SC45/46D5
Mituosi HB35/36D5
Mixinguan ·SX7/8A6
Miyaluo SC45/46C4
Miyi Xian SC45/46E4
Miyu SX7/8D3
Miyun Shuiku BJ3/4B3
Miyun Xian BJ3/4B3
Mizhi Xian SN55/56C6
Mobin HN37/38D2
Mocheng JS19/20B3
Mochiba SC47/48B2

Mochong GZ49/50D6
Mochuan GX43/44B8
Mocun GD39/40C5
Modao Men GD39/40D6
Modaoshi HL15/16E5
Modao Xi SC35/36D1
Modon NM9/10E11
Moganshan ZJ21/22B4
Mogan Shan ZJ21/22B4
Mogoit NM61/62B4
Moguqi NM9/10D14
Moguyu HEB3/4B5
Mohe HL15/16A2
Mohei YN51/52D4
Mohekou AH23/24D4
Mohe Xian(Xilinji) HL15/16A2
Mohuan ZJ21/22C4
Mohurtay XJ63/64B8
Moincêr XZ53/54D3
Moindawang XZ53/54F8
Mojialou NX61/62C2
Mojiang Hanizu Zizhixian(Jiulian)
            YN51/52D4
Molingguan JS17/18E4
Monan SX7/8G2
Monggon Bulag NM9/10G4
Mongh Gol NM11/12B4
Mong Tung Wan HK41B2
Mopanshan JL13/14E10
Mopan Yang ZJ21/22C7
Mopanzhang AH23/24C4
Mopanzhou HB35/36D4
Mopo HEN33/34D5
Mordaga NM9/10B13
Morihong Shan LN11/12B8
Mori Kazak Zizhixian XJ63/64D11
Morin Dawa Daurzu Zizhiqi(Nirji)
            NM9/10C15
(Moron He)Xi He NM9/10F3-G3
Moshan SD31/32E5
Moshi HN37/38B3
Mosuowan XJ63/64C9
Motian Ling LN11/12D7
Motian Ling SC45/46B5
Motou JS17/18D6
Moudao HB35/36D1
Mouding Xian YN51/52C4
Moujiaba SN55/56H3
Mouzi SC47/48C1
Mowu FJ25/26D3
Moxi SC45/46D4
Moxie Dao SD31/32C9
Moxitou JX29/30B3
Moyang Jiang GD39/40D4
Moyu(Karakax)Xian XJ63/64G5
Mozhong QH59/60D5
Moziqiao SN55/56G3
Mozitan AH23/24E3
Mozitan Shuiku AH23/24E3
Mu'ai SC45/46D5
Mubo GS61/62D4
Muchangbu AH23/24E3
Mucheng SC47/48C1

Muchengjian BJ3/4C2
(Mucheng)Wuzhi Xian HEN33/34B5
Muchuan Xian SC45/46D4
Mudan Jiang HL15/16E5 JL13/14D9
Mudanjiang Shi HL15/16E5
Mudan Ling JL13/14D8
Mudong SC47/48C4
Mudu JS17/18E6
Mu'er SC47/48C4
Mufu HB35/36D2
Mufu Shan JX29/30B2
Mufu Shan HN37/38B6
Mugang HB35/36E8
Mugang YN51/52D6
Muge GX43/44E7
Muge GD39/40C5
Mugen SC47/48C5
Mugenqiao HN37/38F6
Mugouhe HL15/16C4
Mug Qu QH59/60D3
Muguaping SC47/48A2
Mugui GX43/44D8
Mugxung QH59/60D4
Muhar QH59/60B6
Muhuang GZ49/50B7
Mui Wo HK41B2
Muji XJ63/64G5
Mujiadian JL13/14B3
Mujingzi NM61/62B2
Mükangsar XZ53/54E6
Mula SC45/46D3
Mulantou HI42A3
Mulan Xi FJ25/26E4
Mulan Xian HL15/16E5
Mule GX43/44D8
Muleng Shi HL15/16E6
Muli Feng JS17/18E6
Mulin BJ3/4B3
Muling HL15/16E6
Muling Guan SD31/32C5
Muling He HL15/16E7
Muling Shi HL15/16E6
Muli Zangzu Zizhixian SC45/46E3
Muma He SX7/8C4-5
Muma He SN55/56H3
Muma Shan FJ72C3 JX72C3
Munai YN51/52D3
Muping Shi SD31/32B8
Muqi LN11/12C8
Muqiao AH23/24E5
Muri QH59/60B7
Muri QH59/60A6
Muruin Sum Shuiku NM13/14D2
Mushihe JL13/14C7
Mutang HI42B2
Mutantsun TW27/28E2
Mutoudeng HEB5/6C7
Mutougou NM5/6A6
Mu Us Shadi NM9/10H7
Muwangping SN55/56G4
Muxihe HB35/36C8
Muyang YN51/52D6
Muyang FJ25/26C5

Muyang Xi FJ25/26C5
Muyudian SD31/32B7
Muyuping HB35/36C3
Muyu Shuiku SD31/32B7
Muzat He XJ63/64E6
Muzhen AH23/24F4
Muzhuang SD31/32C3
Muzi GX43/44E7
Muzidian HB35/36C8
Muz Tag XZ53/54A6 XJ63/64G9
Muz Tag XJ63/64G6
Muztagata XJ63/64F3

N

(Naba)Dan Xian HI42B2
Nabi GX43/44C3
Nabu GX43/44F7
Nachen GX43/44E6
Nadanbo JL13/14D6
Nafu GD39/40D5
Nagarzê Xian XZ53/54E8
Nagjog XZ53/54D11
Nag Qu XZ53/54D9
Nagqu Diqu XZ53/54C7-9
Nagqu Xian XZ53/54D9
Nahuo GD39/40E4
Naij Gol QH59/60B3-C4
Naij Tal QH59/60C4
Nailin NM5/6B7
Naiman Qi(Daqin Tal) NM9/10F13
Naimin Bulak XJ63/64C11
Nai Wai HK41B2
Naizijing JL13/14B4
Naizishan JL13/14D8
(Naji)Arun Qi NM9/10C14
Najin JL13/14B3
Najinkouzi HL15/16B4
Nakan GX43/44E5
Nakou FJ25/26C3
Nalao GX43/44C3
Nali GX43/44F6
Naling GX43/44E5
Nalong GX43/44E5
Nalong GX43/44E6
Nalou GX43/44E6
Naman GX43/44D4
Nam Co XZ53/54D8
Namco XZ53/54D8
Namda SC45-46B3
Namjagbarwa Feng XZ53/54E10
(Namka)Doilungdêqên Xian XZ53/54E8
Namling Xian XZ53/54E7
Namoding XZ53/54D6
Namsê La XZ53/54D4
Nam Sha Po HK41B2
Namtang QH59/60C6
Nanan GX43/44F5
Nan'an SC47/48C4
(Nan'an)Dayu Xian JX29/30F2
Nan'an Shi FJ25/26F4
Nanao TW27/28C3
Nan'ao GD41A3
Nan'ao Dao GD39/40C10

Nan'ao Xian GD39/40C10
Nanba SC45/46C7
(Nanbai)Zunyi Xian GZ49/50C5
Nanbao ZJ21/22C4
Nanbao HI42B2
Nanbaxian QH59/60B4
Nanbeihe HL15/16C4
Nanbian GD41A1
Nanbianzao GD41A4
Nanbu Xian SC45/46C6
Nanbuzi SX7/8B3
Nanbuzi HEB3/4B3
Nancaicun TJ3/4C4
Nancha HL15/16D5
Nanchangshan Dao SD31/32B7
Nanchang Shi JX29/30C3
Nanchangtan NX61/62C1
Nanchang Xian(Liantang) JX29/30C3
Nancheng JS17/18B5
Nancheng FJ25/26E4
Nanchengsi HEB3/4C2
Nancheng Xian JX29/30D4
Nanchengzi Shuiku LN11/12B8
Nanchenji JS17/18C4
Nanchong GD39/40C5
Nanchong Shi SC45/46C6
Nanchuang TW27/28C3
Nanchuan Shi SC45/46D6
Nancun SX7/8B6
Nancun JX29/30D3
Nancun AH23/24F4
Nancun SD31/32C7
Nancun HEN33/34B3
Nancun HEN33/34B5
Nandagang HEB5/6E5
Nandan Xian GX43/44C5
Nandashan HN37/38B5
Nandian LN11/12C8
Nanding SD31/32C5
Nanding Dao FJ25/26F4
Nanding He YN51/52D3
Nandu JS17/18E5
Nandu GX43/44E8
Nandu Jiang HI42B2-3
Nandulehe BJ3/4B4
Nanfan SX7/8F3

Nanfen LN11/12C7
Nanfeng HI42B2
Nanfeng JX29/30B4
Nanfeng GD39/40C4
Nanfengmian JX29/30E2
Nanfeng Xian JX29/30D4
Nangang AH23/24E3
Nangang JS17/18B4
Nangang Shan JL13/14E10
Nangaocun HEB3/4C2
Nangdoi QH59/60B8
Nangezhuang BJ3/4C3
Nangong Shi HEB5/6F3
Nangongyingzi LN11/12D3
Nangou SX7/8G3
Nangou JL13/14D9

Nangqên Xian(Xangda) QH59/60D5
Nangsong YN51/52C3
Nanguan SX7/8E3
Nanguan HEB3/4C3
Nanguan HEB5/6B4
Nanguan SX7/8D4
Nanguang SC45/46D5
Nanguang He SC49/50B3
Nanguanling LN11/12E5
Nanguantou HEB3/4C2
Nangucheng GS57/58C5
Nangunlonggou HEB5/6E1
Nangushanzi LN11/12C8
Nanguzhuang SD29/30E5
Nang Xian XZ53/54E9
Nanhai Shi GD39/40C6
(Nanhaoqian)Shangyi Xian HEB5/6B1
Nanhe SD31/32B5
Nan He HB35/36B4
Nan He SC35/36C1
Nanhedian HEN33/34D4
Nanheng GD41A2
Nanhe Xian HEB5/6F2
Nanhsi TW27/28D2
Nanhsiao Tao TW27/28G5
Nanhu SD31/32D6
Nanhu GS57/58C2
Nanhu GS57/58E7
Nan Hu ZJ21/22B5
Nanhuang SD31/32C8
Nanhuangcheng Dao SD31/32A7
Nanhuatang HB35/36A3
Nanhua Xian(Longchuan) YN51/52C4
Nanhui Xian(Huinan) SH17/18E7
Nan Hulsan Hu QH59/60B4
Nanhu Tashan TW27/28C3
Nanjia GZ49/50D7
Nanjiali JS17/18D6
Nan Jiang SC45/46B6-C6
Nanjiangkou GD39/40C4
Nanjiangqiao HN37/38C6
Nanjiang Xian SC45/46B6
Nanjian Yizu Zizhixian YN51/52C4
Nanjiao SX7/8B5
(Nanjie) Guangning Xian GD39/40C5
Nanjin SC47/48B2
Nanjing JX29/30G2
Nanjing Shi JS17/18D4
Nanjinguan HB35/36D4
Nanjing Xian FJ25/26F3
Nanjishan Liedao ZJ21/22E6
Nanjuma He HEB3/4C2
Nankai HI42B2
Nankai GZ49/50D3
Nanka Jiang YN51/52D3
Nankang TW27/28B3

Nankang Shi JX29/30F2
(Nankang)Xingzi Xian JX29/30B4
Nankeng JX29/30D1
Nankou BJ3/4B3
Nankou FJ25/26D3
Nankouqian LN11/12C8
Nanku JS19/20B3

Nankun HI42B2
Nanla He YN51/52E4
Nanlang GD39/40D6
Nanlan He YN51/52D3-E3
Nanlei He YN51/52D3-E3
Nanle Xian HEN33/34A7
Nanliang SX7/8F3
Nanlin HI42C2
Nanling JX29/30B2
Nan Ling JX29/30F1-2
　　　　HN37/38F5-6
　　　　GD39/40A5-6
　　　　GX43/44B8-9
Nanling GD39/40C8
Nanlingcheng HEB3/4D3
Nanling Xian AH23/24F5
Nanlinqiao HB35/36E7
Nanliu SD31/32C6
Nanliu SX7/8F3
Nanliu Jiang GX43/44F7-E7
Nanlou Shan JL13/14D7
Nanlü HI42B3
Nanluji SD31/32D2
Nanluo HI42B1
Nanma ZJ21/22C5
(Nanma)Yiyuan Xian SD31/32C5
Nanmeng HEB3/4C3
Nanmiao JX29/30D2
Nanming He GZ49/50D5-6
Nanmu SC45/46C6
Nanmuping HN37/38D2
Nanmuyuan HB35/36C3
Nanning Diqu GX43/44E5-7
Nanning Shi GX43/44E6
Nanniwan SN55/56D5
Nanpan Jiang GX43/44C2-3
Nanpeiwei JS17/18C4
Nanpeng Dao GD39/40E5
Nanpeng Liedao GD39/40C10
Nanpiao LN11/12C4
Nanping JL13/14E10
Nanping GD41B1
Nanping SC45/46D6
Nanping HB35/36E5
Nanping SC45/46D6
Nanping HN37/38A3
Nanping HN37/38E6
Nanpingji AH23/24C3
Nanping Shi FJ25/26D4

Nanpi Xian HEB5/6E4
Nanpo GX43/44D4
Nanpu FJ25/26F3
Nanpu HEB5/6D6
Nanpu Xi FJ25/26C4
Nanqi SX7/8D4
Nanqi HEB3/4D2
Nanqiao HB35/36C5
Nanqiao HI42C3
(Nanqiao)Fengxian Xian SH17/18F7
Nanqiu GS61/62D3
Nanquan JS17/18E6
Nanquan SD31/32C7
Nanri Dao FJ25/26E5

Nanri Qundao FJ25/26E5
Nansan Dao GD39/40E3
Nansha GD41A2
Nansha YN51/52D5
Nanshahe SD31/32D4
Nanshahe Shuiku SN55/56H3
Nanshan GD39/40D6
Nanshanba FJ25/26E2
Nanshancheng LN11/12B9
Nanshan Ding HN74E2 GX75A4
Nanshangtun HEB5/6D2
Nanshangzhuang SD31/32C4
Nanshankou XJ63/64D12
Nanshankou QH59/60B4
Nanshanpu HEB3/4B2
Nanshan Shuiku ZJ21/22C5
Nanshao GZ49/50D7
Nansha Qundao HI42F6
Nansheng HI42C2
Nansheng FJ25/26F3
Nansheng GD39/40E3
Nanshenzao JS17/18D6
Nanshi HN37/38F5
Nanshih TW27/28C2
Nanshuang Dao FJ25/26D6
Nanshuangmiao LN11/12C4
Nanshui Shuiku GD39/40B6
Nantai LN11/12D6
Nantang JX29/30E3
Nantang GD39/40D3
Nantian ZJ21/22C6
Nantian ZJ21/22E4
(Nantian Dao)Niutou Shan ZJ21/22C6
Nantonggang JS17/18D6
Nantong Shi JS17/18D6

Nantuo HEB5/6E1
Nantzu TW27/28E2
Nan Wan TW27/28F2
Nanwan TW27/28F2
Nanwang SD31/32D3
Nanwangzhuang HEB5/6E3
Nanwan Shuiku HEN33/34E5
Nanwei Tan GD39/40F8
Nanweng He NM15/16B3
Nanwengkouzi NM15/16B3
Nanwenquan SC47/48C4
Nanxi HEN33/34C6
Nanxi AH23/24E2
Nan Xi ZJ21/22D5
Nan Xian HN37/38B5

Nanxiang GX43/44C9
Nanxiang GX43/44E7
Nanxiang SH17/18E7
Nanxiao GX43/44E6
Nanxi He YN51/52D5
Nanxin SD31/32D4
Nanxing SN55/56G2
Nanxing GD39/40F3
Nanxinji JS17/18C4
Nanxinjie JS19/20A3
Nanxinzhuang(Qiuzhuang) HEB3/4C3
Nanxiong Shi GD39/40A7

Nanxi Xian   SC45/46D5
Nanxu   GX43/44D5
Nanxun   ZJ21/22B5
Nanya   FJ25/26D4
Nanyandang Shan   ZJ21/22E5
Nanyang   FJ25/26C5
Nanyang   JS17/18C6
Nanyang   FJ25/26D3
Nanyang   SD31/32D3
Nanyang   GX43/44E6
Nanyang   HI42B3
Nanyang'an   JS17/18C6
Nanyangcun   JS19/20B4
Nanyang He   SX7/8A6
Nanyanghu   SD31/32D3
Nanyang Pendi   HEN73D2
Nanyang Shi   HEN33/34D4
Nanyang Xian   HEN33/34D4
Nanyi   AH23/24E5
Nanyi   SD31/32D4
Nanyi Hu   AH23/24E5
Nanying   HEB5/6E1
Nanyu   FJ25/26E5
Nanyuan   BJ3/4C3
Nanyuan   ZJ21/22E4
Nanyue   HN37/38D5
Nan Yunhe   SD31/32B3-2
           HEB5/6E4
           TJ3/4D3
Nanzamu   LN11/12C8
Nanzha   JS19/20B3
Nanzhai   GZ49/50D7
Nanzhai   HEN33/34B5
Nanzhang   SX7/8F2
Nanzhang   HEB3/4C2
Nanzhangcheng   HEB5/6F2
Nanzhang Xian   HB35/36C4
Nanzhaofu   HEB3/4D3
Nanzhaoji   AH23/24D2
Nanzhao Xian   HEN33/34D4
Nanzheng Xian   SN55/56G2
Nanzhenjie   JS19/20B2
Nanzhiqiu   HEB5/6F3
Nanzhuang   HEN33/34C4
Nanzhuang   SX7/8D4
Nanzhuang   SX7/8C5
Naodahan   HL15/16A3
Naodehai Shuiku   NM9/10F13
           LN11/12B6
Naoli   HEN33/34B6
Naoli He   HL15/16D7
Naozhou Dao   GD39/40F3
Napeng   GX43/44F6
Napo   GX43/44D4
Napo Xian   GX43/44D3
(Napug)Ge'gyai Xian   XZ53/54C3
Naqin   GX43/44E6
Naran Bulag   NM57/58B8
Naran Bulag   NM9/10E10
Narat   XJ63/64D8
Narhong   JL13/14E7
Narin   NM57/58C10
Narin Gol   QH59/60B3

(Narin He)Dong He   NM9/10F3-G3
Nart   NM9/10F10
Nasa   YN51/52D6
Nashan   JX29/30E2
Nashuixi   HB35/36D1
Natong   GX43/44D5
Natou Hsien   TW27/28D2
Naweiquan   SX7/8E5
Nawu   GD39/40E3
Naxiao   GX43/44E4
Naxi   SC45/46D5·
Nayag   XZ53/54C9
Nayong Xian   GZ49/50D4
Nayü   XZ53/54E10
Nazhou   GD41B2
Nazuo   GX43/44C3
Nêdong Xian   XZ53/54E8
Nehe Shi   HL15/16C3
Neibu   HEN33/34C4
Neiguanying   GS57/58E7
Neihuangji   HEN33/34C6
Neihuang Xian   HEN33/34B6
Neijiang Shi   SC45/46D5
Neiliang   JX29/30F2
Neilingding Dao   GD41B2
Nei Mongol Gaoyuan   NM68D3-C7
Neipu   TW27/28E2
Neiqiu Xian   HEB5/6F2
Neiwan   TW27/28C3
Neixiang Xian   HEN33/34D3
Nemor He   HL15/16C3-4
Nenan   HL15/16C3
Nenbei Nongchang   HL15/16C3
Nen Jiang   JL13/14A5-B5
           NM15/16C3
           HL15/16D2-3
Nenjiang Xian   HL15/16C3
Nêri Pünco   XZ78C4
New Territories   HK41B3
Ngamda   XZ53/54D11
Ngamring Xian   XZ53/54E6
Ngangla Ringco   XZ53/54D4
Nganglong Kangri   XZ53/54C3
Ngangzê Co   XZ53/54D6
Ngaqên Shuiku   XZ78C4
Ngari Diqu   XZ53/54C3-5
Ngari Gaoyuan   XZ78B2
(Ngarrab)Gyaca Xian   XZ53/54E9
Ngola Shan   QH59/60B6
Ngola Shankou   QH59/60C6
Ngom Qu   XZ53/54D11
Ngoring   QH59/60C5
Ngoring Hu   QH59/60C5
Ng Uk Tsuen   HK41B2
Ngüra   GS57/58E5
Nianbadu   ZJ21/22D3
(Nianbai)Ledu Xian   QH59/60B8
Niangniangba   GS57/58E7
Niangniangmiao   LN11/12D4
Niangniangmiao   SN55/56F2
(Niangxi)Xinshao Xian   HN37/38D4
Niangziguan   SX7/8D5
Nianjiagang   AH23/24D4

Nianlipu   QH59/60B7
Niansanli   ZJ21/22C5
Niansidu   JX29/30C6
Niantouji   JS17/18B4
Nianyushan   JX29/30B5
Nianyushan Shuiku   HEN33/34F7
(Nianyuwan)Xingangzhen   LN11/12F5
Nianyuxu   HN37/38B5
Nianzhang   SX7/8F3
Nianzhuang   JS17/18B3
Nianzi   BJ3/4B3
Nianzigang   HB35/36C7
Nianzishan   HL15/16D2
Niao Dao   QH59/60B6
Niaoshu Shan   GS57/58E7
Niao Yu   TW27/28D1
Nicheng   SH17/18F7
Nidong   GX43/44C2
Niedu   JX29/30F2
Niejiahe   HB35/36D4
Nieqiao   JX29/30B3
Ni He   HEN33/34D6
Nihe Shuiku   HL15/16D4
Nihezi   LN11/12C5
Nijiao   YN51/52C5
Nilka Xian   XJ63/64D7
Niluo   GZ49/50E4
Ninepin Group   HK41B3
Ning'an Shi   HL15/16E5
Ningbo Shi   ZJ21/22C6
Ningcheng Xian(Tianyi)   NM9/10G12
Ningde Diqu   FJ25/26D5
Ningde Shi   FJ25/26D5
Ningdun   AH23/24F6
Ningdu Xian   JX29/30E3

Ninggu   SX7/8D4
Ningguo Shi   AH23/24F5
Ninghai Xian   ZJ21/22C6
Ninghe Xian(Lutai)   TJ3/4C4
Ninghezhen   TJ3/4C4
Ninghua   SX7/8C4
Ninghua Xian   FJ25/26D2
Ningjiang   JL13/14B5
Ningjin Po   HEB5/6F3
Ningjinsuo   SD31/32C9
Ningjin Xian   SD31/32B3
Ningjin Xian   HEB5/6F2
Ninglang Yizu Zizhixian(Daxing)
           YN51/52B4
Ningling Xian   HEN33/34C7
Ningming Xian   GX43/44E5
Ningnan Xian   SC45/46E4
Ningqiang Xian   SN55/56H2
Ningshan Xian   SN55/56G4
Ningwu Xian   SX7/8C4
Ningxi   ZJ21/22D5
Ning Xian   GS57/58E8
Ningxiang Xian   HN37/38C5
Ningxia Pingyuan   NX80B5
Ningyang Xian   SD31/32D3
Ningyuan He   HI42C2
Ningyuan Xian   HN37/38F4
Ningzhen Shan   JS19/20A2

Niqiu AH23/24C2
(Nirji)Morin Dawa Daurzu Zizhiqi NM9/10C15
Nishan XZ53/54C5
Nishan Shuiku SD31/32D4
Nishi HN37/38B3
Niubaotun BJ3/4C3
Niubitan HN37/38B4
Niubiziliang QH59/60A2
Niubu AH23/24E4
Niuchang GZ49/50D6
Niuchang GZ49/50E4
Niuchang YN51/52B6
Niuchehe HN37/38B3
Niucun SX7/8C5
Niudouguang JX29/30G3
Niudu SX7/8F2
Niu'erhe NM9/10B13
Niufodu SC47/48C3
Niuguanying HEB5/6D7
Niuhuaxi SC47/48C1
Niujia HL15/16E4
Niujiao'an SX67D2
Niujiaodian SD31/32C3
Niujiaqiao HEB5/6F2
Niujiayingzi NM5/6A6
Niujie YN51/52B6
Niujie YN51/52D5
(Niujing)Binchuan Xian YN51/52C4
Niukong YN51/52D5
Niulang GZ49/50C8
Niulan Jiang GZ49/50C2-D2
          YN51/52B5
Niulanshan BJ3/4B3
Niulou HI42C3
Niululing Shuiku HI42C3
Niumaojing NX61/62C4
Niumaowu LN11/12D8
Niumiao GX43/44C9
Niumutun BJ3/4C3
Niupengzi GZ49/50C2
Niuqibu SD31/32C7
Niuqitou FJ25/26F3
(Niushan)Donghai Xian JS17/18B4
Niushi HN37/38C6
Niushitun HEN33/34B6
Niushou HB35/36B4
Niushou Shan NX61/62C2-3
Niutan SC47/48C3
Niutian JX29/30D3
Niutou Dao GD41B2
Niutoudian SN55/56H5
Niutoushan AH23/24E6
Niutoushan AH23/24F4
Niutou Shan(Nantian Dao) ZJ21/22C6
Niutuo HEB5/6D4
Niuxintai LN11/12C7
Niuxintuo LN11/12C6
Niuzhuang LN11/12D6
Niuzhuang SD31/32B5
Nixi SC47/48B4
Nixi YN51/52A3
Nixizhen SC47/48C2

Niya He XJ63/64G7
Niyu Shan ZJ21/22E6
Nizhai ZJ21/22D4
Nizui HB35/36B5
Nogon Toli NM9/10H5
Nohoit QH59/60A4
Nom XJ63/64D13
Nomhon QH59/60B5
Nomhon He QH59/60B5
Nomin Gol NM9/10C14
Nong'an Xian JL13/14C6
Nongche HN37/38B2
Nonghe HL15/16E5
Nong Jiang HL15/16D7-8
Norcang XZ53/54D5
Nuanquan HEB5/6C3
Nuanquan HEB5/6D2
Nuanquan SX7/8D2
Nuanquan NX61/62B3
Nuanquanzhan NX61/62B3
Nuanshui JX29/30C5
Nü'erhe LN11/12C5
Nü'er He LN11/12C4-D4
Nu Jiang YN51/52C3 XZ53/54E11
Nujiang Lisuzu Zizhizhou YN51/52B3
Nulu'erhu Shan NM9/10G12-F13
          LN11/12C3-B4
Numin He HL15/16D4
Nuotong GX43/44D6
Nuozu YN51/52C5
Nur XJ63/64G6
Nurigai NM57/58C5
Nu Shan YN51/52B3
Nüshan Hu AH23/24D5
Nyagla QH59/60D5
Nyaimai XZ53/54E9
(Nyainbo Yuzê)Golog Shan QH59/60D7
Nyainqêntanglha Feng XZ53/54D8
Nyainqêntanglha Shan XZ53/54D7-10
Nyainrong Xian XZ53/54C9
Nyalam Xian(Congdü) XZ53/54E5
Nyang Qu XZ78C5
Nyang Qu XZ53/54E7
Nyêmo Xian(Tarrong) XZ53/54E8
Nyikog Qu SC45/46B2-3
Nyima XZ53/54D6
Nyima XZ53/54D9
Nyinba GS57/58E6
Nyingchi Diqu XZ53/54E10-11
Nyingchi Xian XZ53/54E10
Nyingzhong XZ53/54D8
(Nyinma)Maqu Xian GS57/58F6

O

Obo QH59/60B7
Obo Liang QH59/60A3
Oiga XZ53/54E9
Oilê SC45/46D3
Oisêr QH59/60D6
Oiyug XZ53/54E7
Olji Moron NM9/10F13
(Oljoq)Otog Qianqi NM9/10H6
Olon Bulag NM9/10G6

Olongt SN55/56A5
Oluanpi TW27/28F2
Oma XZ53/54C4
Ombu XZ53/54D6
Ondor Sum NM9/10F9
Onggon NM9/10J18
Ongniud Qi(Wudan) NM9/10F12
Onor NM9/10C13
Orba Co XZ53/54B3
Ordos Gaoyuan NM68E4-5
Oroqen Zizhiqi(Alihe) NM9/10B14
Orqohan NM9/10C13
Orxon Gol NM9/10C11
Otog Qi NM9/10H6
Otog Qianqi(Oljoq) NM9/10H6
Ouchikou HB35/36E5
Oudong GX43/44C6
Oujiacun SX7/8A4
Ou Jiang ZJ21/22D5
Oujiangcha HN37/38C5
Oumiao HB35/36C5
Oupu HL15/16A4
Ou Shui HN37/38F6
Outang AH23/24D4
Ouyanghai HN37/38E5
Ouyanghai Shuiku HN37/38E5
Oytograk XJ63/64G6

P

Pachao Tao(Wangan Tao) TW27/28D1
Pagri XZ53/54F7
Pahsien TW27/28C3
Pahsien Shan TW27/28C3
Paibi HN37/38C2
Paibu JX29/30C2
Paiho TW27/28D2
Pai Hu HB35/36D6
Paikü Co XZ53/54E5
(Pailing)Chun'an Xian ZJ21/22C4
Pailou HEB5/6B5
Pailou AH23/24F4
Pailou'ao HN37/38D2
Paipu HI42B2
Pairi SC45/46C3
Paisha TW27/28D1
Paishan JX29/30D1
Paisha Tao TW27/28D1
Paishi HB35/36E8
Paitan GD39/40C6
Paitou ZJ21/22C5
Paiyang GZ49/50D7
Paizhou HB35/36D6
Pajiangkou GD39/40C6
Pak A HK41B3
Pak Kok Tsuen HK41B3
Pak Nai HK41B2
Pak Tin Pa HK41B3
Pali TW27/28B3
Palingshe TW27/28C3
Pamir XJ63/64G2-3
Pan'an Xian ZJ21/22C5
(Panchiao)Taipei Hsien TW27/28B3
Pancun AH23/24C5

Pandian SD31/32C3
Pandu FJ25/26D5
Panggezhuang BJ3/4C3
Pangjiabu HEB5/6C3
Pangjiazuo HEB5/6E3
Pangkog Co XZ53/54D7
Pangu HL15/16A2
Panguan GZ49/50E3
Pangu He HL15/16A3-2
Pangushan JX29/30F3
Panhe HEN33/34C2
Panji AH23/24D3
Panjiaba JS19/20B2
Panjiabu NX61/62D3
Panjiadian HEB3/4B4
Panjiakou Shuiku HEB5/6C6
Panjiang GZ49/50D6
Panjiasha SH19/20B4
Panjiawan SN55/56F3
Panjin Shi LN11/12C6
Panlong SC47/48A4
Panlong SC47/48B3
Panlong SN55/56D5
Panlong SH19/20B4
Panlong SX7/8E5
Panlong GZ49/50D4
Panlong SC47/48C4
Panlong Jiang YN51/52D6
Panqiao Shuiku JX29/30D3
Pan Shan TJ3/4B4
Panshan Tequ GZ49/50E3
Panshan Xian LN11/12C6
Panshi SC47/48B2
Panshi Shi JL13/14E7
Panshui GZ49/50C5
Pantang AH23/24E4
Pantian GD39/40C9
Panuokuai GZ49/50D3
Panxi YN51/52C5
Panxi GZ49/50D7
Panxidu SD31/32D2
Panyu Shi GD39/40D6
Panzhihua SC45/46E3
Panzhihua YN51/52D6
Panzhihua SC45/46E3
Panzhuang TJ3/4C4
Panzhuang SX7/8F4
Paoche JS17/18B4
Pao Jiang YN77C3
Paomaping YN51/52B4
Paotaiyingzi NM5/6B3
Paozi LN11/12B6
Paoziyan LN11/12C9
Parlung Zangbo XZ53/54E10-11
Parta XZ53/54D8
Paryang XZ53/54D4
Patian FJ25/26E3
Pêdo La XZ53/54E4
Peicheng HL15/16E6
Peicheng HEN33/34D5
Peihsiao Tao TW27/28G5
Peijiachuankou SX7/8C2
Peikang TW27/28D2

Peikang Hsi TW27/28C2
Peikantang Tao FJ25/26D6
Pei Men TW27/28D2
Peinan TW27/28E3
Peinan Chushan TW27/28D2
Peinan Hsi TW27/28E3
Peiqiao HEN33/34D8
Peishan HEB3/4C2
Peitawu Shan TW27/28E2
Peitou TW27/28D2
Peitou TW27/28B3
Peitun TW27/28C2
Peitun JS17/18B2
Pei Xian JS17/18B2
Peixing SC47/48B5
Peng'an Xian(Zhoukou) SC45/46C6
Pengbu NX61/62D3
Peng Chau HK41B3
Pengcheng HEB5/6G2
Pengchia Yu TW27/28B4
Pengdian HEN33/34C6
Penggong ZJ21/22B4
Penghu FJ25/26E4
Penghu Hsien(Makung) TW27/28D1
Penghu Liehtao TW27/28D1
Penghu Shuitao TW27/28D1
Penghu Tao TW27/28D1
Pengjiaba Shuiku SC47/48A2
Pengjiachang HB35/36D6
Pengjiawan HEN33/34E6
Pengkou FJ25/26E2
Penglai HI42B3
Penglai Shi SD31/32B7

Penglang JS19/20B4
Pengnan SC47/48B3
Pengpozhen HEN33/34C4
Pengqiao HEN33/34E3
Pengshan Xian SC45/46C4
Pengshi HN37/38E6
Pengshi HB35/36D6
Pengshui Miaozu Tujiazu Zizhixian
　SC45/46D7
Pengtan SN61/62C4
Pengting GZ49/50E5
Pengtoucun HEB3/4C2
Pengxi ZJ21/22E5
Pengxi Xian SC45/46C5
Pengyang NX61/62E3
Pengze Xian JX29/30B4
Pengzhai GD39/40B8
Pengzhen SC47/48B1
Pengzhou Shi SC45/46C4
Pêxung XZ53/54C9
Piancheng NX61/62E2
Pianguan He SX7/8B3
Pianguan Xian SX7/8B3
Pianjiao YN51/52B4
Pianliang SX7/8B5
Pianling LN11/12C7
Pianma YN51/52B3
Pianqiao SN55/56E5
Piao'erjing GZ49/50C4

Piao'ertun LN11/12C7
Piaoli GX43/44B7
Piaomiao Feng JS17/18E6
Picheng JS17/18B3
Picheng JS17/18D5
Pi He AH23/24D3-E3
Pihe JL13/14D8
Pikou LN11/12E6
Pilin GZ49/50E8
Ping'an JL13/14B4
Ping'an JL13/14C8
Ping'an JL13/14B3
Ping'an NM9/10B13
Ping'anbu HEB5/6B4
Ping'ancheng HEB5/6C5
Ping'andian SD31/32C3
Ping'anpu LN11/12A8
Ping'an Xian QH59/60B8
Pingba SC45/46C7
Pingba Xian GZ49/50D5
Pingbian Miaozu Zizhixian YN51/52D5
Pingchangguan HEN33/34E5
Pingchang Xian SC45/46C6
Pingchao JS17/18D6
Ping Chau HK41A3
Pingcheng HEN33/34C6
Pingcheng SX7/8F5
Pingchuan SC45/46E3
Pingcun ZJ21/22C3
Ping Dao 31/32D6
Pingdeng GX43/44A7
Pingdi YN51/52C5
Pingdi GZ49/50D3
Pingdijie SC45/46E3
Pingding GD39/40D3
(Pingdingbu)Guyuan Xian HEB5/6B3
Pingdingpu LN11/12B7
Pingding Shan HL15/16D5
Pingdingshan LN11/12C8
Pingdingshan Shi HEN33/34D5
Pingding Xian SX7/8D5
(Pingdu)Anfu Xian JX29/30D2
Pingdu Shi SD31/32C6
Ping'enguan GX43/44E4
Pingfeng NX61/62E2
Pingfu GX43/44E5
Pinggang GD39/40E4
Pinggang LN11/12B8
Pinggang HEN33/34C7
Pingguo Xian(Matou) GX43/44D5
Pinggu Xian BJ3/4B4
Pinghai FJ25/26E5
Pinghai GD39/40D7
Pinghe Xian FJ25/26F5
Pinghu FJ25/26D4
Pinghu GD39/40D7
Pinghu HB35/36D8
Pinghu Shi ZJ21/22B6
Pingji GX43/44E6
Pingjiang GZ49/50E7
Ping Jiang JX29/30E3
Pingjiang Xian HN37/38C6
Pingjing Guan HEN33/34F5

HB35/36C6
Pingjinpu SC45/46C6
Pingjipu NX61/62B3
Pingjipuzhan NX61/62B3
Pingkou HN37/38C4
Pinglang GZ49/50D6
Pinglang GX43/44E6
Pingle GX43/44C4
Pingle HEN33/34C4
Pingle GX43/44E8
Pingle Xian GX43/44C8
Pingli AH23/24G5
Pingliang Diqu GS57/58E8
Pingliang Shi GS57/58E8
Pinglidian SD31/32B7
Pinglin HB35/36C5
Pinglin HB35/36C6
Pinglin TW27/28C3
Pingling HB39/40C7
Pinglingcheng SD31/32C4
Pingli Xian SN55/56H5
Pinglu SX7/8B4
Pinglucheng SX7/8B4
Pingluo SC47/48B1
Pingluo Xian NX61/62B3
Pingluozhan NX61/62B3
Pinglu Xian SX7/8G3
(Pingma)Tiandong Xian GX43/44D5
Pingmu SN55/56G3
Pingmu GX43/44E7
Pingnan Xian GX43/44D8
Pingnan Xian FJ25/26D4
Pingqiao JS17/18C5
Pingqiao HEN33/34E6
Pingquan SC47/48B2
Pingquan GS57/58E8
Pingquan Xian HEB5/6B6
Pingsha GD39/40D6
Pingshan HL15/16E4
Pingshan GD39/40D7
Pingshan GX43/44E5
Pingshan JX29/30E4
Pingshan FJ25/26E3
Pingshan SC47/48B5
Pingshan HN37/38C5
Pingshanba HB35/36D4
Pingshancun GD41A2
Pingshang HN37/38D4
Pingshang SD31/32D6
(Pingshan)Huidong Xian GD39/40D7
Pingshanwei GD41A2
Pingshan Xian HEB5/6E2
Pingshan Xian SC45/46D5
Pingshe SX7/8C4
Pingshi HEN33/34E5
Pingshi GD39/40A6
Pingshi JX29/30E2
Pingshi JX29/30F2
Pingshui ZJ21/22C5
Pingshui HN37/38E6
Pingshun Xian SX7/8E5
Pingsong SX7/8D5
Pingtai JL13/14B3
Pingtan SC47/48C3

Pingtan GD39/40C7
Pingtang GX43/44D7
Pingtang HN37/38C5
Pingtang Xian GZ49/50E6
Pingtan Xian FJ25/26E5
Pingtou SN55/56F2
Pingtou SX7/8D4
Pingtung Hsien TW27/28E2
Pingwang SX7/8A5
Pingwang JS17/18F6
Pingwu Xian SC45/46B5
Pingxiangcheng HEB5/6G2
Pingxiang(Qicun) HEB5/6F3
Pingxiang Shi GX43/44E4
Pingxiang Shi JX29/30D1
Pingxing Guan SX7/8B5
Pingyang HEB5/6E2
Pingyang HL15/16C3
Pingyang GX43/44D6
Pingyang HL15/16D2
Pingyangkeng ZJ21/22E5
Pingyang Xian ZJ21/22E5
Pingyao ZJ21/22B4
Pingyao Xian SX7/8D4
Pingyin GX43/44F6
Pingyin Xian SD31/32C3
Pingyi Xian SD31/32D4
Pingyong GZ49/50D7
Pingyu BJ3/4C2
Pingyuan GZ49/50B6
Pingyuan GZ49/50B5
Pingyuanjie YN51/52D5
Pingyuan Xian SD21/22B3
Pingyuan Xian(Dazhe) GD39/40B8
Pingyu Xian HEN33/34E6
Pingzhai GZ49/50E7
Pingzhen ZJ21/22C5
Pingzheng GZ49/50E7
Pingzheng GX43/44E8
Pingzhou GD41A2
Pingzhuang NM5/6A7
Pipa Dingzi JL13/14D9
Pishan ZJ21/22D6
Pishan(Guma)Xian XJ63/64G5
Pitou Chiao TW27/28B3
Pixa XJ63/64G5
Pi Xian(Pitong) SC45/46C4
Piyun Shan ZJ21/22D3
Pizhou Shi JS17/18B3
Plover Cove Reservoir HK41B3
Pogan JX29/30C4
Pohong GX43/44D4
Po Hu AH23/24F3
Poji GD39/40E3
Po Jiang JX25/26A2
Pojiao GZ49/50F4
Pojiao GZ49/50C4
Pojie GX43/44B5
Pok Fu Lam HK41B3
Poli SD31/32D6
Poli SD31/32D5
Poliangting AH23/24F3
Polu SX7/8A4

Pongda XZ53/54D10
Ponggartang GS57/58E6
Popihe HEN33/34F6
Poping GZ49/50E4
Port Island HK41A3
Potan ZJ21/22D5
Po Toi HK41B3
Po Toi Islands HK41B3
Potou HEN33/34C4
Potzu TW27/28D2
Powo SC45/46B2
Poxi JS19/20A2
Poxin HI42B3
Poxin GX43/44C5
Poyang Hu JX29/30B4
Poyanghu Pingyuan JX72B2-3
Poyue GX43/44C5
Pozao GX43/44D5
Pozhai HI42B3
Pozi SD31/32C6
Pu'an Xian GZ49/50E3
Pubei Xian(Xiaojiang) GX43/44E7
Pucheng HEN33/34B7
Pucheng Xian FJ25/26C4
Pucheng Xian SN55/56F5
Puding Xian GZ49/50D4
Pudong SH17/18E7
Püdog Zangbo XZ53/54D5
Pudu He YN51/52B5-C5
Poindo XZ53/54 D8
Pu'erdu YN51/52A6
Pu'er Hanizu Yizu Zizhixian YN51/52D4
Puge Xian(Puji) SC45/46E4
Pu He GS57/58E8
Pu He LN11/12C6
Pui O HK41B2
Puji SD31/32B8
Puji HN37/38D6
Puji HB35/36E5
Puji SD31/32C4
Pujiang Xian SC45/46C4
Pujiang Xian (Puyang) ZJ21/22C4
(Puji)Puge Xian SC45/46E4
(Puji)Wugong Xian SN55/56F4
Pujue GZ49/50C7
Pukou FJ25/26D5
Pukou JS17/18D4
Pulandian Shi LN11/12E5
Pulandian Wan LN11/12E5
(Pula)Nyingche Xian XZ53/54E10
Pulaoyang GZ49/50C6
Puli TW27/28D2
Puli GX43/44C8
Pulu GX43/44C8
Pulu XJ63/64G6
Puluo GX43/44B6
Puma Yumco XZ53/54E8
(Pumiao)Yongming Xian GX43/44E6
Puming SX7/8C3
Punan FJ25/26F3
Püncogling XZ53/54E6
Puning Shi GD39/40C9
Pupai GD39/40E4
Pupeng YN51/52C4

Pupiao YN51/52C3
Puping GZ49/50E4
Puqi ZJ21/22D6
Puqian HI42A3

Pushang SD31/32C6
Pushang FJ25/26D3
Pushi HN37/38C3
Pushi He LN11/12D8
Putai TW27/28D2
Putang GX43/44E7
Putao GX43/44C8
Putaohua HL15/16E3
Putaoyuan GS57/58E8
Putian Shi FJ25/26E5
Putian Xian FJ25/26E5
Putog XZ53/54E12
Putuo (Shenjiamen) ZJ21/22C7
Putuo Shan ZJ21/22B7
Puwa BJ3/4C2
Puwang SD31/32D5
Puwei SC45/46E3
Puwen YN51/52D4
Puxi SN55/56H4
Pu Xian SX7/8E3
Puxing SC47/48B1
Puxiong SC45/46D4
Puyang ZJ21/22C5
Puyang SC47/48A1
Puyang Jiang ZJ21/22B5-C5
(Puyang)Pujiang Xian ZJ21/22C4
Puyang Shi HEN33/34B6
Puyang Xian HEN33/34B6
Puyuan ZJ21/22B5
Puzai GD39/40E3
Puzhang SX7/8F4
Puzhen SN55/56G3
Puzhen JS17/18D4
Puzhou SX7/8G2
Puzijiao HN37/38E2
Puziling SC47/48A5

Q

Qabnag XZ53/54E10
(Qabqa)Gonghe Xian QH59/60B7
Qagan NM9/10C12
Qagan Bulag NM9/10J21
Qagan Bulag NM9/10H5
Qagan Hua JL13/14C5
Qagan Moron NM69B2
Qagan Nur JL13/14B5
Qagan Nur NM9/10H7
Qagan Nur NM9/10F10
Qagan Nur NM9/10F9
Qagan Nur HEB5/6B1
Qagan Obo NM9/10G8
Qagan Obo NM9/10E8
Qagan Teg NM9/10F9
Qagan Tolgoi NM9/10H7
(Qagan Us)Dulan Xian QH59/60B6
Qagan Us He QH59/60B6-C6
Qagca SC45/46B2
Qagcaka XZ53/54C3
Qahar Youyi Houqi(Bayan Qagan)

NM9/10G9
Qahar Youyi Qianqi NM9/10G9
Qahar Youyi Zhongqi NM9/10G9
Qaidam He QH59/60B5
Qaidam Pendi QH59/60A3-B5
Qaidam Shan QH59/60B4-5
Qakar XJ63/64G6
Qalgar NM61/62C1
Qalgar Nur NM61/62B1
Qamalung QH59/60C6
Qamdo Diqu XZ53/54D10-12
Qamdo Xian XZ53/54D11
Qammê SC45/46B4
Qangdoi XZ53/54C3
Qanglapoila XZ78C3-4
Qangzê XZ53/54D2
Qapqal Xibe Zizhixian XJ63/64D6
Qarag NM61/62A3
Qarak XJ63/64F4
Qarhan QH59/60B4
Qarhan Yanhu QH59/60B4
Qarqan He XJ63/64F8-9
Qarqi XJ63/64E6
Qarqi XJ63/64E8
Qarsan NM9/10D13
(Qasq)Tumd Zuoqi NM9/10K21
Qayü XZ53/54E9
Qedir XJ63/64E8
Qeh NM9/10F3
Qiacun JX29/30D4
Qian'an Shi HEN5/6C6
Qian'an Xian JL13/14B5
Qian'anzhan JL13/14B4
Qianban FJ25/26E3
Qiancang ZJ21/22E5

Qiancun ZJ21/22D5
Qiandeng JS19/20B3
Qiandongnan Miaozu Dongzu Zizhizhou

GZ49/50D6-8
Qiandugu HEN33/34B7
Qianfang JX29/30C4
Qianfangzi NM7/8A3
Qianfeng HL15/16D4
Qianfu SC45/46C6
Qiangbai SN55/56F5
Qian Gorlos Mongolzu Zizhixian

JL13/14B5
Qiangu'ao HN37/38D3
Qiangweihe JS17/18B4
Qiangzilu BJ3/4B4
Qian Hai GD41A2
Qian He AH23/24C3-D3
Qian He SN55/56F2
Qianhe ZJ21/22D3
Qianheshangyuan SN55/56D4
Qianhezhan SN55/56E4
Qianhuang JS19/20B2
Qianji JS17/18C4
Qianjia HI42C2
Qianjiadian BJ3/4B3
Qianjiadian NM13/14D3
Qianjiang GX43/44D6

Qian Jiang SC45/46C7
Qian Jiang GX43/44D7

Qianjiang Shi HB35/36D5
Qianjiang

SC45/46D7
Qianjietou SD31/32D6
Qianjin NX61/62B3
Qianjin HL15/16D7
Qianjin JL13/14D8
Qianjin JL13/14C9
Qianjin SH19/20B4
Qianjing JS19/20B4
Qiankou HEN33/34A7
Qiankou AH23/24G5
Qianligang ZJ21/22C3
Qianlimiao NM9/10J17
(Qianling)Baojing Xian HN37/38C2
Qianling Shan GZ49/50D5
Qianliu YN51/52D4
Qianli Yan SD31/32C8
Qianma JS19/20B2
Qianmotou HEB5/6F3
Qiannan Buyeizu Miaozu Zizhizhou

GZ49/50E3-5
Qianning SC45/46C3
Qianpai GD39/40D4
Qianqi FJ25/26C6
Qianqiao SH19/20C4
Qianqihao JL13/14C4
Qianqili Hai TJ3/4C4
Qianqing ZJ21/22B5
Qianqiu HEN33/34C3
Qianqiu JS17/18C6
Qianqiu Guan AH23/24F6 ZJ21/22B4
Qian Shan LN11/12D6-C7
Qianshan GD41B2
Qianshanlaoba XJ63/64C8
Qianshan Xian(Meicheng) AH23/24F3
Qian Shui AH23/24F3
Qiansuo YN51/52C4
Qiansuo LN11/12D3
Qiansuo ZJ21/22D6
Qiantang SC47/48B4
Qiantang Jiang ZJ21/22B5
Qianwei LN11/12D4
Qianweitang HEB3/4B4
Qianwei Xian SC45/46D4
Qianwu GD39/40D6
Qian Xian SN55/56F4
Qianxi Xian GZ49/50C5
Qianxi Xian(Xingcheng) HEB5/6C6
Qianyang LN11/12E8
Qianyang Xian SN55/56F3

Qianyao JS17/18C4
Qianying HEB3/4C5
Qianyou He SN55/56G5
Qianzhai SX7/8B4
Qianzhan GD39/40D9
Qianzhangzhuang HEN33/34B7
Qi'anzhen JS17/18D7
Qianzhou JS19/20B3

Qianzhouzhen HN37/38C2
Qi'ao GD41B2
Qiaocun SX7/8B4
Qi'ao Dao GD41B2
Qiaodong JX29/30C3
Qiaoduan HEN33/34D4
Qiaodun ZJ21/22E5
Qiaogou HEN33/34E7
Qiaoguan SD31/32C5
Qiaohe SC47/48D4
Qiaohou YN51/52B3
Qiaojian GX43/44D5
Qiaojiang HN37/38D3
Qiaojiang GD39/40C8
Qiaojiapu GZ49/50B7
Qiaojiawan SX7/8E3
Qiaojia Xian YN51/52B5
Qiaokou HN37/38F6
Qiaoli GX43/44D6
Qiaolin JS17/18E4
Qiaomaidi YN51/52B5
Qiaoqi SC45/46C4
Qiaoqi JS17/18E6
Qiaoshan GX43/44C6
Qiaoshe JX29/30C3
Qiaosi ZJ21/22B5
Qiaoting AH19/20C1
Qiaotou HI42B2
Qiaotou HEN33/34D4
Qiaotou HN37/38E7
Qiaotou HN37/38F4
Qiaotou JX29/30E2
Qiaotou SD31/32B9
Qiaotou LN11/12C7
Qiaotou SX7/8C3
Qiaotou NM5/6A6
Qiaotoubu AH23/24F5
Qiaotouhe HN37/38D4
Qiaotouhu ZJ21/22C6
Qiaotouji AH23/24E5
Qiaotoupu HN37/38F4
(Qiaowa)Muli Zangzu Zizhixian
  SC45/46E3
Qiaowan GS57/58B3
Qiaoxiajie ZJ21/22D5
Qiaoxian GX43/44D6
Qiaoxu GX43/44E7
Qiaoyin GX43/44C5
Qiaozhen SN55/56D4
Qiashui GD39/40B5
Qiawan JX29/30D4
Qiazijie SN55/56H5
Qibao SH17/18E7
Qibofang GZ49/50D5
Qibu FJ25/26C5
Qibu FJ25/26D5
Qicha HI42B2
Qichongyan HN37/38B4
Qichun Xian(Caohe) HB35/36D8
Qicun SD31/32E4
Qicun SX7/8C4
(Qicun)Pingxiang Xian HEB5/6F3
Qidao SX7/8D2

Qidaogou JL13/14F7
Qidaohe BJ3/4B3
Qidaoquanzi LN11/12C4
Qidong GX43/44D7
Qidonggang JS17/18E7
Qidong Shi JS17/18E7
Qidong Xian HN37/38E5
Qidu AH23/24F4
Qiemo(Qarqan)Xian XJ63/64F8
Qifang HI42B2
Qifanggang HB35/36B5
Qifengcha BJ3/4B3
Qifengdu HN37/38F6
Qigong GD39/40B5
Qigong JX29/30C5
Qigou HEB5/6B6
Qigzhi QH59/60C4
Qi He HEN33/34B6
Qi He HEN33/34D3
Qihe Xian(Yancheng) SD31/32C3
Qihongtu HL15/16D6
Qihulin He HL71E7-D7
Qiji HEB5/6F3
Qijia HEB5/6B6
Qijia JL13/14D6
Qijiahe SX7/8G3
Qijiahe HN37/38B4
Qijian SC47/48B4
Qi Jiang SC47/48B3
Qi Jiang SC45/46D6
Qijiang Xian SC45/46D6
Qijiaojing XJ63/64D11
Qijiaping HN37/38C3
Qijiapu LN11/12D7
Qijiawan HB35/36D7
Qijiawu HEB5/6E5
Qijiazhuang BJ3/4C2
Qijing GD39/40E4
Qika NM9/10B12
(Qike)Xunke Xian HL15/16C5
Qikou HEB5/6E5
Qikou SX7/8D2
Qiktim XJ63/64D11
Qilaotu Shan HEB5/6B6
          NM9/10F11-G12
Qileng SN55/56B6
Qilian Shan QH59/60C5-7
          GS57/58C3-5
Qilian Xian(Babao) QH59/60A7
Qilicun SN55/56D5
Qili Hai HEB67C6
Qilimiao SN55/56F4
Qiling FJ25/26F2
Qiling GD39/40B8
Qilinhe LN11/12C5
Qilinzhen JS17/18E7
Qiliping HB35/36C7
Qilixia SN55/56G5
Qiliying HEN33/34B5
Qilizhen GS57/58B2
Qiman XJ63/64E7
Qiman XJ63/64E7
Qimantag QH59/60B2-3 XJ63/64G11

Qimeng GZ49/50D8
Qimen Xian AH23/24G4
Qimenzhan AH19/20B1
Qimu Jiao SD31/32B7
Qin'an Xian GS57/58E7
Qincheng BJ3/4B3
Qincheng XJ63/64D13
Qinchi SX7/8F4
Qinchuan GS57/58D6
Qincun HEB5/6F4
Qindeli HL15/16C7
Qindu SN55/56F4
Qinfengying YN51/52C5
Qing'an Xian HL15/16D4
Qingbaijiang SC47/48B2
Qingbai Jiang SC47/48B2
Qingbaikou BJ3/4B2
Qingban JX29/30C5
Qingcaoge AH23/24F3
Qingcheng SX7/8D5
Qingcheng SD31/32B4
Qingcheng SX7/8C5
Qingcheng Shan SC47/48B1
Qingchengzi LN11/12D7
Qingchi GZ49/50C4
Qingchuan Xian SC45/46B5
Qingcun SH19/20C4
Qingdao Shi SD31/32C7
Qingduizi LN11/12C5
Qingduizi LN11/12E7
Qingfeng HB35/36B3
Qingfengdian HEB5/6E3
Qingfengling Shuiku SD31/32D5
Qingfeng Xian HEN33/34B7
Qinggang HEN73C1
Qinggang SC45/46C5
Qinggang ZJ21/22D6
Qinggang Xian HL15/16D4
Qinggelt NM9/10G5
Qinggir XJ63/64E10
Qinggis Han NM9/10D14
Qinggouzi JL13/14D9
Qingguandu HN37/38B3
Qingguji SD31/32E2
Qinghai Hu QH59/60B7
Qinghai Nanshan QH59/60B6-7
Qinghe HL15/16D5
Qing He LN11/12B8
Qinghe JL13/14F6
Qinghe LN11/12B8
Qinghe SX7/8F3
Qinghe BJ3/4B3
Qinghe HL15/16C3
Qinghechang SC47/48B5
Qinghecheng LN11/12C8
Qinghei Shan HL15/16D5
Qingheji HEN33/34C6
Qinghekou NM9/10F2
Qinghemen LN11/12C5
Qinghe (Qinggil) Xian XJ63/64B11
Qinghe Shuiku LN11/12B8
Qinghetou HEN33/34B7
Qinghe Xian(Gexianzhuang) HEB5/6F3

Qinghezhen SD31/32B4
Qinghu ZJ2/22D3
Qinghu GX43/44E8
Qinghua SC47/48B4
Qinghua JL29/30B5
Qinghuabian SN55/56D5
Qingjiang SC55/56I2
Qingjiang ZJ21/22D6
Qing Jiang HB35/36D3
Qingjiangqiao HN37/38E3
Qingjian He SN55/56C5-D6
Qingjian Xian SN55/56C6
Qingjuchang SC47/48B4
Qingkeng GD39/40B5
(Qingkou)Ganyu Xian JS17/18B5
Qinglan HEB5/6F4
Qinglan HI42B3
Qinglan Gang HI42B3
Qinglian GD39/40B5
Qingliangdian HEB5/6F3
Qingliang Jiang HEB5/6F4-3
Qingliangsi SX7/8D2
Qingliu SC47/48B2
Qingliu Xian FJ25/26D2
Qinglong JX29/30F2
Qinglong SC47/48C1
Qinglong YN51/52D5
Qinglongchang SC45/46C4
Qinglonggang JS19/20B4
Qinglong He HEB5/6C7-6
Qinglongji AH23/24B3
Qinglong Manzu Zizhixian HEB5/6C6
Qinglongqiao BJ3/4B3
Qinglongshan NM11/12B5
Qinglongshan NX61/62C3
Qinglongwan He TJ3/4C4
Qinglong Xian(Liancheng) GZ49/50E4
Qinglung XZ53/54D8
Qingmuguan SC45/46D6
Qingnan Gaoyuan QH80C2-3
Qingnian Shuiku HL15/16E6
Qingnian Yunhe GD39/40E3-2
Qingningsi SH19/20B4
Qingong JS17/18C5
Qingping GD39/40E2
Qingping SC47/48B4
Qingping SC47/48C4
Qingping SD31/32C3
Qingping HB35/36E2
Qingpu FJ25/26E5
Qingpu Xian SH17/18E7
Qingshan JL13/14B3
Qingshan JL13/14B7
Qingshan JL13/14E9
Qingshan HL15/16D7
Qingshan JS19/20A2
Qingshan ZJ21/22B5
Qingshan AH23/24E2
Qingshan AH23/24E3
Qingshan ZJ21/22B4
Qingshan HB35/36D7
Qingshan GD39/40C9
Qingshan GX39/40C8

Qingshan GX43/44C8
Qingshan GZ49/50E3
(Qingshan)Dedu Xian HL15/16C4
Qingshanquan JS17/18B3
Qingshanshi HN37/38C6
Qingshan Shuiku ZJ21/22B4
Qingshen Xian SC45/46D4
Qingshi JL13/14F7
Qingshila HEB5/6B4
Qingshitan Shuiku GX43/44B8
Qingshizui QH59/60B7
Qingshizui NX61/62E3
Qingshui BJ3/4C2
Qingshui AH19/20B1
Qingshui SD31/32C2
Qingshui GX43/44B9
Qingshui FJ25/26E3
Qingshuihe QH59/60D5
Qingshui He SX7/8C5
Qingshui He NX61/62C2
Qingshuihe HB35/36D8
Qingshuihe SX7/8B5
Qingshuihe Xian NM9/10H8
Qingshuihezi XJ63/64D9
Qingshuihezi XJ63/64C6
Qingshui Jiang GZ49/50C6-D6
Qingshui Jiang GZ49/50D7-8
Qingshuilang Shan YN51/52B3-C3
Qingshuipu GS57/58C4
Qingshuipu SC47/48B2
Qingshuitai LN11/12B7
Qingshuiwan HB35/36D3
Qingshuixi SC47/48C1
Qingshui Xian GS57/58E8
Qingshuping HN37/38D5
Qingsong HI42B2
Qingta HEB3/4D3
Qingtai HEN33/34E4
Qingtaiping HB35/36D4
Qingtan HB35/36C5
Qingtang GD39/40B6
Qingtangzhen HN37/38C4
Qingtian Xian(Hecheng) ZJ21/22D5
Qingtongguan SN55/56G5
Qingtongxia NX61/62C3
Qingtongxia Shi NX61/62C2
Qingtongxia Shuiku NX61/62C2
Qingtongxiazhan NX61/62C2
Qingtou SX7/8F2
Qingtuan AH23/24C3
Qingtuo SD31/32D5
Qinguan SN55/56E5
Qingxi ZJ21/22C4
Qingxi SC45/46B5
Qingxi GZ49/50C7
Qingxi SC47/48B4
Qingxi SC47/48C5
Qingxi AH23/24E4
Qingxi HL15/16C4
Qing Xian HEB5/6E4
Qingxiang SX7/8E3
Qingxin Xian GD39/40C6
Qingxin Xian GD39/40C5

Qingxu Xian(Qingyuan) SX7/8D4
Qingyan GZ49/50D5
Qingyang HL15/16E5
Qingyang JL13/14C6
Qingyangcha SN55/56C5
Qingyang Diqu GS57/58D8-E8
Qingyangshan NM57/58D7
(Qingyang)Sihong Xian JS17/18C4
Qingyang Xian GS57/58D8
Qingyang Xian AH23/24F4
Qingyangzhen JS17/18E6
Qingyi JS17/18B4
Qingyi Jiang AH23/24E5-F5
Qingyi Jiang SC45/46C4-D4
Qingyuan SC47/48D5
Qingyuan Manzu Zizhixian LN11/12B8
(Qingyuan)Qingxu Xian SX7/8D4
Qingyuan Shan JX29/30D3
Qingyuan Shi GD39/40C6
Qingyuan Xian ZJ21/22E4
Qingyuan Xian HEB5/6E3
Qingyun HEB5/6F5
Qingyun ZJ21/22B4
Qingyundian BJ3/4C3
Qingyunqiao ZJ19/20C2
Qingyun Shan GD39/40B6-7
Qingyun Xian SD31/32B4
Qingzang Gaoyuan XZ78B3-5
Qingzhang Dongyuan SX7/8D5
Qingzhang He HEB5/6G1
Qingzhang Xiyuan SX7/8D5-E5
Qingzhen Shi GZ49/50D5
Qingzhou FJ25/26D4
Qing Zhou GD41B2
Qingzhou Shi SD31/32C5
Qingzu HEN33/34B7
Qingzuizi JL13/14D6
Qin He SX7/8F4
Qinhuai He JS17/18E4-5
Qinhuangdao Shi HEB5/6D7
Qinjian ZJ21/22D3
Qin Jiang GX43/44E6
Qin Jiang JX29/30E4
(Qinjiang)Shicheng Xian JX29/30E4
Qinjiatun JL13/14D5
Qinlan AH23/24D6
Qinling SN55/56G4
Qinling SN55/56F2
Qin Ling SN55/56G3-4
Qinling Shandi SN79E3-5
Qinnancang JS17/18C5
Qin Qu NX61/62B3
Qinquan SX7/8D5
Qinquan SX7/8E5
Qinshan Dao JS17/18B5
Qinshui Xian SX7/8F4
Qintang GX43/44D7
(Qinting)Lianhua Xian JX29/30D1
Qintong JS17/18D6
Qinwang Shan ZJ19/20D3
Qin Xian SX7/8E4
Qinyang FJ25/26C5
Qinyang Shi HEN33/34B4

Qinyu FJ25/26C6
Qinyuan Xian SX7/8E4
Qinzhou Shi GX43/44F6
Qinzhou Wan GX43/44F6
Qiong Hai SC45/46E4
Qionghai Shi HI42B3
Qionglai Shan SC45/46C4
Qionglai Shi SC45/46C4
Qionglong Shan JS19/20B3
Qiongri'asang XZ53/54C7
Qiongshan Shi HI42A3
Qiongzhong Yizu Miaozu Zizhixian
　(Yinggen) HI42B2
Qiongzhou Haixia HI42A2-3
　　　　　GD39/40F2-3
Qipan Guan SC45/46B6 SN55/56H2
Qipanliang HEB3/4B2
Qipanshan HEB5/6A5
Qiping SC45/46C6
Qiping JX29/30C2
Qiputang JS19/20B3-4
Qiqian NM9/10A13
Qiqiao JS17/18E4
Qiqihar Shi HL15/16D2
Qiqin JX29/30D3
Qiqing GS57/58C4
Qiquanhu XJ63/64D10
Qiqu Qundao ZJ21/22B7
Qira Xian XJ63/64G6
Qisha GX43/44F6
Qi Shan SN55/56F3
Qishan Xian SN55/56F3
Qishe GZ49/50F3
Qishi GD39/40C9
Qishui GD39/40F2
Qi shui HB35/36D8
Qishui He SN55/56F3
Qishuyan JS17/18E6
Qitaihe Shi HL15/16E6
Qitai Xian XJ63/64C10
Qitamu JL13/14C7
Qitian Ling HN37/38F5
Qiting HB35/36C7
Qiu'ai ZJ21/22C6
Qiubei Xian YN51/52C6
Qiucheng HEB5/6G3
Qiuchuan ZJ21/22D3
Qiucun ZJ21/22C6
Qiuji JS17/18C3
Qiujiadian HL15/16D4
Qiujiajie JX29/30C2
Qiujin JX29/30B3
Qiukou JX29/30B5
Qiuliguo JL13/14D9
Qiulin SC47/48A3
Qiulin SN55/56D6
Qiulu FJ25/26E5
Qiumuzhuang LN11/12D7
Qiupu He AH23/24F4
Qiuqu HEN33/34D7
Qiushui He SX7/8D3-2
Qiu Xian HEB5/6G3
Qiuxihe SC45/46D5

Qiuxi He SC47/48B2-C2
Qiuyuan ZJ19/20D2
(Qiuzhuang)Nanxinzhuang HEB3/4C3
Qiuzhuang Shuiku HEB5/6D6
Qiwangji SD31/32D1
Qiweigang JS19/20A3
Qixi ZJ21/22C3
Qi Xian SX7/8D4
Qi Xian HEN33/34C6
Qixianji AH23/24C4
Qi Xian(Zhaoge) HEN33/34B6
Qixia Shan JS19/20A1
Qixia Shi SD31/32B7
Qixiaying TW27/28D2
Qixia JS17/18D4
Qixing Dao ZJ21/22E5
Qixinghe HL15/16D6
Qixing He HL15/16D7
Qixingjie HN37/38D4
Qixingpao HN15/16C3
Qixingpao HL15/16D6
Qixingqiao ZJ19/20C3
Qixing Qu NX61/62C2
Qiyahe NM9/10A13
Qiyang Xian HN37/38E4
Qiyi HEN33/34E4
Qiying NX61/62D3
Qiyi Qu SX7/8E3
Qizhong XZ53/54E12
Qizhou HB35/36D8
(Qizhou)Anguo Xian HEB5/6E3
Qizhou Liedao HI42B4
Qizhou Yang HI42B4
Qiziqiao HN37/38D5
Qog Ondor NM9/10J21
(Qog Ondor)Urad Houqi NM9/10J17
Qog Ul NM9/10E11
Qoidê SC45/46C2
Qoigargoinba QH59/60C7
Qoijê QH59/60B6
Qoijêgoin SC45/46B4
Qoltag XJ81C6
Qomolangma Feng XZ53/54E6
Qonggyai Xian XZ53/54E8
Qongj NM9/10G7
Qongkol XJ63/64E9
Qong Muztag XZ78B2 XJ81E4
Qonj QH59/60B6
Qu'ali JX29/30B5
Quanbao Shan HEN33/34C3
Quancun HEB5/6G2
Quancun GX43/44C6
Quandian SX7/8E4
Quangang FJ25/26E4
Quangang JX29/30C3
Quangongting ZJ21/22B6
Quan He AH23/24C2
Quanjiang JX29/30D1
(Quanjiang)Suichuan Xian JX29/30E2
Quanjiaohe HN37/38C5
Quanjiao Xian(Xianghe) AH23/24D5
Quankou JX29/30B3
Quanming GX43/44E5
Quannan Xian JX29/30G2

Quanshang FJ25/26D2
Quanshui LN11/12C8
Quanshuigou XJ63/64H5
Quantou LN11/12B8
Quantou HEB5/6F3
Quanxi HB35/36B2
Quanxi HN37/38E5
Quanyang JL13/14E8
Quanzhou Gang FJ25/26F4
Quanzhou Shi FJ25/26F4
Quanzhou Xian GX43/44B9
Quchaihe JL13/14D7
Quchan He SX7/8D2
Qucun SX7/8F3
Qudi SD31/32B4
Qu'e SX7/8E2
Que'er'ao ZJ21/22D6
Queshan Xian HEN33/34E6
Qufu Shi SD31/32D3
Qugou HEB3/4C3
Qujiadian LN11/12A7
Qujialing HB35/36D5
Qujiang JX29/30C3
Qujiang YN51/52D5
Qu Jiang YN77C4
Qujiang SC45/46C6
Qu Jiang ZJ21/22C4
Qujiang Xian(Maba) GD39/40B6
Qujie GD39/40F3
Qujing Diqu YN51/52B5-C5
Qujingpu NX61/62B3
Qujing Shi YN51/52C5
Qujiu GX43/44E5
Qukou HEB3/4C4
Qukoupu NX61/62C2
Qukoupu NX61/62B3
Qukoupuzhan NX61/62C2
Qul NM9/10C13
Qulan HN37/38D5
Qulho XZ53/54D5
Quli GX43/44E5
Qulin Gol NM9/10D13
Qulut NM9/10F9
Qulut NM9/10J19
Qumar He QH59/60C3-4
Qumar Heyan QH59/60C3
Qumarlêb Xian QH59/60C4
Qumdo XZ53/54D10
Qumigxung XZ53/54D6
Qumo HEB5/6G2
Qu'ngoin He QH59/60C6
Qu'nyido XZ53/54D11
Qunying HI42C2
Qu Shui HN37/38E2
Qusum Xian XZ53/54E9
Qutang JS17/18D6
Qutang Xia SC45/46C7
Quting SX7/8E3
Quwan HB35/36B5
Quwo Xian SX7/8F3
Quwu Shan GS61/62D2
(Quxar)Lhazê Xian XZ53/54E6
Quxi ZJ21/22E5

Qu,Xi SC47/48B5
Qu Xian SC45/46C6
Qu Xian ZJ21/22D3
Quxianzhan SC47/48B5
Qüxü Xian(Xoi) XZ53/54E8
Quyang JX29/30E3
(Quyang)Jingzhou Miaozu Dongzu
  Zizhixian HN37/38E2
Quyang Xian HEB5/6E2
Quzhou Shi ZJ21/22D3
Quzhou Xian HEB5/6G2
Quzi GS57/58D8

R

Rabang XZ53/54C3
Rabga La XZ53/54F6
(Racaka)Riwoqê Xian XZ53/54D11
Ragxi XZ53/54D9
Raka XZ53/54E5
Rangdong HEN33/34E4
Ranghe HEN33/34D4
Ranghulu HL15/16D3
Rangnan GX43/44D9
Rangtag GS57/58F6
Ranguji SD31/32D2
Rangzijing JL13/14B5
Ranzhuang HEB5/6E3
Ranzhuang SX7/8B6
Rao'er JX29/30C5
Raofeng SN55/56G4
Raohe Xian HL15/16D7
Raoliang HEN33/34E5
Raoping Xian(Huanggang) GD39/40C10
Raoqiao JX29/30D5
Raoshi JX29/30D2
Raoyang GD39/40B9
Raoyanghe LN11/12C6
Raoyang He LN11/12C6
Raoyang Xian HEB5/6E3
Rawu XZ53/54E11
Rayü XZ53/54D10
Renao JL13/14E6
Renchaoxi HN37/48B3
Renchundu NX61/62B3
Rencun HEN33/34A5
Rendian HEN33/34E5
Renfeng SD31/32B4
Renfengzhuang TJ3/4C4
Rengezhuang HEB3/4C5
Renhe SC47/48C4
Renhe SC47/48B3
Renhe SX29/30D3
Renhe GX43/44D9
Ren He SC45/46B7-C7 SN55/56H4
Renheji HEN33/34F7
Renheji SD31/32C9
Renhuai Shi GZ49/50C5
Renhua Xian GD39/40A6
Renju GD39/40B8
Renli SC47/48B3
Renliji SD31/32C3
Renlong SC47/48B3
Renmei FJ25/26E3

Renmin HL15/16D3
Renmin Qu SC47/48A2
Renmin Shengli Qu HEN33/34B5
Renqiao AH23/24C4
Renqiu Shi HEB5/6E4
Ren Shan FJ25/26C4
Renshan GD39/40D7
Renshi SC45/46C6
Renshou FJ25/26C3
Renshou Xian SC45/46D5
Rentian JX29/30E4
Rentuo SC47/48C4
Renxian SC47/48B5
Ren Xian HEB5/6F2
Renxing HI42B2
Renyizhen SC47/48C3
Renzhu GX43/44D7
Rê Qu QH59/60C6
Reshi HN37/38B4
Reshui NM5/6A7
Reshui JX29/30F6
Reshui HN37/38F6
Reshui QH59/60B7
Reshuitang NM11/12C2
Richoi XZ53/54D6
Riga XZ53/54E10
Rila XZ53/54E5
Rinbung Xian (Dêgyiling) XZ53/54E7
Rinda SC45/46C3
Rindü XZ53/54E7
Ringtor XZ53/54D4
Ri Qu XZ76C2
Riwoqê Xian(Racaka) XZ53/54D11
Riyue Shan QH59/60B7
Riyue Shankou QH59/60B7
Rizhao Shi SD31/32D6
Rizhao Shuiku SD31/32D6
Rizhe YN51/52C5
Rola Co XZ53/54B7
Rolagang XZ53/54B7
Rong'an Xian(Chang'an) GX43/44B7
Rongbaca SC45/46C2
Rongbang HI42B2
Rongchang Xian SC45/46D5
(Rongcheng)Jieyang Xian GD39/40C9
Rongcheng Shi SD31/32B9
Rongcheng Wan SD31/32B9
Rongcheng Xian HEB5/6D3
Ronghe SX7/8F2
Ronghua GX43/44D4
Ronghuashan LN11/12E6
Rong Jiang GX43/44B7
Rong Jiang GD25/26G2
Rongjiang Xian(Guzhou) GZ49/50E7
Rongkou AH23/24G4
Ronglong SC47/48C3
Rongpu Si XZ53/54E6
Rongqi GD39/40D6
Rongshan SC45/46B6
Rongshan SC47/48D3
Rongshui Miaozu Zizhixian GX43/44B7
Rongshujiao GD41A2
Rongwo He QH80C4

(Rongwo)Tongren Xian QH59/60C7
Rong Xian SC45/46D5
Rong Xian GX43/44E8
Round Island HK41B3
Rouyuanpu NX61/62C2
Ruanxiang SH19/20C4
Ru'ao ZJ21/22C5
Rucheng Xian HN37/38F6
Rucun SX7/8C5
Rudong GD39/40E4
Rudong Xian(Juegang) JS17/18D7
Rugao Shi JS17/18D6
Ruhai Yunhe JS19/20A3
Ru He HEN33/34E6
Rui'an Shi ZJ21/22E5
Ruichang Shi JX29/30B3
Ruicheng Xian SX7/8G2
Ruihong JX29/30C4
Ruijin Shi JX29/30F4
Ruili Jiang YN51/52D2-C2
Ruilin JX29/30E3
Ruili Shi YN51/52C2
Ruitapu HN37/38B3
Ruixi HI42B3
Rujigou NX61/62A3
(Rulin)Chengbu Miaozu Zizhixian
  HN37/38E3
Runanbu HEN33/34E6
Runan Xian HEN33/34D6
Runcheng SX7/8F4
Run He AH23/24D2
Runheji AH23/24D3
Ruoheng ZJ21/22D6
Ruoli GS61/62D1
Ruoqiang He XJ63/64F10
Ruoqiang(Qarkilik)Xian XJ63/64F10
Ruoshui HN37/38D2
Ruo Shui NM9/10G3-2
  GS57/58B5-4
Rushankou SD31/32C8
Rushan Shi SD31/32C8
Rushanzhai SD31/32C8
Rushui NX61/62E3
Rushui He GS55/56E3
Rutog XZ53/54E9
Rutog Xian XZ53/54C2
Ruyang Xian HEN33/34C4
Ruyuan Yaozu Zizhixian GD39/40B6
Ruzhou Shi HEN33/34C4

S

Sabu NX61/62D2
Saga Xian(Gya'gya) XZ53/54E5
Sa'gya Xian XZ53/54E6
Sa He HEB3/4B4-5
Saheqiao HEB5/6C6
Saihan Gobi NM9/10F9
Saihan Olji NM9/10F9
Saihan Tal NM9/10C11
Saihan Tal HL15/16D3
(Saihan Tal)Sonid Youqi NM9/10F9
Saihan Toroi NM9/10G2
Sai Kung HK41B3

Saima LN11/12D8
Sai O HK41B3
Saiqi FJ25/26D5
Sairgaltin Hudag NM61/62B2
Saishiji AH23/24E3
Saiyu SX7/8D5
(Salaqi)Tumd Youqi NM9/10K20
Samai NM9/10E11
Samarz NM9/10E10
Samka XZ53/54D11
Samsang XZ53/54D4
Sanbao LN11/12C4
Sanbastaw XJ81B6
Sanbeiyangchang NM61/62A4
Sanbiao JX29/30F3
Sancang JS17/18D6
Sancha GX43/44C6
Sancha SX7/8B3
Sancha HB35/36D2
Sancha GS57/58D8
Sancha GS57/58E7
Sanchabu HB35/36D7
Sanchadian SD31/32C5
Sanchagang JX29/30B4
Sanchahe HN37/38B5
Sancha He GZ49/50D4-5
Sanchakou HEB5/6C3
Sanchakou NM9/10J22
Sanchakou XJ63/64F5
Sanchang JS17/18E7
Sancha Shuiku SC47/48B2
Sanchazi JL13/14E7
Sanchih TW27/28B3
Sanchuan HEN33/34D3
Sanchuan He SX7/8D2-3
Sanchung TW27/28B3
Sandao JL13/14E9
Sandao HI42C2
Sandaogang HL15/16D6
Sandaogou LN11/12D4
Sandaohe HEB3/4B2
Sandaohe Shuiku HB35/36C4
Sandaohezi HL15/16E5
Sandaohu JL13/14E7
Sandaohu NM61/62B1
Sandaohumiao NM61/62B1
Sandaoling XJ63/64D12
Sandaoqiao NM9/10K16
Sandaowai JL13/14D10
Sandaozhen HL15/16D4
Sandong GZ49/50E6
Sandong SC47/48C1
Sandouping HB35/36D4
Sandu ZJ21/22C5
Sandu JX29/30E2
Sandu HN37/38E6
Sandu ZJ21/22C4
Sandu GX43/44C7
Sandu FJ25/26D5
Sandu JX29/30C2
Sandu JX29/30B2
Sandu HI42B2
Sandu GZ49/50D5

Sanduandi NM61/62B4
Sandu Ao FJ25/26D5
Sanduizi SC45/46E3
Sandun ZJ19/20C3
Sandun HN37/38C6
Sandunzi NX61/62C3
Sanduo SX7/8E2
Sanduo JS17/18D5
Sandu Suizu Zizhixian GZ49/50D6
Sanfang GX43/44B6
Sanfeng SC47/48B3
Sanfengsi HN37/38B5
Sa'ngain XZ53/54D12
Sangang FJ25/26C3
Sangba XZ53/54D9
Sangbi SX7/8E2
Sangcun SD31/32D4
Sang Dao SD31/32B7
Sangejing NM9/10H3
Sangengluo HI42C3
Sangequanzi XJ63/64D11
Sang'ezhen SD31/32C2
Sanggan He HEB5/6C2 SX7/8B5-A6
Sanggarmai SC45/46B4
Sanggin Dalai NM9/10F10
Sanggou Wan SD31/32B9
Sanglang GZ49/50E5
Sanglinzi LN11/12C6
Sangluoshu SD31/32B4
Sangmu GZ49/50B5
Sangngagqoiling XZ53/54E9
Sangou HEB5/6B6
Sang Qu XZ53/54E11
Sangri Xian XZ53/54E8
Sangruma QH59/60D6
Sangsang XZ53/54E6
Sangtian JX29/30D4
Sanguan NM61/62B2
Sanguandian AH23/24E5
Sanguandian HB35/36B4
Sanguanmiao HEN33/34C5
Sanguanmiao HEN33/34E6
Sanguansi HN37/38B3
Sangxung La XZ53/54D8
(Sangyuan)Wuqiao Xian HEB5/6F4
Sangyuan Xia GS57/58D7
Sangyuanzi GS57/58D6
Sangzhidian SD31/32C3
Sangzhi Xian(Liyuan) HN37/38B3
Sangzhou ZJ21/22C6
Sangzhuang HEN33/34E4
Sanhaodi HEB5/6B2
Sanhe JL13/14E10
Sanhe GD41B1
Sanhe GZ49/50B5
San He JS17/18C4-5
Sanheba GD39/40B9
Sanhedian HB35/36B6
Sanhejian HEN33/34E7
Sanhekou JS19/20B3
Sanhekou SC47/48D1
Sanhekou Shuiku HB35/36C8
Sanheshi GZ49/50C5

Sanhe Shi HEB5/6D5
Sanhezhan HL15/16A4
Sanhezhen NX61/62E2
Sanhezhen AH23/24E4
Sanhsia TW27/28C3
Sanhu JX29/30D3
Sanhuang GX43/44C7
Sanhuiba SC47/48B4
Sanhuizhen SC45/46C6
San-i TW27/28C2
Sanjia GD39/30D4
Sanjia HEB5/6B6
Sanjia SC47/48B3
Sanjia HI42B1
Sanjiachang YN51/52C4
Sanjiadian BJ3/4C3
Sanjiang GD39/40D6
Sanjiang GX43/44C8
Sanjiang GX43/44C9
Sanjiang HI42B3
Sanjiang SC45/46D6
Sanjiang SC47/48B1
Sanjiang SC47/48C2
Sanjiang Dongzu Zizhixian(Guyi)
   GX43/44B7
(Sanjiang)Jinping Xian GZ49/50D8
Sanjiangkou LN11/12A7
Sanjiangkou YN51/52B4
Sanjiangkou JX29/30C3
Sanjiangkou SC47/48B1
(Sanjiang)Liannan Yaozu Zizhixian
   GD39/40B5
Sanjiangmen GX43/44B7
Sanjiang Pingyuan HL70D8-7
Sanjiangying JS17/18D5
Sanjiao SX7/8C4
Sanjiao SX7/8D2
Sanjiao GD41A1
Sanjiao SC47/48C4
Sanjiaocheng QH80B4
Sanjiao Dao GD41B2
Sanjiaodi LN11/12D7
Sanjiaolou GD41A2
Sanjiaoping HN37/38C3
Sanjiaotang ZJ21/22D6
Sanjiazi LN11/12B7
Sanjiazi LN11/12D7
Sanjie ZJ21/22C5
Sanjie AH23/24D5
Sanjie YN51/52C4
Sanjie GX43/44B8
Sanjieshou SD31/32D5
Sanjing SX7/8C3
Sanjingzi JL13/14B6
Sanju XJ63/64G5
Sankeng GD41A1
Sankeng Shui GD41A1
Sankeshu HL15/16E4
Sankeyushu JL13/14F6
Sankou AH19/20C1
Sanlang HEB5/6F3
Sanlangyan HN37/38B5
Sanli JX29/30C4

Sanli GX43/44C7	Santai XJ63/64C6	Saya SC45/46B3
Sanli GX43/44D6	Santai LN11/12C7	Sayingpan YN51/52B5
Sanli GX43/44D7	Santai YN51/52B4	Sayram XJ63/64E7
Sanliang NM7/8A3	Santai Shan YN77B4-C4	Sayram Hu XJ63/64C6
Sanlicheng HB35/36C7	Santaishan YN51/52C3	Sayu He YN49/50C2
Sanlidian AH23/24F5	Santai Xian SC45/46C5	Segangdian HEN33/34F6
Sanlifan HB35/36D8	Santaizi LN11/12B7	Sehepu SN55/56G5
Sanligang HB35/36C6	Santaizi LN11/12C3	Sêkog QH59/60D5
Sanlintang SH19/20B4	Santang SD31/32B3	Sêlêpug XZ53/54D4
Sanlixi Shuiku HN37/38B4	Santang JX29/30C4	Sêmnyi QH59/60B8
Sanlong JX29/30B5	Santang HN37/38E5	Sêndo XZ53/54D10
Sanlong JS17/18C6	Santanghu XJ63/64C12	Sêngdoi XZ53/54D3
Sanlou SX7/8B5	Santangjie HN37/38C4	Sênggê QH59/60B6
Sanlousi SX7/8G2	Santangpu HN37/38D4	Sênggê Zangbo(Shiquan He)
Sanmen HN37/38D6	Santi TW27/28E2	XZ53/54C2-D3
Sanmen GX43/44B7	Santiao Chiao TW27/28B4	Sengnian SX7/8E3
Sanmen Liedao GD41B3	Santong He JL13/14E7-6	Senjitu HEB5/6B4
Sanmenpo HI42B3	Santun HEN33/34C4	Senlin Shan JL13/14D11
Sanmen Wan ZJ21/22C6	Santunying HEB5/6C6	(Sêraitang)Baima Xian QH59/60D7
Sanmen Xian(Haiyou) ZJ21/22C6	Sanwan JX29/30E1	Sêrba SC45/46C3
Sanmenxia Shi HEN33/34C3	Sanwang GX43/44C5	Sêrca XZ53/54D10
Sanmenxia Shuiku SX7/8G3	Sanwei Shan GS57/58B2	Serh QH59/60B6
HEN33/34C3	Sanxi AH23/24F5	Serikbuya XJ63/64F4
Sanmianchuan LN11/12B7	Sanxi JX29/30D4	Sêrtar Xian SC45/46B3
Sanmiao SC47/48B4	Sanxiang GD39/40D6	Serteng Shan QH80B2
Sanming Shi FJ25/26D3	Sanxiang HEN33/34C3	Sêrwo Qu QH59/60C4
Sanping HI42C2	Sanxianhu HN37/38B5	Seshufen BJ3/4C2
Sanpu JS17/18B3	Sanxikou HB35/36E7	Sêwa XZ53/54C7
Sanpu AH23/24C4	Sanxikou ZJ21/22B4	Shabian GD41A1
Sanpu GX43/44D8	Sanxing HL15/16D3	Shabu GX43/44C7
Sanpu GS57/58C5	Sanxing JX29/30C2	Shachang GZ49/50C5
Sanqia HL15/16B4	Sanxing SH17/18E7	Sha Chau HK41B2
Sanqiao AH23/24F3	Sanxiqiao JX29/30B3	Shacheng FJ25/26C6
Sanqiao GZ49/50D5	Sanya Gang HI42C2	Shacheng Gang FJ25/26C6
Sanqiaobu ZJ21/22B4	Sanyang JX29/30D2	(Shacheng)Huailai Xian HEB5/6C3
Sanquan SX7/8D3	Sanyang HB35/36C6	Shache(Yarkant)Xian XJ63/64F4
Sanquzhen SC45/46D5	Sanyang JX29/30C4	Shaconggou NX61/62B3
Sanrao GD39/40C9	Sanyanggang HN37/38C4	Shacun JX29/30E3
Sanrenban HL15/16E4	Sanyangkeng AH23/24F5	Shadaogou HB35/36E2
Sansha FJ25/26D6	Sanyangzhen JS17/18E7	Shadaoguan HB35/36D4
Sanshan AH24/25E5	Sanyanjing NX61/62C2	Shadi GD39/40E5
Sanshan HEB5/6B3	Sanyantang HN37/38C5	Shadi JX29/30E2
Sansha Wan FJ25/26D5	Sanyao SN55/56F6	Shadianji HEN33/34B6
Sansheng AH23/24E5	Sanya Shi HI42C2	Shadui HB35/36E6
Sanshengyu JL13/14C5	Sanying YN51/52B4	Shagang HB35/36D5
Sanshi GX43/44C5	Sanying NX61/62D3	Shagang LN11/12D6
Sanshi HN37/38C6	Sanyu JS17/18D7	Shagang GD41B4
Sanshihao JL13/14C4	Sanyuan SC47/48B5	Shagangshi HN37/38B5
Sanshijia LN11/12C3	Sanyuanba SN55/56H3	(Shagedu)Jungar Qi NM9/10H18
Sanshilipu SN55/56D5	Sanyuandian AH23/24E3	Shagou JS17/18C5
Sanshilipu NX61/62E3	Sanyuanpu JL13/14E6	Shagou NX61/62D2
Sanshilipu HEB3/4D3	Sanyuan Xian SN55/56F4	Shagou SD31/32E4
Sanshilipu AH23/24E4	Sanzao GD39/40D6	Shagoujie SN55/56G4
Sanshilipu LN11/12E5	Sanzao Dao GD41C1	Shaguotun LN11/12C4
Sanshipu AH23/24E3	Sanzhan HL15/16E3	Shahai NM9/10K16
Sanshizi NX61/62B2	Sanzhan HL15/16C4	Shahai LN11/12C3
Sanshui SC47/48B2	Sanzhen GD39/40B9	Shahe BJ3/4B3
Sanshui Shi GD39/40C5	Sanzhou GD39/40E5	Shahe HEB5/6G2
Sansi SC47/48B1	Sanzhuang SD31/32D6	Shahe HL15/16D5
Sansui Xian(Bagong) GZ49/50D7	Sapqiao SN55/56F4	Shahe JS17/18B4
Sansumu NM9/10K22	Sarbulak XJ63/64B10	Shahe SC45/46C7
Santa AH23/24D2	Sartal XJ63/64B9	Shahe GX43/44E7
Santai LN11/12E5	(Sartu)Daqing Shi HL15/16D3	Sha He HEB3/4B4

Sha He   HEB5/6F2
Sha He   SD31/32B4
Shahe   SD31/32B6

Shahedian   HEB33/34E5
Shaheji   AH23/24D5
Shahekan   SN55/56H3
(Shahepu)Linze Xian   GS57/58C5
Shaheqiao   HEB5/6E4
Shahe Shi   HEB5/6G2
Shahe Shuiku   JS17/18E5
Shaheyan   JL13/14D9
Shaheyi   HEB5/6D6
Shahezhan   SD31/32D3
Shahezhen   JL13/14E6
Shahezi   HL15/16E4
Shahezi   SN55/56G6
Shahousuo   LN11/12D4
Shahu   HB35/36D6
Shahu   GD41B1
Shahu   GD41A3
Shahukou   SX7/8A4
Shaikou   FJ25/26C3
Shaji   SN55/56D4
Shajiadian   SN55/56C6
Shajian   FJ25/26F3
Shajiang   FJ25/26D5
Shajianzi   LN11/12C9
Shajiao   GD41B2
Shajiao   GD41B2
Shajiao   GD41A2
Shajing   GD41A2
Shajingou   JL13/14E9
Shakou   GD39/40B6
Shala   LN11/12B5
Shalan   HL15/16E5
Shalang   GD39/40E4
Shali   GX43/44C3
Shaliangzi   BJ3/4B3
Shaliangzi   QH59/60B3
Shaling   LN11/12C7
Sha Ling   HK41A3
Shalingzi   HEB5/6C2
Shaliu   ZJ21/22C6
Shaliuhe   HEB5/6D5
(Shaliuhe)Gangca Xian   QH59/60B7
Shalong   GD39/40C9
Sha Lo Tung   HK41B3
Shalu   TW27/28C2
Shaluli Shan   SC45/46C2-D3
Shamao   SN55/56B6
Sham Tseng   HK41B3
Sham Wat   HK41B2
Shanban Zhou   GD41A2
Shanbei   AH23/24E6
Shanbiao   HEN33/34B5
Shanchengbu   GS57/58D8
Shanchengzhen   JL13/14E6
Shandan He   GS57/58C5
Shandan Xian   GS57/58C5
Shandian He   HEB5/6A3-B3
Shandong Bandao   SD31/32C6-B8
Shandong Qiuling   SD73C4-B6

Shang'an   HI42C2
Shangba   GZ49/50B6
Shangbahe   HB35/36D8
Shangbaishi   FJ25/26C5
Shangbali   HEN33/34B5
Shangbancheng   HEB5/6C6
Shangbaomei   GD41A2
Shangbazhen   ZJ19/20C2
Shang Boingor   QH59/60D6
Shangbu   JX29/30D1
Shangcai Xian   HEN33/34D6
Shangcang   TJ3/4C4
Shangchao   GX43/44B6
Shangcheng Xian   HEN33/34F7
Shangchewan   HB35/36E6
Shangchuan Dao   GD39/40E5
Shangdachen Dao   ZJ21/22D6
Shangdang   JS19/20A2
Shangdian   HEN33/34C4
Shangdian   SD31/32B4
Shangdian   HEN33/34D5
Shangdianzi   HB35/36A2
Shangdianzi   BJ3/4B4
Shangdouying   HEB3/4B2
Shangdu   HN37/38F6
Shangdundu   JX29/30D4
Shangdu Xian   NM9/10G9
Shange   FJ25/26F3
Shangen   HI42C3
Shangen   QH59/60B7
Shangfang   HEB5/6E2
Shangfang   ZJ21/22C3
Shangfu   JX29/30C3
Shanggang   JS17/18C6
Shangganling   HL15/16D5
Shanggao Xian (Aoyang)   JX29/30C2
Shanggin Dalai   NM61/62B2
Shanggu   HEB5/6C6
Shanggu   JS19/20B2
Shangguancun   HEN33/34B6
Shanggulin   TJ3/4D4
Shanggunquan   NX61/62C3
Shangguo   SX7/8F2
Shanghaimiao Muchang   NM61/62B3
Shanghai Nongchang   JS17/18C6
Shanghai Shi   SH17/18E7
Shanghang Xian   FJ25/26E2
Shanghe   SC47/48B3
Shanghe   GD41A2
Shanghekou   LN11/12D8
Shanghewan   JL13/14C7
Shanghe Xian   SD31/32B4
Shanghu   SX7/8D5
Shanghu   ZJ21/22C6
Shanghu   ZJ21/22C5
Shanghua   ZJ21/22C4
Shanghuang   JS17/18E5
Shanghuangqi   HEB5/6B4
Shangji   HL15/16D4
Shangji   GZ49/50C5
Shangji   HL15/16D3
Shangjia   LN11/12C8
Shangjiahe   LN11/12C8
Shangjiang   JX29/30F2

Shangjiaodao   ZJ21/22C4
Shangjin   GX43/44E5
Shangjin   HB35/36A3
Shangjing   FJ25/26E3
Shangjiuwu   HEN33/34D4
(Shangji)Xichuan Xian   HEN33/34D3
Shang Kongma   QH59/60D6
Shangkou   SD31/32C5
Shangkuli   NM9/10B13
Shanglancun   SX7/8C4
Shanglaxiu   QH59/60D5
Shanglei   GX43/44C7
Shanglian   FJ25/26D4
Shangliang   SC45/46B6
Shangliao   GD41A2
Shangling   GD39/40B7
Shanglin Xian (Dafeng)   GX43/44D6
Shangli Xian   JX29/30D1
Shangluo Diqu   SN55/56G5-6
Shangluozhen   SN55/56G6
Shangmachang   HL15/16B4
Shangmaying   NX61/62D2
Shangmei   FJ25/26C4
Shangnan Xian   SN55/56G6
Shang Ngawa   SC45/46B3
Shangpan   ZJ21/22D6
Shangpeibu   JS19/20B2
Shangping   GD39/40B8
Shangpu   ZJ21/22C5
Shangqing   JX29/30C5

Shangqiu Shi   HEN33/34C7

Shangrao Diqu   JX29/30C5
Shangrao Shi   JX29/30C5
Shangrao Xian (Xuricun)   JX29/30C5
Shangshan   GD39/40B9
Shangshe   SX7/8C4
Shangshe   SX7/8C4
Shangshe   SX7/8C5
Shangshidian   HB35/36C6
Shangshipeng   NX61/62C2
Shangshiqiao   HN33/34F7
Shangshui Xian   HEN33/34D6
Shangsi   GZ49/50E6
Shangsi   AH19/20B2
Shangsi Xian (Siyang)   GX43/44E5
Shangsong   ZJ19/20C2
Shangsuoqiao   SC45/46C4
Shangta   SH19/20B3
Shangtang   JS17/18C4
Shangtang   JX29/30C3
Shangtang   JX29/30D4
(Shangtang)Yongjia Xian   ZJ21/22D5
Shangtian   AH19/20C1
Shangtun   HEN33/34E4
Shan Guan   FJ25/26C3   JX29/30D5
Shangwang   ZJ19/20D3
Shangxi   ZJ21/22C4
Shangxi   JX29/30E3
Shangxiao   GS61/62E4
Shangxing   JS17/18E5
Shangxinhe   JS17/18D4

Shangyangwu   SX7/8C4
Shangyantan   ZJ21/22C5
Shangye   SD31/32D4
Shangying   GX43/44D4
Shangying   JL13/14C8
Shangyong   FJ25/26E4
Shangyou Jiang   JX72D2
Shangyou Shuiku   JX29/30C3
Shangyou Shuiku   XJ63/64E6
Shangyou Xian(Dongshan)   JX29/30F2
Shangyou Yichang   XJ63/64E6
Shangyuan   LN11/12C4
Shangyun   YN51/52D3
Shangyu Shi   ZJ21/22B5
Shang Zayü   XZ49/50E11
Shangzha   GD41B2
Shangzhage   YN51/52B5
Shangzhai   SX7/8B6
Shangzhenzi   SN55/56E4
Shangzhi Shi   HL15/16E4
Shangzhong   GZ49/50D7
Shangzhou   SC47/48D2
Shangzhoujiahewan   NX61/62C2
Shangzhou Shi   SN55/56G5
Shangzhuang   JX29/30D2
Shangzhuang   HEB5/6D2
Shangzhuang   SX7/8C4
Shangzhuang   SD31/32B8
Shangzhuang   HEN33/34B4
Shangzhuang   SD31/32D6
Shangzhuang   ZJ19/20D4
Shanhaiguan   HEB5/6C7
Shanhe   NX61/62E3
Shanhetun   HL15/16E4
(Shanhe)Zhengning Xian   GS57/58E9
Shanhua   TW27/28D2
Shanhu Tan   TW27/28D2
Shanji   JS17/18B3
Shanjiao   GX43/44C5
Shanjiaodi   AH19/20C2
Shankou   HN37/38C4
Shankou   HI42B2
Shankou   XJ63/64D13
Shankou   ZJ21/22D5
Shankou   JX29/30C2
Shankou   GX43/44F7
Shanli   AH23/24G4
Shanlian   ZJ21/22B5
Shanlin   TW27/28E2
Shanlin   HEB5/6E4
Shan Ling   FJ25/26C3
Shanmatang Ding   GX43/44C9
                            HN37/38G4
Shanmei Shuiku   FJ25/26E4
Shanmen   GS57/58E8
Shanmen   HN37/38D3
Shanmen   JL13/14D5
Shanmuqing   GZ49/50D2
Shannan Diqu   XZ53/54E9-F9
Shannanguan   AH23/24E3
Shanpen   GZ49/50C5
Shanpo   HB35/36D7
Shanqiandian   SD31/3B7

Shanrong   HI42C2
Shanshan(Piqa)Xian   XJ63/64D11
Shanshanzhan   XJ63/64D11
Shanshi   HL15/16E5
Shanshulun   HN37/38C5
Shansonggang   JL13/14E7
Shansuogang   SC45/46D4
Shantangyi   HN37/38D3
Shanting   SD31/32D4
Shantou   JX29/30D3
Shantou Gang   GD25/26G2
Shantouji   AH23/24C5
Shantou Shi   GD39/40C9
Shanwang   SC47/48C2
Shanwanghe   AH23/24E3
Shanwanzi   HEB5/6A5
Shanwei Shi   GD39/40D8
Shanxi   ZJ21/22E5
Shan Xian   HEN33/34C3
Shan Xian   SD31/32E3
Shanxiang   HN37/38F4
Shanxin   GX43/44E7
Shanxu   GX43/44E5
Shanyang   SH19/20C5
Shanyang   FJ25/26D5
Shanyang Xian   SN55/56G5
(Shanyao) Quangang   FJ25/26E4
Shanyincheng   SX7/8B4
Shanyin Xian(Daiyue)   SX7/8B4
Shanyi Xian(Nanhaoqian)   HEB5/6B1
Shanzao   HN37/38D5
Shanzhai   SX7/8B3
Shaobo   JS17/18D5
Shaobo Hu   JS17/18D5
Shaodian   HEN33/34D6
Shaodian   JS17/18B4
Shaodong Xian(Liangshi)   HN37/37D4
Shaogangji   HEN33/34C6
Shaogangpu   NX61/62B3
Shaoguan Shi   GD39/40B6
Shaoguo   JL13/14D6
Shaoguodian   JL13/14D5
Shaoguozhen   JL13/14B4
Shaoleng He   NM67A6
Shaoshan Xian   HN37/38D5
Shaoshanzhan   HN37/38D5
Shaoshui   GX43/44B8
Shaowu Shi   FJ25/26C3
Shaoxing Shi   ZJ21/22B5
Shaoxing Xian   ZJ21/22B5
Shaoyang Shi   HN37/38D4
Shaoyang Xian(Tangdukou)   HN37/38D4
Shaoyuan   HEN33/34B4
Shaoyun   SC47/48B3
Shaozi He   LN11/12D7
Shapa   GD39/40E4
Shaping   GX43/44E6
Shaping   SC47/48B5
Shapingba   SC47/48C4
Shapingguan   SC47/48A1
(Shaping)Heshan Xian   GD39/40D5
Shapotou   NX61/62C1
Shaqiuhe   XJ63/64C10

Shaquan   SX7/8B3
Shaquan   HN37/38D5
Shaquanzi   XJ63/64C7
Sharp Island   HK41B3
Sharqin   NM9/10K21
Shashijie   HN37/38C6
Shashiyu   HEB5/6C6
Shatanchang   SC47/48B5
Shatangpu   NX61/62E2
Shatian   JX29/30E2
Shatian   HN37/38F6
Shatian   GX43/44C9
Shatian   GX43/44E8
Shatou   HN37/38C5
Shatou   GX43/44D9
Shatoujiao   GD41B3
Shatu   GX49/50C5
Shatuji   SD31/32D2
Shatupozi   NX61/62D3
Shawan   ZJ21/22E4
Shawan   HN37/38D3
Shawan   GD41A2
Shawan   GD39/40D4
Shawan   SC45/46D4
Shawan   GZ49/50C5
Shawan Xian   XJ63/64C8
Shawo   HEN33/34F7
Shawo   GZ49/50D4
Shawoli   JX29/30C2
Shawu   FJ25/26D2
Shaxi   JX29/30F2
Shaxi   JX29/30E3
Sha Xi   FJ25/26D3
Shaxi   HN37/38E2
Shaxi   FJ25/26D3
Shaxi   JS17/18E7
Shaxi   GD41A1
Shaxi   JX29/30C6
Sha Xian   FJ25/26D3
Shaxin   GD41B1
Shayang   HB35/36D5
Shayu   HEB5/6E2
Shayu   BJ3/4B3
Shayu   SX7/8D5
Shayugou   HEN33/34C5
Shazaoyuan   GS57/58C2
Shazhen   SD31/32D2
Shazhenxi   HB35/36D3
Shazhou   JX29/30D4
Shazhouba   JX29/30F3
Shazi   GX43/44C8
Shazidi   HB35/36D2
Shaziling   GZ49/50E4
Shazipo   GZ49/50B7
Shebu   GX43/44D8
Shebu   HN37/38D5
Shecheng   SX7/8D4
(She Dao)Xiaolongshan Dao   LN11/12F4
Shefu   JX29/30E3
Shegangshi   HN37/38C6
Shegeng   JX29/30C4
Shehong Xian(Taihezhen)   SC45/46C5
Shejiaping   HN37/38C4

Shek Chung Au   HK41A3
Shekeng   GD39/40B8
Shek Hang   HK41B3
Shek Kong   HK41B3
Shek Kwu Chau   HK41B2
Shek O   HK41B3
Shekou   FJ25/26C5
Shekou   HB35/36D7
Shekou   GD41B2
Sheli   JL13/14B4
Sheling   JL13/14D6
Shen'ao   GD39/40C10
Shenchi Xian   SX7/8B4
Shendang   ZJ21/22B5
Shending Shan   HL15/16D7
Shendu   AH23/24G5
Shendushui   GD39/40B7
Shengang   JS17/18E6
Shengang   JX29/30D4
Shengang   GD41A2
Shengci   JS17/18D6
Shengfang   HEB5/6D4
Shenghang   GD39/40D5
Shengjiaqiao   AH23/24F5
Shengjiaqiao   AH23/24E4
Shengjiatan   NX61/62C2
Shengjing Guan   YN51/52C6
          GZ49/50E3
Shengjinguan   NX61/62C2
Shengjin Hu   AH23/24F4
Shengkang   HB35/36B4
Shengli   SC47/48A2
Shengli   HL15/16E5
Shengli   HB35/36C8
Shengli   NX61/62B3
Shengli   HL15/16E4
Shengli Daban   XJ63/64D9
Shengli Qichang   XJ63/64E6
Shengli Shibachang   XJ63/64E6
Shengli Shuiku   SC35/36F1
Shengmijie   JX29/30C3
Shengping   HL15/16D3
Shengshan   ZJ21/22B7
Sheng Shan   ZJ21/22B7
Shengshan Yang   ZJ21/22B7-8
Shengshuihezi   JL13/14E6
Shengsi Liedao   ZJ21/22B7
Shengsi Xian(Caiyuanzhen)   ZJ21/22B7
Shengtang Shan   GX75C4
Shengze   JS17/18F6
Shengzhong Shuiku   SC45/46C5
Shengzhong Shi   ZJ21/22C5
Shenhe   SN55/56H5
Shenhou   HEN33/34C5
Shenhu   FJ25/26F4
Shenhuguan   YN51/52C2
Shenjia   HL15/16D4
Shenjiahe Shuiku   NX61/62D3
Shenjiaji   HB35/36D5
Putuo (Shenjiamen)   ZJ21/22C7
Shenjiatai   LN11/12C4
Shenjiaxiang   AH23/24E5
Shenjing   HEB5/6C2

Shenjing   GD39/40D5
Shenjing   NX61/62C1
Shenjing   GD41B1
Shenjingzi   JL13/14C5
Shenjingzi   LN11/12C7
Shenkeng   JX29/30F2
Shenlinpu   NX61/62E2
Shenlun   JS17/18D5
Shenmu Xian · SN55/56B6
Shennan   HEB5/6D2
Shennong Ding   HB35/36C3
Shennongjia Linqu（Songbai)
     HB35/36C3
Shenqiucheng   HEN33/34D7
Shenqiu Xian(Huaidian)   HEN33/34D7
Shenquan   GD39/40C9
Shenquanbu   SN55/56B6
Shenquan Gang   GD39/40D9
Shenshiqiao   ZJ21/22B6
Shenshizhuang   HEB3/4C3
Shenshu   HL15/16D5
Shen Shui   HN37/38G4-5
Shentang   GD39/40F3
Shentang   GD41B1
Shentangbu   SX7/8B5
Shentou   SD31/32B3
Shentou   SX7/8B4
Shentu   FJ25/26F3
Shenwan   GD41B1
Shenwo Shuiku   LN11/12C7
Shen Xian   SD31/32C2
Shenxing   HEB5/6D3
Shenyang Shi   LN11/12C7
Shenze Xian   HEB5/6E3
Shenzhen   ZJ21/22C6
Shenzhen He   GD41A3
Shenzhen Shi   GD39/40D7
Shenzhen Shuiku   GD41A2
Shenzhen Wan (Deep Bay)   GD41A2
Shenzhou Shi   HEB5/6D3
Sheqiao   HEN33/34D6
Sheqi Xian   HEN33/34D4
She Shan   SH17/18E8
She Shan   SH19/20B4
Sheshiqiao   HN37/38B4
She Shui   HB35/36C7-D7
Shetan   SC47/48C5
Shetianqiao   HN37/38D4
Shetou   JS19/20B2
Sheung Chung   HK41B3
Sheung Shui   HK41A3
Sheung Wo Hang   HK41A3
Shewei   HEN33/34D3
Shexi   JX29/30F2
She Xian   HEB5/6G1
Shexiang   SD31/32B4
She Xian(Huicheng)   AH23/24G5
Sheyang   JS17/18C5
Sheyang He   JS17/18C6
Sheyanghe Kou   JS17/18C6
Sheyang Xian(Hede)   JS17/18C6
Shezhu   JS17/18E5
Shiba   AH23/24D5

Shibaliji   AH23/24C2
Shiban   SC47/48B2
Shibandong Jing   GS57/58B2
Shibanhe   HB35/36C6
Shiban Jing   NM9/10G2
Shibanqiao   SC47/48B5
Shiban Quan   GS57/58B4
Shibantan   HN37/38B4
Shibantan   SC47/48B2
Shibanxi   SC47/48C1
Shibanyan   HEN33/34A5
Shibaocheng   GS57/58C3
Shibaqing   NM5/6B1
Shibatai   NM9/10K22
Shibazhan   HL15/16A3
Shibei   FJ25/26C4
Shibei   NM61/62D3
Shibi   JX29/30C3
Shibi   HI42B3
Shibie   GX43/44C6
Shibing Xian   GZ49/50C7
Shibu   SD31/32C6
Shibuqiao   HN37/38B6
Shibuzi   SD31/32C6
Shicaoji   HEN33/34D7
Shichang   SD31/32D6
Shichang   GZ49/50C5
Shicheng   SX7/8E5
Shicheng   LN11/12D8
Shicheng   FJ25/26E5
Shicheng Dao   LN11/12E7
Shicheng Xian(Qinjiang)   JX29/30E4
Shichuanchang   SC47/48C4
Shichuan He   SN55/56E4-F4
Shicun   AH23/24C4
Shidao   SD31/32C9
Shidao Wan   SD31/32C9
Shidian Xian   YN51/52C3
Shidixi   HN37/38B3
Shidong   SC47/48D3
Shidong   GZ49/50C5
Shidong   GD39/40C5
Shidong   GZ49/50D7
Shidongzi   BJ3/4A3
Shidu   HN37/38E6
Shidu   BJ3/4C2
Shidu   JX29/30B2
Shi'erdaogou   JL13/14F8
Shi'erwei   JS19/20A2
Shifang   FJ25/26E2
Shifang Shi   SC45/46C5
Shifeng Xi   ZJ21/22C5-D6
Shifosi   BJ3/4C3
Shifosi   HEN33/34D4
Shifu   HI42B3
Shigang   JX29/30C3
Shigang   JS17/18D6
Shigang   HEN33/34E3
Shigaojing   YN51/52D4
Shigezhuang   TJ3/4C4
Shigezhuang   HEB3/4D3
Shigong   GS57/58B2
Shigongji   AH23/24C3

Shigong(Zhenxia) JS19/20B3
Shigouyi NX61/62C3
Shigu GZ49/50C7
Shigu GD39/40E3
Shigu YN51/52B3
Shiguai SX7/8D5
Shiguai NM9/10K20
Shiguan He HEN33/34E7 AH23/24D2
Shiguanji AH23/24D5
Shiguguan HB35/36B4
Shiguizhen AH23/24E5
Shigunhe HEN33/34E5
Shigutang GD39/40B6
Shihahe NM9/10J19
Shihe LN11/12E5
Shihe AH23/24E3
Shi He HEN33/34E7-F7
Shi He HEN33/34E6
Shihechang SC45/46C6
Shiheng SD31/32C3
Shihezi Shi XJ63/64C8
Shihlin TW27/28B3
Shihmen TW27/28B3
Shihmen TW27/28C3
Shihmen Shuiku TW27/28C3
Shihuajie HB35/36B4
Shihudang SH19/20C4
Shihui SC45/46D7
Shihuichang NX61/62B2
Shihuipu GD39/40B6
Shihuiqiao HB35/36D5
Shihuiyao HEB5/6C6
Shiji SD31/32D2
Shijia SC47/48B2
Shijiahu NM15/16D2
Shijian GD39/40C5
Shijian SC47/48C2
Shijianbu AH23/24E4
Shijiang HN37/38D3
Shijiao GD39/40B7
Shijiao GD39/40C5
Shijiao SC47/48D4
(Shijiao)Fogang Xian GD39/40C6
Shijiaotou GD41A3
Shijiapu JL13/14D5
Shijiaqiao JS17/18D5
Shijiaqiao ZJ21/22B5
Shijiaqiao AH23/24E3
Shijiaxiang SC47/48C2
Shijiaying BJ3/4C2
Shijiazhuang Shi HEB5/6E2
Shijiazi LN11/12B6
Shijiedu AH23/24F6
Shijing FJ25/26F4
Shijing SD31/32D5
Shijing HEN33/34C4
Shijingshan BJ3/4C3
Shijiu GD39/40C5
Shijiu Hu JS17/18E4 AH23/24E5
Shijiutuo HEB5/6D6
Shijiuwo HEB3/4C4
Shijiuzhan HL15/16A3
Shikan GD39/40C5

Shikang GX43/44F7
Shikeng GD41A2
Shikengkong GD39/40B5
Shikong NX61/62C2
Shikou JX29/30D3
Shikou SX7/8E3
Shikou JX29/30C4
Shikou SD31/32B5
Shiku He GD39/40B9
Shilai SD31/32D4
Shilanji NM9/10G6
Shilan Zhou GD41B1
Shili SX7/8F4
Shiliang SD31/32B7
Shiliang SX7/8E5
Shiliang ZJ21/22C3
Shiliang HEN33/34D7
Shilianghe Shuiku JS17/18B4
Shilihe LN11/12C7
Shilin SX7/8E3
Shilin YN51/52C5
Shilin Yizu Zizhixian YN51/52C5
Shiling HI42C2
Shiling HEB5/6C7
Shiling JL13/14D5
Shiling GD39/40E3
Shiliping JL13/14D11
Shilipu HB35/36D5
Shilipu AH49/50C3
(Shilipu)Tongchuan Shi SN55/56E5
Shiliu FJ25/26F3
(Shiliu)Changjiang Lizu Zizhixian
  HI42B2
Shiliushu JS17/18B4
Shiliu Shuiku HI42B2
Shilong SC47/48B4
Shilong GX43/44D7
Shilong GD39/40C6
Shilongguojiang Shuiku HB35/36D5
Shilou GD41B2
Shilou BJ3/4C2
Shilou Xian SX7/8E2
Shima JX29/30E3
Shima GD39/40B8
Shima SC47/48C3
Shima JS19/20A2
Shima SC47/48D3
Shima He GD41B3
Shimantan Shuiku HEN33/34D5
Shimatan SC47/48B5
Shimen HEB5/6C5
Shimen HEB5/6D6
Shimen JL13/14D10
Shimen ZJ21/22B5
Shimen HEB5/6C3
Shimen JX29/30D4
Shimen SD31/32D6
Shimen SD31/32E5
Shimen HB35/36C4
Shimen SC47/58C4
Shimen GS61/62C1
Shimenjie JX29/30B4
Shimenji Shuiku HB35/36C4
Shimenkan SC49/50B5

Shimenkan HB35/36E1
Shimenlou JX29/30C2
Shimenqiao HEB5/6E4
Shimenqiao HN37/38C4
Shimenshan AH23/24D4
Shimenshan HN37/38E3
Shimen Shuiku LN11/12D6
Shimen Shuiku HB35/36C5
Shimen Shuiku SN55/56G2
Shimensong SD31/32C2
Shimen Xian HN37/38B4
Shimenying BJ3/4C3
(Shimen)Yunlong Xian YN51/52C3
Shimenzhai HEB5/6C7
Shimenzi SN55/56D5
Shimian Xian SC45/46D4
Shimiao SD31/32B4
Shimiaozi HEB3/4B4
(Shinan)Xingye Xian GX43/44E7
Shiniu Shan FJ25/26E4
Shipai JS19/20B3
Shipai AH23/24F3
Shipai FJ25/26E3
Shipai HB35/36D5
Shipan SX7/8D4
Shipan SC47/48B4
Shipen HEB5/6F1
Shiping Xian YN51/52D5
Shipo SN55/56F6
Shipodian AH23/24E3
Shipu ZJ21/22C6
Shiqia GX43/44E7
Shiqian Xian GZ49/50C7
Shiqiao HEN33/34D4
Shiqiao JS19/20B1
Shiqiao JX29/30E2
Shiqiao SD31/32C5
Shiqiao SD31/32D5
Shiqiao JX29/30D4
Shiqiao HEN33/34D5
Shiqiao HB35/36C5
Shiqiao GX43/44D9
Shiqiao SC45/46C6
Shiqiao AH23/24F6
Shiqiaozhen SC45/46C5
Shiqiu JS19/20B1
Shiqiu HI42B2
Shiqizhan HL33/34A3
(Shiquanhe)Gar Xian XZ53/54C3
(Shiquan He)Sênggê Zangbo
  XZ53/54C2-D3
Shiquan Shuiku SN55/56G4
Shiquan Xian SN55/56G4
Shiqu Xian SC45/46B2
Shiren JL13/14F7
Shirencheng HL15/16D4
Shirengou HEB5/6B5
Shirengou HEB5/6C5
Shiren Shan HEN33/34D4
Shirenzhang GD39/40B7
Shisanjianfang XJ61/62D11
Shisanjingzi HL15/16D4
Shisanling Shuiku BJ3/4B3
Shisanzhan HL15/16B3

Shishan   LN11/12C5
Shishan   HI42B3
Shishan   FJ25/26E4
Shishang   JX29/30E4
Shishankou Shuiku   HEN33/34E6
Shishikou   JX29/30E2
Shishi Shi   FJ25/26F4
Shishou Shi   HB35/36E5
Shisizhan   HL15/16B3
Shisun   SC47/48B4
Shitai Xian   AH23/24F4
Shitan   GD39/40B5
Shitan   JX29/30C2
Shitang   NX61/62D2
Shitang   GX43/44B9
Shitang   JX29/30C5
Shitang   JX29/30D3
Shitang   GD39/40C7
Shitang   GX43/44E7
Shitang   ZJ21/22D6
Shitangling   NX61/62C3
Shitangwan   JS19/20B3
Shitanjing   NX61/62A3
Shitanwu   SD31/32C4
Shiti   SC47/48A5
Shitie   SX7/8D4
Shiting   HEB3/4C2
Shiting Jiang   SC47/48A2
Shitou   HL15/16E5
Shitouhezi   HL15/16D6
Shitoukoumen Shuiku   JL13/14D6
Shitou Shan   NM9/10B15
Shitouzhai   YN51/52D3
Shitouzui   HB35/36D8
Shituan   SC45/46C5
Shituo   SC47/48C5
Shiwan   HN37/38D5
Shiwan   SN55/56C5
Shiwan Dashan   GX43/44F5-6
Shiwang Feng   AH23/24F4
Shiwei   NM9/10B12
Shiwei   GD41A2
Shiwu   JL13/14D5
Shixi   JL13/14D6
Shixi   ZJ21/22D5
Shixi   FJ25/26D3
Shixi   JX29/30C5
Shixi   GD41A2
Shixia   SX7/8D5
Shixiakou Shuiku   NX61/62D2
Shixian   JL13/14D10
Shixianzi   NX61/62C2
Shixiazi   GS57/58D6
Shixing Xian(Taiping)   GD39/40B7
Shiya   GX43/44D7
Shiya   SC47/48B4
Shiyan   JS17/18D6
Shiyan   GD41A2
Shiyan   ZJ21/22E4
Shiyangchang   SC45/46D5
Shiyangchang   SC47/48B1
Shiyang He   GS57/58C6
Shiyanjie   HB35/36B3

Shiyanqiao   SC45/46D5
Shiyan Shi   HB35/36B3
Shiyan Shuiku   GD41A2
Shiye   SC45/46D7
Shiyidu   JX29/30C6
Shiyiwei   JS17/18E6
Shiyizhan   HL15/16B4
Shiyong   GX43/44F7
Shiyong   SC47/48B5
Shiyuetian   HI42B1
Shiyun   HI42C2
Shizhan   HL15/16B3
Shizhe   SX7/8E4
Shizheng   GD39/40B8
Shizhenjie   JX29/30C4
Shizhong   FJ25/26F3
Shizhu   HN37/38D3
Shizhu   HEB3/4C2
Shizhu   ZJ21/22D5
Shizhuang   JS17/18D6
Shizhuang   SX7/8F4
Shizhu Tujiazu Zizhixian   SC45/46D7
Shizi   GS57/58E8
Shizi   SC47/48C2
Shizigou   HEB5/6B3
Shizihe   AH23/24C2
Shizikou   SN55/56G4
Shizilu   NX61/62E3
(Shizilu)Junan Xian   SD31/32D5
Shizipu   AH23/24F6
Shizitan Shuiku   SC45/46C6-D6
Shizong   JS19/20A4
Shizong Xian   YN51/52C5
Shizui   SX7/8C5
Shizui   JL13/14D7
Shizui   GX43/44D8
Shizuishan   NX61/62A3
Shizuishan Shi(Dawukou)   NX61/62A3
Shizuishanzhan   NX61/62A3
Shizuiyi   SN55/56C6
Shou'an   SC47/48B1
Shouchang   ZJ21/22C4
Shouche   HN37/38B2
Shoucheng   GX43/44B7
Shouchia   TW27/28E2
Shoufeng   TW27/28D3
Shouguang Shi   SD31/32C5
Shouning Xian   FJ25/26C5
Shoushan   YN51/52B5
Shouwangfen   HEB5/6C5
Shou Xian   AH23/24D3
Shouyang Shan   SN55/56G4
Shouyang Xian   SX7/8D5
Shouyanxu   HN37/38F4
Shuai Shui   AH23/24G4-5
Shuaizhou   HB35/36E8
Shuaiziwan   JL13/14E11
Shuajingsi   SC45/46B4
Shuangba   HEN33/34C7
Shuangbai Xian(Tuodian)   YN51/52C4
Shuangbanqiao   HN37/38D5
Shuangbao   GZ49/50D5
Shuangchahe   JL13/14F6

Shuangchengpu   JL13/14C5
Shuangcheng Shi   HL15/16E4
Shuangchi   SX7/8E3
Shuangdian   JS17/18D6
Shuangduiji   AH23/24C3
Shuangdunji   AH23/24D4
Shuangfeng   SC47/48B3
Shuangfeng   GX43/44E7
Shuangfeng   JS19/20B4
Shuangfeng   HL15/16D4
Shuangfengsi   HEB5/6B5
Shuangfeng Xian(Yongfeng)
   HN37/38D5
Shuangfengyi   SC47/48C3
Shuangfu   AH23/24C2
Shuangfuchang   SC47/48C1
Shuangfupu   HN37/38C5
Shuanggang   TJ3/4C4
Shuanggang   JL13/14B3
Shuanggou   JS17/18B3
Shuanggou   JS17/18C4
Shuanggou   HB35/36B5
Shuanghan   FJ25/26E4
Shuanghe   AH23/24E3
Shuanghe   HL15/16E6
Shuanghe   HB35/36C5
Shuanghe   HEN33/34E5
Shuanghe   AH23/24E2
Shuanghe   NX61/62D2
Shuanghe   SC45/46C4
Shuanghe   SN55/56D4
Shuanghe   SN55/56G5
Shuanghe   SC47/48C3
Shuanghechang   SC45/46C6
Shuanghedagang   HL15/16C6
Shuanghekou   SC45/46C5
Shuanghezhen   JL13/14D7
Shuanghou   SD31/32D5
Shuanghsi   TW27/28B3
Shuanghu   XZ53/54C6
Shuangjian   ZJ19/20C2
Shuangjiang   GZ49/50E7
Shuangjiang   SC45/46C5
Shuangjiangkou   HN37/38D5
Shuangjiang Lahuzu Vazu Blangzu Daizu
   Zizhixian   YN51/52D3
(Shuangjiang)Tongdao Dongzu Zizhixian
   HN37/38E2
(Shuangjiang)Yunyang Xian   SC45/46C7
Shuangjianji   AH23/24C3
Shuangjiao   GD39/40D4
Shuangjie   GD39/40E4
Shuangji He   HEN33/34C5
Shuangjing   HEB5/6G2
Shuangjing   GZ49/50D7
Shuangliao Shi (Zhengjiatun)
   JL13/14D4
Shuanglin   ZJ21/22B5
Shuanglin   JX29/30D2
Shuangliu   GZ49/50C5
Shuangliu   SC47/48A4
Shuangliuhe   HL15/16D7
Shuangliushu   HEN33/34F7

Shuangliu Xian SC45/46C4
Shuanglong SN55/56E4
Shuanglong SC47/48C5
Shuanglongdong ZJ21/22C4
Shuanglu HL15/16D4
Shuangmiao AH23/24D3
Shuangmiao AH23/24C4
Shuangmiaozi LN11/12B8
Shuangmiaozi LN11/12B6
Shuangmiaozi JL13/14E6
Shuangpaishan HN37/38E6
Shuangpaishi JS19/20B1
Shuangpai Shuiku HN37/38F4
Shuangpai Xian HN37/38F4
Shuangqiao BJ3/4C3
Shuangqiao ZJ19/20C3
Shuangqiao AH23/24D3
Shuangqiao AH23/24F5
Shuangqiao JX29/30B4
Shuangqiao JX29/30E2
Shuangqiao JX29/30C2
Shuangqiao HEN33/34E6
Shuangqiao GX43/44D6
Shuangqiao SC45/46D5
Shuangqiao HEB3/4C5
Shuangqiaoji AH23/24C3
Shuangshan HL15/16C3
Shuangshan SN55/56B6
Shuangshanzi HEB5/6C7
Shuangshipu SC47/48C2
(Shuangshipu)Feng Xian SN55/56G2
Shuangshiqiao SC47/48C2
Shuangshiqiao SC47/48C3
Shuangtaizi JL11/12B7
Shuangtaizihe Kou LN11/12D5
Shuangtang HEB3/4C3
Shuangtang JX29/30C4
Shuangtian JX29/30D4
Shuangxi GD39/40B9
Shuangxi FJ25/26C5
Shuangxi ZJ21/22D4
(Shuangxi)Jing'an Xian JX29/30C3
Shuangxing HL15/16D3
Shuangyang FJ25/26E3
Shuangyang HL15/16D3
Shuangyang SD31/32C6
Shuangyangdian LN11/12C5
Shuangyangdian SD31/32C6
Shuangyang JL13/14D6
Shuangyashan Shi HL15/16D6
Shuangdian JS17/18 B4
(Shuangzhong)Hukou Xian JX29/30B4
Shuangzihe HL15/16D5
Shuankou TJ3/4C4
Shuanshan JL13/14D4
Shucheng HEB5/6E4
Shucheng Xian AH23/24E3
Shufu Xian XJ63/64F3
Shuguan HEB5/6G3
Shuguang HL15/16D6
Shu He JS17/18B4 SD31/32D5
Shuhe SN55/56H5
Shuhezhen JS19/20B4

Shuhong ZJ21/22D5
Shuibatang GZ49/50B6
Shuibei JS17/18E5
Shuibei FJ25/26C3
Shuibei FJ25/26C4
Shuibei JX29/30C3
Shuibian GD39/40B6
Shuibian JX29/30D3
Shuibu GD41B1
Shuiche GD39/40B9
Shuicheng Xian GZ49/50D3
Shuidao SD31/32B8
Shuidaoyang HEN33/34C5
(Shuiding)Huocheng Xian XJ63/64C6
Shuidong AH23/24F5
Shuidongdi HN37/38D4
(Shuidong)Dianbai Xian GD39/40E3
Shuidong Gang GD39/40E4
Shuidongjiang HN37/38D5
Shuifeng Shuiku LN11/12D9
Shuifumiao Shuiku HN37/38D5
Shuifu Xian YN51/52A6
Shuiguan SC47/48A4
Shuiguo SD31/32E4
Shuihouling AH23/24F3
Shuiji FJ25/26C4
(Shuijiahu)Changfeng Xian AH23/24D4
Shuijiang SC45/46D6
Shuijing GX43/44C7
Shuijing SC45/46B5
Shuijingkuang QH59/60D2
Shuijingtou HN37/38D4
Shuikou AH23/24D5
Shuikou GZ49/50E8
Shuikou FJ25/26D4
Shuikou HN37/38E6
Shuikou GD39/40D5
Shuikou SC47/48B1
Shuikou FJ25/26E4
Shuikou HN37/38G4
Shuikouguan GX43/44E4
Shuikoushan HN37/38E4
Shuikoushan HN37/38E5
Shuikouxu GD39/40A7
Shuili TW27/28D2
Shuiliandong LN11/12B9
Shuilong GZ49/50E6
(Shuiluocheng)Zhuanglang Xian
   GS57/58E8
Shuiluo He SC45/46D3
Shuimen FJ25/26D6
Shuimenzi LN11/12E6
Shuiming GX43/44E7
Shuimogou NM61/62B2
Shuinan FJ25/26C4
Shuinan JX29/30E3
Shuinan JX29/30E4
Shuinan SC47/48C2
Shuiping HB35/36B2
Shuipo HEN33/34C6
Shuiqian FJ25/26D2
Shuiquan HEB3/4B1
Shuiquan LN11/12C3

Shuiquan GS57/58D7
Shuiquanzi GS57/58C5
Shuiqiuliu JL13/14C8
Shuitang GZ49/50E3
Shuitianba HN37/38B2
Shuitianhe HN37/38B2
Shuitou ZJ21/22E5
Shuitou FJ25/26F4
Shuitou GD39/40C6
Shuitou SX7/8F3
Shuitun HEN33/34E6
Shuitutuo SC45/46D6
Shuiwan SD31/32B4
Shuiwen GX43/44E8
Shuixi JX29/30D3
Shuiyang AH23/24E5
Shuiyang Jiang AH23/24E5-F5
Shuiye HEN33/34A6
Shuiyuan LN11/12D6
Shuiyuan GX43/44C6
Shuizhai SD31/32C4
(Shuizhai)Wuhua Xian GD39/40C8
Shuizhan QH59/60A2
Shujie YN51/52C4
Shulan Shi JL13/14C7
Shulehe HL15/16D5
Shulehe GS57/58B3
Shule He QH59/60A5-6 GS57/58B2-3
Shule Nanshan QH50/60A5-6
Shule Xian XJ63/64F4
Shulin TW27/28C3
(Shulinzhao)Dalad Qi NM9/10G8
Shulinzi NM9/10K18
Shun'an AH23/24F4
Shunchang Xian FJ25/26D3
Shunde Shi GD39/40D6
Shundian HEN33/34C5
Shunhe JS17/18B2
Shunhe SC47/48C3
Shunheji HEN33/34C8
Shunping Xian HEB5/6E3
Shunxi ZJ21/22B3
Shunyi Xian BJ3/4B3
Shuoji JS17/18C5
Shuoliang GX43/44D5
Shuolong GX43/44E4
Shuozhou Shi SX7/8B4
Shuren SC47/48C5
Shushan AH23/24E4
Shushanbei GD41A2
Shushe GZ49/50D3
Shu Shui JX29/30E2
Shutai NX61/62D2
Shu Xi AH23/24F5
Shuxi ZJ21/22D5
Shuyang Xian JS17/18B4
Shuzhang SX7/8F5
Si'an ZJ21/22B4
Siba GX43/44C6
Sichakou HEB5/6B4
Sichuan Pendi SC76C4-5
Sidangkou TJ3/4D4
Sidaogou JL13/14F8

Sidaohezi   LN11/12C9
Siding   GX43/44B7
Sidu   FJ25/26G3
Sidu   HN37/38F6
Sidu   GZ49/50C5
(Si'en)Huanjiang Maonanzu Zizhixian
   GX43/44C6
Si'erpu   LN11/12D4
Sifang   SD31/32C7
Sifang Ling   GX43/44E5
Sifangtai   HL15/16D4
Sifangtuozi   JL13/14A4
Sifen   HN37/38D6
Sigeng   HI42B1
Sigu   HN37/38D4
Siguanyingzi   LN11/12C3
Sihai   BJ3/4B3
Sihaidian   HL15/16D4
Sihe   JL13/14C7
Si He   SD31/32D3-4
Sihe   GD41A2
Sihedun   JS19/20A1
Siheyong   HEB5/6B5
Sihong Xian (Qingyang)   JS17/18C4
Sihui Shi   GD39/40C5
Sihu Zongganqu   HB35/36E6
Sijia   HN37/38E6
Sijiaba   JS17/18D7
Sijiao   SX7/8F3
Sijiao Shan   ZJ21/22B7
Sijiazi   HL15/16D3
Sijiazi   LN11/12B7
Sijiazi   NM11/12C4
Sijiemei Dao   ZJ21/22B7
Sijing   SH17/18E7
Sijingzi   JL13/14C3
Sijiqing   BJ3/4C3
Sijiu   GD39/40D5
Sikou   SD31/32B7
Sikou   JX29/30B5
Sikouzi Shuiku   NX61/62D2

Silaogou   SX7/8B5
Sili   JX29/30C5
Silian   GX43/44C6
Silin   GX43/44D5
Siling Co   XZ53/54D7
Siliping   HN37/38F5
Silong   GX43/44D6
Silukou   ZJ21/22C5
Silun   GD39/40D4
Simajia   JL13/14B6
Simao Diqu   YN51/52D4
Simao Shi   YN51/52D4
Simaqiao   HN37/38F4
Simawat   XJ63/64G6
Simen   ZJ21/22B6
Simeng   SC47/48C1
Simenqian   HN37/38D3
Simianshan   SC47/48D3
Siminghu Shuiku   ZJ19/20D4
Siming Shan   ZJ21/22C5
Simudijie   SN55/56G4

Sinan Xian   GZ49/50C7
Sinda   XZ53/54D11
Sinüsi   SD31/32B3
Sipai   GX43/44C7
Sipingjie   LN11/12C8
Siping Shi   JL13/14D5
Sipu   AH23/24C3
Sipu   GX43/44B6
Sipu   JX20/30C5
Siqian   FJ25/26C3
Siqian   GD39/40B7
Siqian   JX29/30C4
Siqiao   FJ25/26C5
Siqin Jiang   GX43/44C9-8
Siqu   GZ49/50B7
Sishibadu   JX29/30C6
Sishilijie   JX29/30B4
Sishilipu   SD31/32D5
Sishilipu   SN55/56C6
Sishilipu   GS57/58E8
Sishuang Liedao   FJ25/26D6
Sishui   HEN33/34C5
Sishui Xian   SD31/32D4
Sishun   JX29/30F2
Sitang   GX43/44B8
Sitang   GX43/44D4
Sitang   GX43/44E6
Sitian   XJ63/64D13
Siting   GZ49/50E6
Siting   SX7/8E4
Sitou   SX7/8E5
Siu A Chau   HK41B2
Siu Kau   HK41B3
Siu Lam   HK41B3
Siu Mo To   HK41B2
Siwang   GX43/44D8
Sixi   JX29/30C3
Sixia   JX29/30F2
Si Xian   AH23/24C4
Sixiangkou   JS17/18D5
(Siyang)Cengong Xian   GZ49/50C7
(Siyang)Shangsi Xian   GX43/44E5
Siyang Xian(Zhongxing)   JS17/18C4
Siyitang   NM9/10G7
Sizao   JS17/18D6
Sizhoutou   ZJ21/22C6
Sizhuang   SX7/8F4
Sizhuang   HEB3/4C3
Siziwang(Dorbod)Qi   NM9/10G8
Sogcanggoinba   SC45/46B4
Sogmai   XZ53/54C2
Sogo Nur   NM9/10F3
Sog Qu   XZ78B5-C5
Sogruma   QH59/60D7
Sog Xian   XZ53/54D9
Sokang   TW27/28D1
Soko Islands   HK41B2
Solon   NM9/10D13
Somang   SC45/46C4
Somang Qu   SC76C4
(Sonag)Zêkog Xian   QH59/60C7
Song'acha He   HL15/16E7
Song'ao   ZJ21/22C6

Songbai   HN37/38E5
Songbaichang   HN37/38C5
Songbai Guan   GD39/40B9
Songbailin   SD31/32D6
(Songbai)Shennongjia Linqu   HB35/36C3
Songbu   HB35/36C7
Songcun   ZJ21/22C3
Songcun   SD31/32B8
Songdong   GD39/40B9
Songgai   SC45/46D5
Songgang   GD39/40D6
Songgang   SC45/46C4
Songgui   YN51/52B4
Songhe   HB35/36C6
Songhu   JX29/30C3
Songhua Hu   JL13/14D7-8
Songhuajiang   JL13/14C6
Songhua Jiang   HL15/16D6-7

Songjiagou   SX7/8C3
Songjiang   JL13/14D8
Songjiang   JL13/14E8
Songjiang   JL13/14E9
Songjianghe   JL13/14E8
Songjiang Xian   SH17/18E7
Songjiapu   SC45/46D5
Songjiaqiao   JS17/18D5
Songjiaying   HEB5/6D6
Songjiayu   HEB5/6E2
Songjiazhuang   SX7/8B5
Songkan   GZ49/50B5
Songkou   GD39/40B9
Songkou   FJ25/26D2
Songlin   SD31/32C2
Songlin   YN51/52B6
Songlindian   HEB5/6D3
Song Ling   LN11/12C4
Songlingzi   LN11/12D3
Songlou   JS17/18B2
Songmen   ZJ21/22D6
Songming Xian   YN51/52C5
Songmuping   HB35/36D4
Songnen Pingyuan   JL69A4-5
                  HL70D2-4
Songpan Caodi   SC45/46B4
Songpan(Sungqu)Xian(Jin'an)
   SC45/46B4
Songshan   LN11/12C5
Songshan   JX29/30D2
Songshan   SD31/32B7
Songshan   GX43/44E8
Songshan   GX43/44F7
Songshan   GS57/58D6
Song Shan   HEN33/34C5
Songshanpu   LN11/12B8
Songshan Shuiku   SD31/32C5
(Songshan)Ziyun Miaozu Buyeizu
   Zizhixian   GZ49/50E5
Songshanzui   HB35/36D8
Songshaoguan   YN51/52C5
Songshi   JX29/30D4
Songshu   LN11/12E6
Songshuzhen   JL13/14E8

Songta   SX7/8D5
Songtao   HI42B2
Songtao Ganqu   HI42B2
Songtao Miaozu Zizhixian   GZ49/50B8
Songtao Shuiku   HI42B2
Songtuan   AH23/24C3
Song Xi   FJ25/26C4
Songxi   ZJ21/22B4
Songxi   FJ25/26D2
Songxia   FJ25/26E5
Songxia   ZJ21/22B5
Song Xian   HEN33/34C4
Songxi Xian   FJ25/26C4
Songyan   SX7/8D5
Songyan   GZ49/50C6
Songyang Xi   ZJ21/22D4
Songyang Xian(Xiping)   ZJ21/22D4
Songyankou   SX7/8C5
Songyin   SH19/20C4
Songyu   FJ25/26F4
Songyuan   GD39/40B9
Songyuan Shi   JL13/14B5
Songzhai   HEN33/34C5
Songzhan   HL15/16D3
Songzhangzi   LN11/12C3
Songzhuang   BJ3/4C3
Songzi Guan   AH23/24E2
    HB35/36C8
Songzi He   HB35/36D5-E5
Songzikou   HB35/36D4
Songzi Shi   HB35/36D4
Sonid Youqi(Saihan Tal)   NM9/10F9
Sonid Zuoqi(Mandalt)   NM9/10F9
South China Sea   39/40F5-8
Sowa   SC45/46D2
Ssuchung Hsi   TW27/28E2
Ssuyuanyakou   TW27/28C3
Stonecutters Island   HK41B3
Su'ao   FJ25/26E5
Suao   TW27/28C3
Suao Wan   TW27/28C3
Suban   FJ25/26E3
Subang   FJ25/26E3
Subao Ding   HN37/38D3
Subei Guangai Zongqu   JS17/18C5-B6
Subei Mongolzu Zizhixian(Dangchengwan)
  GS57/58C2
Subrag   NM9/10E12
Subujing   NX61/62B4
Suchen   JS19/20A3
Sucheng   SX7/8E5
Sucun   HEB5/6F3
Sucun   SD31/32D5
Sugehe   NM9/10C13
Sugongtuo   JL13/14C4
Sugu   HB35/36B4
Sugun   XJ63/64F4
Suhai Hu   QH59/60A3
Suhait   NM9/10H5
Suibin Xian   HL15/16D6
Suichang Xian(Miaogao)   ZJ21/22D4
Suicheng   HEB5/6D3
Suichuan Jiang   JX29/30E2

Suichuan Xian(Quanjiang)   JX29/30E2
Suide Xian   SN55/56C6
Suidong   HL15/16D7
Suifengyuan   GD41B1
Suifen He   HL15/16E6-F6
Suifenhe Shi   HL15/16E6
Sui He   AH23/24C4
Suihua Diqu   HL15/16D4-3
Suihua Shi   HL15/16D4
Sui Jiang   GD39/40C5
Suijiang Xian(Zhongcheng)   YN51/52A5
Suileng Xian   HL15/16D4
Suining Shi   SC45/46C5
Suining Xian   JS17/18C3
Suining Xian(Changpu)   HN37/38E3
Suiping Xian   HEN33/34D5
Sui Xian   HEN33/34C7
Suixi Xian   GD39/40E3
Suixi Xian   AH23/24C3
Suiyang   HL15/16E6
Suiyangchang   GZ49/50B6
Suiyangdian   HB35/36B5
Suiyang Xian(Yangchuan)   GZ49/50C6
Suizhong Xian   LN11/12D4
Suizhou Shi   HB35/36C6
Suji   AH23/24C2
Sujiabu   AH23/24E3
Sujiatun   LN11/12C7
Sujiazui   JS17/18C5
Suli Hu   QH59/60B4
Sulin Gol   QH59/60B5
Suliuzhuang   SD31/32B3
Sumba Xia   QH59/60B7
Sumdo   SC45/46D3
Sumxi   XZ53/54B3
Sumzom   XZ53/54E11
Sunan Yugurzu Zizhixian   GS57/58C4
Suncun   SD31/32D4
Sundian   HEN33/34D6
Sunduan   ZJ19/20C3
Sunfang   JX29/30D4
Sungeng   SD31/32C4
Sung Kong   HK41B3
Suning Xian   HEB5/6E3
Sunji   SX7/8F2
Sunjiaba   GZ49/50C7
Sunjiabu   AH23/24F5
Suyu Xian   JS17/18 C4
Sunjiaqiao   HB35/36C6
Sunjiaquan   HEB3/4C4
Sunjiatan   NX61/62C3
Sunjiazhuang   HEB3/4C2
Sunshi   HEB3/4D3
Sunshidian   SD31/32D3
Suntiepu   HEN33/34E6
Suntuanji   AH23/24C3
Sunwu Xian   HL15/16C4
Sunxi He   SC47/48C4-D4
Sunzhen   SN55/56F5
Sunzhen   SD31/32B4
Suocheng   HN37/38F5
Suognang   SX7/8D5
Suolong   GS57/58E7

Suoshi   HN37/38B3
(Suozhen)Huantai Xian   SD31/32C5
Suqian Shi   JS17/18C4
Suqian Xian   AH23/24F3
Suqiao   HEB3/4C3
Suqiao   JX29/30C4
Suqiao   HEN33/34C5
Suqiao   GX43/44B8
Suqu   GD39/40C8
Sushan Dao   SD31/32C9
Sushui He   SX7/8F2
Sutuo   BJ3/4C3
Suxi   ZJ21/22C5
Suzhou Shi   AH23/24C4
Suxik   QH59/60A4
Suxiong   SC45/46D4
Suxu   GX43/44E6
Suyahu Shuiku   HEN33/34D6
Suyangshan   JS17/18B3
Suyukou   NX61/62B2
(Suzhou Creek)Wusong Jiang
    SH19/20B4
Suzhou Shi   AH23/24C3
Suzhou Shi   JS17/18E6
Suzhuang   ZJ21/22C3
Suzigou   LN11/12D7
Suzi He   LN11/12C8

T

Taan   TW27/28D3
Taan Hsi   TW27/28C2-3
Tachakou   XJ63/64C8
Tacheng   TW27/28D2
Tacheng   YN51/52B3
Tacheng Diqu   XJ63/64B8-9
Tacheng(Qoqek)Shi   XJ63/64B7
Tachia   TW27/28C2
Tachia Hsi   TW27/28C2-3
Tachien   TW27/28C3
Tachoshui   TW27/28C3
Tadou   FJ25/26D4
Ta'erling   NM61/62A2
Ta'erqi   NM9/10D13
Ta'erwan   HB35/36C6
Tagdaxman   XJ63/64G6
Taha   HL15/16D3
Tahan Hsi   TW27/28C3
Ta He   HL15/16A3-B3
Tahe Xian   HL15/16A3
Tahsi   TW27/28C3
Tahu   TW27/28C2
Tai A Chau   HK41B2
Tai'an   SC47/48B3
Tai'an Shi   SD31/32C4
Tai'an Xian   LN11/12C6
Taiba   FJ25/26F2
Taibai   JX29/30B5
Taibai   GS57/58D9
Taibai   GZ49/50B6
Taibai Ding   HEN33/34E5   HB35/36B6
Taibai Shan   SX7/8B6
Taibai Shan   SN55/56G3
Taibai Xian(Zuitou)   SN55/56F3

Taibo Ding SD31/32B8
Taibus Qi(Baochang) NM9/10G10
Taicang Shi JS17/18E7
Tai Chuen HK41B3
Taichung Hsien(Fengyuan) TW27/28C2
Taichung Shih TW27/28C2
Taidong HL15/16D3
Tai'erzhuang SD31/32E4
Taigemu NM9/10K21
(Taigong)Taijiang Xian GZ49/50D7
Taigu Xian SX7/8D4
Taihang Shan HEN33/34A5-B5
　　　　　SX7/8C5-E5
　　　　　HEB5/6D2-G1
Taihe SC45/46E6
Taihe SD31/32C5
Taihe JX29/30D4
Taihe SC45/46C6
Taihechang SC47/48B1
Taihe Xian AH23/24C2
Taihe Xian(Chengjiang) JX29/30E2
Taihexu HN37/38F5
(Taihezhen)Shehong Xian SC45/46C5
Taihsi TW27/28D2
Tai Hu JS17/18E6
Taihuai SX7/8B5
Taihu He AH23/24F3
Taihu Xian AH23/24F3
Taijiang Xian(Taigong) GZ49/50D7
Taijihe SN55/56G6
Taijnar He QH59/60B3
(Taikang)Dorbog Mongolzu Zizhixian
　　HL15/16D3
Taikang Xian HEN33/34C6
Tailai Xian HL15/16D2
Tailiang NM9/10K19
Tailie GZ49/50D7
Tailing BJ3/4B3
Tai Long HK41B3
Tailuko TW27/28C3
Taimali TW27/28E3
Taimei GD39/40C7
Tai Mei Tuk HK41B3
Tai Mong Tsai HK41B3
Tai Mo Shan HK41B3
Tai Mo To HK41B2
Taimu Shan FJ25/26C5-D5
Tainan Hsien(Hsinying) TW27/28D2
Tainan Shih TW27/28E2
Taining Xian FJ25/26D3
Tainya HI42C2
Taipa Island MC41B2
Taipei Hsien(Panchiao) TW27/28B3
Taipei Shih TW27/28B3
Taiping FJ25/26D4
Taiping FJ25/26G3
Taiping HB35/36B5
Taiping GD39/40D4
Taiping NM13/14D2
Taiping GX43/44C7
Taiping GX43/44D5
Taipingxu HN37/38B4
Taiping HN37/38F5

Taiping GD39/40B5
Taiping GX43/44E5
Taiping GX43/44E6
Taiping HI42B3
Taiping SC47/48A3
Taiping SC47/48B1
Taiping SC47/48B2
Taiping SC47/48B4
Taiping SC47/48B5
Taiping SC47/48C1
Taiping SC47/48C3
Taiping SC47/48C4
Taiping GZ49/50B8
Taiping GS61/62E4
Taiping GX4/44D8
Taipingbu HEB3/4B2
Taipingchang GD39/40C6
Taipingchang SC47/48C4
(Taiping)Chongzuo Xian GX43/44E5
Taipingchuan JL13/14C4
Taipingchuan JL13/14E8
Taipingcun TJ3/4D4
Taipingdian HB35/36B4
Taipingdu SC45/46D6
Taipinggou LN11/12C3
Taipinggou HL15/16C6
Taipingguan JX29/30B4
Taipinghu Shuiku HL15/16C3
Taipingkou HB35/36D5
Taipingling JL13/14D9
Taipingling HN37/38F6
Taiping Ling NM9/10D13
Taiping Ling HL15/16E6
Taipingpu HN37/38D4
Taipingpu GS57/58C5
Taipingqiao SD31/32D3
Taipingshan JL13/14C5
Taiping Shan TW27/28C3
Taipingshan LN11/12D6
Taipingshao LN11/12D9
Taipingshao Shuiku LN11/12D9
(Taiping)Shixing Xian GD39/40B7
Taipingsi HN37/38D5
Taipingxu HN37/38F5
Taipingzhai HEB5/6C6
Taipingzhen SD31/32B5
Taipingzhen HEN33/34D3
Taipingzhen HB35/36E2
Taipingzhuang HEB5/6B5
Taipo HI42B2
Tai Po HK41B3
Tai Po Kau HK41B3
Tai Po Tsai HK41B3
Taiqian Xian HEN33/34B7
Tairi SH19/20C4
Tai Shan SD31/32C4
Taishang JL13/14F6
Taishan Liedao FJ25/26D6
Taishan Shi GD39/40D5
Taishanxincun JS19/20A1
Taishitun BJ3/4B4
Tai Shui Hang HK41B2
Tai Shui Hang HK41B3

Taishun Xian(Luoyang) ZJ21/22E4
Taitou SX7/8E3
Taitouying HEB5/6C7
Taitung Hsien TW27/28E3
Taitung Kang TW27/28E3
Tai Wai HK41B3
Tai Wan HK41B3
Taiwan Chientan TW72E4
Taiwan Haixia TW27/28C1-B2
　　　　　　FJ25/26G4-F6
Taiwan Shan TW72D5-E5
Taiwan Tao TW27/28C3-D3
Tai Wan Tau HK41B3
Taixi FJ25/26D4
Taixing SC47/48B2
Taixing Shi JS17/18D6
Taiyang ZJ19/20C2
Taiyangcun SX7/8F2
Taiyangcun GX43/44C7
Taiyangdong HN37/38F4
Taiyangfan AH23/24E3
Taiyanghe HB35/36D2
Taiyangmiao NM9/10K16
Taiyangshan NX61/62C3
Taiyi SC47/48B3
Taiyong GZ49/50D7
Taiyu SN55/56F4
Taiyuan Shi SX7/8D4
Taiyuansi HN37/38D5
Taiyue Shan SX7/8D4-E3
Taizhao XZ53/54D9
Taizhimiao HN37/38D4

Taizhou Liedao ZJ21/22D6
Taizhou Shi JS17/18D5
Taizhou Shi ZJ21/22D6
Taizhou Wan ZJ21/22D6
Taizi He LN11/12C6-7
Taizimiao HN37/38C4
Tajen TW27/28E2
Takangkou TW27/28D3
Taklimakan Shamo XJ63/64F6-8
Talangkong NM9/10B14
Tali TW27/28C3
Talin TW27/28D2
Talin Hiag HL15/16D3
Taman Shan TW27/28C3
Tanbin GD39/40D4
Tanbo HN37/38D5
Tanbu GD41A2
Tanbu SD31/32D5
Tanbu JX29/30C2
Tancheng Xian SD31/32E5
Tandang He HB35/36C4
Tandian LN11/12D8
Tandou GD39/40F2
Tanei TW27/28D2
Tanfang JX29/30D4
Tangang JX29/30C3
Tangba SC45/46C5
Tangbai He HB35/36B5
Tangbakol Shuiku XJ63/64B9
Tangbu JX29/30C3

Tangchang SC45/46C4
Tangcheng SX7/8E4
Tangchi HL15/16D2
Tangchi LN11/12D6
Tangchizi LN11/12D8
Tangchuan FJ25/26D4
Tangcun SD31/32D4
Tangcun ZJ21/22C4
Tangcun ZJ21/22C3
Tangcun GD39/40A6
Tangcun Shuiku SD31/32D4
Tangcunxu HN37/38F5
Tangdan YN51/52B5
Tangdaohe HEB5/6C6
(Tangdukou)Shaoyang Xian HN37/38D4
Tang'erli HEB5/6D4
Tangfang HEB5/6D6
Tangfang JX29/30E4
Tangfu GD41B2
Tanggangzi LN11/12C6
Tanggarma QH59/60B6
Tanggeng AH19/20C2
Tanggor SC45/46B4
Tanggou AH23/25F4
Tanggou JS17/18C4
Tanggu TJ3/4C4
Tangguantun TJ3/4D3
Tanggula(Dangla)Shan QH59/60D2-4
                     XZ53/54C7-9
Tanggula Shankou(Dang La) XZ53/54C8
                     QH59/60D2
Tanggulashan(Togton Heyan)
  QH59/60C3
Tanghai Xian HEB5/6D6
Tang He BJ3/4B3 HEB5/6B4-C4
Tang He SX7/8B6 HEB5/6E3
Tang He AH23/24C4
Tang He HEN33/34E4
Tanghekou BJ3/4B3
Tangheng GD41A2
Tanghe Shuiku LN11/12C7
Tanghe Xian HEN33/34E4
Tangheyan LN11/12C7
Tanghu JX29/30E2
Tanghu HEB5/6D3
Tangji JS17/18C5
Tangjia GD39/40D6
Tangjia GD39/40F2
Tangjiagou AH23/24E5
Tangjiang JX29/30F2
Tangjiapo SD31/32B8
Tangjiawan ZJ21/22B4
Tangjiawan HN37/38E4
Tangjia Wan GD41B2
(Tangkeng)Fengshun Xian GD39/40C9
Tangkou AH23/24F5
Tangkou FJ25/26D5
Tangkoubang ZJ19/20C3
Tangku GX43/44B7
Tanglag QH59/60D6
Tanglai Qu NX61/62B3
Tanglou JS17/18B2
Tangmai XZ53/54D10

Tangnag QH59/60C7
Tangnange AH19/20B1
Tangnanji AH23/24C4
Tangpeng GD39/40E3
Tangpu ZJ21/22C5
Tangpu JX29/30C2
Tangqi ZJ21/22B5
Tangqiao JS17/18E6
Tangquan JS19/20A1
Tangquan FJ25/26E3
Tangra Yumco XZ53/54D6
Tangshan JS17/18D5
Tangshancheng LN11/12D8
Tangshan Shi HEB5/6D6
Tangshi JS17/18E6
Tangtang YN51/52B6
Tangtian HN37/38E6
Tangtianshi HN37/38E4
Tangtou SD31/32D5
Tangtou GZ49/50C7
Tangtouxia GD39/40D7
Tangwan HN37/38D3
Tangwan JX29/30C5
Tangwan JS19/20A2
Tangwanghe HL15/16C5
Tangwang He HL15/16D5
Tangwu SD31/32C5
Tangxi ZJ21/22C4
Tangxi AH23/24E4
Tangxia ZJ21/22E5
Tangxia GD39/40D6
Tangxian ZJ21/22C5
Tang Xian HEB5/6E2
Tangxianzhen HB35/36C6
Tangxi Shuiku GD39/40C9
Tangya ZJ21/22C4
Tangyang JS17/18D6
Tangyan He SC35/36E1
Tangyi SD31/32C2
Tangyin JX29/30D4
Tangyin Xian HEN33/34B6
Tangyu SN55/56F5
Tangyuan Xian HL15/16D5
Tangzha JS17/18D6
Tangzhuang SD31/32E5
Tangzi YN51/52C5
Tangzizhuang BJ3/4B4
Taniantaweng Shan XZ53/54C10-D11
Tanjiafang SD29/30C5
Tanjiajing GS57/58D6
Tanjiang GD39/40B9
Tan Jiang GD39/40D5
Tanjiaqiao AH23/24F5
Tanjiawan HN37/38C3
Tankou JX29/30F2
Tankou FJ25/26F3
Tanlin TW27/28E2
Tanluo GX43/44E5
Tanmen HI42B3
Tanniu HI42B3
Tanqiao HB35/36D5
Tanqiu JX29/30D3
Tanshan NX61/62D3

Tanshan JX29/30C2
Tanshang SX7/8C5
Tanshi ZJ21/22D3
Tanshi HN37/38D5
Tanshui TW27/28B3
Tanshui GD39/40D4
Tanshui Kang TW27/28B3
Tantou YN51/52A6
Tantou ZJ21/22C6
Tantou ZJ21/22C4
Tantou FJ25/26D5
Tantou GD39/40D3
Tantou JX29/30E3
Tantou HEN33/34C3
Tantou Shan ZJ21/22C7
Tantu JL13/14A4
Tanwan HN37/38D3
Tanwen HI42B3
Tanxi JX29/30C3
Tanxi JS19/20B3
Tanxi HN37/38C2
Tanxia GX43/44B8
Tanxu GX43/44E7
Tanxu Shan ZJ21/22B6
Tanyi SD31/32D5
Tanzaichong GD41A2
Tanzhesi BJ3/4C3
Tanzhou GD41B1
Tanzhuang HEN33/34D6
Tanzishan HN37/38E5
Taobao JL13/14B4
Taocheng HEN33/34D6
Taocheng AH23/24E5
(Taocheng)Daxin Xian GX43/44E5
Taochuan HN37/38F4
Taocun SD31/32B8
Tao'er He NM9/10D13 JL13/14B4-3
Taofu GZ49/50B6
Tao He GS57/58E6
(Taohong)Longhui Xian HN37/38D4
Taohua HEB5/6C2
Taohua Dao ZJ21/22C7
Taohuadian HB35/36C7
Taohuatu LN11/12C4
Taohuayu HEN33/34C5
Tao Jiang JX29/30F3-2
Taojiang Xian HN37/38C5
Taojiatun LN11/12B7
Taojiatun JL13/14D6
Taolaizhao JL13/14C6
Taole Xian(Mataigou) NX61/62B3
Taolin HEN33/34E7
Taolin HN37/38B6
Taolin HN37/38C6
Taolin JS17/18B4
Taolin HN37/38D5
Taolin SD31/32D6
Taoluo SD31/32D6
Taonan Shi JL13/14B3
Taosha JX29/30C4
Taoshan NX61/62C2
Taoshan HL15/16D5
Taoshan ZJ21/22E5

Taoshanji AH23/24B4
Taowu JS17/18E4
Taoxi ZJ21/22D4
Taoxi AH23/24E4
Taoxi FJ25/26E2
Taoxing SX7/8D4
Taoxu GX43/44E7
Taoyan ZJ21/22B5
Taoyao GD39/40B9
Taoying GZ49/50C7
Taoyuan FJ25/26E3
Taoyuan TW27/28D2
Taoyuan SD31/32E2
Taoyuan JS17/18C3
Taoyuan Hsien TW27/28B3
Taoyuan Xian HN37/38C4
Taozhou HN37/38E6
Taozhu ZJ21/22D6
Taozhuang SD31/32E4
Tapu TW27/28D2
Taqian JX29/30B5
Taqiao HEN33/34D6
Tarbagatai Shan XJ81B4-5
Targan Obo NM9/10D11
Tarhu NM9/10G6
Tarian Gol NM9/10G7
Tarim XJ63/64E7
Tarim Erchang XJ63/64E9
Tarim He XJ63/64E7-8
Tarim Liuchang XJ63/64E9
Tarim Pendi XJ63/64F6-8
Tarim Qichang XJ63/64E9
Tarmar XZ53/54E7
(Tarrong)Nyêmo Xian XZ53/54E8
Tart QH59/60B3
Tashan LN11/12D6
Tashan LN11/12D4
Tashi SN55/56F2
Tashi ZJ21/22C4
Tashi HI42A3
Tashi GS57/58B2
Tashiyi HN37/38B5
Tatalin Gol QH59/60B5
Tata Shan TW27/28D2
Tathong Channel HK41B3
Tàtrang XJ63/64F8
Tatu TW27/28C2
Tatu Hsi TW27/28C2
Tatun Shan TW27/28B3
Tawo HN37/38B2
Tawu TW27/28E2
Taxi HL15/16C4
Taxkorgan Tajik Zizhixian XJ63/64G3
Tayang HI42B3
Tayayi HEB3/4C2
Tayuan TW27/28B3
Tayuan HL15/16B3
(Ta Yu)Chimei Yu TW27/28D1
Tayuling TW27/28C3
Tazhuang FJ25/26D4
Taziba SC45/46C3
Tazishan SC47/48A3
Techi Shuiku TW27/28C3

Tei Tong Tsai HK41B2
Tekes He XJ63/64D6
Tekes Xian XJ63/64D6
Telashi Hu QH59/60C3
Temet NM61/62B2
Têmpung QH59/60B6
Teng'aopu LN11/12C6
Tengchong Xian YN51/52C3
Tengger Els NM9/10I5
Tengger Feng XJ81C5
Tengger Shamo NM9/10H4-5
Tengjiaji SD31/32B9
Tengqiao JX29/30D4
Tengqiao HI42C2
Tengtian JX29/30D3
Tengtiao Jiang YN51/52D5
Teng Xian GX43/44D8
Tengzhai HI42B2
Tengzhou Shi SD31/32D4
Tengzhuang HEB5/6E5
Tengzhuang SD31/32B3
Tergun Daba QH59/60A4-5
Têring XZ53/54D7
Têwo SC45/46A4
Têwo Xian(Dêngka) GS57/58E6
Tian'an HI42B1
Tianba YN51/52D4
Tianba YN51/52B6
Tianba YN49/50D3
Tianbao FJ25/26F3
Tianbaoshan JL13/14E9
Tianbei JL13/14C7
Tiancang GS57/58B4
Tianchang HB5/6E2
Tianchang Shi AH23/24D6
Tiancheng NM7/8A4
Tiancheng GS57/58C4
Tianchi GS57/58D8
Tianchi NX61/62C4
Tianchi XJ63/64C10
Tianciwan SN55/56C4
Tiancun JX29/30E3
Tiande LN11/12A8
Tiande JL13/14C7
Tiandeng Xian GX43/44D5
Tiandong Xian(Pingma) GX43/44D5
Tiandu SN55/56F3
Tiandu HI42C2
Tian'erhe HB35/36D6
Tian'e Xian(Liupai) GX43/44B5
Tianfanjie JX29/30B4
Tianfengping SX7/8B3
Tianfu'an JS19/20B4
Tiangang JL13/14D7
Tiangongmiao SD31/32E2
Tiangongsi HEB3/4C2
Tianhe JX29/30D2
Tianhe HB35/36B3
Tianhe GX43/44C6
Tian He HB35/36A3-B3
Tian He BJ3/4B3
Tianhekou HB35/36B6
Tianheng Dao SD31/32C7-8
Tianhu HEN33/34C4

Tianhua JX29/30G3
Tianhuang SD31/32D4
Tianhuizhen SC47/48B2
Tianhushan FJ25/26E3
Tianjia LN11/12E6
Tianjia SC47/48C3
Tianjia'an AH23/24D4
Tianjiaba HB35/36B3
Tianjialaozhuang NX61/62C3
Tianjiaping NX61/62D2
Tianjiazhen HB35/36E8
Tianjiazhen LN11/12C6
Tianjin Shi TJ3/4C4
Tianjin Xingang TJ3/4C4
Tianjun Xian(Xinyuan) QH59/60B6
Tianjunzhan QH59/60B6
Tianliao GD41A3
Tian Ling HL70E5
Tianlin Xian GX43/44C4
Tianliu SD31/32C5
Tianlou JS17/18B5
Tianlu Shan GD75C4-5
Tianma HN37/38D4
Tianma GZ49/50C7
Tianmen He HB35/36D5-6
Tianmenhe HB35/36D6
Tianmen Shi HB35/36D6
Tianmu Shan ZJ21/22B4
Tianmu Xi ZJ21/22B4-C4
Tianning ZJ21/22B5
Tianpan GD39/40D5
Tianping GX43/44D8
Tianping GZ49/50C8
Tianping HN37/38D4
Tianqiao HEB3/4B3
Tianqiao HB35/36D2
Tianqiaoling JL13/14D10
Tianquan Xian SC45/46C4
Tian Shan XJ63/64D5-10
(Tianshan)Ar Horqin Qi NM9/10F13
Tianshencun GD39/40F2
Tianshenggang JS17/18D6
Tianshengqiao SC47/48A5
Tianshengqiao YN51/52C5
Tianshifu LN11/12C8
Tianshuibu GS57/58D8
Tianshuihai XJ63/64H5
Tianshui He NX61/62C3
Tianshuijing GS57/58B2
Tianshui Shi GS57/58E7
Tiantai Shan ZJ21/22C6
Tiantai Xian ZJ21/22C6
Tiantaiyong NM9/10F11
Tiantang HN37/38F4
Tiantang GD39/40D5
Tiantang SN55/56F3
Tiantangshao GZ49/50B7
Tiantangwei GD41A3
Tiantangzhai HB35/36C8
Tiantou GD39/40A6
Tianwan HN37/38C3
Tianwangsi JS17/18E5
Tianxi GX43/44E5

Tongshan   JS17/18E4
Tongshan   JL13/14F8
Tongshan Xian   HB35/36E7
Tongshan Xian   JS17/18B3
Tongshanyuan Shuiku   ZJ21/22C3
Tongshi   SD31/32D4
Tongshi Shi   HI42C2
Tongshuping   JX29/30D2
Tongsi   SC47/48C3
Tongtan   SC47/48D3
Tongtian He(Zhi Qu)   QH59/60C4-D5
Tongwan   GX43/44D7
Tongwaxiang   HEN33/34C6
Tongwei Xian   GS57/58E7
Tongxi   SC47/48C4
Tongzhou   BJ3/4C3
Tongxian   SC47/48B3
Tongxiang Shi   ZJ21/22B5
Tongxing   SC47/48B4
Tongxing   JS17/18C6
Tongxing   GD41A2
Tongxingjie   JS17/18B5
Tongxin Xian   NX61/62D2
Tongxu Xian   HEN33/34C6
Tongyanggang   JS17/18C6
Tongyanghe   AH23/24E4
Tongyang Yunhe   JS17/18D5-6
Tongyi   NX61/62B3
Tongyu   SX7/8E5
Tongyuan   JX29/30C4
Tongyuan   ZJ21/22B5
Tongyuanpu   LN11/12D7
Tongyu Xian(Kaitong)   JL13/14C4
Tongyu Yunhe   JS17/18C6
Tongzhaipu   HEN33/34E4
Tongzhong   SC47/48C2
Tongzhong   HEN33/34E6
Tongzhou   GZ49/50E5
Tongzhou Shi   JS17/18D7
Tongzi   SC45/46D6
Tongzicun   HN37/38C4
Tongzi Xian   GZ49/50B5
Toro Co   XZ53/54D5
Toson Hu   QH59/60B5
Tost   NM9/10G6
Toucheng   TW27/28C3
Toudao   JL13/14F6
Toudao Chuan   SN55/56C3-D4
Toudaodun   NX61/62B3
Toudaogou   JL13/14E10
Toudaohezi   SN55/56B5
Toudaohu   NM61/62B2
Toudao Jiang   JL13/14E8
Toudaokan   NX61/62A3
Toudaoqiao   NM9/10K17
Tou'erying   HEB3/4B2
Toufang   GS57/58F7
Toufen   TW27/28C2
Touguan   NX61/62B2
Toulin   HL15/16D7
(Touliu)Yunlin Hsien   TW27/28D2
Toulu Zhou   GD41B2
Toumen Shan   ZJ21/22D6

Tounan   TW27/28D2
Toupai   GX43/44C8
Toupao   HEB3/4B2
Toupeng   ZJ21/22B5
Toupi   JX29/30E4
Touqiao   JS19/20A2
Toutai   HL15/16E3
Touying   NX61/62E3
Touzeng   JS17/18B6
Touzha   NX61/62B3
Touzhai   GS61/62D1
Toxkan He   XJ63/64E5
Toyêma   QH59/60C7
Toyun   XJ63/64E3
Tsak Yue Wu   HK41B3
Tsaotun   TW27/28D2
Tseng Lan Shue   HK41B3
Tsengwen Hsi   TW27/28D2
Tsengwen Shuiku   TW27/28D2
Tsin Shui Wan   HK41B3
Tsin Yue Wan   HK41B2
Tsoying   TW27/28E2
Tuanbaosi   HB35/36D2
Tuanbokou   HEB5/6E1
Tuancun   JX29/30D4
Tuanfeng   HB35/36D7
Tuan He   HEN33/34E3
Tuanjie   JL13/14C3
Tuanjie   NM9/10J17
Tuanjie   HL15/16D4
Tuankou   ZJ21/22B4
Tuanlin   JL13/14E7
Tuanlinpu   HB35/36D5
Tuannian   SC47/48C4
Tuanpi   HB35/36D8
Tuanpo   TJ3/4D4
Tuanshansi   HB35/36E5
Tuanwan   SD31/32C7
Tuanwang   SD31/32C7
Tuanxi   GZ49/50C6
Tuban   SX7/8C2
Tubao   FJ25/26D4
Tubo   GX43/44C7
Tubxin   NM15/16C2
Tuchang   TW27/28C8
Tuchang   GX49/50E6
Tucheng   HB35/36C3
Tucheng   GZ49/50B4
Tucheng   GZ49/50D3
Tuchengzi   LN11/12D8
Tuchengzi   HEB5/6B4
Tuchengzi   HEB5/6B2
Tuchengzi   JL13/14C7
Tudian   ZJ19/20C3
Tudi'ao   GZ49/50B7
Tuding   JL13/14D6
Tuditang   HB35/36D7
Tuen Mun   HK41B2
Tufang   FJ25/26E2
Tugao   GS57/58D7
Tuguancun   YN51/52B3
Tuhai He   SD31/32B4
(Tujiabu)Yongxiu Xian   JX29/30B3

Tujiezi   GZ49/50C3
Tujingzi   NM61/62B2
Tuku   TW27/28D2
Tulagt Ar Gol   QH59/60B2
Tulai   QH59/60A6
Tulai He   QH59/60A6
Tulai Nanshan   QH59/60A5-6
Tulai Shan   QH59/60A6
Tulan   TW27/28E3
Tulantai   NM9/10H5
Tule Mod   NM9/10E13
Tulihe   NM9/10B13
Tulongshan   HL15/16D6
Tumain   XZ53/54C8
Tumd Youqi   NM9/10G8
Tumd Zuoqi   NM9/10G8
Tumen   HB35/36A3
Tumen   SC47/48C1
Tumen   SN55/56G6
Tumen   SC47/48A4
Tumen Jiang   JL13/14E11
Tumenling   JL13/14C7
Tumen Shi   JL13/14E10
Tumenya   HB35/36D4
Tumenzi   HEB5/6C7
Tumenzi   GS57/58D6
Tumenzi Shuiku   LN11/12D7
Tumu   HEB3/4B2
Tumulu   HEB5/6B2
Tumxuk   XJ63/64E5
Tunbao   HB35/36D2
Tuncang   AH23/24D5
Tunchang Xian   HI42B3
Tungan   TW27/28D1
Tungchi Yu   TW27/28D1
Tungchuan Tao   FJ25/26E5
Tung Chung   HK41B2
(Tungdor)Mainling Xian   XZ53/54E10
Tunggalag Nur   NM61/62B2
Tungho   TW27/28E3
Tunghsiao   TW27/28C2
Tungkang   TW27/28E2
Tungmen   TW27/28D3
Tung O   HK41B3
Tungshan   TW27/28C3
Tungsha Tao   FJ25/26D6
Tungshih   TW27/28C2
Tungshih   TW27/28D2
Tung Wan   HK41B2
Tungyin Tao   FJ25/26D6
Tunjiao   GZ49/50E4
Tunken   HEB5/6B2
Tunli   SX7/8E2
Tunli   GX43/44E6
Tunliu Xian   SX7/8E4
Tunqiu   GX43/44C7
Tunshuzhen   HL15/16D8
Tuntou   SD31/32C3
(Tunxi)Huangshan Shi   AH23/24G5
Tunzi   HEN33/34B6
Tuocheng   GD39/40B8
Tuochuanbu   JX29/30C3
(Tuodian)Shuangbai Xian   YN51/52C4

Tuodong GD39/40D4
Tuo He AH23/24C4
Tuoji AH23/24C4
Tuo Jiang SC76D5
(Tuojiang)Fenghuang Xian HN37/38D2
Tuoji Dao SD31/32A7
Tuokou HN37/38D2
Tuoli BJ3/4C3
Tuolu GX43/44E5
Tuomugou SC45/46E4
Tuoniang Jiang GX43/44C3
Tuo Shui HN37/38F4
Tuowu SC45/46D4
Tuozhaminnutuke NM9/10B14
Tuping GZ49/50B6
Tupo NX61/62C2
Tuqiang HL15/16A2
Tuqiao AH23/24E4
Tuqiao HN37/38E3
Tuqiao SC47/48B2
Tuqiao SN55/56E4
Tuqiao JS17/18E5
Tuqiao BJ3/4C3
Tuqiao SD31/32B3
Tuqiaozi JL13/14C7
Tuquan Xian NM9/10E13
Tura XJ63/64G9
Turpan Diqu XJ63/64D10-11
Turpan Pendi XJ81C6
Turpan Shi XJ63/64D10
Turpan Zhan XJ63/64D10
Turugart Shankou XJ63/64E3
Tushan JS17/18B3
Tutang JX29/30B4
Tuwei He SN55/56B6
Tuxi GZ49/50B6
Tuxi SC47/48A5
Tuxiang SC45/46C7
Tuzhuchang SC47/48C1

U

Uher Hudag NM9/10J20
Ujur Gol NM9/10G7
Ujur Gol NM9/10J18
Ulan NM9/10K19
Ulan Buh Shamo NM9/10G6-H6
Ulan Had NM61/62C1
Ulan Had NM9/10J23
Ulan Had NM9/10D12
Ulanhot Shi NM9/10D14
Ulan Hua JL13/14C3
(Ulan Hua)Siziwang(Dorbod)Qi
   NM9/10J21
Ulan Hudag NM9/10J20
Ulan Jalag JL13/14C5
Ulanlinggi XJ63/64D9
Ulan Moron SN55/56A6-B6
Ulan Obo NM61/62C1
Ulanqab Meng NM9/10G8 − 9
Ulan Suhai NM9/10K17
Ulan Suhai NM9/10G5
Ulansuhai Nur NM9/10G7
Ulan Sum He NM9/10F8

Ulan Tohoi NM9/10G3
Ulan Tug NM9/10K17
Ulan Ul Hu QH59/60C2
Ulan Xian(Xireg) QH59/60B6
Ulgai NM9/10E12
Ulgain Gobi NM9/10E11-12
Ulgain Gol NM9/10E12
Uljir NM11/12B4
Ulugqat XJ63/64F3
Ulungur He XJ63/64B10
Ulungur Hu XJ63/64B9
Unuli Horog QH50/60C2
Urad Houqi NM9/10G6
Urad Qianqi NM9/10G7
Urad Zhongqi(Haliut) NM9/10G7
Urho XJ63/64B8
Urt Moron QH59/60B3
Ürümqi Shi XJ63/64D9
Ürümqi Xian XJ63/64D9
Usu Shi XJ63/64C8
Utbulak XJ63/64B9
Uxin Ju NM9/10H7
Uxin Qi(Dabqig) NM9/10H7
Uxxaktal XJ63/64D9
Uzbel Shankou XJ63/64F2
Üztag XJ63/64C8
Uzunbulak XJ63/64E10

W

Wabu AH23/24D3
Wabu Hu AH23/24D3
Wadi SX7/8F3
Wadian HEN33/34E4
Wafang JL13/14B3
Wafangdian SN55/56H4
Wafangdian Shi LN11/12E6
Wagang SC45/46E4
Wahei SC47/48D1
Wah Fu HK41B3
Waian TW27/28D1
Waichen ZJ21/22C5
Waifang Shan HEN33/34D4
Waikuatang JS19/20B3
Wailingding Dao GD41B3
Wailuo GD39/40F3
Waishe ZJ21/22D4
Waitoushan LN11/12C7
Waiyang FJ25/26D3
Waiyang FJ25/26C6
Waizizhen HEN33/34E4
Walagan HL15/16A3
Walêg SC45/46D3
Wali HEB5/6D6
Walongqiao AH23/24F3
Walung XZ53/54E11
Wamiao HB35/36D6
Wan'an FJ25/26D3
Wan'an SX7/8E3
Wan'an Xi FJ25/26E2-3
Wan'an Xian JX29/30E2
Wanba SC45/46D4
Wanbanqiao GX43/44B8
Wanbao JL13/14E9

Wanbao JL13/14C6
Wanbei GD39/40B6
Wanbi YN51/52B4
Wanchang SC47/48C2
Wanchong HI42C2
Wanda Shan HL15/16D7
Wande SD31/32C3
Wandi SD31/32C7
Wandianzi LN11/12C9
Wanding Shi YN51/52C3
Wanfa JL13/14B6
Wanfotang BJ3/4C2
Wanfu JX29/30D2
Wanfu LN11/12D6
Wanfu He SD31/32D3
Wangan TW27/28D1
Wangan Tao TW27/28D1
Wang'anzhen HEB3/4C1
Wangben JL13/14D4
Wangbi SX7/8F4
Wangbuzhuang TJ3/4C4
Wangcang Xian SC45/46B6
Wangcao GZ49/50B6
Wangchang SC47/48C2
Wangcheng Xian(Gaotangling)
   HN37/38C5
Wangchuan FJ25/26E4
Wangcun GS61/62E4
Wangcun SN55/56E6
Wangcun HN37/38C2
Wangcun SD31/32C7
Wangcun SD31/32C4
Wangcun AH23/24G5
Wangcun AH23/24G4
Wangcundian SD31/32B3
Wangcunkou ZJ21/22D3
Wangdain XZ53/54E7
(Wangda)Zogang Xian XZ53/54E11
Wangdian ZJ21/22B5
Wangdian GX43/44C4
Wangdingdi TJ3/4C4
Wangdu Xian HEB5/6E3
Wang'er JX29/30C5
Wangfan HEN33/34C3
Wangfeng SD31/32C2
Wangfengqiao SN55/56E6
Wangfu JL13/14C6
Wangfu LN11/12B5
Wangfu GD39/40E4
Wangfutai NX61/62C3
Wanggao GX43/44C9
Wang Gaxun QH59/60B5
Wanggezhuang SD31/32C7
Wanggong SX7/8D4
Wanggou SD31/32D5
Wangguantun SX7/8A5
Wangguanying HEB3/4C5
Wanghai Shan LN11/12C5
Wanghaotun SD31/32D2
Wanghe SX7/8E4
Wanghongpu NX61/62B3
Wanghu SD31/32D6
Wanghu SX7/8B5

Wanghua JX29/30D2
Wangji JS17/18C3
Wangji JS17/18C4
Wangji HB35/36C5
Wangjiachang HN37/38B4
Wangjiachang Shuiku HN37/38B4
Wangjiadian HB35/36C6
Wangjiadian LN11/12D3
Wangjiafangqian SD31/32D6
Wangjiajin HEB5/6F3
Wangjiangjing ZJ21/22B5
Wangjiang Xian AH23/24F3
Wangjiaping HN37/38E2
Wangjiapu LN11/12D7
Wangjiapu JX29/30B3
Wangjiawan SN55/56C5
Wangjiawopu LN11/12D5
Wangjiaxu JX29/30C3
Wangjiayao SN55/56D5
Wangjiaying HB35/36D1
Wangjiayu SX7/8E5
Wangjiazhuang YN51/52C5
Wangjiazhuang SX7/8C4
Wangjie YN51/52D4
Wangjing HEB3/4D2
Wangkou TJ3/4D3
Wangkuai Shuiku HEB5/6E2
Wangkui Xian HL15/16D4
Wanglang SC45/46B5
Wanglaorenji AH23/24C2
Wanglejing NX61/62C4
Wangling HN37/38D6
Wangliu HEN33/34E7
Wanglong SC47/48D3
Wanglongchang GZ49/50B4
Wangmao GX43/44E7
Wangminbu NX61/62E2
Wangmo Xian GZ49/50E5
Wangmu GD41A3
Wangmudu JX29/30F2
Wangou JL13/14E7
Wangpan HEB3/4D2
Wangpan Shan ZJ21/22B6
Wangping HB35/36D2
Wangqi JL13/14D7
Wangqiao HEN33/34C7
Wangqiao HB35/36E5
Wangqingmen LN11/12C9
Wangqingtuo TJ3/4C3
Wangqing Xian JL13/14D10
Wangqu SN55/56F4
Wangquze SN55/56C4
Wangshi AH23/24C3
Wangshiwa SN55/56E5
Wangshiwan HN37/38D5
Wangshu HEB5/6F5
Wangsi GZ49/50D6
Wangsi HEB5/6E4
Wangsitan NX61/62C4
Wangtai FJ25/26D3
Wangtai SD31/32C6
Wangtan ZJ21/22C5
Wangtao SX7/8E4

Wangtian'e JL13/14F8
Wangtien TW27/28C2
Wangting JS17/18E6
Wangtuan HEB5/6F4
Wangtuan SD31/32B8
Wangtuanji AH23/24C3
Wangtuanzhuang NX61/62D2
Wangu SC47/48B4
Wanguchang SC47/48C3
Wangwa NX61/62D3
Wangwu HI42B2
Wangwu HEN33/34B4
Wangwuqiao HEN33/34E6
Wangwu Shan SX7/8F4 HEN33/34B4
Wangwu Shuiku SD31/32B7
Wangxia HI42B2
Wangxian HN37/38D6
Wangxian SX7/8F2
Wangxian JX29/30D3
Wangxuzhuang HEB5/6E5
Wangyang HL15/16D4
Wangyang SC47/48C2
Wangyao Shuiku SN55/56D4-5
Wangyedian NM9/10G12
Wangyin SD31/32D3
(Wangying)Huaiyin Xian JS17/18C5
Wangyuanqiao NX61/62B3
Wangzhai ZJ21/22D4
Wangzhai AH23/24B3
Wangzhai SX7/8F4
Wangzhai LN11/12D6
Wangzhu SD31/32C7
Wangzhuang SX7/8E3
Wangzhuang SX7/8F3
Wangzhuangbu SX7/8B5
Wangzhuangji JS17/18B4
Wangziguan GS57/58F7
Wangzizhuang SD31/32C3
Wan He AH23/24F3
Wanhedian HB35/36B6
Wanjiabu JX29/30C3
Wanjialing LN11/12E6
Wanjiamatou TJ3/4D4
Wanjiatun LN11/12D3
Wanjiazhai SX7/8B3
Wanjinta JL13/14C6
Wanli AH23/24E5
Wanli TW27/28B3
Wanli JX29/30C3
Wanliang JL13/14E8
Wanling HI42B2
Wannian Xian(Chenying) JX29/30C5
Wanning Shi HI42C3
Wanqingsha GD41B2
Wanqiu SC45/46E4
Wanquan HI42B3
Wanquan He HI42B3
Wanquansi HEB3/4B3
Wanquan Xian(Kongjiazhuang)
  HEB5/6C2
Wanrong Xian SX7/8F2
Wanshan SC47/48B4
Wanshan Qundao GD39/40D6-7

Wanshan Tequ GZ49/50C8
Wansheng SC45/46D6
Wanshengchang SC47/48B1
Wanshi ZJ19/20C2
Wanshou LN11/12C3
Wanshou SC47/48B4
Wan Shui AH71C2
Wanshunpu JL13/14C5
Wanta TW27/28D3
Wantan TW27/28E2
Wantan HEN33/34C5
Wantan HB35/36D3
Wantang ZJ19/20D4
Wantang YN51/52D5
Wanta Shuiku TW27/28D3
Wantouqiao HN37/38E3
Wan Tuk HK41B3
Wanzhou SC45/46C7
Wanyang Shan JX29/30E2-1
          HN37/38E7-6
Wanyuan Shi SC45/46B7
Wanzai GD41B2
Wanzai Xian(Kangle) JX29/30C2
(Wanzhi)Wuhu Xian AH23/24E5
Wanzhuang HEB5/6D4
Wanzi Hu HN37/38C5
Waqên SC45/46B4
Warzhong SC45/46D3
Washi SC47/48C2
Watang SX7/8C2
Watang GX43/44E7
Wating NX61/62E3
Wawu HEN33/34D4
Wawutang HN37/38E3
Waxi GD39/40C8
Waxingzhen HL15/16D4
Waxü GS57/58E6
Waxxari XJ63/64F9
Wayao YN51/52C3
Wayao JS17/18B4
(Wayaobu)Zichang Xian SN55/56C5
Wayuan HN37/38E5
Wazidian HEB5/6B6
Wazijie SN55/56E5
Weibo HEB5/6E3
Weichang Manzu Mongolzu Zizhixian
  HEB5/6B5
Weicheng GZ49/50D5
Weicheng SC45/46E3
Weicheng SC45/46C5
Weichuan HEN33/34C5
Weicun JS17/18E5
Weidoushan Shuiku HB35/36C7
Weidu GX43/44D7
Weifang Shi SD31/32C6
Weifangxi SD31/32C6
Weiganbao HB35/36D2
Weigan He XJ63/64E7-8
Weihai Shi SD31/32B9
Wei He HEN33/34B6 SD31/32C2
Weihe HL15/16E5
Wei He GS57/58E8 SN55/56F5
Wei He SD31/32C6

Weihe Pingyuan   SN79D3-4
Weihui Qu   SN55/56F4
Weihui Shi   HEN33/34B6
Weihuling   JL13/14D8
Weihu Ling   JL13/14D8
Weijiaqiao   SD31/32B4
Weijiatan   SX7/8C3
Weijiaying   HEB3/4C2
Weijiazhuang   GZ49/50D6
Weijin   JL13/14E6
Weijingtang   JS17/18E6
Weiling   HL15/16D5
Weilu   SX7/8A4
Weiluo   GX43/44E6
Weima   SX7/8D5
Weimin   FJ25/26C3
Weinan Shi   SN55/56F5
Weining Yizu Huizu Miaozu Zizhixian
    GZ49/50D3
Weiqiao   JS17/18C4
Weiqiuji   HEN33/34B6
Weirong   GS57/58E7
Weishan   HN37/38C4
Weishan   ZJ21/22C5
Weishan Hu   SD31/32E4   JS17/18B3
Weishan Xian(Xiazhen)   SD31/32E4
Weishan Yizu Huizu Zizhixian
    YN51/52C4
Weishanzhuang   BJ3/4C3
Weishi Xian   HEN33/34C6
Wei Shui   HN37/38C5
Wei Shui   HB35/36E4
(Weishui)Jingxing Xian   HEB5/6E2
(Weitang)Jiashan Xian   ZJ21/22B5
Weitian   FJ25/26C4
Weiting   JS17/18E6
Weitou   FJ25/26F4
Weitou Wan   FJ25/26F4
Weiwan   SD31/32C2
Weiwan   SD31/32E2
Weixi   SC47/48B4
Wei Xian   HEB5/6G3
Weixian   HEN33/34B6
Wei Xian   HEB5/6G2
Weixi Lisuzu Zizhixian   YN51/52B3
Weixin   GZ49/50C4
Weixinchang   HN37/38B4
Weixin Xian(Zhaxi)   YN51/52B6
Weiya   XJ63/64E13
Weiying   JS17/18C4
Weiyuanbu   SX7/8B4
Weiyuan Jiang   YN77D3
Weiyuankou   HB35/36D8
Weiyuanpu   LN11/12B8
Weiyuan Xian   GS57/58E7
Weiyuan Xian(Yanling)   SC45/46D5
Weizha   NX61/62A3
Weizhangzi   LN11/12D3
Weizhou   NX61/62C3
Weizhou   HEB5/6E2
Weizhou   GX43/44F7
Weizhou Dao   GX43/44F7
(Weizhou)Wenchuan Xian   SC45/46C4

Weizhuang   SN55/56F5
Weizi   LN11/12D7
Weiziyu   LN11/12C8
Weizizhen   SX7/8E5
Wen'an   HB35/36D4
Wen'an Wa   HEB5/6E4
Wen'an Xian   HEB5/6E4
Wenbo   SC45/46B2
Wenbu   NX61/62E2
Wenchang   ZJ21/22C4
Wenchang Shi   HI42B3
Wencheng Xian(Daxue)   ZJ21/22E5
Wenchuan Xian(Weizhou)   SC45/46C4
Wenchun   HL15/16E5
Wendeng Shi   SD31/32B9
Wendi   GX43/44F8
Wendou   HB35/36E1
Wenfang   JX29/30C5
(Wenfeng)Jishui Xian   JX29/30D3
Wenfengzhen   GS57/58E7
Weng'an Xian   GZ49/50C6
Wengcheng   GD39/40B6
Wengdong   GZ49/50C8
Wengjiang   HN37/38C6
Wengjiang   GD39/40B6
Wengong   SC47/48B2
Wengshui   YN51/52A3
Wengtian   HI42B3
Wenguangxiang   GD41A2
Wengyang   ZJ21/22D5
Wengyuan Xian(Longxian)   GD39/40B7
Wen He   SD31/32D5
Wenheng   FJ25/26E2
Wenhua   SC47/48C3
Wenjia   FJ25/26E5
Wenjiadian   GZ49/50C6
Wenjiadian   SD31/32B4
Wenjiang Xian   SC45/46C4
Wenjiao   HI42B3
Wenjiashi   HN37/38C6
Wenjiazhen   JX29/30C4
Wenjing   SC47/48B3
Wenjiyu   YN51/52C4
Wenkutu   NM9/10C14
Wenling Shi   ZJ21/22D6
Wenlong   JX29/30G2
Wenluo   HI42C2
Wenming   HN37/38F6
Wenmingpu   HN37/38E4
Wenping   GZ49/50B7
(Wenping)Ludian Xian   YN51/52B5
Wenqiao   JX29/30B4
Wenqiao   ZJ21/22D6
Wenqu   HEN33/34E3
Wenquan   AH19/20C1
Wenquan   QH59/60D2
Wenquan   QH59/60C6
Wenquan   GZ49/50C5
Wenquan   GZ49/50B6
Wenquan   SC45/46C7
Wenquan   GD39/40C6
Wenquan   BJ3/4B3
Wenquan   JX29/30B3

Wenquan (Arixang)Xian   XJ63/64C6
Wenquancun   GZ49/50D7
Wenquan Hu   XZ53/54B4
Wenquansi   LN11/12C8
Wenquantang   SD31/32B9
Wenquanzhen   HB35/36E7
Wenren   HEB5/6E3
Wenru   HI42B3
Wenshang Xian   SD31/32D3
Wenshan Xian   YN51/52D6
Wenshan Zhuangzu Miaozu Zizhizhou
    YN51/52D6
Wenshi   GX43/44B9
Wenshi   HI42B3
Wenshui   GZ49/50B5
Wenshui Xian   SX7/8D4
Wensu Xian   XJ63/64E6
Wentang   HEB5/6E1
Wentang   JX29/30D2
Wentang   JX29/30B2
Wentang Xia   SC47/48C4
Wenxi   ZJ21/22D5
Wen Xian   GS57/58F7
Wen Xian   HEN33/34C5
Wenxingchang   SC47/48B5
Wenxi Xian   SX7/8F3
Wenyan   ZJ19/20C3
Wenying   JX29/30F2
Wenyu   HEN33/34C3
Wenyu He   SX7/8D3-4
Wenyu He   BJ3/4B3
Wenyu Shuiku   SX7/8D3
Wenzhou Shi   ZJ21/22D5
Wenzhou Wan   ZJ21/22E5
Wenzhu   JX29/30E1
Wenzu   SD31/32C4
West Lamma Channel   HK41B3
Wing Ning Lei   HK41B3
Wofotang   HEB3/4D3
Wohutun   JL13/14D4
Woken   HL15/16D6
Woken He   HL15/16D5-E6
Wolong   JL13/14E9
Wolongguan   SC45/46C4
Woluogu   HEB3/4C4
Wong Chuk Hang   HK41B3
Wong Ka Wai   HK41B2
Wong Uk   HK41B3
Wong Yue Tan   HK41B3
Woniushi   LN11/12B7
Woniutu   HL15/16D2
Wopi   JL13/14C6
Woshi   HB35/36D5
Woyangchang   SX7/8C4
Wu'anji   SD31/32D2
Wu'an Shi   HEB5/6G2
Wubairha   NM9/10G6
Wubao   SC47/48C2
Wubu   HEB3/4B2
Wubu Xian   SN55/56C6
Wuchang   HB35/36D7
Wuchang Hu   AH23/24F3
Wuchang Shi   HL15/16E4

Wucheng   AH23/24G5
Wucheng   SX7/8E2
Wucheng   SX7/8B5
Wucheng   HEN33/34D5
Wucheng   JX29/30B3
Wucheng   SX7/8D3
Wucheng   HEN33/34E5
Wucheng   SD31/32B2
Wuchen Xian   SD31/32B3
Wuchi   TW27/28C2
Wuchiu Yu   FJ25/26F5
Wuchuan Gelaozu Miaozu Zizhixian(Duru)
   GZ49/50B6
Wuchuan Xian   NM9/10G8
Wuchuan Shi   GD39/40E3
Wucun   GX43/44D4
Wucun   HEN33/34B5
Wucun   SD31/32D4
Wuda   NM9/10H6
Wudabao   ZJ21/22E4

Wudalianchi   HL15/16C4
(Wudan)Ongniud Qi   NM9/10F12
Wudang   GZ49/50D5
Wudang Shan   HB35/36B3
Wudao   LN11/12E5
Wudaogou   JL13/14D11
Wudaogou   JL13/14E6
Wudaogou   HL15/16B4
Wudaojiang   JL13/14F7
Wudaoliang   QH59/60C3
Wudaoshui   HN37/38B2
Wudaoying   HEB3/4B3
Wude   GX43/44E4
Wudian   HB35/36C5
Wudian   ZJ21/22C4
Wudian   AH23/24E2
Wudian   AH23/24D4
Wuding He   SN55/56C6
Wuding Xian(Jincheng)   YN51/52C5
Wudi Xian   SD31/32B4
Wudong   SC47/48B5
Wudongzha   ZJ19/20C4
Wudu   ZJ21/22E4
Wudu   JX29/30C6
Wudu   SC45/46C5
Wuduhe   HB35/36C4
Wuduizi   NX61/62B3
Wudu Xian   GS57/58F7
Wufeng   TW27/28C3
Wufeng   LN11/12B6
Wufeng   TW27/28D2
Wufeng   TW27/28C2
Wufengpu   HN37/38E4
Wufeng Tujiazu Zizhixian   HB35/36D3
Wufengxi   SC47/48B2
Wufosi   GS57/58D7
Wufu   FJ25/26C4
Wufu   SC47/48A2
Wufu   SC47/48C4
Wugai   NM9/10J17
Wugang   JS17/18C5
Wugang Shi   HEN33/34D5

Wugang Shi   HN37/38E3
Wugong   HEB5/6E3
Wugong Shan   JX29/30D1-2
          HN37/38D6-7
Wugong Xian(Puji)   SN55/56F4
Wugouying   HEN33/34D6
Wuguan   SN55/56G6
Wuguanhe   SN55/56G2
Wuguanzhai   HEB5/6F3
Wugui   SC47/48C3
Wuhai Shi(Haibowan)   NM9/10H6
Wuhan Shi   HB35/36D7
Wuhe   AH23/24F3
Wuhe Xian   AH23/24C4
Wuhuanchi   LN11/12B5
Wuhuang   SC47/48C2
Wuhua Xian(Shuizhai)   GD39/40C8
Wuhubei   AH19/20B1
Wuhu Shi   AH23/24E5
Wuhu Xian(Wanzhi)   AH23/24E5
Wüjang   XZ53/54C2
Wuji   SD31/32D6
Wuji   SD31/32B8
Wuji   HEB5/6G2
Wuji   JS17/18B5
Wujia   HL15/16E4
Wujia   GX43/44F7
Wujiaba   SC47/48A2
Wujiachuan   GS61/62D1
Wujiadian   HEN33/34E5
Wujiagang   AH23/24D5
Wujiang   GX43/44C8
Wujiang   AH23/24E5
Wujiang   JX29/30D3
Wu Jiang   SC45/46D6-7   GZ49/50C6
Wujiang   GZ49/50C5
Wujiang Shi   JS17/18E6
Wujiapu   SC47/48C3
Wujiaqu   XJ63/64C9
Wujiatang   FJ25/26C3
Wujiazhan   JL13/14C6
Wujimi   HL15/16E4
Wujing   SD31/32C5
Wujing   GD39/40A7
Wujingfu   GD39/40C9
Wujin Shi   JS17/18E5
Wuji Xian   HEB5/6E2
Wu Kai Sha   HK41B3
Wukang   ZJ21/22B4
Wu Kang Tang   HK41A3
Wukeshu   JL13/14A4
Wukeshui   NM61/62C2
Wukou   HN37/38C6
Wulaga   HL15/16C6
Wulai   TW27/28C3
Wulajie   JL13/14C7
Wula Shan   NM9/10K19
Wuleidao Wan   SD31/32C8
Wuli   GD39/40F3
Wuli   QH59/60C3
Wuli   GX43/44E7
Wulian   SC45/46C5
Wulian Feng   YN51/52A5-B5

Wuliangdian   LN11/12C6
Wuliang He   SC45/46D3
Wuliang He   AH19/20C2
Wuliang Shan   YN51/52C4-D4
Wulian Shan   SD73C5
Wulian Xian(Hongning)   SD31/32D6
Wuliba   SN55/56H3
Wuliba   SN55/56H4
Wulichuan   HEN33/34D3
Wulidian   HEN33/34E6
Wulie   HI42B1
Wulie He   HEB5/6B6-5
Wuli Jiang   GX43/44E7-F7
Wulin   HL15/16E5
Wulin   GX43/44D8
Wuling   HN37/38B4
Wuling   HEN33/34B6
Wuling   GX43/44D6
Wulingchang   SC45/46C7
Wuling Shan   GZ49/50C7-B9
          HN37/38C2-B4
Wuling Shan   HEB5/6C5
Wulingyuan   HN37/38B3
Wulipai   HN37/38F4
Wuliping   HB35/36E3
Wulipo   NX61/62C3
Wulipu   HB35/36D5
Wulipu   SN55/56H4
Wulitun   HEB3/4C5
Wulong   LN11/12C8
Wulongbei   LN11/12D8
Wulong He   SD31/32C7
Wulongpu   SN55/56C6
Wulongquan   HB35/36D7
Wulong Xian(Xiangkou)   SC45/46D6
Wulubutie   NM15/16C3
Wuluo   GZ49/50B7
Wumahe   HL15/16D5
Wumang Dao   LN11/12E7
Wumatang   XZ53/54D8
Wumei Shan   JX29/30C2
Wumeng Shan   YN51/52B6-5
          GZ49/50C3-D2
Wumin   FJ25/26E2
Wuminghe   GX43/44D6
Wuming Xian   GX43/44D6
Wuning Shui   JX29/30C2
Wuning Xian(Xinning)   JX29/30B3
Wunüdian   HEN33/34C5
Wuping Xian   FJ25/26E2
Wuqiang   HEN33/34C7
Wuqiang   HEB5/6E3
Wuqiang Xian(Xiaofan)   HEB5/6E3
Wuqiao   JS19/20A2
Wuqiao   HEB5/6F4
Wuqiao Xian(Sangyuan)   HEB5/6F4
Wuqia(Ulugqat)Xian   XJ63/64F3
Wuqing Xian(Yangcun)   TJ3/4C4
Wuqi Xian   SN55/56D4
Wurenqiao   HEB5/6E3
Wusha   GZ49/50E3
Wusha   AH23/24F4
Wu Shan   SC45/46C8   HB35/36C3-D3
Wushan   AH23/24D4

Wushan HB35/36B6
Wushan Xian SC45/46C7
Wushan Xian GS57/58E7
Wushaoling GS57/58D6
(Wushe)Jenai TW27/28C3
Wusheng Guan HB35/36C7
　　　　　　　HEN33/34F6
Wusheng Xian(Yankou) SC45/46C6
Wushi GD39/40C8
Wushi GD39/40F2
Wushi GX43/44E8
Wushi HI42B2
Wushi JX29/30D4
Wushi GD39/40B6
Wushi JS19/20B3
Wushih Pi TW27/28C3
Wushi(Uqturpan)Xian XJ63/64E5
Wushu JX29/30E2
Wu Shui HN37/38D3-E3
Wu Shui HN37/38D2
Wu Shui HN37/38F6-G6
　　　　　GD39/40A6-B6
Wu Shui HN37/38C2-3
Wushulin TW27/28E2
Wusi SH19/20C4
Wusijiang Shuiku GX43/44E7
Wusong SH17/18E7
Wusong Jiang (Suzhou Creek)
　SH19/20B4
Wusong Kou SH17/18E7
Wusu HN37/38C3
Wusuli HL15/16A2
Wusuli Jiang HL15/16D8-7
Wuta JS19/20B3
Wutai XJ63/64C7
Wutai SD31/32D4
Wutaimiao HEN33/34D7
Wutai Shan SX7/8C4-B5
Wutai Xian SX7/8C5
Wutan HN37/38C4
Wutang GX43/44E6
Wutang FJ25/26E5
Wutong GX43/44B8
Wutong SX7/8D3
Wutong FJ25/26E4
Wutonggou XJ63/64E10
Wutonggou NM9/10G2
Wutong He HL15/16D6
Wutonghe HL15/16D6
Wutongqiao SC45/46D4
Wutongshu NX61/62B3
Wutongwozi Quan XJ63/64D13
Wuwei Diqu GS57/58C6-D6
Wuwei Shi GS57/58D6
Wuwei Xian AH23/24E4
Wuxi AH19/20B1
Wuxi AH19/20C1
Wu Xia SC45/46C8 HB35/36C3
Wuxiangpu NX61/62B3
Wuxiangqi ZJ21/22C6
Wuxiang Xian SX7/8E4
Wuzhong Qu JS17/18E6
Wuxi Jiang ZJ21/22D3

(Wuxi)Luxi Xian HN37/38C3
Wuxiqiao AH23/24F4
Wuxi Shi JS17/18E6
Wuxi Xian SC45/46C7
Wuxu GX43/44E6
Wuxuan Xian GX43/44D7
Wuxue Shi HB35/36E8
Wuxun JS17/18C6

Wuyang SX7/8E5
Wuyang HN37/38E3
Wuyang JX29/30F3
Wuyang He GZ49/50C7
Wuyang Xian HEN33/34D5
(Wuyang)Zhenyuan Xian GZ49/50C7
Wuyapao HL15/16E5
Wuyi AH23/24D5
Wuyigong FJ25/26C3
Wuyi He AH19/20A1
Wuyiling HL15/16C5
Wuying HL15/16C5
Wuying NX61/62D3
Wuyi Shan JXC29/30D6-F4
　　　　　FJ25/26B4-E2
Wuyishan Shi FJ25/26C4
Wuyi Xian HEB5/6F3
Wuyi Xian(Hushan) ZJ21/22D4
Wuyou JS17/18C6
Wuyuancun HEN33/34C3
(Wuyuan)Haiyan Xian ZJ21/22B5
Wuyuan Xian NM9/10G7
Wuyuan Xian JX29/30B5
Wuyuanzhan NM9/10K18
Wuyue Shuiku HEN33/34F6
(Wuyun)Jinyun Xian ZJ21/22D5
Wuyunqiao JX29/30E2
Wuyur He HL15/16D3-C4
Wuzhai ZJ21/22C4
Wuzhai Xian SX7/8C3
Wuzhan HL15/16E4
Wuzhan HL15/16B3
Wuzhen ZJ21/22B5
Wuzhen HB35/36C5
Wuzhen SN55/56C5
Wuzhi Shan HI42C2
Wuzhishan HI42C2
Wuzhi Shan HEB5/6C6
Wuzhi Xian(Mucheng) HEN33/34B5
Wuzhong Shi NX61/62C3
Wutaishan SX7/8 B5
Wuzhou Shi GX43/44D9
Wuzong JS19/20A4

X

Xabyai XZ53/54D11
Xagquka XZ53/54D9
Xaidulla XJ63/64G4
Xainza Xian XZ53/54D7
Xaitongmoin Xian XZ53/54E7
Xajing NM55/56A4
Xakur XJ63/64F5
(Xamba)Hanggin Houqi NM9/10K17
Xangd NM9/10G5

(Xangda)Nangqên Xian QH59/60D5
Xangdoring XZ53/54C3
Xangzha XZ53/54D10
Xaomafang HEB3/4B4
Xarag QH59/60B6
Xarag Mori NM9/10H7
Xar Burd NM9/10G5
Xardong XZ53/54D5
Xar Gut NM9/10D12
Xarlag NM9/10H7
Xar Moron NM9/10F12
Xar Obot NM9/10E12
Xarru XZ53/54E6
(Xarsingma)Yadong(Chomo)Xian
　　XZ53/54F7
Xaxa XZ53/54C4
Xayag XZ53/54D11
Xayar Xian XJ63/64E7
Xebert NM9/10E13
(Xêgar)Tingri Xian XZ53/54E6
Xênkyêr XZ53/54D7
Xia'ao GX43/44C5
Xia Awat XJ63/64F4
Xiaba HB35/36B3
Xiaba JS19/20B2
Xiabahe HB35/36D8
Xiabaishi FJ25/26D5
(Xiabancheng)Chengde Xian HEB5/6C6
Xiabaoping HB35/36C4
Xia Bazar XJ63/64F4
Xiabuji JX29/30C4
Xiacang TJ3/4C4
Xiacaowan JS17/18C4
Xiacengpu HN37/38F4
Xiachabu HB35/36D6
Xiache GD39/40B8
Xiachengzi HL15/16E6
Xiachong GD39/40D7
Xiachuan SX7/8F4
Xiachuan Dao GD39/40E5
Xiacun HN37/38E6
(Xiacun)Rushan Xian SD31/32C8
Xiadachen Dao ZJ21/22D6
Xiadao FJ25/26D4
Xia Dawo QH59/60C6
Xiadian SD31/32B7
Xiadian HB35/36C7
Xiadian SX7/8E4
Xiadian HEB5/6D4
Xiadian SD31/32C6
Xiadingjia SD31/32B7
Xiadong GS57/58B2
Xiadu SC47/48Ci
Xiafang AH19/20C1
Xiafangqiao ZJ21/22B5
Xiafeidi LN11/12B8
Xiagang JS17/18E6
Xiagaochuan SN55/56H4
Xiage AH23/24E4
Xiagezhuang SD31/32C7
Xiagou SD31/32C3
Xiaguan ZJ21/22C6
Xiaguan SX7/8B6

Xiaguan HEN33/34D3
Xiaguan ZJ21/22E5
Xiaguantun SD31/32D3
Xiaguanying GS57/58E7
Xiagui SN55/56F5
Xiahecheng SD31/32D6
Xiahe Xian(Labrang) GS57/58E6
Xiaheyan NX61/62C2
Xiahu FJ25/26D5
Xiahuaqiao HN37/38E4
Xiahuayuan HEB5/6C3
Xiajia GX43/44C4
Xiajiabian JS19/20B2
Xiajiang GZ49/50E7
Xiajiang Xian(Shuibian) JX29/30D3
Xiajiapu LN11/12B8
Xiajiayuan JS19/20A3
Xiajin ZJ21/22D3
Xiajin Xian SD31/32C3
Xia Kongma QH59/60D7
Xiakou SD31/32B3
Xiakou ZJ21/22C3
Xiakou NX61/62C3
Xiakou SN55/56H3
Xiakou HB35/36C4
Xiakou ZJ21/22D3
Xiakou HEB5/6F4
Xialaxiu QH59/60D5
Xialiang SX7/8E5
Xialilang GD41A2
Xia Lingka XZ53/54E11
Xialiushi HN37/38D5
Xialiushui NX61/62C2
Xialuhe LN11/12D9
Xiamaguan NX61/62C3
Xiamao FJ25/26D3
Xiamaoshan BJ3/4A3
Xiamatang LN11/12C7
Xiamaya XJ63/64D13
Xiameilin GD41A3
Xiamen Gang FJ25/26F4
Xiamen Shi FJ25/26F4
Xi'an GD39/40B5
Xianan GX43/44C5
Xianchuankou SN55/56D6
Xiancun FJ25/26D5
Xiandi GX43/44E8
Xiandu FJ25/26E3
Xiandu SC47/48B4
Xi'anfeng JS17/18C5
Xianfeng SC47/48C4
Xianfengqiao HEB5/6G3
Xianfeng Xian HB35/36E2
Xiang'an AH23/24E4
Xiangba GX43/44C6
Xiangbi SC47/48D2
Xiangcheng SD31/32E4
Xiangcheng JX29/30C3
Xiangchenggu HEB5/6G3
Xiangcheng(Qagchêng)Xian SC45/46D2
Xiangcheng Shi HEN33/34D6
Xiangcheng Xian HEN33/34D5
Xiangdong JX29/30D1

Xiangdu GX43/44D4
Xiangfan Shi HB35/36B5
Xiangfen Xian SX7/8F3
Xiangfu SC47/48B2
Xiangfuguan JX29/30C3
Xianggongzhuang SD31/32D5
Xiangguanji AH19/20A1
Xianghai JL13/14B3
Xianghe SN55/56G6
Xiang He AH19/20A1
Xiangheguan HEN33/34D5
(Xianghe)Quanjiao Xian AH23/24D5
Xianghe Xian HEB5/6D4
Xianghongdian AH23/24E3
Xianghongdian Shuiku AH23/24E3
Xianghu JX29/30B5
Xianghua SH19/20B4
Xianghua FJ25/26E3
Xianghua Ling HN37/38F5
Xianghuang(Hobot Xar)Qi(Xin Bulag)
   NM9/10F9
Xiangjia ZJ21/22D3
Xiang Jiang GX43/44A9-B9
         HN37/38D6-5
Xiang Jiang GZ49/50C6
Xiangjiangkou HN37/38F4
Xiangkou AH23/24F3
(Xiangkou)Wulong Xian SC45/46D6
Xianglan HL15/16D5
Xiangling SX7/8E3
Xianglinpu HN37/38F4
Xiangning Xian SX7/8F2
Xiangongzhen SN55/56F3
Xiangqi GX43/44D8
Xiangqian FJ25/26E5
Xiangqiao SN55/56F5
Xiangquan AH19/20B1
(Xiangquan He)Langqên Zangbo
   XZ53/54D2-3
Xiangride QH59/60C5
Xiangride He QH59/60C6
Xiangshan AH23/24E5
Xiang Shan NX61/62C2
Xiangshan BJ3/4C3
Xiangshan JS29/30D4
Xiangshan SC47/48B3
Xiangshan Gang ZJ21/22C6
Xiangshan Xian(Dancheng) ZJ21/22C6
Xiangshao HN37/38D5
Xiangshizhen SC47/48C3
Xiangshui GX43/44E5
Xiangshui GZ49/50C4
Xiangshui HI42C2
Xiangshui SN55/56B5
Xiang Shui JX29/30F3
Xiangshuiba HN37/38E2
Xiangshuihe SX7/8F3
Xiangshui Xian JS17/18B5
Xiangtandong HN37/38D5
Xiangtang JX29/30C3
Xiangtang QH59/60B8
Xiangtangpu HEB5/6G1
Xiangtangshan Grottoes HEB5/6G2

Xiangtan Shi HN37/38D5
Xiangtan Xian(Yisuhe) HN37/38D5
Xiangxi JX29/30C3
Xiang Xi HB35/36C3
Xiangxi HB35/36D3
Xiangxian GX43/44D6
Xiangxiang Shi HN37/38D5
Xiangxi Tujiazu Miaozu Zizhizhou
   HN37/38B2-C2
Xiangyang GX43/44B4
Xiangyang SC47/48B2
Xiangyang SX7/8D3
Xiangyang JL13/14C7
Xiangyang HL15/16E4
Xiangyang JL13/14E6
Xiangyangchuan HL15/16D7
Xiangyangcun JS17/18E7
Xiangyangdian SX7/8D4
Xiangyangqiao HN37/38E5
Xiangyang Xian HB35/36B5
Xiangyin Xian HN37/38C5
Xiangyuan Xian SX7/8E5
Xiangyun Xian YN51/52C4
Xiangzhi FJ25/26F4
Xiangzhou SD31/32C6
Xiangzhou GX43/44D5
Xiangzhou Xian GX43/44D7
Xiangzhouzai GD41B1
(Xiangzhou)Zhuhai Shi GD39/40D6
Xiangzikou HN37/38C4
Xianhe YN51/52D4
Xianhepu HB35/36B2
Xianing HN37/38C5
Xianjiang ZJ21/22E5
Xianjin HL15/16D6
Xianju HB35/36C5
Xianjuemiao Shuiku HB35/36C6
Xianju Xian ZJ21/22D5
Xianlai HI42B3
Xianlinbu ZJ19/20C2
Xianmahe Shuiku NX61/62D3
Xianmawan NX61/62E3
Xianning Diqu HB35/36E7
Xianning Shi HB35/36E7
Xianrencun SX7/8C5
Xianrendu HB35/36B4
Xianrewan HN37/38D2
Xi'an Shi SN55/56F4
Xianshui GX43/44B8

Xianshui He SC45/46C3
Xiantan SC45/46D6
Xiantang GZ49/50E5
Xiantao Shi HB35/36D6
Xianxi HN37/38C4
Xianxia AH23/24F6
Xianxiaguan JX29/30E3
Xianxia Ling ZJ21/22D3-4
Xian Xian HEB5/6E4
Xianxiang ZJ21/22C6
Xianxizhen HN37/38E2
Xianyan ZJ21/22C5
Xianyang FJ25/26B4

Xianyang Shi SN55/56F4
Xianyou Xian FJ25/26E4
Xianyu HEB3/4C2
Xianyuan AH23/24F5
Xianyuan JX29/30C2
Xianzhong HN37/38C6
Xi'anzhou NX61/62D2
Xianzijiao HN37/38F4
Xianzong AH23/24E4
Xi'ao GD39/40B8
Xiao'an Xi SC47/48C4
Xiao'ao FJ25/26D5
Xiaobai HL15/16D5
Xiaoban HB35/36D6
Xiaobole Shan HL15/16B3
Xiaobu JX29/30E3
Xiaocang FJ25/26D5
Xiaocha NX61/62D3
Xiaochan Dao GD41A2
Xiaochang HEB5/6B3
Xiaochang GX43/44B5
Xiaochang(Huayuan) HB35/36C7
Xiaochangshan Dao LN11/12E6
Xiaocheng JL13/14C8
Xiaocheng FJ25/26D5
Xiaochengzi JL13/14D5
Xiaochengzi NM5/6B6
Xiaochengzi LN11/12B7
Xiaochengzi JL13/14C6
Xiaochi AH23/24F3
Xiaochikou HB35/36E8
Xiaochuan GS57/58F7
Xiaodanyang AH23/24E5
Xiaodanyang JS17/18E4
Xiaodian SX7/8D4
Xiaodian HEN33/34C4
Xiaodian TJ3/4C4
Xiaodian JS17/18B4
Xiaodong LN11/12B6
Xiaodong GX43/44E6
Xiaodong ZJ21/22B6
Xiaodu SC47/48C3
Xiao'ergou NM9/10C14
Xiao'ertang XJ63/64G8
(Xiaofan)Wuqiang Xian HEB5/6E3
(Xiaogang)Dongxiang Xian JX29/30C4
Xiaogangkou JX29/30C3
Xiaogan Shi HB35/36D6
Xiaoganzhan HB35/36D6
Xiaogu SC47/48C2
Xiaoguai XJ63/64C8
Xiaoguan HB35/36E2
Xiaoguan GS57/58D8
Xiaogujia JL13/14D8
Xiaogushan LN11/12E7
Xiaogushan JL13/14D5
Xiaogu Shan JX29/30B4
Xiaohai JS17/18C6
Xiaohaizi GZ49/50D3
Xiaohaizi Shuiku XJ63/64F5
Xiaohe NX61/62D2
Xiaohe SN55/56G5
Xiaohe HB35/36C5

Xiaohe SC47/48D5
Xiaohe SN55/56C5
Xiao He HEB5/6F2
Xiao He SX7/8D4-5
Xiaohei Jiang YN77D3
Xiaohekou HB35/36B2
Xiaohekou SN55/56G3
Xiaohenan HEB3/4B4
Xiaohenglong HN37/38D3
Xiaohetou SX7/8B3
Xiaohexi HB35/36C7
Xiaoheyan NM11/12B3
Xiaohezhen NX61/62E2
Xiaohezi HEB5/6B3
Xiaohezi NM9/10B12
Xiao Hinggan Ling HL15/16C4-D5
Xiaohongshan NX61/62C1
Xiaohu FJ25/26C4
Xiaohuan Jiang GX43/44B6-C6
Xiaoji SD31/32C7
Xiaoji JS17/18D5
Xiaoji HEB5/6D6
Xiaoji HN37/38D6
Xiaoji HEN33/34B5
Xiaojiagang HB35/36C6
Xiaojiahe HL15/16D7
Xiao Jiang SC45/46C7
Xiaojiang JX29/30F2
Xiao Jiang YN51/52B5
Xiaojiang ZJ21/22E5
Xiaojiangbian JX29/30D2
Xiaojiangkou HN37/38E5
(Xiaojiang)Pubei Xian GX43/44E7
Xiaojiang Shuiku GX43/44E7
Xiaojianji AH23/24C3
Xiaojieji NM13/14D2
Xiaojieling HB35/36C8
Xiaojiemiao LN11/12D6
Xiaojin GS57/58E8
Xiaojin Chuan SC45/46C4
Xiaojingzhuang SX7/8B4
Xiaojin He SC45/46E3
Xiaojinkou GD39/40C7
Xiaojin(Zainlha)Xian(Meixing)
　SC45/46C4
Xiaoji Shan ZJ19/20C5
Xiaojue HEB5/6E1
Xiaokouzi NX61/62B2
Xiaolan GD39/40D6
Xiaoliangshan LN11/12B6
Xiaoliji JS17/18B5
Xiaolin ZJ21/22B6
Xiaolindian HB35/36B6
Xiaoling HL15/16E4
Xiaoling He LN11/12C4-5
Xiaolingwei JS19/20A1
Xiaolipu SD31/32C3
Xiaoliuji SD31/32D2
Xiaoliuxiang AH23/24C5
Xiaolizhuang HEN33/34C5
Xiaolong GX43/44C6
Xiaolongshan Dao(She Dao) LN11/12F4
Xiaolongtan YN51/52D5

Xiaoluan He HEB5/6B4-5
Xiaolu Dao LN11/12E7
Xiaomaqiao JS19/20A3
Xiaomei ZJ21/22E3
Xiaomei Guan JX29/30F2 GD39/40A7
Xiaomengtong YN51/52C3
Xiaomian SC45/46C6
Xiaomudong GD41A1
Xiaomuhe HL15/16D7
Xiaonanchuan QH59/60C4
Xiaonanhai SC47/48C4
Xiaoniuzhuang HEB3/4D4
Xiaopaozi NM9/10E11
Xiaopikou SD31/32D2
Xiaoping HN37/38C3
Xiaopingshan GX43/44E8
Xiaopingyang GX43/44D7
Xiaopu ZJ19/20B2
Xiaopuzi YN51/52B5
Xiao Qaidam QH59/60B4
Xiao Qaidam Hu QH59/60B4
Xiaoqi GD39/40B7
Xiaoqiao FJ25/26D4
Xiaoqiao SC47/48A4
Xiaoqin Dao SD31/32A7
Xiaoqing He SD31/32B5
Xiaoqinghe HL15/16D7
Xiaoqiu SN55/56F4
Xiaoquan SC47/48A2
Xiaoqu Shan ZJ19/20C5
Xiaosanjiang GD39/40B5
Xiaoshakou HB35/36E6
Xiaoshan HEB5/6E5
Xiao Shan HEN33/34C2-3
Xiaoshangqiao HEN33/34D5
Xiaoshan Shi ZJ21/22B5
Xiaoshetai NM9/10J19
Xiaoshidian HEN33/34D5
(Xiaoshi)Lu Xian SC45/46D5
Xiaoshu ZJ21/22B4
Xiaoshui SC47/48A4
Xiao Shui HN37/38E4-F4
Xiaoshuipu HN37/38E5
Xiaoshun ZJ21/22C4
Xiaosigou HEB5/6C6
Xiaosiping JL13/14E6
Xiaosong FJ25/26C4
Xiaosong JX29/30E4
Xiaosuan SX7/8D2
Xiaosuangou HEB5/6C2
Xiaosuifen He HL13/14C11
Xiaosunzhuang TJ3/4D4
Xiao Surmang QH59/60D5
Xiaotangshan BJ3/4B3
Xiaotao FJ25/26E3
Xiaotashan Shuiku JS17/18B4
Xiaotian AH23/24E3
Xiaotianji AH23/24D2
Xiaotianlong AH23/24G5 ZJ21/22C3
Xiaowangying AH23/24D5
Xiaowanshan Dao GD41C2
Xiaowei AH23/24C4
Xiaowutai Shan HEB5/6D3

Xiaowuzhan HL15/16E6
Xiao Xi ZJ21/22D5
Xiaoxi JX29/30F3
Xiaoxi AH23/24C4
Xiao Xian AH23/24B3
Xiaoxiang Ling SC45/46D4
Xiaoxiang Shuiku YN43/44B1
Xiaoxiba SC45/46C5
Xiaoxihe AH23/24D4
Xiaoxingkai Hu HL15/16E7
Xiaoxiqiao JS19/20B2
(Xiaoxita)Yichang Shi HB35/36D4
Xiaoya GZ49/50B6
Xiaoyan HB35/36C4
Xiaoyanghe LN11/12D7
Xiaoyangqi NM9/10B15
Xiaoyang Shan ZJ21/22B7
Xiaoyaozhen HEB33/34D6
Xiaoyi GX43/44E7
(Xiaoyi)Gongyi Xian HEN33/34C4
Xiaoyiji AH23/24D4
Xiaoying SD31/32B5
Xiaoyingpan XJ63/64C6
Xiaoyi Shi SX7/8D3
Xiaoyu SX7/8B4
Xiaoyuan SC47/48C2
Xiaoyuan HN37/38F6
Xiaoyue ZJ19/20C3
Xiaozhai HEB5/6G2
Xiaozhaiba GZ49/50C5
Xiaozhan TJ3/4D4
Xiaozhangzhuang HEN33/34D5
Xiaozhao NM9/10K17
Xiaozhen ZJ21/22C6
Xiaozhi SD31/32C3
Xiaozhi Zhou GD41B2
Xiaozhongdian YN51/52B3
Xiaozuo FJ25/26F4
Xiaping HB35/36D3
Xiapu JX29/30D2
Xiapu HB35/36E7
Xiapu Xian FJ25/26D6
Xiaqiao GD39/40F3
Xiaqiaotou YN51/52B4
Xiaqiupu SD31/32B6
Xiaruo YN51/52B3
Xiaruyue SX7/8B5
Xiashan GZ49/50E4
Xiashankou JX29/30D1
Xiashan Shankou SD31/32C6
Xiashan GD39/40E3
Xiashe SX7/8B5
Xiashesi HN37/38D5
Xiashi GX43/44E4
Xiashu JS17/18D5
Xiashuitou SX7/8B4
Xiasi GZ49/50D6
Xiasi GZ49/50E6
Xiasifen GS57/58C6
Xiataizi HEB3/4B4
Xiatang HEN33/34D4
Xiatang HN37/38E6
Xiatangji AH23/24D4

Xiatun BJ3/4B2
Xiawa NM9/10F13
Xiawan GX43/44D8
Xiawei SD31/32D5
Xiawentan JX29/30F3
Xiawuxing AH23/24E3
Xiaxi SC47/48D1
Xiaxi JS19/20B2
Xia Xian SX7/8F3
Xiaxiaoyuchuan NX61/62C2
Xiayang FJ25/26E3
Xiayang FJ25/26F2
Xiayang GD39/40F3
Xiayang FJ25/26D4
Xiayao NX61/62D2
Xiaye SX7/8E3
Xiaying BJ3/4B3
Xiaying TJ3/4B4
Xiaying SD31/32B6
(Xiayingpan)Luzhi Tequ GZ49/50D4
Xiayi Xian HEN33/34C8
Xiayizhan HEN33/34C8
Xiayukou HN37/38B5
Xiayukou SN55/56E6
Xiayunling BJ3/4C2
Xiayuqiao ZJ21/22B4
Xia Zanggor QH59/60D7
Xiazha GD41B2
Xiazhai FJ25/26F3
Xiazhai SC45/46C3
Xiazhai NX61/62E2
Xiazhang AH19/20C1
Xiazhang SD31/32C3
Xiazhen JX29/30C6
(Xiazhen)Weishan Xian SD31/32E4
Xiazhi Dao ZJ21/22C7
Xiazhuang SD31/32C6
Xiazhuang SD31/32D5
Xiazhuang HEN33/34E7
Xiazichang GZ49/50C6
Xiazongyang AH23/24F4
Xibaipo HEB5/6E1
Xibali HEB3/4B2
Xibaoyu SX7/8C3
Xibaxa Qu XZ53/54E9-F10
Xibdê SC45/46D2
Xibei FJ25/26E3
Xibeikou HB35/36C4
Xibing FJ25/26D5
Xibo He NM5/6A6-B6
Xibozi BJ3/4B2
Xibu AH23/24E5
(Xibu)Dongshan Xian FJ25/26G3
Xichahe SN55/56G3
Xichang HI42B3
Xichang JS19/20A3
Xichang GX43/44F6
Xichang Shi SC45/46E4
Xichang Xian SC45/46E4
Xichatou HEB5/6E2
Xiche HN37/38B2
Xicheng YN51/52C5
Xicheng HEN33/34B7

Xicheng HL15/16C3
Xicheng Shan SX7/8F4
(Xicheng)Yangyuan Xian HEB5/6C2
Xichong GD41A3
Xichong Xian SC45/46C5
Xichou Xian YN51/52D6
Xi Chuan HEN33/34D3
Xichuan Xian(Shangji) HEN33/34D3
Xicun JX29/30D2
Xidamiao HEB3/4B4
Xidatan NX61/62B3
Xidawa JL13/14B5
Xidayang Shuiku HEB5/6E2
Xidayingzi LN11/12C4
Xide Xian SC45/46D4
Xidian ZJ21/22C6
Xiditou TJ3/4C4
Xidongting Shan JS17/18E6
Xidoupu NM9/10G7
(Xidu)Hengyang Xian HN37/38E5
Xie Chi SX7/8G2-3
Xiefang JX29/30F3
Xiehe GZ49/50C5
Xie He AH23/24C3-4
Xieji HEN33/34C7
Xiejia SC47/48B1
Xiejia JL13/14E6
Xiejiagou SN55/56C6
Xiejiaji JS17/18D5
Xiejiatan JX29/30B4
Xiejiaya HN37/38C3
Xiema SC47/48C4
Xiemahe HB35/36C4
Xiemating SD31/32D4
Xiepu ZJ21/22B6
Xieqiao AH23/24D3
Xieqiao JS17/18D6
Xieqiao ZJ21/22B5
Xi'er YN51/52C5
Xie Shan JX29/30B4
Xie Shui HN37/38B2
Xietan FJ25/26C5
Xietang ZJ19/20C3
Xietun LN11/12C5
Xietun LN11/12E5
Xiewu SD31/32D5
Xiexing SC47/48B4
Xieyang Dao GX43/44G7
Xiezhou SX7/8G2
Xiezhuang HEN33/34C5
Xifangcheng SX7/8B5
Xifeng HL15/16D7
Xifengling HEN33/34C6
Xifeng Shi GS57/58E8
Xifeng Xian LN11/12B8
Xifeng Xian(Yongjing) GZ49/50C5
Xifo LN11/12C6
Xifu SD31/32C7
Xifu Shan ZJ19/20C5
Xifuying BJ3/4B3
Xigang SD31/32E4
(Xigang)Helan Xian NX61/62B3
Xigangzi HL15/16C4

Xi Ganqu NX61/62B3
Xigazê Diqu XZ53/54E5-7
Xigazê Shi XZ53/54E6
Xi Golog SC45/46C3
Xigongyi GS61/62E1
Xigou SX7/8E5
Xiguanyingzi LN11/12C4
Xigubu GD41A1
Xihan Shui SN55/56G1
        GS57/58E7-F7
Xihaoping HB35/36C3
Xihe AH23/24F5
Xi He LN11/12C5
Xihe SC45/46D4
Xi He NX61/62D2
Xihe SD31/32C4
Xihe SD31/32C7
Xihe NM9/10J20
Xi He AH23/24E4
Xi He JX29/30B4
Xi He SC45/46C5
Xi He SC47/48B1
Xihe SN55/56H4
Xihe HB35/36C6
Xihekou SN55/56D5
Xi He(Moron) NM9/10F3-G3
Xihe Shuiku YN49/50E2
Xihe Xian GS57/58E7
Xiheying HEB5/6D2
Xihou FJ25/26D3
Xi Hu ZJ19/20C3
Xihu JX29/30B5
Xihu HN37/38B5
Xihu GS57/58B2
(Xihuachi)Heshui Xian GS57/58E9
Xihuancun HEB5/6F2
Xihua Xian HEN33/34D6
Xihuo Shan ZJ19/20C4
Xiji BJ3/4C3
Xiji HL15/16D4
Xiji SD31/32E4
Xijiadian HB35/36B4
Xijiang JX29/30F3
Xi Jiang GD39/40C4-5
Xijiaozi SX7/8D3
Xijie SC47/48D2
Xijin FJ25/26C4
Xijin GX43/44E7
Xijing SX7/8E5
Xijin He AH19/20C1
Xijin Shuiku GX43/44E6
Xijir QH59/60C2
Xijir Ulan Hu QH59/60C2
Xijishui GS57/58D7
Xijitan NX61/62E2
Xiji Xian NX61/62E2
Xikelin HL15/16C5
Xikeng HB35/36E7
Xikeng ZJ21/22E4
Xikeng GD39/40C8
Xikengdawei GD41A3
Xikou FJ25/26D2
Xikou HN37/38B3

Xikou SC47/48B4
Xikou AH23/24G5
Xikou ZJ21/22D4
Xikou ZJ21/22D3
Xikou ZJ21/22C6
Xikou ZJ21/22B4
Xikou JX29/30B2
Xikou FJ25/26E3
Xikou HN37/38E2
Xikou AH23/24F5
Xikuangshan HN37/38D4
Xil NM9/10F9
Xilai SC47/48B1
Xilaizhen JS19/20A3
Xilang He JL13/14C8
Xilaotou Shan NM9/10E13
Xilian GD39/40F2
Xiliang Shan AH19/20B1
Xiliangzi QH59/60A3
Xiliao He NM9/10F13-14
Xilin HL15/16D5
Xilingjing SX7/8C4
Xilin Gol NM9/10E10-F11
Xilin Gol Gaoyuan NM68C6-7
Xilin Gol Meng NM9/10E9-11
Xilingsi HEN33/34C6
Xiling Xia HB35/36D3
Xilinhe HL15/16E6
Xilinhot Shi NM9/10F11
(Xilinji)Mohe Xian HL15/16A2
Xilin Xian GX43/44C3
Xilinzi HL15/16D7
Xili Shuiku GD41A2
Xiliu HEB5/6F3
Xiliuhe HB35/36D6
Xiliyu SN55/56C6
Xiluga He NM5/6A6 HEB5/6A6
Xilühua Shan ZJ19/20C5
Xiluoqi HL15/16A3
Ximafan HB35/36D8
Ximahe GZ49/50D6
Ximalin HEB5/6C2
Ximao Zhou HI42C2
Ximayi Dao NL11/12E5
Ximei SC47/48B3
Ximeng Vazu Zizhixian YN51/52D3
Ximing SX7/8D4
Ximo SX7/8G2
Ximu LN11/12D6
Xin'an SD31/32B5
Xin'an GD39/40D6
Xinan FJ25/26D5
Xinan FJ25/26E3
Xin'an SD31/32C7
Xin'an HEB5/6D4
Xin'an GD39/40C8
Xin'an JS17/18E6
Xin'an HL15/16E5
Xin'an JX29/30E4
Xin'an JL13/14C8
Xin'an HN37/38B4
Xin'an NM9/10G7

(Xin'an)Anxin Xian HEB5/6E3

Xinanban FJ25/26F3
Xin'anbian SN55/56C4
Xin'ancun HEB5/6E2
Xin'andian HEN33/34E6
Xin'andu AH23/24F3
(Xin'an)Guannan Xian JS17/18B5
Xinanhe HEB3/4D2
Xin'anji HEN33/34D7
Xin'an Jiang AH23/24G5 ZJ21/22C3
Xin'anjiang ZJ21/22C4
Xin'anjiang Shuiku ZJ21/22C3
(Xin'an)Lai'an Xian AH23/24D5
Xin'ansuo YN51/52D5
Xinanwanzi NM5/6A7
Xin'an Xian HEN33/34C4
Xin'anzhen JL13/14C4
Xin'anzhen JL13/14C7
Xin'anzhen TJ3/4C4
Xin'anzhuang SD31/32B6
Xinba JS19/20A2
Xinba JS17/18B5
Xinbao'an HEB5/6C3
Xin Barag Youqi(Altan Emel)
        NM9/10C11
Xin Barag Zuoqi(Amgalang)
        NM9/10C12
Xinbian He AH23/24C4
Xinbin GX43/44D6
Xinbin Manzu Zizhixian LN11/12C9
Xinbo HEB5/6A5
Xinbu HEB5/6C2
Xin Bulag Dong NM9/10C12
(Xin Bulag)Xianghuang(Hobot Xar)Qi
        NM9/10F9
Xincai Xian HEN33/34E6
Xincang ZJ19/20C4
Xincang ZJ21/22B5
Xinchang JX29/30B5
Xinchang HB35/36E5
Xinchang HN37/38E2
Xinchang SH17/18E7
Xinchang SC47/48B1
Xinchang SC47/48C2
Xinchang Xian ZJ21/22C5
(Xinchang)Yifeng Xian JX29/30C2
Xincheng TJ3/4D4
Xincheng HEB5/6F3
Xincheng SX7/8D4
Xincheng HL15/16D6
Xincheng HL15/16E6
Xincheng JS17/18D5
Xincheng GS57/58C5
Xincheng ZJ21/22B5
Xincheng GS61/62E3
Xincheng JX29/30F2
Xincheng JX29/30E2
Xincheng HB35/36C7
Xincheng GS57/58E6
Xincheng NX61/62B3
Xincheng HB35/36B6
Xinchengbu SN55/56C4
Xinchengpu HEB5/6E2
Xincheng Xian GX43/44C6

Xinchengzhen HEB5/6D3
Xinchengzi BJ3/4B4
Xinchengzi LN11/12B7
Xinchepaizi XJ63/64C8
Xinci FJ25/26F3
Xincun SX7/8C3
Xincun GX43/44C7
Xincun HEB5/6E5
Xincun GD41A2
Xincun GD41A3
Xincun GD41A2
(Xincun)Dongchuan Shi YN51/52B5
Xindai ZJ21/22B6
Xindeng ZJ21/22C4
Xindi NM11/12B3
Xindi GX43/44D9
Xindian SD31/32B4

Xindian SD31/32C5
Xindian SD31/32B3
Xindian HEB5/6F2
Xindian GS57/58E6
Xindian HL15/16E4
Xindian YN51/52C5
Xindian SX7/8E4
Xindian JS17/18B4
Xindian JX29/30D2
Xindian HEN33/34D4
Xindian SC47/48B1
Xindian SC47/48C2
Xindian FJ25/26F4
Xindian HB35/36E6
Xindianbu AH23/24D3
Xindianping HN37/38D2
Xindianpu HEN33/34E4
Xindianzi GZ49/50D5
Xindianzi SC45/46C7
Xindianzi HEB5/6C6
Xindong GD39/40E4
Xindong GD41A2
Xindu GX43/44C9
(Xindu)Luhuo(Zhaggo)Xian SC45/46C3
Xinduqiao SC45/46C3
Xindu Xian SC45/46C5
Xin'e HL15/16C4
Xinfan SC45/46C4
Xinfang JX29/30D2
Xinfeng JS19/20A2
Xinfeng JS17/18C6
Xinfeng JS17/18D5
Xinfeng GD39/40B9
Xinfeng HI42B3
Xinfeng ZJ21/22B5
Xinfeng GX43/44E8
Xinfeng Jiang GD39/40B7
Xinfengjiang Shuiku GD39/40C7
Xinfengjie JX29/30D4
Xinfengshi JS19/20A3
Xinfeng Xian GD39/40B7
Xinfeng Xian(Jiading) JX29/30F2
Xinfengzhen SN55/56F5
Xing'an SC47/48B2
Xing'an HEB5/6E2

Xingang JS19/20A3
Xingang AH23/20E5
Xingang Linchang GD39/40B5
Xingangzhen JS19/20B4
Xingangzhen(Nianyuwan) LN11/12F5
Xing'anli NM9/10C14
Xingan Xian JX29/30D3
Xing'an Xian GX43/44B8
Xingao SX7/8B4
(Xingba)Lhünzê Xian XZ53/54E9
Xingcheng SX7/8E5
(Xingcheng)Qianxi Xian HEB5/6C6
Xingcheng Shi LN11/12D4
Xingcun SD31/32C7
Xingcun HEB3/4D2
Xingcun HL15/16E6
Xingcun SD31/32D4
Xingdi XJ63/64E9
Xingdian JS17/18D4
Xingdong HL15/16D6
Xingfu SD31/32B5
Xingfu Qu SD31/32B4
Xingfushan JX29/30B3
Xingguo HL15/16D4
Xingguo Xian JX29/30E3
Xinghai Xian(Ziketan) QH59/60C6
Xinghe Xian NM9/10G9
Xinghu YN51/52B4
Xinghua HEN33/34C3
Xinghua HL15/16D4
Xinghua HL15/16A4
Xinghua JL13/14E7
Xinghuacun SX7/8D3
Xinghua Shi JS17/18D5
Xinghua Wan FJ25/26E5
Xinghuaying HEN33/34C6
Xingji HEN33/34E5
Xingji HEB5/6E4
Xingjiabu HEB3/4B2
Xingjiashe SX7/8D4
Xingjiawan HEB5/6F2
Xingkai HL15/16E7
Xingkai Hu HL15/16E7
Xingkaihu HL15/16E7
Xinglang GZ49/50E6
Xinglin FJ25/26F4
Xinglinbu HEB3/4B2
Xingliu AH23/24C2
Xinglong AH23/24F5
Xinglong SD31/32B3
Xinglong HEN33/34C6
Xinglong HL15/16B3
Xinglong SC47/48C2
Xinglong SC47/48C4
Xinglong GD39/40H5
Xinglong SC47/48B4
Xinglongchang SC45/46D6
Xinglongchang SC47/48C3
Xinglongchang HN37/38C2
Xinglongchang GZ49/50C6
Xinglongchang SN55/56H4
Xinglongcun GD41A1
Xinglongdian LN11/12C7

Xinglongji AH23/24D5
Xinglongji HB35/36B5
Xinglongjie HN37/38C4
Xinglong Nongchang HI42C3
Xinglongquan HL15/16D3
Xinglongshan JL13/14D6
Xinglongshan JL13/14C3
Xinglongtai LN11/12B8
Xinglong Xian HEB5/6C5
Xinglongzhen NX61/62E2
Xinglongzhen JS19/20A2
Xinglongzhen HL15/16D6
Xinglongzhen HL15/16D4
Xinglongzhen GS57/58E7
Xingmin GZ49/50B4
Xingnan HEB3/4D2
Xingning HN37/38F6
Xingning GX43/44D5
Xingning Shi GD39/40B8
Xingnong HL15/16D3
Xingou HB35/36D5
Xingou HB35/36D6
Xingping GX43/44C8
Xingping NX61/62E2
Xingping Shi SN55/56F4
Xingren SC47/48B5
Xingren GZ49/50D6
Xingren JS19/20A3
Xingrenbu NX61/62D2
Xingrenbu HEB3/4B2
Xingren Xian GZ49/50E4
Xingsagoinba QH59/60C7
Xingshan HL15/16E3
Xingshan HL15/16D2
Xingshan HEN33/34C5
(Xingshan)Majiang Xian GZ49/50D6
Xingshan Xian (Gufu) HB35/36C3
Xingshengzhuang NX61/62E3
Xingshizhen SN55/56F5
Xingshunxi NM9/10J19
Xingshutun LN11/12E6
Xingtai Shi HEB5/6F2
Xingtai Xian HEB5/6F2
Xingtangji AH23/24C2
Xingtang Xian HEB5/6E2
Xingtian FJ25/26C4
Xinguangwu SX7/8B4
Xingwang SC47/48B4
Xingwei GD41A2
Xingwen Xian SC45/46D5
Xing Xian SX7/8C3
Xingxingshao Shuiku JL13/14D7
Xingxingxia XJ63/64E13
Xingxiu Hai QH59/60C5
Xingyang Xian HEN33/34C5
Xingyi HEB5/6E3
Xingyi Shi GZ49/50E3
Xingzhou JX29/30E2
Xingzhou HEB3/4A4
Xingzhou He HEB5/6B4-5
Xingzi GD39/40A5
Xingzi Xian(Nankang) JX29/30B4
Xinhai SH19/20B4

Xinxing JL13/14C3
Xinxing JL13/14D10
Xinxing JL13/14E9
Xinxing HL15/16D3
Xinxing JS17/18C6
Xinxing SC47/48A1
Xinxingji AH23/24C3
Xinxing Jiang GD39/40D5
Xinxing Xian GD39/40D5
Xinxu FJ25/26F3
Xinxu GD39/40B8
Xinxu GX43/44E9
Xinxu GX43/44C8
Xinxu GX43/44D4
Xinxu GX43/44E8
Xinxu GD41A4
Xinxu GX43/44B9
Xinyang Diqu HEN33/34E6-7
Xinyanggang JS17/18C6
Xinyang Gang JS17/18C6
Xinyanggang Kou JS17/18C6
Xinyang Shi HEN33/34E6

Xinyangzhen GS57/58E7
Xinye Xian HEN33/34E4
Xinyi SX7/8D3
Xinyi He JS17/18B5
Xinying NX61/62D2
Xinying JX29/30C5
Xinying HI42B2
Xinyi Shi JS17/18B4
Xinyi Shi GD39/40D3
Xinyuan(Künes)Xian XJ63/64D7
(Xinyuan)Tianjun Xian QH59/60B6
Xinyu Shi JX29/30D2
Xinzaozhen JS19/20B4
Xinzhai SD31/32C5
Xinzhai SD31/32C4
Xinzhai ZJ21/22D4
Xinzhai HEB5/6D6
Xinzhan GZ49/50B5
Xinzhan HL15/16E3
Xinzhan JL13/14D8
Xinzhan JL13/14C6
Xinzhan HEN33/34D6
Xinzhang HEB3/4C3
Xinzhangfang NM9/10B13
Xinzhangzi HEB5/6C5
Xinzhazhen JS19/20B2
Xinzhelin JX29/30B3
Xinzhen SD31/32B5
Xinzhen HEN33/34B6
Xinzhen HEB5/6D4
Xinzheng HI42C2
Xinzheng SC45/46C6
Xinzheng Shi HEN33/34C5
Xinzhi SX7/8E3
Xinzhi JX29/30D2
Xinzhou HN37/38B4
Xinzhou GZ49/50B6
Xinzhou GD39/40E5
Xinzhou GZ49/50C6
Xinzhou HI42B2

Xinzhou Diqu SX7/8C3-4
(Xinzhou)Longlin Gezu Zizhixian
    GX43/44C3
Xinzhou Shi SX7/8C4
Xinzhou Xian HB35/36D7
Xinzhu HI42B3
Xinzhuang SD31/32C4
Xinzhuang SD31/32B7
Xinzhuang SD31/32D4
Xinzhuang JS19/20B3

Xinzhuang SD31/32D4
Xinzhuangji NX61/62C3
Xinzhuangzi HEB5/6C3
Xinzhuangzi NX61/62C4
Xinzhuangzi LN11/12C5
Xinzuotang GD39/40C7
Xiongcun JX29/30D5
Xiongdian AH23/24E2
Xiongdi Yu FJ25/26G3
Xiong'er Shan HEN33/34D3-C3
Xiong'erzhai BJ3/4B4
Xionghe Shuiku HB35/36C5
Xiongjiang FJ25/26D4
Xiongjiashui NX61/62C2
Xiongkou HB35/36D5
Xionglu AH23/24F5
(Xiongshi)Guixi Xian JX29/30C5
Xiong Xian HEB5/6E4
Xiongyuecheng LN11/12D6
Xiongzhai HEN33/34E6
Xipan SX7/8C5
Xi Paozi LN11/12B7
Xiping SC47/48A2
Xiping SX7/8F4
Xiping FJ25/26E3
Xiping LN11/12D4
Xiping HEN33/34D3
(Xiping)Datong Xian SX7/8A5
(Xiping)Songyang Xian ZJ21/22D4
Xiping Xian HEN33/34D6
Xipu SC47/48B1
Xipucun HEB5/6DC6
(Xipucun)Jianming HEB3/4B5
Xiqiao YN49/50F2
Xiqiao JS17/18C5
Xiqin FJ25/26D4
Xiqin HL15/16E4
Xiqing TJ3/4C4
Xiqing Shan GS57/58E5-6 QH59/60C7
Xiqu GS57/58C6
Xiquan SX7/8D3
Xiquanjie AH23/24D4
Xiquele YN51/52B6
(Xireg)Ulan Xian QH59/60B6
Xirong SC47/48C1
Xisanshilidian AH23/24D4
Xi Shan BJ3/4C2-B3
Xishan JX29/30C3
Xishan GD39/40B7
Xishanbei HEB5/6D3
Xishanqiao JS19/20B1
Xishan Shi JS17/18E6
(Xishanzui)Urad Qianqi NM9/10K18

Xisha Qundao HI42E5-6
Xishe SX7/8D3
Xishiqiao JS17/18E6
Xishu HEB5/6G1
Xishuangbanna Daizu Zizhizhou
    YN51/52E4
(Xishuanghe)Kenli Xian SD31/32B5
Xishui HI42B2
Xi Shui HB35/36D8
Xishuibei HEB3/4C2
Xishui Xian HB35/36D8
Xishui Xian(Donghuang) GZ49/50B5
Xisi LN11/12D6
Xisipo AH23/24C4
Xita JX29/30C2
Xi Taijnar Hu QH59/60B3
Xitan FJ25/26G3
Xitang ZJ21/22B5
Xitangchi AH23/24E3
Xitiangezhuang BJ3/4B3
Xitianmu Shan ZJ21/22B4
Xitiao Xi ZJ21/22B4
Xitieshan QH59/60B4
Xiting JS17/18D7
Xitou JX29/30C3
Xitou GD39/40E4
Xitou AH19/20C1
Xituchengzi LN11/12D7
Xituozhen SC45/46C7
Xiuduan GD39/40B7
Xi Ujimqin Qi (Bayan Ul Hot)
    NM9/10E11
Xi Ulan Bulag NM9/10J20
Xiuning Xian(Haiyang) AH23/24G5
Xiuren GX43/44C8
Xiu Shan ZJ21/22B7
Xiushan Tujiazu Miaozu Zizhixian
    SC45/46D7
Xiushui JL13/14C7
Xiushui JL13/14D4
Xiushui GZ49/50D2
Xiu Shui JX29/30B2
Xiushui He LN11/12B7
Xiushuihezi LN11/12B7
Xiushui Xian(Yining) JX29/30B2
Xiuwen Xian GZ49/50D5
Xiuwu Xian HEN33/34B5
Xiuxikou HN37/38D3
Xiuyan Manzu Zizhixian LN11/12D7
Xiwagebu NM9/10K18
Xiwaizi JL13/14D10
Xiwan HEN33/34B4
Xiwanbu HEB5/6C2
Xiwangji AH23/24D4
Xiwangshan HEB5/6C3
(Xiwanzi)Chongli Xian HEB5/6C3
Xiwei SX7/8D2
Xiwei Shuiku SD31/32D4
Xiwengzhuang BJ3/4B3
Xiwu ZJ21/22C6
Xiwu QH59/60D5
Xiwujiang SX7/8F4
Xixabangma Feng XZ53/54E5

Xushui Xian HEB5/6D3
Xutangzhuang JS17/18B4
Xuwei JS17/18B5
Xuwen Xian GD39/40F3
Xuyi Xian JS17/18C4
Xuyong Xian SC45/46D5
Xuzhen HEN33/34B7
Xuzhou Shi JS17/18B8
Xuzhuang SD31/32D4

Y

Ya'an Diqu SC45/46C4-D4
Ya'an Shi SC45/46D4
Yabai SN55/56F4
Yabrai Shan NM9/10H4-G4
Yabrai Yanchang NM9/10H4
Yabuli HL15/16E5
(Yacha)Baisha Lizu Zizhixian HI42B2
Yachang GX43/44C4
Yacheng FJ25/26D6
Yacheng HI42C2
Yachi He GZ49/50D5-C5
Ya Dian TJ3/4D4
Yadong(Chomo)Xian(Xarsingma)
  XZ53/54F7
Ya'ergou NX61/62C3
Ya'erya SX7/8B4
Yafan ZJ21/22C4
Yagan NM9/10F4
Yagang GD41B1
Yageying HEB5/6F2
Yagkêng QH59/60B6
Yagkêng Qu QH59/60A6-B6
Yag Qu QH59/60C4
Yagradagzê Shan QH59/60C4
Yahekou HEN33/34D4
Yahekou Shuiku HEN33/34D4
Yahongqiao HEB5/6D5
Ya Jiang SC47/48C5
Yajiang SC47/48C5
Yajiang(Nyagquka)Xian SC45/46C3
Yajiangqiao HN37/38D6
Yaji Shan JS19/20B2
Yakatograk XJ63/64F9
Yakeshi Shi NM9/10C13
Yakou FJ25/26F4
Yakou GD41B2
Yalakan SC45/46C3
Yalang Wan HI42C2
Yali HB35/36C3
Yalian YN51/52C3
Yaliang HI42C2
Yaliji HEB5/6G2
Yalong Jiang SC45/46D3
Yalu NM9/10C14
Yalu He NM9/10C14-D14 HL15/16D2
Yalu Jiang LN11/12D8-9 JL13/14F7
Yalujiang Kou LN11/12E8
Yamat XJ63/64D6
Yamat LN11/12C5
Ya Men GD39/40D6
Yamzho Yumco XZ53/54E8
Yandu Xian JS17/18 C6

Yan'an Shi SN55/56D5
Yanbeiqiao HN37/38D5
Yanbian Chosenzu Zizhizhou
  JL13/14D9-11
Yanbian Xian SC45/46E3
Yanbodu HN37/38B3
Yanbutou HB35/36E8
Yanchangbu SN55/56C3
Yanchang Xian SN55/56D6
(Yancheng)Qihe Xian SD31/32C3
Yancheng Shi JS17/18C6
Yancheng Xian HEN33/34D5
Yanchi XJ63/64D13
Yanchi XJ63/64B9
Yanchi BJ3/4B3
Yanchiwan GS57/58C3
Yanchi Xian NX61/62C4
Yanchuan Xian SN55/56D6
Yandang Shan ZJ21/22E4-D5
Yandaxkak XJ63/64F10
Yandian NM9/10G8
Yandian SD31/32C2
Yandong GX43/44D4
Yandong GX43/44C5
Yanduhe HB35/36C3
Yandun XJ63/64D13
Yandunbu AH23/24F5
Yanfang YN51/52C6
Yanfeng SC47/48A4
Yanfeng YN51/52C4
Yanfeng HI42B3
Ya'ngamdo XZ53/54D10
Yang'an GX43/44C8
Yang'an SD31/32B4
Yangang SC47/48C1
Yangba GZ49/50F4
Yangbajain XZ53/54D8
Yangbi Jiang YN77B2
Yangbi Yizu Zizhixian YN51/52C3
Yangbu HEN33/34E6
Yangce HEN33/34E5
Yangchang GZ49/50E5
Yangchang GZ49/50D4
Yangchang NM11/12B3
Yangchang GZ49/50C7
Yangchang GZ49/50D6
Yangchang GZ49/50D5
Yangchangba GZ49/50C4
Yangchangzi He NM5/6A7
Yangcheng HEB3/4D2
Yangcheng Hu JS17/18E6
Yangcheng Xian SX7/8F4
Yangchu SD31/32B7
(Yangchuan)Suiyang Xian GZ49/50C6
Yangchun Shi GD39/40D4
Yangcun AH19/20D1
Yangcun JX29/30C5
Yangcun JX29/30G2
Yangcun GD39/40C7
Yangcun HEB5/6D3
Yangcunqiao ZJ21/22C4
(Yangcun)Wuqing Xian TJ3/4C4
Yangdachengzi JL13/14D5

Yangdang HB35/36B5
Yangdeng GZ49/50B5
Yangdian HEN33/34C2
Yangdian JS17/18E5
Yangdian HB35/36C7
Yangdianzi HEB5/6C6
Yangdong Xian GD39/40D4
Yang'erzhuang HEB5/6E5
Yangezhuang HEB5/6D6
Yangezhuang TJ3/4C4
Yangfang BJ3/4B3
Yangfangbu NX61/62D2
Yangfangkou SX7/8B4
Yangfanglin HB35/36E7
Yangfengang HEB3/4C3
Yanggang HL15/16E7
Yanggao Xian SX7/8A5
Yanggezhuang BJ3/4B3
Yanggu HEN33/34C6
Yangguo SN55/56F5
Yanggu Xian SD31/32C2
Yanghe NX79B3
Yanghe JS17/18C4
Yang He HEB5/6C2-3
Yanghe Shuiku HEB5/6D7
Yanghua JS17/18C4
Yanghua He SC47/48B2
Yanghulun HEB5/6B3
Yanghuzhen AH23/24D3
Yangji SD31/32E5
Yangji HEN33/34B7
Yangji HEN33/34C8
Yangji JS17/18B5
Yangjia SC47/48C3
Yangjia SC47/48B5
Yangjiabanqiao HEB3/4C4
Yangjiadian SN55/56E4
Yangjiagou SN55/56C6
Yangjiahe SN55/56H4
Yangjiajiang HB35/36D5
Yangjialing SN55/56D5
Yangjiang JX29/30D2
Yangjiang Shi GD39/40E4
Yangjiao SC47/48C5
Yangjiaogou SD31/32B5
Yangjiaotang HN37/38E5
Yangjiapu LN11/12D7
Yangjiatan HN37/38D4
Yangjiawan GZ49/50C3
Yangjiaxie SN55/56G5
Yangjiayao NX61/62C3
Yangjiayuanzi SN55/56C5
Yangjiazhai SD31/32D5
Yangjiazhai HB35/36C7
Yangjiazhangzi LN11/12D4
Yangjiazhuang SX7/8D3
Yangjie YN51/52C5
Yangjiezi GZ49/50C3
Yangjing SN55/56C3
Yangjingdi SX7/8E5
Yangjuanzi LN11/12C5
Yangkou JX29/30C6
Yangkou JS19/20A3

Yangkou FJ25/26D3
Yangkoushi ZJ21/22D3
Yanglan HI42C2
Yanglang NX61/62D3
Yanglaowa SX7/8A5
Yanglin HB35/36E5
Yanglin YN51/52C5
Yangling SN55/56F4
Yanglinqiao HN37/38D6
Yanglinwei HB35/36D6
Yanglinzhai HN37/38C5
Yangliu GD39/40C5
Yangliuchi HB35/36D3
Yangliudian SD31/32C4
Yangliudian SD31/32D3
Yangliujie GZ49/50D6
Yangliujing YN51/52D6
Yangliupu AH23/24F5

Yangliuxue SD31/32B4
Yangliuzhuang HEB3/4C5
Yanglongsi GZ49/50C5
Yanglou SD31/32E3
Yanglou AH23/24B3
Yangloudong HB35/36E6
Yanglousi HN37/38B6
Yangluo HB35/36D7
Yangluwa NX61/62D3
Yangma SC47/48B1
Yangma Dao SD31/32B8
Yangmahe SN55/56C5
Yangmahe SC47/48B2
Yangmaowan Shuiku SN55/56F4
Yangmei GX43/44E8
Yangmei TW27/28C3
Yangmeishu GZ49/50D3
Yangmeisi JX29/30F2
Yangmiao HEN33/34C6
Yangmingbu SX7/8B4
Yangmingbu NX61/62D2
(Yangming)Heping Xian GD39/40B7
Yangming Shan HN37/38E4
Yangmingshan TW27/28B3
Yangmugang HL15/16E7
Yangmulin JL13/14E6
Yangmuzhazi HEB3/4B3
Yangongtang AH23/24F5
Yangou HB35/36D5
Yangping GZ49/50C7
Yangping SX7/8C3
Yangping HEN33/34C2
Yangping SN55/56F3
Yangping HB35/36C4
Yangpingguan SN55/56H2
Yangpo SX7/8C4
Yangpu Gang HI42B2
Yangqiao HN37/38C5
Yangqiao AH23/24C2
Yangqiao HEB5/6G3
Yangqiao JX29/30D2
Yangqiaopan SN55/56C5
Yangqu SX7/8D4
Yangquan SN55/56E5

Yangquan HN37/38E5
Yangquanqu SX7/8D3
Yangquan Shi SX7/8D5
Yangqu Shan SX7/8D5
Yangqu Xian (Huangzhai) SX7/8C4
Yangshan SD31/32D3
Yangshan LN11/12C4
Yangshan HEN33/34F7
Yangshan Xian GD39/40B5
Yangshao HEN33/34C3
Yangsha Pao JL13/14A4
Yangshuba NM9/10K20
Yangshuiwu HEB3/4C3
Yangshuling HEB5/6C6
Yangshuo Xian GX43/44C8
Yangtan AH23/24F6
Yangtian HEB3/4B2
Yangting SD31/32B9
Yangtouyan YN51/52C4
Yangtuanji AH23/24C4
Yanguan ZJ21/22B5
Yanguan GS57/58E7
Yanguanxiang GX43/44B8
Yanguo Xia GS80C4
Yangwei HB35/36B3
Yangwu YN51/52D5
(Yangwu)Yuanyang Xian HEN33/34B5
Yangxi AH23/24F5
Yangxi ZJ21/22C4
Yangxi FJ25/26D3
Yangxi JX29/30D2
Yangxi HN37/38D4
Yangxi SC47/48B3
Yangxi HB35/36D4
Yang Xian SN55/56G3
Yangxiang JS17/18E5
Yangxiangjing JS19/20B4
Yangximu He LN11/12B6
Yangxing SX7/8C4
Yangxin Xian HB35/36E8
Yangxin Xian SD31/32B4
Yangxi Xian(Zhilong) GD39/40E4
Yangxu GX43/44D4
Yangxu JX29/30C3
Yangxu GX43/44D6
Yangyi HEB5/6G1
Yangyi SX7/8D4
Yangyuan Xian(Xicheng) HEB5/6C2
Yangzhai JS17/18C5
Yangzhong FJ25/26D4
Yangzhong Shi JS17/18D5
Yangzhou Shi JS17/18D5
Yangzhuang SD31/32E4
Yangzhuang SX7/8B5
Yangzhuang HEN33/34D5
Yangzhuangji SD31/32D3
Yangzi HB35/36C5
Yangziqiao JX29/30B4
Yangzishao JL13/14E7
Yanhai HI42B3
Yan He SN55/56D6
Yanhe HB35/36C8
Yanhecheng BJ3/4B2

Yanhe Tujiazu Zizhixian GZ49/50B7
Yanhewan SN55/56D5
Yanheying HEB5/6C7
Yanhu(Caka) XZ53/54C4
Yanhui SX7/8D5
Yanji HEN33/34C7
Yanji JS17/18B4
Yanjia SC47/48B5
Yanjia SC47/48C4
Yanjia HL15/16D6
Yanjia LN11/12D5
Yanjiadian LN11/12E5
Yanjiahe HEN33/34F6
Yanjiahe SN55/56F2
Yanjiang HL15/16C4
Yanjiang JL13/14B4
Yanjiang GX43/44D5
Yanjiao GZ49/50D4
Yanjiao HEB3/4C3
Yanjiapu HEB3/4C5
Yanjiazhuang SD31/32C4
Yanjing SX7/8F2
Yanjing SC45/46D6
Yanjing XZ53/54E12
Yanjingping SC45/46C4
Yanjin Xian HEN33/34B6
Yanjin Xian YN51/52A6
Yanji Shi JL13/14E10
Yankou HEB3/4B5
Yankou AH23/24D3
(Yankou)Wusheng Xian SC45/46C6
Yanli SX7/8F4
Yanliang SN55/56F5
Yanling JS17/18E5
Yanling GD39/40B6
(Yanling)Weiyuan Xian SC45/46D5
Yanling Xian HEN33/34C6
Yanliumiao AH23/24D3
Yanma Shuiku SD31/32D4
Yanmeidong HEB5/6D2
Yanmen HN37/38D2
Yanmen YN51/52A3
Yanmenba SC45/46B5
Yanmen Guan SX7/8B4
Yanmu JS17/18F6
Yanqian FJ25/26D3
Yanqian FJ25/26F2
Yanqiao SC47/48C1
Yanqiao HN37/38D2
Yanqiao JS19/20B3
Yanqi Huizu Zizhixian XJ63/64D9
Yanqing Xian BJ3/4B2
Yanqiu HEN33/34C4
Yanshan GZ49/50D6
Yan Shan BJ3/4B3 HEB5/6C4-6
Yanshan BJ3/4C2
Yanshan GX43/44B8
Yanshan Xian HEB5/6E5
Yanshan Xian(Hekou) JX29/30C5
Yanshan Xian(Jiangna) YN51/52D6
Yanshi FJ25/26E3
Yanshiping QH59/60D3
Yanshi Shi HEN33/34C4

Yanshi Xi FJ25/26E3
Yanshou HN37/38F6
Yanshou Xian HL15/16E5
Yanshuiguan SN55/56D6

Yantai Shi SD31/32B8
Yantan ZJ21/22D5
Yantan SC47/48C2
Yantang HN37/38D2
Yantang HN37/38E6
Yantang HI42B3
Yantang SC45/46E3
Yantian JX29/30D2
Yantian FJ25/26D5
Yantian GD41A3
Yantian GD41A3
Yantietang JS19/20B3-4
Yanting Xian SC45/46C5
Yantongshan JL13/14D7
Yantongshan HEB5/6C3
Yantongtun HL15/16D3
Yantou SX7/8B5
Yantou ZJ21/22D5
Yanwa YN51/52B3
Yanweigang JS17/18B5
Yanwodao HL15/16D7
Yanwu SX7/8D3
Yanwuping GZ49/50C8
Yanxi FJ25/26F3
Yanxi JX29/30D3
Yanxi HN37/38C3
Yanxia HB35/36E7
Yanxidu JX29/30E2
Yanxing HL15/16D6
Yanyuan Xian SC45/46F3
Yanzao GD39/40E2
Yanzhao HEB5/6E2
Yanzhou HEN33/34B6
Yanzhou Shi SD31/32D3
Yanzhuang SX7/8C4
Yanzhuang HEN33/34C5
Yanzhuang SD31/32C4
Yanzibian SN55/56H1
Yanzidun NX61/62A3
Yanziji JS17/18D4
Yanzikou GZ49/50C4
Yanziwo HB35/36D7
Yao'an Xian(Dongchuan) YN51/52C4
Yaoba NM9/10H5
Yaocheng HEB5/6F2
Yaocun HEB5/6D3
Yaocun HEN33/34A5
Yaocun SD31/32D3
Yaocun AH23/24F6
Yaodian SN55/56D5
Yaodian GS57/58E8
Yaodian SN55/56F4
(Yaodu)Dongzhi Xian AH23/24F4
Yaofupu NX61/62B3
Yaogangxian HN37/38F6
Yaogezhuang SD31/32C6
Yaogou SD31/32C5
Yaogou AH23/24E4

Yaogou NM7/8B3
Yaogu GD39/40D5
Yaoguan HEB5/6E4
Yaoguan YN51/52C3
Yaojiaba HN37/38D6
Yaojiadianzi SD31/32D5
Yaojiafang HEB3/4B1
Yaojiaji HB35/36C7
Yao Jiang ZJ19/20D4
Yaojiaqiao JS19/20A2
Yaojiata AH19/20C2
Yaojie GS57/58D6
Yaojie Shuiku HEN33/34B5
Yaokouji AH23/24D3
Yaoli JX29/30B5
Yaolimiao AH23/24E3
Yaolindong ZJ21/22C4
Yaoling GD39/40B6
Yaolugou LN11/12D3
Yaoluoping AH23/24F3
Yaomangmiao LN11/12D4
Yaopi HN37/38E6
Yaopu GZ49/50D4
Yaopu LN11/12B6
Yaopu AH23/24D5
Yaoqianhutun LN11/12C7
Yaoqu SX7/8E2
Yaoquan HL15/16C4
Yaoquanzi GS57/58C3
Yao Shan NX61/62D3
Yao Shan GD75B5
Yaoshang HEB5/6C5
Yaoshao GZ49/50D5
Yaoshi HN37/38D2
Yaotan SC47/48B4
Yaotou SX7/8C3
Yaotou JX29/30E2
Yaotun HL15/16C4
Yaowan JS17/18B4
Yaoxian SN55/56E5
Yaoxian Qu SX7/8G2
Yao Xiao SN55/56F4
Yaoxu JX29/30D3
Yaozhai GX43/44C5
Yaozhan HL15/16B3
Yaozhen SN55/56B6
Yaozitou SX7/8B4
Yaqian JX29/30E2
Yaqian JX29/30C4
Yaqueling HB35/36D4
Yaqueshui HB35/36D2
Yarga XZ53/54 D4
Yarkant He XJ63/64F5 – E6
Yarlung Zangbo Daxiagu XZ53/54E10
Yarlung Zangbo Jiang XZ53/54E8 – 10
Yarwa SC45/46C2
Yarzhong XZ53/54E11
Yashanjie AH23/24F5
Yatunbu HN37/38E2
Yau Tong Estate HK41B3
Yawangkou SD31/32C4
Yawatongguzlangar XJ63/64G7
Yaxi GZ49/50C5
Yaxigang JS17/18E5
Yaxilt NM9/10K18

Yaxing HI42B2
Yayu GZ49/50C8
Yayuan JL13/14F7
Yazai Shan GD41A2
Yazhong ZJ21/22E5
Yazhou GZ49/50E6
Yazhou JS17/18D6
Ya Zhou GD41A3
Ya Zhou GD41A4
Yazhuang SD31/32C5
Yazi SD31/32B8
Yazigang HN37/38C5
(Yebaishou)Jianping Xian LN11/12C3
Yecaowan HEB5/6F2
Yecheng(Kargilik)Xian XJ63/64G4
Yecun SN55/56G6
(Yêgainnyin)Henan Mongolzu Zizhixian
   QH59/60C7
Yehe JL13/14E5
Ye He HEB5/6E2
Yeji AH23/24E2
Yejigang HEN33/34C7
Yejituo HEB5/6D6
Yeliguan GS57/58E6
Yellow Sea 17/18B7-D8
Yema JL13/14B3
Yemachuan GZ49/50C3
Yema He GS80B2
Yema Nanshan GS57/58C2-3
Yemaotai LN11/12B6
Yematan QH59/60C6
Yematan QH59/60B6
Yematu JL13/14B2
Yenchao TW27/28E2
(Yêndum)Zhag'yab Xian XZ53/54D11
Yengierik XJ63/64E6
Yengiostang XJ63/64F8
Yengisar XJ63/64E8
Yengisar Xian XJ63/64F4
Yengisu XJ63/64E9
Yeniugou QH59/60C5
Yeniugou QH59/60A6
Yenpu TW27/28E2
Yenshui TW27/28D2
Yeping JX29/30F4
Yepingjie SN55/56G4
Yesanguan HB35/36D3
Yeshan JS19/20A1
Yeshengpu NX61/62B3
Yetai Shan SN55/56F4
Yetan GD39/40C8
(Yêtatang)Baqên Xian XZ53/54D10
Ye Xian HEN33/34D5
Yexie SH19/20C4
Yeyik XJ63/64G7
Yeyuan SD31/32C5
Yeyuan Shuiku SD31/32C5
Yeyungou XJ63/64E8
Yezhuang SX7/8C4
Yi'an SX7/8D3
Yi'an Xian HL15/16D3
Yiban FJ25/26E4
Yibang YN51/52D4

Yibin Shi SC45/46D5
Yibin Xian(Baixi) SC45/46D5
Yibug Caka XZ53/54C6
Yibutan SC47/48D2
Yichang Caohe JS19/20B2
Yichang Shi HB35/36D4
Yichang Xian(Xiaoxita) HB35/36D4
Yicheng SD31/32E4
Yicheng Shi HB35/36C5
Yicheng Xian SX7/8F3
Yichexun YN51/52B5
Yichuan Xian HEN33/34C4
Yichuan Xian SN55/56D6
Yichun Diqu JX29/30C2-3
Yichun Shi HL15/16D5
Yichun Shi JX29/30D2
Yidan JL13/14D6
Yidao SD31/32B7
Yidian SN55/56F3
Yidie SX7/8D2
Yidouquan SX7/8B6
Yidu FJ25/26E3
Yidu FJ25/26E5
Yidu JX29/30C3
Yidu HB35/36D4
Yidun SC45/46C2
Yidushui HN37/38E4
Yifeng Xian(Xinchang) JX29/30C2
Yigang GS61/62E2
Yigaolou ZJ19/20C3
Yigou HEN33/34B6
Yihatuoli GS57/58A3
Yi He HEN33/34C4
Yihe SN5/6C6
Yi He SD31/32D5-E5
Yi He JS17/18B4
Yihe SD31/32B5
Yihuang Xian(Fenggang) JX29/30D4
Yijiadian JL13/14B6
Yijialing HB35/36D5
Yijiangshan Dao ZJ21/22D6
(Yijiang)Yiyang Xian JX29/30C5
Yijiangzhen AH23/24F5
Yijianpu JL13/14C6
Yijiawan HN37/38D6
Yijing HEB5/6G2
Yijing SX7/8B4
Yijinqiao AH23/24F4
Yijun Xian SN55/56E5
Yiketian NM61/62A2
Yikou FJ25/26D3
Yilan Xian HL15/16D5
Yilehuli Shan HL15/16B2-4
       NM9/10B14-15
Yi'lhung SC45/46C2
Yiliang Xian YN51/52C5
Yiliang Xian(Jiaokui) YN51/52B6
Yiliekede NM9/10C13
Yili He YN51/52B5
Yilin JS17/18C5
Yiling JS17/18D5
Yiliping QH59/60B3

Yiliu HN37/38F5
Yilong HL15/16D3
Yilong Hu YN77D4
Yilong Xian SC45/46C6
Yiluo He HEN7/8G4
Yima JL13/14D7
Yima GS61/62E4
Yimaling HEB5/6D2
Yima Shi HEN33/34C3
Yimatu HEB5/6B3
Yimatu He HEB5/6B5
Yimen AH23/24C3
Yimen SN55/56F3
Yimen SC45/46E4
Yimen Xian YN51/52C5
Yimianpo HL15/16E5
Yimianshan LN11/12D8
Yimin He NM9/10C12
Yiminzhan NM9/10C12
Yim Tin Tsai HK41B3
Yimuhe NM9/10A13
Yinajia GZ49/50D4
Yinan Xian (Jiehu) SD31/32D5
Yincha GX43/44D5
Yincheng SX7/8F5
Yinchuan Shi NX61/62B3
Yinchuanzhan NX61/62B2
Yincun HEB5/6F2
Yindi GZ49/50C4
Yindian HB35/36B6
Yinfang HEB5/6D2
Yinfengqiao HN37/38C5
Yingbifeng JL13/14E8
Yingcheng JL13/14C6
Yingcheng Shi HB35/36D6
Yingchengzi JL13/14D6
Yingchuan ZJ21/22E4
Yingchun HL15/16D7
Yingde Shi GD39/40B6
Yingdu FJ25/26F4
Ying'ebu JL13/14F6
Ying'e Ling JL13/14E9
Ying'emen LN11/12B9
Yingfang SD31/32C7
Yinggehai HI42C1
Yingge Ling HI42B2
(Yinggen)Qiongzhong Lizu Miaozu
   Zizhixian HI42C2
Yinggezui SN55/56F3
Yinghao HEN33/34C3
Yinghe AH23/24D3
Ying He AH23/24C2-D3 HEN33/34C5
Yinghua JL13/14B4
(Yinghuayuan) Fan Xian HEN33/34B7
Yingjia GX43/44C9
Yingjiakou JX29/30C6
Yingjiang Xian YN51/52C2
Yingjing Xian SC45/46D4
Yingjin He NM5/6A7
Yingko TW27/28C3
Yingkou Shi LN11/12D6
Yingli GD39/40F3
Yingli HEB5/6E1

Yingpan LN11/12C8
Yingpan YN51/52C3
Yingpan YN51/52D4
Yingpan GX43/44F7
Yingpan SN55/56G5
Yingpanjie YN51/52C3
Yingpanshan SC45/46E5
Yingpanshui NX61/62C1
Yingpanwan NM9/10K19
Yingpanxu JX29/30E2
Ying Pun HK41B3
Yingqian FJ25/26E5
Yingqian JX29/30F2
Yingqiao HEN33/34D5
Yingrenshi GD41A2
Yingshang SD31/32C7
Yingshang Xian AH23/24D3
Yingshan Xian HB35/36D8
Yingshan Xian SC45/46C6
Yingshouyingzi HEB5/6C5
Yingshuiqiao NX61/62C2
Yingtan Shi JX29/30C5
Yingtian HN37/38C5
Yingwang SN55/56D5
Yingwanzhen HN37/38C5
Yingwuxi GZ49/50B7
Yingxi SC47/48B4
Ying Xian SX7/8B5
Yingxiangjie SC47/48D4
Yingxin TJ3/4D4
Yingxiu SC47/48A1
Yingyang HEN33/34C4
Yingyang Guan GX43/44C9
          GD39/40B4
Yingyang Shi HEN33/34C5
Yingzhou HI42C2
Yinhao NM9/10J20
Yinhar NM9/10F9
Yin He NM5/6A6
Yin He NM70C2-D2
Yining(Gulja)Shi XJ63/64D6
Yining(Gulja)Xian(Jililyüzi) XJ63/64C6
(Yining)Xiushui Xian JX29/30B2
Yiniu SC45/46B2
Yinji SD31/32C3
Yinji AH23/24C4
Yinji JS17/18C5
Yinjiahui AH23/24F4
Yinjiang ZJ21/22C6
Yinjiang Tujiazu Miaozu Zizhixian
      GZ49/50B7
Yinju HEN33/34B6
Yinkengxu JX29/320E3
Yinliu TJ3/4C4
Yinma SD31/32C6
Yinma SD31/32D2
Yinma He JL13/14C6-D6
Yinmahe JL13/14C6
Yinmin YN51/52B5
Yinnan Diqu NX61/62C3
Yinping JS17/18B4
Yinqueshan SD31/32D5
Yin Shan NM9/10G6-8

Yinshanzhen SC45/46D5

Yinta SX7/8B3

Yintian HN37/38E5

Yĭntian HN37/38D5

Yin Xian ZJ21/22C6

Yinxiang SD31/32B4

Yinxianji AH23/24D3

Yinxu HEN33/34A6

Yinyang JS17/18E7

Yinying SX7/8D5

Yinzhan'ao GD39/40C6

Yinzhen SN5/56F5

Yinzikuang SD31/32B9

Yinzu HB35/36E7

Yi O HK41B2

Yi'ong Nongchang XZ53/54D10

Yi'ong Zangbo XZ53/54D9-10

Yipin SC47/48C4

Yipinglang YN51/52C4

Yipingyuan SX7/8E3

Yiqian JX29/30E4

Yiqiao ZJ21/22B5

(Yiquan)Meitan Xian GZ49/50C6

Yiran Co QH59/60D3

Yirtkuq Bulak XJ63/64E10

Yirxie NM9/10D12

Yisha GD41A2

Yi shan SD31/32D4

Yi Shan SD31/32C5

Yishan ZJ21/22E5

Yisheng ZJ19/20C3

Yi Shui HEB3/4C2

Yishui Xian SD31/32D5

Yitang SD31/32D5

Yitang SX7/8E3

Yitang HB35/36C6

Yiting ZJ21/22C4

Yitong He JL13/14E6

Yitong He JL13/14C6

Yitong Manzu Zizhixian JL13/14D6

Yitulihe NM9/10B13

Yiwanquan NX61/62C1

Yiwanquan XJ63/64D12

Yiwu YN51/52E4

Yiwu(Aratürük)Xian XJ63/64D13

Yiwulü Shan LN11/12C5

Yiwu Shi ZJ21/22C5

Yixi GD25/26G2

Yi Xian LN11/12C5

Yi Xian HEB5/6D3

Yi Xian AH23/24G4

Yixiang YN51/52D4

Yixiken HL15/16A3

Yixing SC47/48A3

Yixingbu TJ3/4C4

Yixing Shi JS17/18E5

Yixu FJ25/26D5

Yixun He HEB5/6B5

Yiyang SD31/32C3

Yiyang Shi HN37/38C5

Yiyang Xian HEN33/34C4

Yiyang Xian(Yijiang) JX29/30C5

Yiyuankou HEB5/6C7

Yiyuan Xian(Nanma) SD31/32C5

Yizhang Xian HN37/38F5

Yizheng Shi JS17/18D5

Yizhou Shi GX43/44C6

Ynxiang SX7/8G2

Yoigilanglêb Qu QH59/60C5

Yolin Mod NM13/14C3

Yong'an HL15/16D4

Yong'an AH23/24C4

Yong'an SD31/32B5

Yong'an HN37/38F5

Yong'an GZ49/50B6

Yong'an SC47/48C2

Yong'anbu GD41A2

Yong'anguan HN37/38F4

Yong'anpu LN11/12D3

Yong'an Shi FJ25/26E3

Yong'anshi HN37/38C6

Yong'an Xi ZJ21/22D5

Yong'anxiang HL15/16E6

Yongbi HEB5/6F2

Yongchang XZ21/22C4

Yongchang JX29/30E2

Yongchangbu GS57/58C6

Yongchang Xian GS57/58C5

Yongcheng GZ49/50B6

Yongcheng Shi   HEN33/34D8

Yongchuan Shi SC45/46D5

Yongchun JL13/14D6

Yongchun Xian FJ25/26E4

Yongcong GZ49/50D8

Yongdeng Xian GS57/58D6

Yongde Xian (Dedang) YN51/52C3

Yongdian LN11/12D8

Yongding He BJ3/4C3 HEB5/6D4

Yongding Xian FJ25/26F2

Yongding Xinhe TJ3/4C4

(Yongding)Yongren Xian YN51/52B4

Yongfa HI42B3

Yongfeng SN55/56F5

Yongfeng SN55/56F6

Yongfeng GD39/40C5

Yongfeng GD39/40B5

(Yongfeng)Guangfeng Xian JX29/30C6

(Yongfeng)Shuangfeng Xian HN37/38D5

Yongfeng Xian(Enjiang) JX29/30D3

Yongfu FJ25/26E3

Yongfu Xian GX43/44C7

Yonggu GD39/40C5

Yonghan GD39/40C6

Yonghe HEB5/6C6

Yonghe HN37/38C6

Yonghe GD39/40B5

Yongheguan SX7/8E2

Yonghe Xian SX7/8E2

Yongji SC47/48B3

Yongjia SC47/48C3

Yongjiabu SX7/8A6

Yong Jiang GX43/44E6

Yong Jiang ZJ19/20D4

Yongjia Xian(Shangtang) ZJ21/22D5

Yongjing Xian GS57/58E6

(Yongjing)Xifeng Xian GZ49/50C5

Yongjin Qu SX7/8E5

Yongji Shi SX7/8G2

Yongji Xian(Kouqian) JL13/14D7

Yongkang AH23/24D4

Yongkang YN51/52C3

Yongkangpu NX61/62C2

Yongkang Shi ZJ21/22D5

Yongle HEB3/4C2

Yongle GX43/44B7

Yongle GX43/44D4

Yongle GZ49/50D7

Yongledian BJ3/4C3

Yongledian SN55/56F4

Yonglegong SX7/8G2

Yongle Jiang HN37/38E6

Yongling LN11/12C8

Yonglonghe HB35/36D5

Yonglong Sha JS19/20B4

Yongming HI42C2

Yongmo GD41B1

Yongnian HEB5/6G2

Yongnian Xian (Linmingguan)
  HEB5/6G2

Yongning BJ3/4B3

Yongning JL13/14D7

Yongning JS17/18D4

Yongning FJ25/26F4

Yongning GZ49/50E4

Yongning YN51/52B4

Yongning He SC49/50B4

Yongningjian LN11/12E5

(Yongning)Tonggu Xian JX29/30C2

Yongning Xian NX61/62B3

Yongning Xian(Pumiao) GX43/44E6

Yongping JX29/30C5

Yongping SN55/56C5

Yongping Xian YN51/52C3

Yongqiang ZJ21/22E5

Yongqing SC47/48B3

Yongqing Xian HEB5/6D4

Yongquan ZJ21/22D6

Yongren Xian(Yongding) YN51/52B4

Yongshan JX29/30B5

Yongshan Xian (Jingxin) YN51/52A5

Yongshanzhuang NM9/10K23

Yongsheng NM9/10J17

Yongsheng Xian YN51/52B4

Yongshou SC47/48C1

Yongshou Xian(Jianjun) SN55/56F4

Yongshun SC47/48B3

Yongshun Xian(Lingxi) HN37/38B2

Yongsui GX43/44A9

Yongtai JX29/30D3

Yongtai SC47/48A2

Yongtai Xian FJ25/26E4

Yongxiang SN55/56E5

Yongxin SC47/48D4

Yongxing HB35/36D6

Yongxing SC47/48B2

Yongxing SC47/48B4

Yongxing FJ25/26C4

Yongxing GZ49/50C6

Yongxing HI42B3

Yongxing SC47/48A2
Yongxing NM7/8A4
Yongxing SC45/46C5
Yongxing YN51/52B4
Yongxing SN55/56B6
Yongxing GS57/58E7
Yongxing SC47/48A5
Yongxingchang SC47/48C2
Yongxing Dao HI42E6
Yongxingqiao JX29/30D4
Yongxing Xian HN37/38E6
Yongxin Xian(Hechuan) JX29/30E2
Yongxiu Xian (Tujiabu) JX29/30B3
Yongyang JX29/30E2
Yongzhen AH19/20B1
Yongzhou Shi HN37/38E4
Yopurga Xian AH23/24F3
Youbu ZJ21/22C4
Youcheng JX29/30B4
Youcun JX29/30D3
Youdunjie JX29/30B4
Youdunzi QH59/60A2
Youfang HEB5/6F3
Youfanggou SN55/56F2
Yougang HN37/38B5
Youguzhuang TJ3/4C4
Youhao HL15/16D5
Youji AH23/24C4
Youjiabian JX29/30D4
You Jiang GX43/44D5
Youjiang He SC47/48C5
Youjiawan HN37/38D4
Youju JX29/30C2
Youlan GX43/44C7
Youlan JX29/30C4
Youlaxi SC45/46C3
Youli GX43/44C4

Youma GX43/44D8
Youmakou GX43/44C8
Youqing SC47/48B4
Youquanzi QH59/60A2
You Shan JX29/30F2 GD39/40A7
Youshashan QH59/60A2
Youshui JX29/30F3
You Shui HN37/38C3 SC45/46D7
Youtian JX29/30D2
Youtingpu SC45/46D5
Youtingxu HN37/38E4
You Xi FJ25/26D4
Youxi ZJ21/22D6
Youxi SC45/46D6
Youxiu HN37/48D4
You Xian HN37/38D6
Youxi Xian FJ25/26D4
Youxizhen SC45/46C6
Youyang FJ25/26E4
Youyang Tujiazu Miaozu Zizhixian
  SC45/46D7
Youyi Feng XJ63/64A9
Youyiguan GX43/44F4
Youyi Shuiku HEB5/6C2
Youyi Xian HL15/16D6

Youyu SX7/8A4
Youyu Xian SX7/8B4
Youzai SX7/8B5
Youzhagou AH19/20B1
Youzhahe HEN33/34F6
Youzhaping GX43/44B8
Youzhou HEB3/4B2
Yuan'an Xian HB35/36C4
Yuanba SN55/56H2
Yuanbao Shan GX43/44B7
Yuanbaoshan NM11/12B3
Yuancun HEN33/34A7
Yuan Dao LN11/12F6
Yuanfang HEN33/34C6
Yuangezhuang SD31/32B8
Yuangtung TW27/28C3
Yuanhou GZ49/50B4
Yuanhua ZJ19/20C3
Yuanjiacun SX7/8C3
Yuanjiahui ZJ19/20C3
Yuan Jiang HN37/38C3
Yuan Jiang YN51/52D4-5
Yuanjiang Hanizu Yizu Daizu Zizhixian
  YN51/52D4
Yuanjiang Shi HN37/38C5
Yuankeng FJ25/26D3
Yuankou GZ49/50D8
Yuanli TW27/28C2
Yuanlin TW27/28D2
Yuanlin NM9/10C13
Yuanling Xian HN37/38C3
(Yuanma)Yuanmou Xian YN51/52C4
Yuanmen HI42B2
Yuanmou Xian(Yuanma) YN51/52C4
Yuanping Shi SX7/8C4
Yuanqiang AH23/24C2
Yuanqiao ZJ21/22D6
Yuanquan SD31/32C5
Yuanqu Xian SX7/8F3
Yuanquzhan SX7/8F3
Yuansha SH19/20B4
Yuanshan SC45/46C5
Yuanshan TW27/28C3
(Yuanshan)Lianping Xian GD39/40B7
Yuanshanzi GS57/58C4
Yuanshi SC47/48B5
Yuanshi Xian HEB5/6F2
Yuan Shui JX29/30D2
Yuantan HN37/38B6
Yuantan GD39/40C6
Yuantan HEN33/34E4
Yuantan AH23/24F3
Yuantianba GZ49/50B5
Yuantongchang SC47/48B1
Yuantou GX43/44C8
Yuantou HEB5/6F2
Yuantouzhu JS19/20B3
Yuanwu HEN33/34B5
Yuanxiang HEN33/34C7
Yuanxiang SX7/8D4
Yuanxiangzhen JS19/20B2
Yuanyangchi Shuiku GS57/58C4
Yuanyang Xian YN51/52D5

Yuanyang Xian(Yangwu) HEN33/34B5
Yuanyangzhen GS57/58E7
Yuanyi SC45/46C6
Yuanyongjing YN51/52C4
Yuanzhou GD41A4
Yuanzi He SX7/8B4
Yucai HI42C2
Yucheng ZJ19/20C3
Yucheng SD31/32E3
Yucheng Shi HEN33/34C7
Yucheng Xian SD31/32C3
Yuching TW27/28D2

Yucun AH23/24F5
Yudaokou HEB5/6A4
Yudaokou Muchang HEB5/6A5
Yudi Shan HL15/16A1 NM9/10A13
Yudong JS17/18D7
Yudu GS61/62E4
Yuduba SN55/56H3
Yudu Xian JX29/30F3
Yuecheng HEN33/34E6
Yuecheng HEB5/6G2
Yuecheng GD39/40C5
Yuecheng Ling GX43/44A8-B8
                 HN37/38E4-F4
Yuecheng Shuiku HEB5/6G2
Yuechi Xian SC45/46C6
Yuehedian HEN33/34E5
Yuejiajing NM61/62C1
Yuejiang HN37/38C6
Yuejiashan SC45/46C4
Yuejin Qu NX61/62C2
Yuejin Shuiku XJ63/64C9
Yuekou JX29/30D4
Yuekou HB35/36D6
Yuelai SC45/46C7
Yuelai SC47/48B4
Yuelaichang SC45/46C6
(Yuelai)Huachuan Xian HL15/16D6
Yuele GS57/58D8
Yueli GX43/44B5
Yueliang Pao JL13/14B4
Yuelongshi HN37/38C6
Yuelu Shan HN37/38C5
Yuen Long HK41B3
Yuen Long HK41B3
Yuepu SH19/20B4
Yueqing Wan ZJ21/22D6
Yueqing Shi ZJ21/22D5
Yu'erya HEB5/6C6
Yueshan HN37/38D5
Yueshan AH23/24F3
Yuetangji JS19/20A2
Yuetian HN37/38B6
Yuetuo HEB5/6D6
Yuexi SC47/48C2
Yuexi ZJ21/22C6
Yuexi He SC47/48C2
Yuexi He SC45/46D4
Yuexi Xian SC45/46D4
Yueyahu NX61/62B3
(Yueyang)Gu Xian SX7/8E3

Yueyang Shi HN37/38B6
Yueyang Xian HN37/38B6
Yuezhou YN51/52C5
Yuezhuang SD31/32C5
Yuezi JX29/30G3
Yufa BJ3/4C3
Yufang FJ25/26D3
Yufeng GX43/44D5
Yufeng SC47/48B3
Yufengchang SC47/48B3
Yufen He SX7/8C3
Yugan Xian JX29/30C4
Yugê QH59/60C4
Yugong HL15/16D6
Yugou JS17/18C4
Yugou AH23/24C4
Yuguan HEB5/6D7
Yuhang Shi ZJ21/22B5
Yuhangzhen ZJ21/22B4
Yuhe GZ49/50C6
Yuhe HEN33/34B5
Yu He SX7/8A5-B5
Yuhebu SN55/56C5
Yuhong GX43/44C4
Yuhu GD39/40C9
Yuhu ZJ21/22E5
Yuhua JS17/18C6
Yuhuan Dao ZJ21/22D6
Yuhuang Ding SD31/32C4
Yuhuan Xian(Huanshan) ZJ21/22D6
Yuhua Shan JX29/30D3
Yuhui ZJ19/20C3
Yuji HEB5/6F4
Yuji SD31/32C3
Yuji LN11/12C5
Yujia JX29/30C5
Yujiabu HB35/36D5
Yujiacun JS19/20B4
Yujiafang LN11/12C6
Yujiajing AH23/24F3
Yu Jiang GX43/44E7-D7
Yu Jiang SC45/46D7
Yujiang Xian(Dengjiabu) JX29/30C4
Yujiaxi HN37/38B3
Yujiazhuang HEB3/4D2
Yujing SX7/8B4
Yujing Feng JX29/30C6
Yujuncun NM9/10D12
Yuke SC45/46C3
Yuke HEB5/6F3
Yukou SX7/8D3
Yukou BJ3/4B4
Yulao GD39/40C4
Yuli TW27/28D3
Yuli SD31/32B8
Yuliangpu NM11/12A5
Yuli(Lopnur)Xian XJ63/64E9
Yulin JL13/14G6
Yulin HL15/16E5
Yulin HI42C2
Yun'an Xian GD39/40 C4
Yulin Diqu SN55/56C5-6
Yu Ling ZJ21/22C3-4 AH23/24G5-F6

Yuling Guan ZJ21/22B3 AH23/24F5
Yulin He SC47/48C4
Yulin He SN55/56B5
Yulin Shi GX43/44E8
Yulin Shi SN55/56B5
Yulong SC45/46C5
Yulong Xueshan YN51/52B4
Yulü GD41A2
Yumco XZ53/54D5
Yumendongzhan GS57/58C3
Yumenguan GS57/58B1
Yumenkou SX7/8F2
Yumen Shi GS57/58C3
Yumenzhen GS57/58B3
Yumin Xian(Karabura) XJ63/64B7
Yunan Xian(Ducheng) GD39/40C4
Yun'anzhen SC45/46C7
Yunbiao GX43/44E7
Yuncao AH23/24E5
Yuncheng Diqu SX7/8F2-3
Yuncheng Shi SX7/8F2
Yuncheng Xian SD31/32D2
Yunfeng Shuiku JL13/14F7
Yunfu Shi GD39/40D5
Yungang SX7/8A5
Yung Long HK41B2
Yung Shue O HK41B3
Yungui Gaoyuan GZ77C4-B6
　　　　　　　　YN77C4-B6
Yunhe JS17/18B5
Yunhe Xian ZJ21/22D4
Yunhuqiao HN37/38D5
Yunjiang GX43/44C7
Yunjin SC47/48C3
Yunkai Dashan GD39/40D3-4
　　　　　　　　GX43/44E8-9
Yun Ling YN51/52A3-B3
Yunling AH23/24F5
Yunlin Hsien(Touliu) TW27/28D2
Yunlong HI42B3
Yunlong SC47/48B5
Yunlong SC47/48B3
Yunlong YN51/52C4
Yunlong Xian(Shimen) YN51/52C3
Yunlu GD39/40C9
Yunmen SC47/48B4
Yunmeng Shan BJ3/4B3
Yunmeng Xian HB35/36C6
Yunnanyi YN51/52C4
Yunshan JX29/30C4
Yunshan GS55/56F1
Yunshang YN51/52C6
Yun Shui HB35/36C6
Yuntai SC47/48B5
Yuntai JS17/18B5
Yuntai Shan JS17/18B5
Yuntian GS57/58E7
Yunting JS19/20B3
Yunwu GZ49/50D6
Yunwudong GD39/40A5
Yunwu Shan GD39/40D4
Yunwu Shan HEB5/6B4
Yunwu Shan GZ49/50D6
Yunxi HN37/38B6

Yunxi SC47/48A2
Yun Xian HB35/36B3
Yun Xian YN51/52C4
Yunxiao Xian FJ25/26G3
Yunxi Xian HB35/36B3
Yunyan SN55/56D6
Yunyang HN33/34D4
Yunyang SC45/46C7
Yunyang Diqu HB35/36B3
Yunyang Xian（Shuangjiang） SC45/46C7
Yunyan He JS17/18B5-C5
Yunyan He SN55/56D6
Yunzhong Shan SX7/8C4
Yunzhou HEB5/6B3
Yunzhou Shuiku HEB5/6B3
Yunzhouxicun SX7/8D4
Yuping Dongzu Zizhixian GZ49/50C7
Yuqi JS19/20B3
Yuqian ZJ21/22B4
Yuqiao NX61/62E2
Yuqiao Shuiku TJ3/4B4
Yuqing Shui GZ49/50C6
Yuqing Xian(Baini) GZ49/50C6
Yu Qu XZ53/54E12
Yuquan HL15/16E4
Yuquansi HB35/36D4
Yuquanying NX61/62B2
Yurungkax He XJ63/64G5-H6
Yu Shan JX29/30D4-F3
Yu Shan TW27/28D2
Yushan FJ25/26D4
Yushan HEN33/34D5
Yu Shan JS17/18E6
(Yushan)Changshu Shi JS17/18E6
Yushan Liedao ZJ21/22D7
Yushan Xian JX29/30C6
Yushanzhen SC45/46D7
Yushe GZ49/50D3
Yushe Xian SX7/8D4
Yushi HN37/38D2
Yushi GZ49/50C8
Yushu LN11/12C8
Yushuchuan JL13/14E10
Yushugou JL13/14C8
Yushugou XJ63/64D9
Yushulinzi HEB5/6B7
Yushulinzi LN11/12C3
Yushu Shi JL13/14C7
Yushutai LN11/12C7
Yushutai JL13/14D5
Yushutun HL15/16D2
Yushuwan NM7/8B3
Yushu Xian(Gyêgu) QH59/60D5
Yushu Zangzu Zizhizhou QH59/60C2-D5
Yusi LN11/12B5
Yutai Xian(Guting) SD31/32D3
Yutan JX29/30B5
Yutang HN37/38D5
Yutanzhai SD31/32D2
Yutian JX29/30E2
Yutiangao NM11/12B3
Yutian(Keriya)Xian XJ63/64G6
Yutian Xian HEB5/6D5

Yuting   AH23/24G4
Yutog   SC45/46B3
Yutou   ZJ21/22D3
Yuwan   GD39/40B6
Yuwang   SX7/8F3
Yuwang   NX61/62D3
Yuwangcheng   HB35/36C7
Yuweng Tao   TW27/28D1
Yuwu   SX7/8E4
Yuxi   SC47/48B3
Yuxi   JS19/20A4
Yuxi   SC47/48C2
Yuxi   FJ25/26E5
Yuxi   HB35/36D4
Yuxia   YN51/52C6
Yuxia   SN55/56F4
Yuxiakou   HB35/36D3
Yu Xian   HEB5/6D2
Yu Xian   SX7/8C5
(Yuxi)Daozhen Gelaozu Miaozu Zizhixian
   GZ49/50B6

Yuxi He   AH23/24E4-5
Yuxikou   AH23/24E5
Yuxin   ZJ19/20C3
Yuxin   HB35/36D5
Yuxi Shi   YN51/52C5
Yuyan   LN11/12F5
Yuyangguan   HB36/36D4
Yuyang He   HB35/36D4
Yuyao Shi   ZJ21/22B6
Yuyi   JX29/30C4
Yuyingzi   HEB3/4B4
Yuza   SC45/46C3
Yuzaokou   SX7/8C5
Yuzhang   GZ49/50E4
Yuzhen   HEN33/34C6
Yuzhong Xian   GS57/58E7
Yuzhou Shi   HEN33/34C5
Yuzhuang   SX7/8F2
Yuzhuang   SX7/8C4
Yuzui   SC47/48C4

Z

Zabqung   XZ53/54D6
Zadoi   QH59/60D5
Zadoi Xian   QH59/60D4
(Zagunao)Li Xian   SC45/46C4
Za'gya Zangbo   XZ53/54C7-8
Zaibian   GZ49/50E7
Zaima   GZ49/50D7
Zaimiao   GX43/44E5
Zaiyang   SC45/46D4
Zalantun Shi   NM9/10C14
Zamtang Xian   SC45/46B3
Zanda Xian(Toling)   XZ53/54D2
Zangang   HEB5/6F2
Zangbei Gaoyuan   XZ78B2-4
Zanggezhuang   SD31/32B7
Zangguy   XJ63/64G5
Zangnan Gudi   XZ78C3-5
Zangqênrong   SC45/46D2
Zangqiao   HEB5/6E4

Zanhua Xian   HEB5/6D4
Zaohe   JS17/18B4
Zaoheshi   JX29/30E2
Zaohuli   SD31/32B4
Zaolin   SX7/8B5
Zaolin   JX29/30E2
Zaolinping   SN55/56C6
Zaoqiang Xian   HEB5/6F3
Zaosheng   GS57/58E9
Zaoshi   HN37/38B4
Zaoshi   HB35/36D6
Zaoshi   HN37/38E5
Zaoxi   ZJ21/22B4
Zaoyang Shi   HB35/36B5
Zaoyangzhan   HB35/36B5
Zaoyuan   XJ63/64C9
Zaoyuan   HEB5/6G3
Zaoyuan   SD31/32C4
Zaoyuan   SN55/56D5
Zaoyuanpu   NX61/62C2
Zaozhuang Shi   SD31/32E4
Zapug   XZ53/54C3
Zaqên   QH59/60D4
Za Qu   QH59/60D5
Za Qu   QH59/60D4-5
Zawa   XJ63/64G5
Zawa   QH59/60B7
Zayü   XZ53/54E11
Zayü Qu   XZ53/54E11-F11
Zayu Xian(Gyigang)   XZ53/54E11
Zeguo   ZJ21/22D6
Zejiahu   HN37/38C2
Zêkog Xian(Sonag)   QH59/60C7
Zekti   XJ63/64D7
Zênda   SC45/46B1
Zengcheng Shi   GD39/40C6
Zengfeng Shan   JL13/14G9
Zenggang   NX61/62B3
Zengjiaba   SN55/56H5
Zeng Jiang   GD39/40C6
Zengmu Ansha   HI42F5-6
Zengsheng   JL13/14C6
Zengtian   GD39/40B7
Zengtian   JX29/30D3
Zepu (Poskam) Xian   XJ63/64F4
Zêsum   XZ53/54E6
Zêtang   XZ53/54E8
Zetouji   SD31/32B8
Zezhang   SX7/8F3
Zhag'yab Xian(Yêndum)   XZ53/54D11
Zhaiba   GZ49/50B5
Zhaidian   SX7/8F2
Zhaigang   GD39/40B5
Zhaihao   GZ49/50D7
Zhai He   HEN33/34E6
Zhaihe   HEN33/34E6
Zhaijiasuo   GS61/62E2
Zhaike   NX61/62D3
Zhaikou Shuiku   HEN33/34C2
Zhaili   FJ25/26C3
Zhaili   SD31/32B7
Zhaili   SD31/32C4
Zhailing   HEB5/6B4

Zhaiqian   HN37/38F6
Zhaiqiao   JS19/20B2
Zhaisha   GX43/44C7
Zhaishizhen   HN37/38E3
Zhaitang   BJ3/4C2
Zhaixi   ZJ21/22C4
Zhaixidian   HEB5/6E2
Zhaixu   GX43/44E7
Zhaizi   HEB5/6F4
Zhaizitan   GS57/58D6
Zhajiang   HN37/38D5
Zhajin   JX29/30C2
Zhakou   HB35/36E5
Zhalanying   LN11/12B5
Zham   XZ53/54E5
(Zhamo)Bomi(Bowo)Xian   XZ53/54E10
Zhanang Xian(Chatang)   XZ53/54E8
Zhanbei   HL15/16C4
Zhancheng   SD31/32B4
Zhandanzhao   NM9/10K19
Zhandian   HEN33/34B5
Zhandian   HB35/36C7
Zhan'erxiang   GS57/58F8
Zhang'an   ZJ21/22D6
Zhangbaiwan   HEB5/6C5
Zhangba Ling   AH23/2FD5
Zhangbaling   AH23/24D5
Zhangbaotun   SD31/32C3
Zhangbeitun   AH19/20C1
Zhangbei Xian   HEB5/6B2
Zhangcun   HEN33/34E3
Zhangcun   JX29/30C5
Zhangcun   ZJ21/22B4
Zhangcun   ZJ21/22C5
Zhangcun   ZJ21/22D4
Zhangcun   JX29/30D4
Zhangcunping   HB35/36C4
Zhangcunpu   AH23/24C2
Zhangcunyi   SN55/56E5
Zhangdang   LN11/12C8
Zhangdeng   HEB5/6E3
Zhangdian   JS17/18D6
Zhangdian   SX7/8E4
Zhangdian   SX7/8F4
Zhangdian   SX7/8G3
Zhangdiyingzi   HL15/16B4
Zhangdu   AH23/24F5
Zhangdu Hu   HB35/36D7
Zhang'enpu   NX61/62C2
Zhangfang   BJ3/C2
Zhangfeng   YN51/52C2
Zhangfengji   SD31/32D3
Zhanggang   JS19/20A2
Zhanggang   HB35/36D5
Zhanggang   FJ25/26E5
Zhanggezhuang   SD31/32C7
Zhanggezhuang   BJ3/4B3
Zhanggong   HEN33/34C7
Zhanggongdong   JS19/20B2
Zhanggongdu   JX29/30B3
Zhangguan   SD31/32B3
Zhangguangcai Ling   HL15/16E5
Zhangguangji   AH23/24D4

Zhangguanji   AH23/24D2
Zhangguizhuang   TJ3/4C4
Zhanggutai   LN11/12B6
Zhang He   HEB5/6G2
Zhang He   AH19/20B1
Zhanghedian   HEB5/6G2
Zhanghe Shuiku   HB35/36C4
Zhanghuang   GX43/44E7
Zhanghuanggang   JS19/20A3
Zhanghuban   FJ25/26D4
Zhangji   AH23/24D4
Zhangji   JS17/18B5
Zhangji   AH23/24C2
Zhangji   AH23/24D3
Zhangji   HEN33/34D5
Zhangji   JL17/18B4
Zhangjia   SC47/48C2
Zhangjiaba   JS19/20A2
Zhangjiabang   HB35/36D8
Zhangjiabian   GD41A1
Zhangjiabu   SD31/32B9
Zhangjiachuan Huizu Zizhixian
   GS57/58E8
Zhangjiadian   JL13/14D10
Zhangjiadian   AH23/24E3
Zhangjiadu   ZJ21/22D5
Zhangjiafang   HN37/38C7
Zhangjiagang   JS19/20B3
Zhangjiagang Shi   JS17/18E6
Zhangjiahe   SN55/56G2
Zhangjiaji   HB35/36C5
Zhangjiajie   HN37/38B3
Zhangjiajie Shi   HN37/38B3
Zhangjiajing   NX61/62D3
Zhangjiakounan   HEB3/4B1
Zhangjiakou Shi   HEB5/6C2
Zhangjialing   JX29/30B4
Zhangjialou   SD31/32D6
Zhang Jiang   FJ25/26F3
Zhangjiaping   HN37/38C3
Zhangjiaqiao   JS19/20A3
Zhangjiashan   JX29/30C3
Zhangjiawan   BJ3/4C3
Zhangjiawan   NX61/62D3
Zhangjiayan Shuiku   SC47/48B2
Zhangjiayingzi   LN11/12C3
Zhangjiayuan   NX61/62D3
Zhangjiazhuang   HEB5/6D7
Zhangjiazhuang   SX7/8E3
Zhangjiazuitou Shuiku   NX61/62E2
Zhangjicun   HEB5/6B2
Zhangjingqiao   JS19/20B3
Zhangjinhe   HB35/36D5
Zhangjiying   LN11/12C4
Zhangjunmu   HEN33/34C7
Zhangla   SC45/46B4
Zhanglan   SX7/8D4
Zhangli   SX7/8F3
Zhangliangdian   HEN33/34D5
Zhangling   SD31/32C6
Zhangling   HL15/16A2
Zhanglou   JS17/18B4
Zhanglou   AH23/24D3

Zhanglu   SD31/32C2
Zhangmao   HEN33/34C3
Zhangmu   GX43/44C9
Zhangmu   GX43/44D7
Zhangmu   GX43/44E8
Zhangmuqiao   AH23/24E3
Zhangmushi   HN37/38D5
Zhangmutou   GD39/40D7
Zhangouji   AH23/24D3
Zhangping Shi   FJ25/26E3
Zhangpu   JS17/18E6
Zhangpu Xian   FJ25/26F3
Zhangqiangzhen   LN11/12B6
Zhangqiao   HEN33/34D6
Zhangqiao   AH23/24D4
Zhangqiu   SD31/32C2
Zhangqiu Shi   SD31/32C4
Zhangsanying   HEB5/6B5
Zhangsanzhai   HEN33/34B6
Zhangshanji   AH23/24D5
Zhangshanying   BJ3/4B2
Zhangshe   SD31/32C6
Zhangshi   HEB3/4 C2
Zhangshi   HEN33/34C6
Zhangshu   HN37/38E6
Zhangshudun   JX29/30C5
Zhangshugang   HN37/38C5
Zhang Shui   JX29/30F2
Zhangshui   HB35/36C4
Zhangshu Shi   JX29/30C3
Zhangshutan   ZJ21/22D3
Zhangshuxia   HN37/38F5
Zhangtai   HEB5/6F3
Zhangtao   HEN33/34E6
Zhangting   ZJ21/22B6
Zhangwan   FJ25/26D5
Zhangwei Xinhe   SD31/32B3-4
                 HEB5/6F4-5
Zhangwu   ZJ21/22B4
Zhangwu Xian   LN11/12B6
Zhangxi   AH23/24F4
Zhangxi   ZJ21/22D5
Zhangxi   GD39/40C9
Zhangxia   SD31/32C3
Zhang Xian   GS57/58E7
Zhangxin   BJ3/4B3
Zhangxing   SD31/32B7
Zhangyan   SH17/18F7
Zhangyaoxian   SN55/56D3
Zhangye Diqu   GS57/58C4-5
Zhangye Shi   GS57/58C5
Zhangyi   NX61/62E3
Zhangyuan   SX7/8E4
Zhangze Shuiku   SX7/8E5
Zhangzhen   ZJ21/22C5
Zhangzhengqiao   NX61/62B3
Zhangzhishan   JS17/18E6
Zhangzhou Shi   FJ25/26F3
Zhangzhu   JS17/18E5
Zhangzhuang   SD31/32B3
Zhangzhuang   SD31/32C5
Zhangzhuang   JX29/30D2
Zhangzhuang   HEN33/34E7

Zhangzhuang   SD31/32D4
Zhangzi Dao   LN11/12E6-F6
Zhangzihu   NM61/62C1
Zhangzi Xian   SX7/8E4
Zhanhe   YN51/52B4
Zhan He   HL15/16C4
Zhanhua Xian(Fuguo)   SD31/32B5
Zhanji   HEN33/34C7
Zhanjiang Gang   GD39/40E3
Zhanjiang   GD39/40E3
Zhanjiaqiao   ZJ19/20C3
Zhanjiatan   SN55/56D6
Zhanshang   SX7/8D5
Zhan Shui   SX7/8D5
Zhanyi Xian   YN51/52C5
Zhanyu   JL13/14C3
Zhao'an Wan   FJ25/26G3
Zhao'an Xian   FJ25/26G3
Zhaobao   HEN33/34C5
Zhaobei   SX7/8B6
Zhaobeikou   HEB5/6E4
Zhaobi   SX7/8D5
Zhaobishan   NX61/62C2
Zhaocheng   SX7/8E3
Zhaochuan   HEB5/6C3
Zhaochuan   SN55/56G6
Zhaochuan   SN55/56G6
Zhaocun   BJ3/4C3
Zhaocun   HEN33/34D4
Zhaodong Shi   HL15/16D3
(Zhaoge)Qi Xian   HEN33/34B6
Zhaogezhuang   SD31/32B7
Zhaogezhuang   TJ3/4C4
Zhaogezhuang   SD31/32C6
Zhaoguan   AH23/24E5
Zhaoguang   HL15/16C4
Zhaoguanzhen   SD31/32C3
Zhao He   HEN33/34E4
Zhaohe   HEN33/34D4
Zhaohua   SC45/46B5
Zhaohua   SC47/48C3
Zhaoji   JS17/18B4
Zhaoji   AH23/24C3
Zhaoji   HEN33/34E7
Zhaojiachang   SC45/46C6
Zhaojiadian   HB35/36C4
Zhaojiahe   NX61/62E3
Zhaojiapeng   HEB3/4C2
Zhaojiapu   HEB5/6E5
Zhaojiazui   SD31/32B5
Zhaojin   SN55/56E4
Zhaojue Xian   SC45/46D4
Zhaojun   HN37/38D6
Zhaojun Tomb   NM9/10K21
Zhaokang   SX7/8F3
Zhaokua   YN51/52C5
Zhaolaihe   HB35/36D3
Zhaolianzhuang   TJ3/4D4
Zhaoliqiao   HB35/36E6
Zhaomiao   AH23/24C2
Zhaopingtai Shuiku   HEN33/34D4
Zhaoping Xian   GX43/44C8
Zhaopo   NM9/10K20

Zhaoqiao HEB5/6F3

Zhaoqing Shi GD39/40C5

Zhaoqizhuang TJ3/4D4

Zhaoqu SX7/8F3

Zhaoshi HN37/38B2

Zhaoshipan SN55/56C5

Zhaosishui HEB5/6G2

Zhaosu(Mongolküre)Xian XJ63/64D6

Zhaosutai He LN11/12A7-B7

Zhaotan AH23/24G3

Zhaotong Diqu YN51/52B5-6

Zhaotong Shi YN51/52B5

Zhaotun AH23/24C3

Zhaowan SN55/56H5

Zhaowang He SD31/32D3

Zhaowan Shuiku HEN33/34D4

Zhaoxian SX7/8D2

Zhaoxian ZJ21/22D3

Zhaoxian SN55/56F3

Zhaoxian SD31/32D5

Zhao Xian HEB5/6F2

Zhaoxiang SH19/20B4

Zhaoxie JX29/30D3

Zhaoxing HL15/16D6

Zhaoya SC47/48D3

Zhaoyang Hu SD31/32D3-E3

Zhaoyiwei GD41B1

Zhaoyuan Shi SD31/32B7

Zhaoyuan Xian HL15/16E3

Zhaozhangjianlao SX69D3

(Zhaozhen)Jintang Xian SC45/46C5

Zhaozhou Xian HL15/16E3

Zhaozhuang AH23/24B3

Zhaozhuang JS17/18B2

Zhapo GD39/40E4

Zhapu ZJ19/20C5

Zhapu ZJ21/22B6

Zhapu SC47/48C5

Zhari Namco XZ53/54D5

Zhashui Xian SN55/56G5

Zhashuping HB35/36D3

Zhawo SC45/46B4

Zhaxi Co XZ53/54C5

Zhaxigang XZ53/54C2

(Zhaxi)Weixin Xian YN51/52B6

Zhaxizê XZ53/54D11

Zhaze JS19/20A2

Zhazuo GZ49/50D5

Zhebao GX43/44C3

Zhecheng Xian HEN33/34C7

Zheduo Shan SC45/46C3-D3

Zheduo Shankou SC45/46C3

Zhegao AH23/24E4

Zhegao AH23/24E4

Zhegou SD31/32D3

Zhehai YN51/52B5

Zhêhor SC45/46C3

Zhejiahe Shuiku SN55/56E5

Zhejiaping SN55/56C6

Zhelang GD39/40D8

Zhelin GD39/40C10

Zhelin SH17/18F7

Zhelin Shuiku JX29/30B3

(Zhelou)Ceheng Xian GZ49/50E4

Zhemi GZ49/50E6

Zhen'an SC47/48C5

Zhen'an YN51/52C3

Zhen'an GD39/40D4

Zhen'an Xian SN55/56G5

Zhenbao Ding GX43/44A8

Zhenba Xian SN55/56H3

Zhenbeipu NX61/62B3

Zhenchaigang JL13/14C6

Zhenchang HEB5/6D3

Zhenchengdi SX7/8D4

Zhenchuanbu SN55/56C6

Zhenchuanbu SX7/8A5

Zhenfang YN51/52C3

Zhenfeng Xian GZ49/50E4

Zheng'an HEN33/34C5

Zhengang JX29/30F3

Zheng'anpu LN11/12C5

Zheng'an Xian(Fengyi) GZ49/50B6

Zhengbatun SD31/32C2

Zhengcheng SD31/32D4

Zhengchong HN37/38F4

Zhengcun JX29/30C2

Zhengcun AH19/20B1

Zhengde JL13/14C4

Zhengdian SD31/32B4

Zhengding Xian HEB5/6E2

Zhengdong YN51/52D4

Zhengdun FJ25/26C4

Zhengfang JX29/30C5

Zhengguo GD39/40C6

Zhenghe Xian FJ25/26C4

Zhengji JS17/18B3

Zhengjiadian LN11/12C6

(Zhengjiakou)Gucheng Xian HEB5/6F3

Zhengjiao Zui GD41A3

(Zhengjiatun)Shuangliao Xian JL13/14D4

Zhengjiawu ZJ21/22C5

Zhengjiayi HN37/38C4

Zhengjiazhai SD31/32B3

Zhengjiazhuang HEB3/4C1

Zhenglan(Xulun Hoh)Qi(Dund Hot) NM9/10F11

Zhenglu SD31/32B4

Zhenglubu GS57/58D6

Zhengmu SD31/32C5

Zhengning Xian(Shanhe) GS57/58E9

Zhengping JX29/30F2

Zhengqibu NX61/62D2

Zheng Shui HN37/38D5

Zhengtian Shuiku ZJ19/20D3

Zhengtun GZ49/50E4

Zhengwang SD31/32D5

Zhengwuji AH23/24D2

Zhengxiangbai(Xulun Hobot Qagan)Qi NM9/10F10

Zhengxing SC47/48C4

Zhengyang JS19/20A4

Zhengyangguan AH23/24D3

Zhengyang Xian HEN33/34E6

Zhengyi JS17/18E6

Zhengzhou Shi HEN33/34C5

Zhengzhuang ZJ21/22D3

Zhengzhuang SX7/8F4

Zhengzichang SC47/48C2

Zhenhai FJ25/26F4

Zhenhai GD39/40E5

Zhenhai Jiao FJ25/26F4

Zhenhai Xian ZJ21/22C6

Zhenjaping HN37/38B3

Zhenjiang HL15/16D7

Zhenjiangguan SC45/46B4

Zhenjiang Shi JS17/17D5

Zhenjiazhuang SX7/8B5

Zhenjing SN55/56C4

Zhenjinqiao SC47/48B2

Zhenkang Xian YN51/52D3

Zhenlai Xian JL13/14B4

Zhenlong GX43/44E6

Zhenlong GD39/40D3

Zhenlong GX43/44D7

Zhenlong Shan GX75C3

Zhenluopu NX61/62C2

Zhenluoying BJ3/4B4

Zhennan GZ49/50B6

Zhennan JL13/14B4

Zhennei HEB5/6F2

Zhenning Buyeizu Miaozu Zizhixian GZ49/50D4

Zhenningbu HEB3/4B2

Zhenping Xian HEN33/34D4

Zhenping Xian SN55/56I5

Zhenqian FJ25/26C5

Zhenru SH19/20B4

Zhenshang JX29/30C5

Zhenshang HN37/38G4

Zhen Shui GD39/40A6-7

Zhentou AH23/24F5

Zhentou He HEN33/34E6

Zhentoushi HN37/38C6

(Zhenwudong)Ansai Xian SN55/56D5

Zhenxi SC47/48C5

Zhenxi JL13/14B3

Zhenxi SC47/48C2

Zhenxiang HL15/16D3

(Zhenxia)Shigong JS19/20B3

Zhenxing LN11/12B8

Zhenxiong Xian YN51/52B6

Zhenxipu LN11/12B7

Zhenyuan Xian GS57/58E8

Zhenyuan Xian(Wuyang) GZ49/50C7

Zhenyuan Yizu Hanizu Lahuzu Zizhixian YN51/52D4

Zhenze JS17/18F6

Zhenzhumen JL13/14F7

Zhenzhuquan BJ3/4B3

Zhenzhushan JX29/30B5

Zhenzichang SC47/48C3

Zhenziling HB35/36C3

Zhenzizhen HEB5/6D6

Zheqiao HN37/38E5

Zherong Xian FJ25/26C5

Zhesang YN51/52D6

Zhesi Gou NX61/62D3

Zhetai YN51/52C6

Zhetang   JS17/18E4
Zhewang   JS17/18A5
Zhexi   HN37/38C4
Zhexiang   GZ49/50F5
Zhexiang   GZ49/50E4
Zhexi Shuiku   HN37/38C4
Zheyuanbu   GD41A2
Zhibu   ZJ21/22C5
Zhicheng   SC45/46C5
Zhicheng   HB35/36D4
(Zhicheng)Changxing Xian   ZJ21/22A4

Zhicheng Xian(Majiadian)   HB35/36D4
Zhichuan   SN55/56E6
Zhicun   YN51/52D5
Zhidan Xian(Bao'an)   SN55/56D4
Zhidian   HEN33/34D7
Zhidoi Xian(Gyaijêpozhanggê)
    QH59/60D4
Zhifang   HEN33/34C4
Zhifu Dao   SD31/32B8
(Zhigong)Yangzi Xian   GD39/40E4
Zhigou   SD31/32D6
Zhigung   XZ53/54E8
Zhi He   HEB5/6F2
Zhijiang Dongzu Zizhixian   HN37/38D2
Zhijin Xian   GZ49/50D4
Zhikun   GZ49/50D4
Zhilang   GX43/44F5
Zhili   ZJ21/22B5
Zhiluozhen   SN55/56E5
Zhima   FJ25/26C3
Zhimushan   HN37/38D4
Zhinü Qu   SN55/56C6
Zhiqu   QH59/60C4
(Zhi Qu)Tongtian He   QH59/60C4-D5
Zhishan   HL15/16E5
Zhishan   HN37/38E4
Zhitan   JX29/30B5
Zhitang   JS17/18E6
Zhitang   JS19/20B3
Zhitian   SN55/56E4
Zhiwan Dao   GD41C3
Zhixi   FJ25/26E2
Zhixia   ZJ21/22C4
Zhixia   JX29/30E3
Zhixin   JL13/14E10
Zhixiqiao   JS17/18E5
Zhixitou   ZJ21/22D5
Zhiyi   HL15/16E6
Zhiying   ZJ21/22D5
Zhizhong   HI42C2
Zhiziluo   YN51/52B3
Zhnya   SD31/32C5
(Zhong'an)Fuyuan Xian   YN51/52C6
Zhong'anpu   LN11/12C5
Zhong'anqiao   ZJ19/20C3
Zhong'ao   SC47/48C3
Zhongba   GD39/40C8
Zhongban   JX29/30C5
Zhongbao   HB35/36E2
Zhongba Xian   XZ53/54E5
Zhongbu   AH23/24E4
Zhongbujie   JX29/30C5

Zhongcang   AH23/24E4
Zhongce   SD31/32D4
Zhongchao   GZ49/50D8
Zhongcheng   GZ49/50D7
(Zhongcheng) Suijiang Xian   YN51/52A5
Zhongcun   HN37/38E6
Zhongcun   SN55/56G6
Zhongcun   JX29/30F3
Zhongcun   SD31/32D4
Zhongcun   GD41B2
Zhongcun   SD31/32E5
Zhongdai   ZJ19/20C4
Zhongde   JL13/14C6
Zhongdian   AH23/24E3
Zhongdian Xian   YN51/52B3
Zhongdong   GX43/44E5
Zhongdu   FJ25/26F2
Zhongdu   GX43/44C7
Zhongfang   Xian   HN37/38 D2
Zhongfang   FJ25/26D5
Zhongfeng   HB35/36B2
Zhonggang   AH23/24D2
Zhonggong   SD31/32C4
Zhongguan   ZJ21/22B5
Zhonghe   HL15/16E5
Zhonghe   JX29/30G3
Zhonghe   HEN33/34B5
Zhonghe   HL15/16D3
Zhonghe   HI42B2
Zhonghe   SC47/48B4
Zhonghe   SC47/48B2
Zhonghe   GX43/44C5
Zhong He   NX61/62D2-3
Zhongheying   YN51/52D5
Zhonghuang   GZ49/50D8
Zhonghuopu   HB35/36E6
Zhongjiang Xian   SC45/46C5
Zhongjian He   HB35/36E2
Zhongjieshan Liedao   ZJ21/22B7
Zhongling   JX29/30C4
Zhonglu   HB35/36D1
Zhongluotan   GD41A2
Zhonglupu   HN37/38D5
Zhongmiao   AH23/24E4
Zhongming   AH23/24F5
Zhongmou Xian   HEN33/34C6
Zhongnan   SN55/56F4
Zhongnan Shan   SN55/56G5
Zhongning Xian   NX61/62C2
Zhongping   HI42B3
Zhongping   GZ49/50C6
Zhongpu   GS57/58D6
Zhongqiao   JS19/20B3
Zhongrangkou   SC45/46B4
Zhongrong   GX43/44B8
Zhongsha   HI42C1
Zhongsha   FJ25/26D2
Zhongshan   FJ25/26E2
Zhongshan   SC47/48C1
Zhongshan Shi   GD39/40D6
Zhongshan Xian   GX43/44C9
Zhongsha Qundao   HI42E6
(Zhongshu)Huairen Xian   GZ49/50C5

Zhongshuihe   NX61/62D3
(Zhongshu)Luxi Xian   YN51/52C5
Zhongtanpu   SC47/48A1
Zhongtiao Shan   SX7/8G2-F3
Zhongtou   HEN33/34D5
Zhongwang   TJ3/4D4
Zhongwei Xian   NX61/62C2
Zhongxian   FJ25/26E4
Zhongxian   JX29/30D4
Zhong Xian   SC45/46C7
Zhongxiangchang   SC47/48C2
Zhongxiang Shi   HB35/36C5
Zhongxin   HL15/16D3
Zhongxin   GZ49/50C5
Zhongxin   GD39/40C6
Zhongxin   GZ49/50B6
Zhongxin   FJ25/26B4
Zhongxin   GD39/40B7
Zhongxindian   SD31/32D3
Zhongxing   SC47/48B1
Zhongxing   HI42B2
Zhongxing   GD39/40B8
Zhongxing   HL15/16D2
Zhongxing   GD41C1
Zhongxing   AH23/24D4
Zhongxing   AH23/24D3
Zhongxing   SD31/32E3
Zhongxingchang   SC45/46C5
Zhongxingji   AH23/24D3
Zhongxingqiao   JS17/18C6
Zhongxing Shuiku   AH23/24D4
(Zhongxing)Siyang Xian   JS17/18C4
(Zhongxin)Huaping Xian   YN51/52B4
Zhongxinzhan   QH59/60C6
Zhongxinzhen   SC45/46C6
Zhongxin Zhou   GD41B2
Zhongxinzhuang   TJ3/4C4
Zhongyangpu   JL13/14E7
Zhongyang Xian   SX7/8D3
Zhongyaozhan   HL15/16B3
Zhongyi   HB35/36C7
Zhongyicun   YN51/52C5
Zhongyicun   HEB5/6B2
Zhongying   GZ49/50D4
Zhongyu   ZJ21/22C4
Zhongyu   SX7/8E4
Zhongyuan   HI42B3
Zhongyun   JX29/30B5
Zhong Yunhe   JS17/18C4
Zhongzhai   GS57/58F7
Zhongzhai   GX43/44B7
Zhongzhai   HN37/38D2
Zhongzhai   ZJ21/22C7
Zhongzhai   GZ49/50D4
Zhongzhou   GD39/40B5
Zhongzhuangpu   SX7/8B5
Zhorongwo   QH59/60C8
Zhouba   SC47/48C1
Zhoucao   HN37/38D4
Zhoucheng   NX61/62B3
Zhoucheng   SD31/32D3
Zhoucun   SD31/32C4
Zhoucun   SX7/8F4

Zhoudangfan   HEN33/34F6
Zhoudian   SD31/32C4
Zhougou   SD31/32C7
Zhouguanqiao   HN37/38D4
Zhou He   TJ3/4C4
Zhou He   SC45/46C6
Zhouhu   JX29/30D2
Zhouji   AH23/24B3
Zhouji   AH23/24D2
Zhoujia   SC47/48B5
Zhoujia   HL15/16E4
Zhoujia   ZJ21/22B4
Zhoujiadian   HN37/38B4
Zhoujiagang   AH23/24D5
Zhoujiajing   GS57/58C6
Zhoujiang   GD39/40C8
Zhoujiapo   SC47/48C2
Zhoujiatian   NM61/62B2
Zhoujiatun   LN11/12C5
Zhoujiawan   SN55/56C4
Zhoujiaxian   SN55/56C5
Zhoujiazhen   SC47/48B5
Zhoukoudian   BJ3/4C2
Zhoukou Diqu   HEN33/34D6-7
(Zhoukou)Peng'an Xian   SC45/46C6
Zhoukou Shi   HEN33/34D6
Zhoulaozui   HB35/36D5
Zhouliangzhuang   TJ3/4C4
Zhoulichang   SC45/46D5
Zhoulu   GX43/44D5
Zhouning Xian   FJ25/26C5
Zhoupeng   AH23/24D2
Zhoupu   SH17/18E7
Zhouqin   GZ49/50E6
Zhouqingzhuang   HEB3/4D4
Zhouquan   ZJ19/20C3
Zhoushan Dao   ZJ21/22B7
Zhoushan Qundao   ZJ21/22B6-7
Zhoushan Shi   ZJ21/22B7
Zhoushi   JS19/20B3
Zhoushizhuang   SX7/8A5
Zhoushuizi   LN11/12F5
Zhoutan   JX29/30C5
Zhoutian   JX29/30F3
Zhoutian   JX29/30B3
Zhoutian   JX29/30F3
Zhoutieqiao   JS17/18E5
Zhoutou   AH23/24G3
Zhouwangcun   AH19/20C1
Zhouwangpu   HN37/38D4
Zhouxiang   ZJ21/22B6
Zhouxijie   JX29/30B4
Zhouxin   GD41A2
Zhouying   SD31/32E4
Zhouzhai   AH23/24B3
Zhouzhi Xian   SN55/56F4
Zhouzhuang   JS17/18E6
Zhouzhuang   JS17/18D5
Zhuaji   HL15/16C8
Zhuandian   HEN33/34E6
Zhuanghe Shi   LN11/12E6
Zhuangkou   JX29/30F3
Zhuanglang He   GS57/58D6

Zhuanglang Xian(Shuiluocheng)
   GS57/58E8
Zhuangli   SN55/56F5
Zhuangmo   SX7/8C4
Zhuangmu   AH23/24D4
Zhuangqiao   ZJ21/22C6
Zhuangta   HN37/38B3
Zhuangtang   JS17/18B4
Zhuanjiao   SN55/56E4
Zhuanjiaolou Shuiku   LN11/12E7
Zhuanjing   SN55/56C3
Zhuanlu   HEB3/4D1
Zhuanqiao   SH19/20B4
Zhuantang   ZJ21/22B5
Zhuanyaowan   SN55/56D5
Zhubgyügoin   QH59/60D5
Zhubi Jiang   HI42B1-2
Zhubuyuan   AH23/24E3
Zhucang   GZ49/50D4
Zhucheng Shi   SD31/32D6
Zhuchengzi   JL13/14C6
Zhucnag   GZ49/50C6
Zhu Dao   LN11/12E5
Zhudongshe   SX7/8C4
Zhudun   AH23/24F3
Zhugan He   HEN33/34E6
Zhuganpu   HEN33/34E6
Zhugao   SC45/46C5
Zhugaotang   HN37/38D3
Zhuge   ZJ21/22C4
Zhuge   SD31/32D5
Zhugkyung   QH59/60B6
Zhugou   HEN33/34E5
Zhugqu   GS57/58F7
Zhuguang Shan   JX29/30E2-F1
Zhuguanzhai   SN55/56B6
Zhugusi   QH59/60B8
Zhuhai Shi(Xiangzhou)   GD39/40D6
Zhuhe   HB35/36E6
Zhuhushan   JX29/30C4
Zhuji   AH23/24D3
Zhuji   GD39/40A7
Zhujiaba   SN55/56H3
Zhujia Chuan   SX7/8C3-B3
Zhujiafang   LN11/12C6
Zhujia Jian   ZJ21/22C7
Zhujiajiao   SH17/18E7
Zhujiakeng   JX29/30C5
Zhujiang Kou   GD39/40D6
Zhujiang Nongchang   GD41A2
Zhujiangqing   JX29/30D2
Zhujiaqiao   AH19/20C2
Zhujiatun   LN11/12C7
Zhujiawan   AH23/24D4
Zhujiawan   HB35/36D7
Zhujiayu   SX7/8E2
Zhujing   SH17/18 F7
Zhuji Shi   ZJ21/22C5
Zhukeng   GD39/40C5
Zhukou   FJ25/26D3
Zhukou   HEN33/34C7
Zhulanbu   JX29/30F3
Zhuli   HEN33/34D6

Zhuliang   JX29/30D4
Zhuliao   GD39/40C6
Zhulin   JS17/18E5
Zhulin   HB35/36B6
Zhulin   YN51/52D6
Zhulinguan   SN55/56G6
Zhuliudian   SD31/32C5
Zhulong He   HEB5/6E3
Zhulongqiao   AH23/24D5
Zhuluke   LN11/12C3
Zhumadian Diqu   HEN33/4E5-6
Zhumadian Shi   HEN33/34E6
Zhuogang   HB35/36D8
Zhuokeji   SC45/46C4
Zhuolu Xian   HEB5/6C3
Zhuoshui   SC45/46D3
Zhuoshui   GZ49/50B6
Zhuoshui   SC45/46D7
Zhuotian   FJ25/26E2
Zhuozhang Beiyuan   SX7/8D4-E5
Zhuozhang He   SX67D3
Zhuozhang Xiyuan   SX7/8E4
Zhuozhou ShiHEB5/6D3
Zhuozi Shan   NM9/10H6
Zhuozi Xian   NM9/10G9
Zhuping   GZ49/50C7
Zhuqi   FJ25/26D5
Zhuqiao   SD31/32B7
Zhuqiao   JS17/18C5
Zhuqiao   SH17/18E7
(Zhuquan)Jiahe Xian   HN37/38F5
Zhurushan   HB35/36D6
Zhusha   GD39/40D3
Zhushan   JX29/30G2
Zhushan   JX29/30C3
Zhushanqiao   JX29/30D3
Zhushan Xian   HB35/36B3
Zhushi   HN37/38F5
Zhushi   HEN33/34D5
Zhushui He   SD31/32D3
Zhutai   SD31/32C5
Zhutan   JX29/30C2
Zhutang   JS17/18E6
Zhutian   SD31/32D4
Zhuting   HN37/38D6
Zhuting   JX29/30D2
Zhutuo   SC47/48C3
Zhuwantou Dao   GD41B3
Zhuwapu   SC47/48B1
Zhuwo   BJ3/4B2
Zhuwu   SD31/32C8
Zhuxi   ZJ21/22D3
Zhuxi   SC47/48C3
Zhuxiang   AH23/24D4
Zhuxianzhen   HEN33/34C6
Zhuxichang   JX29/30C2
Zhuxi Xian   HB35/36B2
Zhuyang   SD31/32C4
Zhuyangguan   HEN33/34D3
Zhuyangxi   SC47/48C3
Zhuyangzhen   HEN33/34C2
Zhuyu   SC45/46B6
Zhuyuan   SC47/48C2

Zhuyuan   YN51/52C5
Zhuzeqiao   JS17/18E5
Zhuzhao Xinhe   SD31/32D2-3
Zhuzhen   JS17/18D4
Zhu Zhou   GD41B2
Zhuzhoujiang   HN37/38E3
Zhuzhou Shi   HN37/38D6
Zhuzhou Xian(Lukou)   HN37/38D6
Zhuzhuang   SD31/32C2
Zhuzhuang Shuiku   HEB5/6F2
Zhuzikou   HN37/38B5
Zibo Shi   SD31/32C5
Zichang Xian(Wayaobu)   SN55/56C5
Zichuan   SD31/32C4
Zidutai   LN11/12B5
Zigê Tangco   XZ53/54C8
Zigong Shi   SC45/46D5
Zigui Xian   HB35/36C3
Zihag   SC45/46D3
Zi He   SD31/32C5
Zihedian   SD31/32C5
Zihong   SX7/8D4
Zihukou   JX29/30C6
Zijiao   SD31/32B4
Zijin   HB35/36B4
Zijingguan   HEB5/6D3
Zijingguan   GZ49/50C7
Zijin Shan   JS17/18D4
Zijin Xian   GD39/40C8
(Ziketan)Xinghai Xian   QH59/60C6
Zilaiqiao   AH23/24D5
Ziliang   GX43/44D8
Ziliangping   HN37/38A4
Zimenqiao   HN37/38D5
Zindo   SC45/46C3
Zini Hu   NM9/10H5
Zin Qu   SC45/46C2
Ziqiu   HB35/36D3
Zi Qu   QH59/60D5
Ziqudukou   QH59/60D4
Zirun   SX7/8B4
Zishan   HB35/36C5

Zishan   JX29/30F3
Zishi   SC45/46C4
Zishikou   HEB3/4C2
Zi Shui   HN37/38C4-5
(Zito)Lhorong Xian   XZ53/54D10
Zitong He   SC47/48A3
Zitong Xian   SC45/46C5
Ziwei   HEB5/6E3
Ziwu   SN55/56F4
Ziwu He   SN55/56G4
Ziwu Ling   GS57/58E9
Zixi   HN37/38E4
Zixi   JX29/30C5
Zixing Shi   HN37/38F6
Zixiqiao   JX29/30D4
Zixi Xian(Hecheng)   JX29/30D5
Ziya He   HEB5/6E4   TJ3/4D3
Ziyang   AH23/24C5
Ziyang Shi   SC45/46C5
Ziyang Xian   SN55/56H4
Ziya Xinhe   HEB5/6E4-5   TJ3/4D3-4
Ziyou   GD41A2
Ziyuan Xian   GX43/44A8
Ziyun   SC47/48D4
Ziyundong Shan   FJ25/26E3
Ziyun Miaozu Buyeizu Zizhixian
    (Songshan)   GZ49/50E5
Ziyunshan Shuiku   JX29/30D3
Zizhong Xian   SC45/46D5
Zizhou Xian   SN55/56C6
Zoco   XZ53/54C3
Zogang Xian(Wangda)   XZ53/54E11
Zogqên   SC45/46B2
Zoidê Lhai   XZ53/54C7
Zoigê Xian(Dagcagoin)   SC45/46B4
Zong'ai   SX7/8D5
(Zongga)Gyirong Xian   XZ53/54E5
Zongjiafangzi   QH59/60B5
Zongjiangkou   GX43/44F7
Zongkou   HB35/36D5
Zongpu   AH23/24D4

Zongyang Xian   AH23/24F4
Zongza   SC45/46D2
Zongzhai   GS57/58C4
Zoucheng Shi   SD31/32D3
Zouhui   SX7/8E5
Zoujia   JL13/14C7
Zoulang Nanshan   GS57/58C4
                QH59/60A6
Zouma   GX43/44C8
Zoumaping   HB35/36E3
Zoumayi   HEB5/6D2
Zouping Xian   SD31/32C4
Zouqiao   JX29/30B3
Zoushi   HN37/38B4
Zouwu   SD31/32E4
Zouxu   GX43/44D6
Zuguan   HI42C2
(Zuitai)Kang Xian   GS57/58F7
(Zuitou)Taibai Xian   SN55/56F3
Zuli He   GS57/58D7-E7
Zulou   AH23/24B3
Zezhou Xian   SX7/8 F4
Zunhua Shi   HEB5/6C5
Zuntan   HI42B3
Zunyi Shi   GZ49/50C5
Zunyi Xian(Nanbai)   GZ49/50C5
Zuo'an   JX29/30E2
Zuoba   AH23/24F3
Zuocheng   HEN33/34B6
Zuodeng   GX43/44D5
Zuogezhuang   HEB3/4C3
Zuo Jiang   GX43/44E5
Zuojiawu   HEB3/4C5
Zuolong   SN55/56H14
Zuoquan Xian   SX7/8D5
Zuoshan   SD3132C6
Zuotan   GD39/40C7
Zuowei   HEB5/6C2
Zuoyun Xian   SX7/8B4
Zuozhou   GX43/44E5
Zurhen Ul Shan   QH59/60C2 – D2
Zurong   GX43/44D4

图书在版编目(CIP)数据

中国地图册:英文版/刘斌主编. - 2版. - 北京:中国
地图出版社,1998.10
　ISBN 7 - 5031 - 2148 - 3

　Ⅰ.中…Ⅱ.刘…Ⅲ.①行政区地图 - 中国 - 地图集②地
形图 - 中国 - 地图集　Ⅳ.K992.2

中国版本图书馆 CIP 数据核字(98)第 29469 号

Responsible Editor: Liu Bin

Drawers: Wang Jingli　He Hongyan

Checker: Liu Yi

Translator: Fan Yi

Cover designer: Wu Lingyun

Processing Designer: Chen Honglie

Examiner: Lu Yongsen

Reviser: Lu Jinwei

ISBN 7-5031-2148-3

ATLAS OF CHINA (English Edition)

Compiled and Published by China Cartographic Publishing House

Distributed by China Cartographic Publishing House

787 × 1092　　16mo　　12¼ Printing Sheets

3rd Edition 3rd Impression　May 2001

ISBN 7 - 5031 - 2148 - 3/K·781

GS(1998)145 号

07000

Printed in the People's Republic of China